HANDBOOKS
❖
NUMBER SIX

Introduction to Combinatorics

Gerry Leversha
and
Dominic Rowland

**United Kingdom
Mathematics Trust**

Introduction to Combinatorics

© 2015, 2019 United Kingdom Mathematics Trust

All rights reserved. No part of this publication may be reproduced or transmitted in any form or by any means, electronic or mechanical, including photocopy, recording, or any information storage and retrieval system, without permission in writing from the publisher.

Published by The United Kingdom Mathematics Trust.
School of Mathematics, University of Leeds,
Leeds, LS2 9JT, United Kingdom
http://www.ukmt.org.uk

First published 2015.
Reprinted 2019

ISBN 978-1-906001-24-7

Printed in the UK for the UKMT by The Charlesworth Group, Wakefield.
http://www.charlesworth.com

Typographic design by Andrew Jobbings of Arbelos.
http://www.arbelos.co.uk

Typeset with LaTeX.

The books published by the United Kingdom Mathematics Trust are grouped into series.

❖

The EXCURSIONS IN MATHEMATICS series consists of monographs which focus on a particular topic of interest and investigate it in some detail, using a wide range of ideas and techniques. They are aimed at high school students, undergraduates and others who are prepared to pursue a subject in some depth, but do not require specialised knowledge.
  1. *The Backbone of Pascal's Triangle*, Martin Griffiths
  2. *A Prime Puzzle*, Martin Griffiths

❖

The HANDBOOKS series is aimed particularly at students at secondary school who are interested in acquiring the knowledge and skills which are useful for tackling challenging problems, such as those posed in the competitions administered by the UKMT and similar organisations.
  1. *Plane Euclidean Geometry: Theory and Problems*, A D Gardiner and C J Bradley
  2. *Introduction to Inequalities*, C J Bradley
  3. *A Mathematical Olympiad Primer*, Geoff C Smith
  4. *Introduction to Number Theory*, C J Bradley
  5. *A Problem Solver's Handbook*, Andrew Jobbings
  6. *Introduction to Combinatorics*, Gerry Leversha and Dominic Rowland
  7. *First Steps for Problem Solvers*, Mary Teresa Fyfe and Andrew Jobbings
  8. *A Mathematical Olympiad Companion*, Geoff C Smith
  9. *Topics in Combinatorics*, Gerry Leversha and Dominic Rowland

❖

The PATHWAYS series aims to provide classroom teaching material for use in secondary schools. Each title develops a subject in more depth and in more detail than is normally required by public examinations or national curricula.
  1. *Crossing the Bridge*, Gerry Leversha
  2. *The Geometry of the Triangle*, Gerry Leversha

❖

The PROBLEMS series consists of collections of high-quality and original problems of Olympiad standard.
  1. *New Problems in Euclidean Geometry*, David Monk

❖

The CHALLENGES series is aimed at students at secondary school who are interested in tackling stimulating problems, such as those posed in the Mathematical Challenges administered by the UKMT and similar organisations.

1. *Ten Years of Mathematical Challenges: 1997 to 2006*,
2. *Ten Further Years of Mathematical Challenges: 2006 to 2016*,
3. *Intermediate Problems*, Andrew Jobbings
4. *Junior Problems*, Andrew Jobbings
5. *Senior Problems*, Andrew Jobbings

❖

The YEARBOOKS series documents all the UKMT activities, including details of all the challenge papers and solutions, lists of high scorers, accounts of the IMO and Olympiad training camps, and other information about the Trust's work during each year.

Contents

Series Editor's Foreword   ix

Preface   xi

1 Counting   1
    1.1   Listing   1
    1.2   Rearranging   5
    1.3   Ranking   8
    1.4   Colex ordering   8
    1.5   Tabulating   11

2 Arranging   19
    2.1   Permuting   19
    2.2   Conditions   21
    2.3   Round tables and necklaces   23
    2.4   Repeated letters   25

3 Choosing   29
    3.1   Grouping   29
    3.2   Expanding   32
    3.3   Coding   36
    3.4   Combinations with replacement   42

4 Enumerating   47
    4.1   Double-counting   47
    4.2   Bijecting   52
    4.3   Partitioning   55
    4.4   Making PIE   57

4.5	Factors and multiples	61
4.6	Primes	62
4.7	Deranging	66

5 Forming recurrences 71
5.1	Iterating	71
5.2	Fibonacci	74
5.3	Counting in Catalan	80
5.4	Metamorphosis	87
5.5	Voting	92
5.6	Going directly	96

6 Solving recurrences 99
6.1	Linear with constant coefficients	99
6.2	Non-linear	105

7 Generating 109
7.1	Generating functions	109
7.2	Power series	111
7.3	Solving recurrences using generating functions	117

8 Pigeonholing 123
8.1	The pigeonhole principle	123
8.2	Bounding	128
8.3	Pigeons and pigeonholes	132
8.4	Single objects	137
8.5	Averaging	141
8.6	Generalising	147
8.7	Number theory	150

9 Tiling and colouring 155
9.1	Dominoes	155
9.2	Trominoes and Tetrominoes	159
9.3	Alternative colourings	164
9.4	Tiling large boards	170
9.5	Multiple colourings	173
9.6	Knight's tours	177

10	**Using invariants**	**183**
10.1	Parity	184
10.2	Finding other invariants	189
10.3	Using monovariants	193
10.4	More subtle arguments involving variation	198
10.5	Solitaire games	207
11	**Going to extremes**	**215**
11.1	Using extremal objects	215
11.2	Arranging things	218
11.3	Geometrical problems	222
11.4	Number theory	229
11.5	Harder geometrical problems	232

Appendices

A	Sets	243
B	Sigma notation	247
C	Polynomials	253
D	Mathematical induction	255
E	Finite and infinite series	259
F	Congruences	263

Hints	267
Solutions	271
Bibliography	373
Index	375

Series Editor's Foreword

This book is part of a series whose aim is to help young mathematicians prepare for competitions, such as the British Mathematical Olympiad, at secondary school level. Like other volumes in the Handbooks series, it provides cheap and ready access to directly relevant material. All these books are characterised by the large number of carefully constructed exercises for the reader to attempt.

I hope that every secondary school will have these books in its library. The prices have been set so low that many good students will wish to purchase their own copies. Schools wishing to give out large numbers of copies of these books, perhaps as prizes, should note that discounts may be negotiated with the UKMT office.

London, UK   GERRY LEVERSHA

About the Authors

Gerry Leversha taught mathematics in secondary schools before retiring in 2011. He has also been involved in the work of the UKMT, both in the setting and marking of various Olympiads and as Chair of the Publications Committee. He is also the editor of *The Mathematical Gazette*, the journal of the Mathematical Association, and is a regular speaker at conferences and summer schools. His interests include music, film and literature, wine and cooking as well as playing tennis and mountain walking.

Dominic Rowland participated in his first UKMT maths challenge when he was eight years old. Over the next decade he took part in various challenges, Olympiads and maths camps. He began teaching mathematics at secondary school in 2011 and is a regular speaker at UKMT summer schools and mathematical circles as well as helping to set and mark the British Mathematical Olympiads. He enjoys backgammon, cycling and hill walking.

Preface

It is quite hard to give a precise definition of what combinatorics is. At one level it can be thought of as a sort of *extreme counting*—how do we enumerate the number of different ways of doing something? Here are some examples.

- How many permutations are there of the letters of the word BANANARAMA?
- Twelve tennis players split up to play three games of doubles. In how many ways can this be done?
- How many ways are there of dividing an octagon into six triangles using five diagonals?

The aim, of course, is to ensure that everything is counted exactly once, and when the numbers are getting big this can be quite challenging. In the school curriculum, this subject is only just touched on, but you might find yourself working with permutations and combinations. In the first seven chapters of this book, we delve much more deeply than this into what is properly called enumerative combinatorics.

However, as you will see by looking at later chapters, the subject is much broader than that. The best way to explain this is to list some of the problems which are addressed.

- There are 99 seats in a circle. Prove that, if 80 people sit down, then five consecutive seats will be occupied.
- For which n can an $n \times n$ chessboard be completely tiled with L-tetrominoes?
- Suppose that n identical cars are stopped on a circular track. Together, they have enough fuel to complete one lap. Show that one of the cars can complete a lap by collecting fuel from the other cars on the way.

♦ Prove that a cube cannot be split up into a finite number of cubes of different sizes.

What do all these problems have in common? They all begin with a practical situation which involves organising things so as to satisfy certain criteria—placing tiles on a chessboard, seating people in a circle, chopping up a cube—and then ask whether or not a certain outcome is possible. In general, the answer to this question is one of three alternatives:

(i) whichever way you carry out the instructions, something will always happen;
(ii) whichever way you carry out the instructions, you can never make it happen;
(iii) if you carry out the instructions in an ingenious way, it is possible to achieve a desired outcome.

The arguments needed to answer such questions are often very subtle, but there are general principles and methods which can be applied, and these form the focus of the second half of the book.

The structure of this book is, as befits the subject, problem-based. Each chapter proceeds through a series of challenges which introduce the important ideas slowly and carefully. In particular, we have tried to show how to tackle each problem from first principles but building on previously acquired knowledge and technique. You should be prepared to put the book down regularly and spend some time with pencil and paper thinking about how to proceed with a problem. The first step, obviously, is to understand what exactly the problem means. What are we being asked to do? How are we going to tackle a situation which, it seems, has so many different variations that it is impossible to consider each of them one by one? What sort of insights will lead to finding the key to the puzzle?

As authors, we have tried to avoid simply presenting the reader with a clinically perfect solution which comes 'out of the blue'. Instead, we have attempted to explain the experiences which led to its discovery. The activity by which someone discovers or learns something for themselves is known as *heuristics* and we hope that our experience as teachers has helped us to convey the steps in this journey. With this aim in mind, many of the problems posed have been trialled at summer schools or used in the classroom.

Our target audience includes secondary school students and their teachers, and we have aimed to make this volume as self-contained as possible. If you have a basic knowledge of algebra, then you should be able to follow all the arguments in the book. In a handful of places we assume some understanding of quadratic equations, but apart from that all the techniques and notation used are explained either in the text or in one of the six appendices.

Each chapter is broken up by several Exercises and it is important that you make an attempt to engage with the questions. Some of these have Hints, so you can glance at these to help you get started on a problem without giving the whole game away. Harder questions are starred. There are full solutions provided and sometimes alternative approaches are discussed. Hence it is worth looking at the solution even if you have solved the problem.

If you have already encountered combinatorics you may realise that there are many areas of the subject which are not covered in this book. These include graph theory, Ramsey theory and Polya counting. We hope to produce a follow-up volume which covers this and other topics at a more theoretical level.

Acknowledgements

This book would have been impossible without the support of a large number of people. We would like to thank James Gazet and Rosemary Emanuel for reading the text and making many useful suggestions for improving it, particularly in the early chapters. Imre Leader has been a great help in commentating on the style and warning us of the danger of 'moving too fast'. We would also like to thank all those who proofread sections of the book, notably Tom Lyster, who found numerous errors we would certainly have missed ourselves. The junior author would also like to thank his wife Camilla for her unfailing support and encouragement, and his son James for slowing the final stages of the writing process by his birth.

It is inevitable in a book of this nature that many of the problems will have appeared elsewhere in other books, example sheets or websites. Some of these constitute a sort of mathematical 'folklore' which it is impossible to attribute to a single source. However, we have included a list of well-known books in the bibliography. In addition there are many useful websites on the internet which include combinatorial problems, particularly *The Art of Problem Solving* and *Cut-the-Knot*. We have also drawn on national and international competitions for some of the problems and exercises; these are acknowledged by means of the codes in the following table. Note that in some cases we have taken the liberty of modifying the wording.

Code	Competition
BMO1	British Mathematical Olympiad Part One*
BMO2	British Mathematical Olympiad Part Two
Balkan MO	Balkan Mathematical Olympiad
Cayley	Intermediate Mathematical Olympiad, Year 9
CGMO	China Girls Mathematical Olympiad
Hamilton	Intermediate Mathematical Olympiad, Year 10
IMO	International Mathematical Olympiad
KMO	South Korean Mathematical Olympiad
Maclaurin	Intermediate Mathematical Olympiad, Year 11
Putnam	William Lowell Putnam Mathematical Competition
USAMO	USA Mathematical Olympiad

Last but by no means least we are indebted to Andrew Jobbings, not only for his elegant typesetting and exquisite diagrams but for his meticulous criticism of errors and textual infelicities. He also introduced us to some vital software which allowed us to cooperate in annotating successive versions of the manuscript. Without his contribution this book would not have been possible.

London, UK   Gerry Leversha
London, UK   Dominic Rowland

---

* Before 1992 this was known simply as BMO, since the second round was called the Further International Selection Test or FIST. For clarity we refer to it in this period as BMO1.

Chapter 1

Counting

At a very basic level, combinatorics addresses the question:

How many different ways are there of doing something?

In this chapter we will discuss a number of problems of this type.

1.1 Listing

One obvious way of tackling such problems is to make a list of all the possible outcomes.

Problem 1.1

A coin is tossed four times in succession.

How many different outcomes can there be?

You might attack this by writing out the outcomes as in table 1.1.

HTHH	TTTH	HHHT	THHT
HTHT	THTH	HHHH	TTHH
TTTT	HTTH	HHTT	THHH
HHTT	TTHT	HTHT	HTTT

Table 1.1

Hence there would appear to be sixteen outcomes when a coin is tossed four times.

COUNTING CRITERIA

A successful listing of cases will satisfy two conditions:

(i) every case is counted at least once;
(ii) no case is counted twice.

We can merge these conditions into a single statement: every case is counted exactly once.

So how well does the attempt above fare under these criteria? It turns out that it fails on both. If you look carefully, you will see that the outcomes HHTH and THTT are not counted at all, and the cases HHTT and HTHT are counted twice. The fact that the correct 'answer' of sixteen has been reached is entirely accidental; this is not a successful solution to the problem.

This attempt at a solution may strike you as inept, but it is very easy to make mistakes of this kind. With a long list of cases, it can be tricky to spot repetitions. Even when you have checked that this does not happen, how do you know that you have not overlooked one or more cases? How do you know when you are finished?

The trouble with this ad hoc listing is that it is not *systematic*. The outcomes must be arranged in such a way that it is clear that every option is being considered and that there is no possibility of repetition. One way of achieving this is to list the outcomes as shown in table 1.2; the table should be read row by row.

HHHH	HHHT	HHTH	HHTT
HTHH	HTHT	HTTH	HTTT
THHH	THHT	THTH	THTT
TTHH	TTHT	TTTH	TTTT

Table 1.2

Now the outcomes are arranged in *increasing alphabetical order*, as they would appear in a dictionary. It would be equally appropriate to list them in the opposite order, which is *decreasing* alphabetical order, particularly if you enjoy reading dictionaries backwards. But why is this any better? Why does such a strategy ensure that both criteria have been met?

It is pretty clear that there are no repetitions, since the outcomes are in a prescribed order. It is a bit harder to convince yourself that the list is *exhaustive*—there are no omissions. You could argue this by trying to interpolate another outcome into the list, and then you realise that there is not enough 'space'—the outcomes are as tightly packed as possible.

Another way is to imagine a row of four people, unimaginatively named 1, 2, 3 and 4, who each have a card marked H and a card marked T. They perform a routine which has the rules shown in figure 1.1.

At the start, all four people display card H.

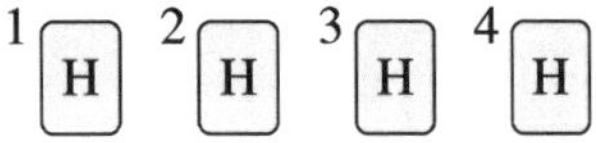

$$^1[H] \quad ^2[H] \quad ^3[H] \quad ^4[H]$$

At each step in the routine, 4 switches cards, so the second stage is

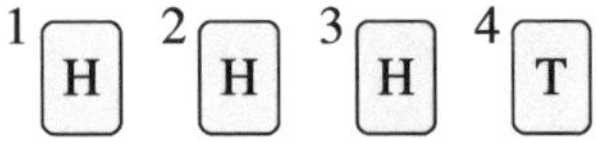

$$^1[H] \quad ^2[H] \quad ^3[H] \quad ^4[T]$$

When 4 changes cards from T to H, 3 switches cards, so the next stage is

$$^1[H] \quad ^2[H] \quad ^3[T] \quad ^4[H]$$

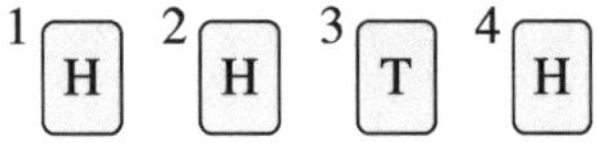

Now 4 switches, so we have

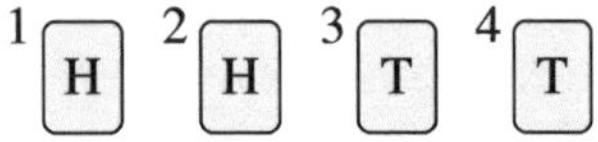

$$^1[H] \quad ^2[H] \quad ^3[T] \quad ^4[T]$$

When 3 changes from T to H, 2 switches cards, so the next stage is

$$^1[H] \quad ^2[T] \quad ^3[H] \quad ^4[H]$$

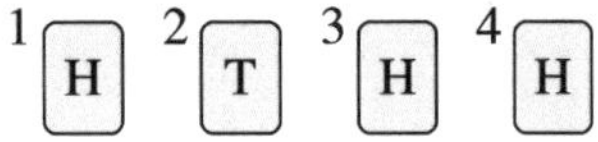

with only 1 keeping the same card, and when they reach the stage

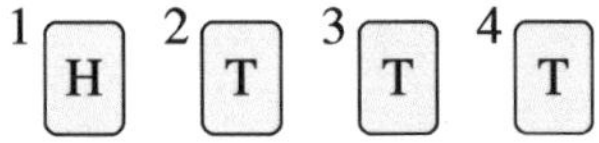

$$^1[H] \quad ^2[T] \quad ^3[T] \quad ^4[T]$$

and so 2 changes from T to H, 1 switches as well, and we have

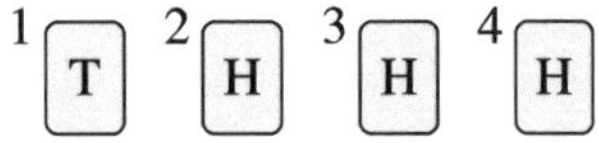

$$^1[T] \quad ^2[H] \quad ^3[H] \quad ^4[H]$$

They keep going until they arrive at the situation

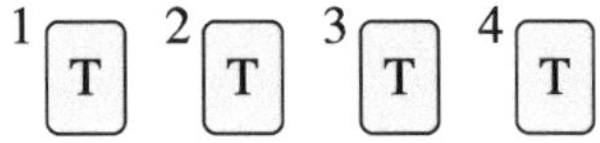

$$^1[T] \quad ^2[T] \quad ^3[T] \quad ^4[T]$$

at which point they stop.

Figure 1.1

Focus on 3 and 4. Notice that 3 does not make a change until 4 has used both cards, so after four steps it is obvious that they have used up all the possibilities open to them. Now bring in 2, who does not switch until both 3 and 4 have run through all their options, so after eight steps these three have exhausted their potential. Finally 1 only switches when 2, 3 and 4 have run the gamut of their possibilities.

This is known as a *recursive argument*, in which we proceed from the case k to the case $k+1$. Such arguments are very common in combinatorics.

If the writing on the cards were changed so that H became 0 and T became 1, then the sequence would consist of the binary numbers from 0000 (which is 0 in base 10) to 1111 (which is 15 in base 10) and it would then be clear that there were 16 different outcomes. Note that the process is similar to the way an odometer (a distance gauge) works on a car, except there each counter runs through the numbers 0 to 9 before clicking back to 0 as the counter to its left moves on by one. If we think of the terms in the sequence as binary numbers, it is very clear that we have not left any possibilities out (since the numbers are consecutive) and that none are repeated.

However, tempting as this argument is, there are going to be scenarios in which it is not available, and sometimes it can be quite tricky to write out a list using alphabetical ordering, and even harder to explain how to move from one outcome to the next.

The fact that you can think of the problem in two different ways is also common in combinatorics. It often happens that two questions which look superficially different turn out to be exactly the same. In this case, the problem of counting the outcomes when a coin is tossed four times is exactly the same as that of counting all binary numbers with up to four digits. We shall see again and again that a new problem can be reduced to an older one, which has already been solved, by coding some aspect of the new question in a particular way. The symbols H/T and 0/1 are codes for the two states that something has, and need have no intrinsic meaning in themselves.

The process of generating the list gives us an easy way of calculating the number of outcomes. This method is based on a fundamental idea in combinatorics, known as the multiplication principle:

> if there are a ways of performing action A and b ways of performing action B, then there are $a \times b$ ways of performing both actions.

Clearly this generalises to any number of actions. In the case of problem 1.1, each coin can come to rest either as a head or a tail, so the number of outcomes is $2^4 = 16$. This easily generalises to n coins where the number of outcomes is 2^n.

1.2 Rearranging

Problem 1.2

In how many different ways can the letters of the acronym UKMT be arranged?

Here we are required to find rearrangements of the letters U, K, M and T, where no repetitions are allowed. The alphabetical ordering is given in table 1.3.

KMTU	KMUT	KTMU	KTUM	KUMT	KUTM
MKTU	MKUT	MTKU	MTUK	MUKT	MUTK
TKMU	TKUM	TMKU	TMUK	TUKM	TUMK
UKMT	UKTM	UMKT	UMTK	UTKM	UTMK

Table 1.3

Hence there are 24 acronyms altogether. The order is that which would appear in some universal dictionary of acronyms. Readers with time on their hands can speculate as to what they might stand for. Again, you can justify the fact that the listing is exhaustive by beginning with two letters and then working up to three and four, and so on.

This time, there are four ways of choosing the first letter, but only three ways of choosing the second, since the first choice cannot be repeated. Similarly there are two ways of choosing the third and only one way of choosing the fourth. So, by the multiplication principle, the total number of acronyms is $4 \times 3 \times 2 \times 1 = 24$. This number is known as 4 *factorial*, which is written as 4!. With N different letters, there would be $N!$ acronyms.

Note that we are now using the multiplication principle in a more sophisticated way than in problem 1.1. In that problem, we said that every coin could be either H or T, so the number of outcomes for four coins was $2 \times 2 \times 2 \times 2$. In this one, each letter can be either K or M or T or U. But the number of outcomes is not $4 \times 4 \times 4 \times 4$, because we are not allowing repetitions. The choices are no longer independent; what is possible for the second letter depends on what happened for the first, and what is possible for the third depends on what happened for the first and second. So the multiplication principle needs a little tweaking to make it correct.

THE MULTIPLICATION PRINCIPLE

If there are a ways of performing action A and b ways of performing action B (once action A has happened), then there are $a \times b$ ways of performing both actions.

At this point, it is worth introducing the correct terminology for these acronyms. Rearrangements of sequences of objects where order matters are known as *permutations*. The same word is used when two or more of the objects are the same; for example, ADMIRER is a permutation of MARRIED.

We can also have permutations with replacement, where the same object can be chosen several times. The 16 outcomes in problem 1.1 are permutations with replacement of the objects H and T. We will return to this subject in chapter 2.

Let us analyse problem 1.2 a little further. As in problem 1.1, we can reduce the case of four letters to that of three letters, and we shall assume that you know how to deal with that. Begin by choosing the first letter K. Now follow this with the alphabetical ordering of the permutations of M, T and U. Now start with M and follow it with the six permutations of K, T and U, and do the same beginning with T and U.

These could also be represented as numbers, taking K as 1, M as 2, T as 3 and U as 4, as shown in table 1.4.

1234	1243	1324	1342	1423	1432
2134	2143	2314	2341	2413	2431
3124	3142	3214	3241	3412	3421
4123	4132	4213	4231	4312	4321

Table 1.4

Problem 1.3

In how many ways can four pieces of fruit be selected from a large pile of apples, oranges and pears?

As in many situations in combinatorics, various assumptions must be made to clarify what you have to do. The first assumption is that all apples look the same, so you cannot distinguish them from each other, and the same applies to oranges and pears. The second is that it does not matter what order you select the fruit. So, using initial letters for the different types of fruit, a selection like AOPA is the same as AAOP. It follows that we might as well put the letters in alphabetical order in each foursome. If you are familiar with set notation, you might think we should use it in this situation. However, sets cannot contain repeated elements, so that {A, O, O, P} and {A, A, O, P} would both be represented as {A, O, P}. A third assumption is that you do not have to select at least one piece of each fruit. Hence AAAA is a valid selection. Finally, the word 'large' is to be taken as meaning that there are at least four pieces of each kind of fruit available.

Once we have established exactly what the problem is, we have to figure out how to list the possibilities. Now we could start by using the multiplication principle to find out how many ways there are of choosing the fruit in order. This is exactly like problem 1.1 and the answer is 3^4, that is, 81. However, we now have to collect all selections which have the same items in a different order so that they appear as only one choice. This is not very easy to do, since it depends on what the selection looks like. For instance, a selection such as AAAA will only appear once in our list of 81, but AAAP will appear four times with the P in first, second, third and fourth place, and, if you take the trouble, you will see that AAPP appears six times.

In fact, alphabetical ordering works effectively, as shown in table 1.5, and there are 15 choices.

AAAA	AAAO	AAAP	AAOO	AAOP
AAPP	AOOO	AOOP	AOPP	APPP
OOOO	OOOP	OOPP	OPPP	PPPP

Table 1.5

1.3 Ranking

When combinatorial objects are arranged in some order, there are two processes we can carry out.

- Given a particular object in the list, find the place in the order which it occupies. This is known as *ranking*.
- Given a particular rank, find the object which lies in this position in the list. This is *unranking* and is the inverse operation of ranking.

For problem 1.1, the key to ranking is the binary coding. To rank an outcome, convert it to binary and add one to the decimal equivalent. For instance, THHT converts to 1001, which represents the number 9 in base ten, and so THHT has rank 10. To find the outcome which has rank 13, subtract one to give 12 and convert this to binary. The result is 1100 and so the item in the list is TTHH.

For problem 1.2, we must split the rank up as a sum of factorials. Take, for example, the permutation TMUK. As it starts with a T, there are $2 \times 3!$ before it which start with either K or M. The second letter is M, so there are also $1 \times 2!$ permutations before which start with TK. Finally, the third letter is U, so there is $1 \times 1!$ permutation before it starting TMK. Putting all this together we see that the ranking is $2 \times 3! + 1 \times 2! + 2 \times 1! = 16$. To find the 8th permutation we note that it is preceded by $1 \times 3! + 0 \times 2! + 1 \times 1!$ permutations. That is all those starting with a K or with MKT. Thus the 8th is MKUT.

1.4 Colex ordering

We have focussed so far on alphabetical ordering, but that is not the only sensible way to make systematic lists.

Problem 1.4

How many subsets are there of the set $\{1, 2, \ldots, 5\}$ that contain exactly three elements?

As the order of elements in a subset does not matter, we might as well list their elements in increasing numerical order. Now the alphabetical

Chapter 1: Counting

ordering of the subsets is shown in table 1.6, and there are clearly ten of them.

$$\{1,2,3\} \quad \{1,2,4\} \quad \{1,2,5\} \quad \{1,3,4\} \quad \{1,3,5\}$$
$$\{1,4,5\} \quad \{2,3,4\} \quad \{2,3,5\} \quad \{2,4,5\} \quad \{3,4,5\}$$

Table 1.6

However, we could also have listed these according to the size of their largest element. This is known as *colexicographic ordering* or *colex*, and it produces table 1.7.

$$\{1,2,3\} \quad \{1,2,4\} \quad \{1,3,4\} \quad \{2,3,4\} \quad \{1,2,5\}$$
$$\{1,3,5\} \quad \{2,3,5\} \quad \{1,4,5\} \quad \{2,4,5\} \quad \{3,4,5\}$$

Table 1.7

Thus we begin with the one subset whose largest element is 3, then the three whose largest element is 4 and finally the six whose largest element is 5. Note that this criterion also applies within these groups, so that $\{1,2,4\}$ precedes $\{1,3,4\}$ since $2 < 3$.

In fact, subsets can be represented by binary codes. The subset $\{2,3,5\}$ is chosen from the set $\{1,2,\ldots,5\}$. Counting in both cases from right to left, this is done by selecting the set's first, third and fourth elements. Hence, using a 1 to indicate that a number is chosen and a 0 to indicate that it is not chosen, it can be coded by the binary number 10110.

Exercise 1a

1. A restaurant menu offers a three-course lunch consisting of a choice of three starters, four main courses and two desserts.
   List the different outcomes in increasing alphabetical order, coding the starters as A, B and C, the main courses as P, Q, R and S and the desserts as X and Y.

2. List, in increasing alphabetical order, the different ways in which the letters of the word COCOA can be arranged.

3. Three indistinguishable dice, each having the numbers 1 to 6 on their six faces, are thrown simultaneously. The fact that they are indistinguishable means that their order does not matter. If they landed showing 3, 5 and 6 that would count as the same outcome as if they landed 6, 3 and 5. Since the order does not matter, we can represent the outcome where the dice show 6, 3 and 5, say, as the three-digit number 356.
   (a) List, in increasing numerical order, the different outcomes when three indistinguishable dice are thrown.
   (b) How many outcomes would there be if the dice were coloured red, white and blue and so were distinguishable?

4. Sanskrit verse has syllables which can be either light (with a length of one *mora*) or heavy (with a length of two *moras*). A line in a Vedic hymn consists of a variable number of syllables with a fixed total length.
   List the syllabic schemes for a line of length six *moras* in increasing alphabetical order, using L to denote a light syllable and H a heavy one.

5. A *partition* of a number is a way of expressing it as a sum of positive integers, where the order of the parts does not matter.
   For instance, some of the partitions of 9 are $4+5$, 9, $6+1+1+1$ and $3+3+2+1$. Note that $4+5$ and $5+4$ count as the same partition. Omitting the $+$ signs, so that 3 3 2 1 stands for $3+3+2+1$, list the partitions of 6.

6. Convert the alphabetical and colex orderings of the outcomes for problem 1.4 to binary numbers using the binary coding system mentioned on page 9, and comment on the result.

7. Suppose that the 256 results of tossing eight coins are listed in increasing alphabetical order.
   (a) What is the rank of HTHTTHHT?
   (b) Which outcome has rank 141?

8. Suppose that the 720 permutations of the letters of MONDAY are listed in increasing alphabetical order.
   (a) What is the rank of DYNAMO?
   (b) Which permutation has rank 666?

9. The restaurant in question 1 expands its menu to have five starters (A, B, C, D, E), six mains (P, Q, R, S, T, U), and three desserts (X, Y, Z). The 90 options are listed in alphabetical order.
   (a) What is the rank of CRY?
   (b) Which option has rank 50?

*10. For the list given in table 1.4 of problem 1.2, devise a method for generating each term from the previous one.

1.5 Tabulating

Listing all possible arrangements may not always be practical, since the numbers involved are often very large. For instance, there are 15 120 permutations of the word BANANARAMA, and listing these would try the patience of even the most avid enthusiast of this all-girl vocal group, which was popular in the 1980s.

However, it is not always easy to find a quick way of calculating numbers of outcomes, and often it is simpler to draw a useful diagram which manages to track combinatorial objects without listing every one of them.

Problem 1.5

Consider a standard 8 × 8 chessboard consisting of 64 small squares coloured grey and white in the usual pattern, so 32 are grey and 32 are white. A zig-zag path across the board is a collection of eight white squares, one in each row, which meet at their corners.

How many different zig-zag paths are there? [BMO1 2008]

It is natural to start by looking at the board. There are four possible starting points for a zig-zag path, namely the four white squares in the top row. We can indicate this by placing a 1 in each of these four squares; this tells us that there is exactly one zig-zag path which starts with these squares. Now look at the white squares in the second row. The first three of these can be reached in two ways from the line above, since the paths can zig either to the left or the right, but the fourth can only be reached in one way, from the square to its left. For the first three rows this produces figure 1.2.

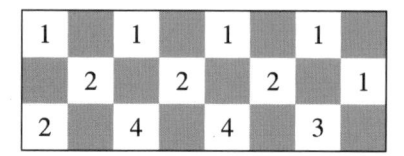

1		1		1		1	
	2		2		2		1
2		4		4		3	

Figure 1.2

This method can now be continued as we move down the board. In each white square, we place the sum of the numbers in the white squares immediately above it. With an edge square, there is only one number to add, but with all other squares there are two. It is this *edge effect* which makes the problem unsuitable for more sophisticated methods of enumeration. The resulting numbers are shown in figure 1.3.

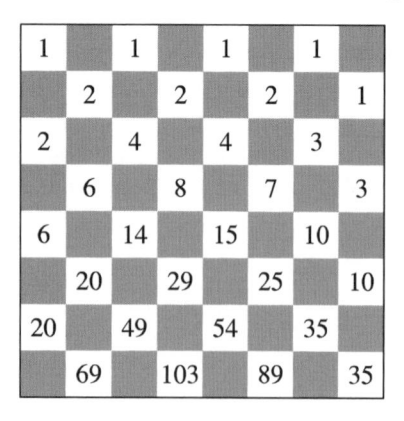

1		1		1		1	
	2		2		2		1
2		4		4		3	
	6		8		7		3
6		14		15		10	
	20		29		25		10
20		49		54		35	
	69		103		89		35

Figure 1.3

All we have to do now to complete the solution is to add up the four numbers in the bottom row. Hence there are 296 zig-zag paths.

The quincunx

A quincunx is a device invented by the scientist Francis Galton. It consists of a vertical board with a triangle of pegs driven into its upper half (figure 1.4).

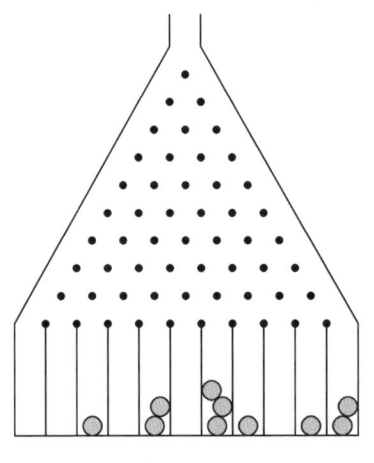

Figure 1.4

A ball dropped through a funnel at the top of the board will strike the central peg in the top row and bounce either left or right with equal probability, only to strike another peg in the row below. This process continues as the ball falls through the device. Eventually the ball reaches the lower half of the machine where it lands in one of a number of evenly spaced rectangular slots. The front of the device is covered with a glass panel to allow viewing of the balls and the slots.

Devices such as the quincunx used to be common in the games arcades on the piers which were a major attraction of many seaside towns, but instead of a ball a coin was inserted at the top of the machine. The customer then saw it descend through the pins until it finished up in one of the slots at the bottom. Occasionally, but not often, you got your money back. This mechanism served the worthy purpose of separating children from their pocket money.

Problem 1.6

How many different paths are there from the funnel to the fifth slot?

In problem 1.5, we used the chessboard to enumerate zigzag paths up to a particular square, and a similar approach can be used here. The funnel and each gap between two pegs in the machine is replaced by the number of routes which end there. Hence the funnel is replaced by 1 and the same is true for the two gaps on either side of the top peg. The middle gap of the next row is replaced by 2, since it can only be reached via either of the two gaps above it. As in the chessboard problem, each value in the array is calculated as the sum of the two above (figure 1.5).

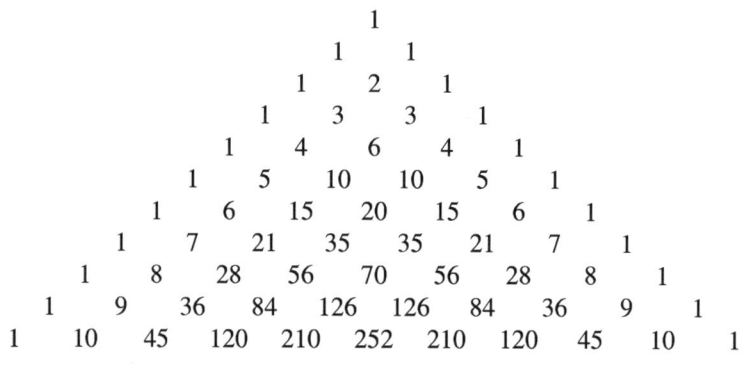

```
                              1
                          1       1
                      1       2       1
                  1       3       3       1
              1       4       6       4       1
          1       5      10      10       5       1
      1       6      15      20      15       6       1
  1       7      21      35      35      21       7       1
1     8      28      56      70      56      28       8       1
  1     9     36     84    126    126     84     36      9      1
1    10    45    120    210    252    210    120    45     10     1
```

Figure 1.5

The pattern generated is one of the most familiar in mathematics and is known as *Pascal's triangle*, after the French mathematician and philosopher Pascal (1623–1662). However, it was known long before the seventeenth century and is called the Yang Hui (杨辉) triangle in China and Khayyam's triangle in Iran. We shall return to Pascal's triangle in chapter 2.

From this array, we can read off the fact that the number of routes through the machine to the fifth slot is 210.

However, this approach is not only applicable to problems which involve a physical diagram such as a chessboard or a grid of pins. It is also useful in a situation in which choices have to be made at stages in a process, but they are not independent choices, since what has happened at previous stages limits what is possible at the next.

Chapter 1: Counting

Problem 1.7

How many six-digit numbers are there in which adjacent digits differ by at most one?

There is a free choice for the first digit, which can be anything between 1 and 9. However, our options for the second digit are limited. If we had chosen 5 for the first digit, it can only be 4, 5 or 6, and a similar statement can be made for any first choice between 1 and 8 inclusive. However, if we had chosen 9 as the first digit, the second can only be 8 or 9. Later, when a digit can be 0, the next digit can only be 0 or 1. If there were three choices for each new digit, this would be a straightforward enough exercise, but there are edge effects, rather like in problem 1.5.

So a tabular approach which mimics the solution to the chessboard problem is likely to be effective. We therefore draw up table 1.8.

Final digit	One digit	Two digits	Three digits	Four digits	Five digits	Six digits
0	0	1	3	9	26	75
1	1	2	6	17	49	141
2	1	3	8	23	66	191
3	1	3	9	26	76	222
4	1	3	9	27	80	237
5	1	3	9	27	81	241
6	1	3	9	27	80	236
7	1	3	9	26	75	216
8	1	3	8	22	61	171
9	1	2	5	13	35	96

Table 1.8

The second column shows the number of one-digit numbers ending in each of the digits 0 to 9; there is, of course, no such number ending in 0. The next column shows the number of two-digit numbers ending in each digit, including 0, and is found by summing either two or three of the entries in the previous column. For example, there is only one such number ending in 0 (namely 10) but there are two such numbers ending in 1 (namely 11 and 21) and three ending in 2 (namely 12, 22 and 32). The other columns are constructed in the same way, and now the solution to the problem is the sum of the entries in the final column, which is 1826.

Exercise 1b

1. This problem concerns the TV quiz show Blockbusters which was popular in the 1980s and 1990s. The game uses an array of twenty hexagons with four rows and five columns, as shown.

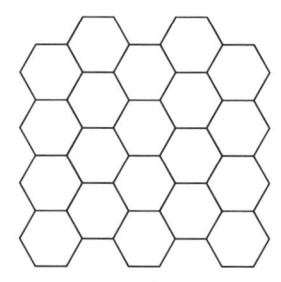

   Two hexagons are adjacent if they share a side, and a path consists of a sequence of adjacent hexagons.
   (a) How many shortest paths are there from the left to the right?
   (b) How many shortest paths are there from the top to the bottom?

2. Isaac is planning a nine-day holiday. Every day he will go surfing or water-skiing, or else he will rest. On any given day he does just one of these three things. He never does different water-sports on consecutive days.
   How many different schedules are possible for the holiday?
   [BMO1 2013]

3. In how many different ways is it possible to make up £1 using 1p, 2p, 5p, 10p, 20p and 50p coins? [HINT]

4. The diagram shows a cube with opposite vertices A and B, made up of eight smaller cubes with sides of one unit.

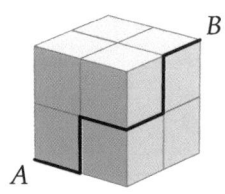

How many routes are there from A to B on the surface of the cube made up of six unit segments in directions parallel to the edges of the cube? An example of such a route is shown. [HINT]

5. All the faces of three identical cubes are to be painted so that nine faces are green and nine are yellow. After the paint has dried, the cubes are going to be placed in a velvet bag and given as a gift. Only the colouring can be used to tell two cubes apart. How many different gifts are possible? [Maclaurin 2013]

6. In how many distinct ways can a cubical die be numbered from 1 to 6 so that consecutive numbers are on adjacent faces? Numberings that are obtained from each other by rotation or reflection are considered indistinguishable. [Hamilton 2011]

7. What is the answer to question 6 if there are no restrictions on the placement of the numbers?

Chapter 2

Arranging

The previous chapter solved problems without using algebra; it contained no formulae and used virtually no algebraic notation. The price paid for that was that the approaches used were somewhat crude and time-consuming, and in this chapter we begin to build up some methods which are more sophisticated and, perhaps, more satisfying. However, be warned that combinatorics is not a subject where you can always rely on using neat formulae, and you will often need to go back to first principles in order to solve a problem which looks familiar but turns out to be quite new.

2.1 Permuting

We have already used the term *permutation* to describe a rearrangement of the letters of a word. The words 'merits', 'mitres', 'remits', 'smiter' and 'timers' are distinct permutations of the word 'mister'. In this chapter we will extend the term to include a rearrangement of some, as well as all, of the letters, so 'rest', 'emit', 'item', 'sire', 'tier' and 'trim' are all permutations of four letters from the word 'mister'.

However, there is no need for a permutation to be a real word in a language such as English; it is a letter jumble rather than an anagram. In this book, we will use the term 'word' to mean any sequence of letters, which does not have to make linguistic sense.

Moreover, you can have permutations of any sort of objects, not just letters of the alphabet. The usual condition is that the objects are distinguishable, so that you can tell them apart. For example, picking the first, second and third horses to finish a race (assuming that there are no dead heats) is going to involve permutations, since (a) the horses participating in the race are distinguishable and (b) the order in which the horses finish is significant. In general it should be clear in the context of a question whether the objects are distinguishable or not. However, things like beads of the same colour, books with the same title and pieces of the same kind of fruit will be assumed to be indistinguishable.

Problem 2.1

How many words can be made with all six letters of WOMBAT?

This depends only on the multiplication principle. There are six choices for the first letter, five for the second, four for the third, three for the fourth, two for the fifth and only one for the sixth. Hence the solution to the problem is $6 \times 5 \times 4 \times 3 \times 2 \times 1 = 720$, that is, 6!. When a word consists of N different letters, it is easy to see that there are $N!$ permutations of all of its letters. In problem 1.2 on page 5, the 24 permutations of the four letters of UKMT were listed.

Problem 2.2

How many words with four different letters can be made from the letters of WOMBAT?

This is solved in exactly the same way. There are six choices for the first letter, five for the second, four for the third and three for the fourth, so the answer is $6 \times 5 \times 4 \times 3 = 360$. We have found the number of permutations of four letters from six, which is sometimes denoted by $_6P_4$. There is a neat way of formulating this. We 'complete' the factorial by multiplying and dividing by 2×1 to produce the expression

$$\frac{6 \times 5 \times 4 \times 3 \times 2 \times 1}{2 \times 1} = \frac{6!}{2!}.$$

Hence the general formula for the number of permutations of r objects from n objects is

$$\frac{n!}{(n-r)!}.$$

Chapter 2: Arranging

Problem 2.3

How many words with four letters, not necessarily different, can be made from the letters of WOMBAT?

Here we drop the requirement that each letter chosen is different. Now we have each of six choices four times, and so the answer is $6^4 = 1296$. Arrangements like this are known as *permutations with replacement*, since whenever you choose a particular letter it is replaced in the list of objects and can be selected again. However, the order in which you select the objects still matters.

It follows that the number of permutations with replacement of r objects from n objects is n^r. An example of this was problem 1.1 on page 1 about coin tosses, which is a matter of listing the 16 four letter permutations with replacement of the two objects H and T.

In general, permutations do not allow replacement, and it will be made clear in a problem when they do.

2.2 Conditions

Sometimes we are asked to count permutations which are restricted by extra conditions.

Problem 2.4

How many permutations of WOMBAT begin and end with a vowel?

In this problem the vowels of WOMBAT are required to be at the ends of the word. This situation is quite easy to deal with using the multiplication principle. There are only two choices for the first letter, which is either O or A. Now there are four choices for the second letter, which can be any consonant, three for the third letter, two for the fourth letter, one for the fifth letter (which is the remaining consonant) and one for the final letter (which is the remaining vowel). So the solution to this problem is $2 \times 4 \times 3 \times 2 \times 1 \times 1$, which is 48.

Problem 2.5

How many permutations of the letters of the word WOMBAT have the vowels separated?

It is not quite so straightforward to deal with this problem, since there are many ways in which the vowels can be separated. There are, however, only two ways in which the vowels can be together, as they will be in one of the orders OA or AO. Now we can treat this as a 'supervowel' (AO) and find the permutations of (AO), W, M, B and T. There are 5! or 120 of these, so if the supervowel is 'unwrapped' this gives 240 arrangements. However, we want to count the cases where the vowels are separated, and this is just the complementary situation, so there are $720 - 240 = 480$ such permutations.

Of course permutations need not be of letters. Many problems, such as the next one, ask us to count integers of a particular type, and these can be thought of as permutations of the digits 0 to 9.

Problem 2.6

How many five-digit multiples of 5 are there in which all the digits are different and the second digit is odd?

Now we have three conditions. The first digit cannot be zero (since otherwise it is not a five-digit number), the second digit is 1, 3, 5, 7 or 9 and the last digit is either 0 or 5. Unfortunately these restrictions 'interfere' with each other, in that the digits 0 and 5 figure in more than one of them, so we have to be very careful about organising the count. One way to tackle this problem is to start with the final digit and split the problem into two cases. If the final digit is 0, there are 5 choices for the second, 8 for the first, 7 for the third and 6 for the fourth, so there are $5 \times 8 \times 7 \times 6 = 1680$ such numbers. If the final digit is 5, there are 4 choices for the second, 7 for the first, 7 for the third and 6 for the fourth, so there are $4 \times 7 \times 7 \times 6 = 1176$ numbers of this type. Altogether there are 2856 numbers which satisfy the conditions.

Chapter 2: Arranging

2.3 Round tables and necklaces

There are a couple of conventions in combinatorial problems that you ought to be aware of.

Problem 2.7

In how many ways can twelve diners be seated around a round table?

If twelve people are arranged on a bench, then there are clearly 12! orders in which they can be seated. If that bench is placed alongside a dining table and the twelve people are having a meal together, there are still 12! different ways in which to organise them. If the table is round, does this change the number of ways in which diners can be seated?

In reality, dinner parties tend to take place in rooms which have a distinguishing feature, such as a prominent picture hanging on the wall. The seat directly beneath the picture is distinguishable from the other places at the table, and so we can analyse the situation by focussing on that chair and choosing somebody to sit in it. We can then count off the other eleven places clockwise and assign people to them one by one. The round table becomes, effectively, a bench, so the number of ways the people can be seated is still 12!.

In the fantasy world of combinatorics, however, round tables are assumed to be floating around in a cosmic void, so that no particular seat is special. This is the context of problem 2.7. Now it is sensible to promote one of the diners to be at the head of the table, and now the other eleven people can be counted off from this person in clockwise order. So the number of ways of organising twelve people around a round table is, by convention, 11!.

Problem 2.8

In how many ways can twelve beads of different colours be threaded onto a necklace?

The situation here is rather unrealistic, since most necklaces contain indistinguishable beads, but it is a good starting point. Again, there are conventions. The necklace is assumed to have no clasp, which would allow us to determine a starting point from which to count, so in this respect it begins to resemble a round table. However, it has the additional property that it can be turned upside down, which is not true of round tables unless the diners are nailed to their seats. This means that the clockwise and anticlockwise senses are indistinguishable, and it follows that the twelve beads can be arranged in $\frac{1}{2}(11!)$ ways.

It will be seen that these variations allow plenty of scope for setting challenging problems which involve counting permutations.

Exercise 2a

1. An outdoor pursuits centre offers the five activities rock-climbing, orienteering, canyoning, kayaking and yoga. Each activity uses up a whole day.
   (a) A participant on a five-day course must experience all these activities, but in any order. In how many ways can they organise their programme?
   (b) If, instead, they are allowed a free choice of activities, but are not allowed to do the same one on two consecutive days, in how many ways can they plan their holiday?
   (c) If they must experience all five activities, but must do rock-climbing before canyoning, in how many ways can they plan their holiday?
   (d) If they must experience all five activities, but must do rock-climbing before canyoning and orienteering before yoga, in how many ways can they plan their holiday?

2. An exclusive dining club has twelve female members, and at its annual general meeting it must elect the chairwoman, secretary and treasurer. If these must be different people, in how many ways can this be done?

3. In how many ways can a black and a white square be chosen on a chessboard in such a way that the two squares are not in the same row or column?

4. In how many ways can eight rooks be placed on a chessboard so that no two are in the same row or column?

5. (a) How many seven-digit numbers have even and odd digits alternating? [HINT]
   (b) How many of these have distinct digits and are divisible by 5?

6. How many numbers divisible by 6 can be made by arranging four different digits from 1, 2, 3, 4 and 5?

7. How many numbers between 1000 and 9999 contain at least one repeated digit?

8. James has three blue, four red and five green snooker balls, and he decides to place four of them in a row on his mantelpiece to make a stunning conversation piece.
   In how many different ways can this be done?

9. In how many ways can four married couples be arranged around a round table so that every couple sits together?

10. (a) In how many ways can four Arsenal fans, three Liverpool fans and two Chelsea fans be arranged around a round table for a philosophical discussion of the ethics of football?
    (b) In how many ways can the protagonists of the previous part be arranged if fans of the same team must all sit together?

2.4 Repeated letters

Problem 2.9

How many permutations are there of the letters of the word TUMULUS?

A tumulus is a burial mound. The word has seven letters but three of them are Us. It makes perfect sense to talk about a jumble of the letters of TUMULUS; an example is STUMULU. We must use the U three times and the other letters once each. Note that we no longer have a permutation of the type discussed so far in the chapter, since the objects we permute are no longer distinguishable. However, we can amend our definition to allow this to happen, and talk about a permutation which contains one item three times.

Consider what happens if the second and third occurrence of U are changed to B and E. Now we would be counting permutations of the word TUMBLES. This is familiar, since it has seven distinct letters, and we know that there are 7! permutations of this word. Suppose that we select one of these, for example STUMBLE, and replace the B and the E by Us. The result will be STUMULU, which is indeed a permutation of TUMULUS. The trouble is that we would obtain exactly the same result if we started with STUMELB, STBMELU, STBMULE, STEMBLU or STEMULB. Six *different* permutations of TUMBLES would yield STUMULU, the *same* permutation of TUMULUS. What is happening is that the letters B, E and U, which were distinct, become indistinguishable. Since there are 3! = 6 permutations of these three letters, this means that six different words become the same word.

Instead of finding a word which closely resembles TUMULUS but avoids the repeated letters, we could have distinguished the Us by printing them in different colours. This is impractical in this book, so we adopt another strategy and add subscripts to them. The word becomes $TU_1MU_2LU_3S$, and there are 7! distinct permutations of this. Now remove the subscripts, and then distinct permutations such as $STU_1MU_2LU_3$ and $STU_1MU_3LU_2$ become indistinguishable as STUMULU. There are 3! such permutations which all turn into STUMULU, and this happens wherever in the word the U_1, U_2 and U_3 occur, so it will have the effect of reducing the number of permutations by a factor of 6.

Hence there are $\dfrac{7!}{3!} = 840$ permutations of TUMULUS.

Problem 2.10

How many permutations are there of the letters of the word BANANARAMA?

Chapter 2: Arranging

Now we generalise the method of dealing with repeated letters. We distinguish both the As and the Ns by adding subscripts, so the initial word becomes $BA_1N_1A_2N_2A_3RA_4MA_5$ which has ten distinct letters. There are 10! distinct permutations of this word. When the subscripts are removed from the Ns, these become indistinguishable in pairs, so $BA_1NA_2NA_3RA_4MA_5$ has $\frac{10!}{2!}$ different permutations, and when the subscripts are removed from the five As, we must divide by a further 5!. Hence the solution to the problem is $\frac{10!}{2!5!} = 15\,120$.

We have a general result. The number of permutations of n objects which consist of r_1 objects of one type, r_2 of another, and so on up to r_k of the last (so $1 \le r_i \le n$ and $n = r_1 + r_2 + \cdots + r_n$) is

$$\binom{n}{r_1\, r_2\, \ldots\, r_k} = \frac{n!}{r_1!r_2!\cdots r_n!}. \qquad (2.1)$$

Note that if the r_i are all equal to 1, this reduces to $n!$ as before. The notation used on the left of equation (2.1) will be explained in the next chapter.

It is worth pausing for a moment to compare two situations. The first is that of counting permutations with replacement of four letters of the word WOMBAT. In that case WWWW is a possible outcome. The second is counting permutations of all the letters of the word TUMULUS. This case is quite different since every permutation will use exactly three Us.

We shall distinguish the two situations by referring to the outcomes in the first situation as permutations with replacement and those in the second as permutations of objects some of which are repeated. The point being made is that we have to be very careful in combinatorics about using language precisely, since the sloppy use of words such as 'repeated' can be very confusing.

Exercise 2b

1. How many ways are there to place three copies of *Introduction to Number Theory*, four copies of *Introduction to Inequalities* and five copies of *Crossing the Bridge* next to one another on a bookshelf?

2. How many permutations of the word BANANARAMA have
   (a) the letters in alphabetical order?
   (b) all the vowels together?
   (c) all the consonants together?
   (d) the two Ns separated?
   (e) the two Ns separated and the vowels together?
   (f) all the As preceding both the Ns?
   (g) each N surrounded by two As? [HINT]

3. How many permutations of the letters of the word SUCCESS have no two Ss together?

4. How many permutations are there of three letters of the word BANANARAMA?

5. In how many ways could the letters of the word BANANARAMA sit around a round table? [HINT]

Chapter 3

Choosing

In this chapter we introduce the concept of combinations, which are permutations where the order in which objects are selected does not matter.

3.1 Grouping

> **Problem 3.1**
> Ten management trainees are spending a bonding weekend together.
> In how many ways can four of them engage in an ice-breaking group hug?

One way to attack this is to replace the management trainees with a row of 10 boxes, and to place a 1 in a box if the trainee is to be selected and a 0 in the box if not. The result of this is a permutation of four 1s and six 0s, such as 1001010100, which can be thought of as a word. This particular word would indicate that the first, fourth, sixth and eighth trainees would be enjoying their hug.

The problem reduces to counting such words, but this is by now familiar from the work in the last chapter. Using equation (2.1), we see that the number of such permutations is

$$\binom{10}{4\ 6} = \frac{10!}{4!6!},$$

that is, 210.

It is worth comparing this problem with those we have already tackled. We are choosing four out of ten distinguishable objects (which happen to be management trainees). If we were choosing them so that they won prizes of £500, £200, £100 and £50, then there would be $10 \times 9 \times 8 \times 7 = 5040$ ways of doing so. But with group hugs, rather than different financial rewards, the order in which we make the choice does not matter. In the example given, it is irrelevant whether we choose the trainees in the order 1, 4, 6, 8 or 8, 4, 1, 6; the result is the same.

Choices of this kind are known as *combinations*. Nowadays the number of such combinations is written as $\binom{10}{4}$; in the past, the notation $_{10}C_4$ was sometimes used.

It should be plain that combinations can be thought of as permutations where some of the objects are repeated. But this scenario is so common in combinatorics that is given a special name and notation.

So $\binom{n}{r}$ stands for the number of ways of choosing a set of r objects from a set of n objects, where the order in which the objects are picked is irrelevant. We have already encountered this scenario in problem 1.4 on page 8, which asked for the number of ways of choosing a subset containing three elements from a set of five elements. This is $\binom{5}{3}$, which is equal to 10.

The general formula is

$$\binom{n}{r} = \frac{n!}{r!(n-r)!} \qquad (3.1)$$

and is, of course, an immediate consequence of equation (2.1). It is clear that there is only one way to choose n things from n (choose all of them) and we also see that there is one way to choose zero things from n (omit all of them). In symbols we have $\binom{n}{n} = 1$ and $\binom{n}{0} = 1$. This is consistent with equation (3.1) provided we use the standard convention that $0! = 1$. If r is negative or greater than n then equation (3.1) no longer makes sense and it is conventional to take $\binom{n}{r} = 0$ in these cases.

Chapter 3: Choosing

Problem 3.2
Anne has four different T-shirts and six different polo shirts.
How many ways can she choose exactly six of them to take to a mathematics summer school?

This problem includes some noise—that is, redundant information. After thinking about this for a moment, you will realise that the question of whether a garment is a T-shirt or a polo shirt is irrelevant. Anne simply has to select six shirts from ten. So again we have ten cells (the shirts) and we use 0 and 1 as selection indicators, and the answer is $\binom{10}{6} = \frac{10!}{6!4!} = 210$.

This shares the same answer with problem 3.1, and it is not hard to see why. Anne can either choose the shirts she wants to wear or set aside the ones she does not want. In terms of the codes used earlier, we are simply swapping the interpretation of 0 and 1. It also follows from the fact that the right-hand side of equation (3.1) does not change when r is replaced by $n - r$.

However, the combinatorial explanation as to why $\binom{10}{4}$ and $\binom{10}{6}$ are the same is much more enlightening than obtaining the result from the formula. This is true in general; it is much better to use arguments which rely on the meaning of $\binom{n}{r}$ than to get involved in algebraic manipulation. Not only is the algebra involving factorials often rather messy and technical, but the combinatorial argument gives much more insight into why something is true.

In general, we have

$$\binom{n}{r} = \binom{n}{n-r}. \tag{3.2}$$

At this point, we will revisit problem 1.6 on page 14 which introduced the quincunx machine. Suppose we wanted to count the number of ways in which a ball could reach the fifth slot. Let us analyse what happens in such a path. At each stage, the ball (imagined as a sentient being) can move either to the left or to the right. Let us code these choices by L and R. In order to reach the eleventh row, the ball has to make ten choices. We imagine these choices to be ten cells, and we are therefore indicating the route of the ball by placing either L or R in each cell.

Alternatively, the route is shown by a word such as LRLRLLRRLL. To reach the fifth slot, the ball must have moved leftwards six times and rightwards four times. So the number of routes will be the same as the number of ways of placing four Rs in ten cells, and this is $\binom{10}{4} = 210$.

It follows that the entries in Pascal's triangle count combinations. In order to avoid the inconvenience of thinking of the fifth entry in the eleventh row as $\binom{10}{4}$, it is usual to label the first row of the triangle as the 0th row and also the first entry in any row as the 0th entry. Equation (3.2) indicates that the array is symmetrical.

In chapter 1, we generated Pascal's triangle by calculating each entry in the array as the sum of the two entries above it. The first and last in each row were automatically assigned the value 1, which is equivalent to imagining the triangle floating in a sea of zeros. How does this tabulating method relate to combinations? On investigation, it yields the formula

$$\binom{n+1}{r+1} = \binom{n}{r} + \binom{n}{r+1}, \qquad (3.3)$$

which is known in the trade as *Pascal's identity*.

It is not too hard to prove this using equation (3.1), but that is only worth doing if you need practice in manipulating algebraic fractions with factorials. A far better way to tackle it from first principles is by imagining a row of $n + 1$ objects from which you have to select $r + 1$. Unfortunately the last object in the row is a Portkey and will transport you somewhere disagreeable if you do decide to choose it. You have a democratic choice either to select this object or not.

If you do select the Portkey, then you must also choose r out of the remaining n objects, and there are $\binom{n}{r}$ ways of doing this.

If you decide to postpone your meeting with Lord Voldemort, then you must make all your $r + 1$ selections from the first n objects and there are $\binom{n}{r+1}$ ways of doing so.

Adding the two expressions gives the value of $\binom{n+1}{r+1}$.

3.2 Expanding

The next problem concerns algebraic manipulation. If you are not used to working with algebraic expressions such as polynomials, you will find some guidance in appendix C.

Chapter 3: Choosing　　33

Problem 3.3

If $(x+1)^{10}$ is multiplied out to give a polynomial, what is the coefficient of x^4?

As suggested in the appendix, we tackle this by considering how the coefficients arise. The ten brackets to be multiplied look like this:

$$(x+1)(x+1)(x+1)(x+1)(x+1)(x+1)(x+1)(x+1)(x+1)(x+1).$$

Suppose now that we select either x or 1 in the first bracket, multiply it by either x or 1 in the second bracket, multiply the result by either x or 1 in the third bracket, and so on until the end. The result will be a power of x. If we chose 1 every time, the result would be 1, which is x^0, and if we chose x every time, the result would be x^{10}, but in between these extreme cases we would obtain a power of x between 1 and 9 inclusive.

In order to multiply out all ten brackets, we have to make every possible choice, and then collect like terms. So the coefficient of x^4 would be the number of ways in which the selection process yields a term with x^4 in it. This is equivalent to starting with a row of ten cells, which represent the brackets, and then placing a 1 or a 0 in each cell according to whether you choose x or 1 from the corresponding bracket. The number of ways of choosing 1 four times and 0 six times is $\binom{10}{4}$, and it follows that this is also the coefficient of x^4 in the expansion.

This means that we can read off the expansion of $(x+1)^{10}$ from Pascal's triangle simply by 'filling in' the gaps. What we then see is that

$$(x+1)^{10} = x^{10} + 10x^9 + 45x^8 + 120x^7 + 210x^6 + 252x^5$$
$$+ 210x^4 + 120x^3 + 45x^2 + 10x + 1.$$

This is a special case of the *binomial theorem*, which says that

$$(x+y)^n = \binom{n}{0}x^n + \binom{n}{1}x^{n-1}y + \binom{n}{2}x^{n-2}y^2 + \cdots$$
$$+ \binom{n}{k}x^{n-k}y^k + \cdots + \binom{n}{n}y^n. \quad (3.4)$$

For this reason, the numbers $\binom{n}{r}$ are also known as *binomial coefficients*.

To summarise, we now have several interpretations of this symbol. It represents

(i) the coefficient of $x^r y^{n-r}$ in the expansion of $(x+y)^n$;
(ii) the number of combinations of r objects from n objects;
(iii) the number of subsets of size r in a set with n elements.

We return now to the notation $\binom{n}{r_1 \, r_2 \, \ldots \, r_k}$ from equation (2.1) on page 27, where $r_1 + r_2 + \cdots r_k = n$. It is clear from the formula that

$$\binom{n}{r \; n-r} = \binom{n}{r} \tag{3.5}$$

and also that

$$\binom{n}{r_1 \, r_2 \, \ldots \, r_k} = \binom{n}{r_1} \times \binom{n-r_1}{r_2} \times \binom{n-r_1-r_2}{r_3} \times \cdots \times \binom{r_k}{r_k}. \tag{3.6}$$

The last equation can be interpreted in the following way. First of all, we select an r_1-set from the full set of n elements. Then we select an r_2-set from the remaining $n - r_1$ elements. We continue doing this until we have $n - (r_1 + r_2 + \cdots + r_{k-1}) = r_k$ elements left, and we have to select all of these.

Finally, we can also consider the expansion $(x_1 + x_2 + \cdots + x_k)^n$ and consider how various terms arise, in the same way as with the binomial expansion.

The coefficient of $x_1^{r_1} x_2^{r_2} \cdots x_k^{r_k}$ will be the number of ways of choosing x_1 in r_1 of the brackets, x_2 in r_2 of the brackets, and so on up to x_k in r_k of the brackets. Hence it is $\binom{n}{r_1 \, r_2 \, \ldots \, r_k}$, which is known as a *multinomial coefficient*.

In summary, then, we have several interpretations of this symbol. It represents

(i) the coefficient of $x_1^{r_1} x_2^{r_2} \cdots x_k^{r_k}$ in the expansion of $(x_1 + x_2 + \cdots + x_k)^n$;
(ii) the number of ways of splitting up a set with n elements into an ordered sequence of disjoint subsets with $r_1, r_2, \ldots, r_k$ elements;
(iii) the number of permutations of n objects which consist of r_1 objects of one type, r_2 of another, and so on up to r_k of the last.

Note that the subsets in the second bullet point are chosen in a particular order. For example, if the original set is $\{1,2,3,4\}$, then the split $\{1,4\}$, $\{2,3\}$ would be counted as different from $\{2,3\}$, $\{1,4\}$.

So we are not counting the number of ways of splitting a set into subsets. This is a more difficult problem and will be addressed later.

Exercise 3a

1. In how many ways can a quiz team of six people be selected from a group of twelve people?

2. In how many ways can an A and a B team, both of six people, be selected from a group of fifteen people?

3. In the national lottery, a player buys a ticket which lists six out of the numbers 1 to 49 inclusive. A machine selects six balls, without replacement, from a set of forty-nine balls which are numbered 1 to 49.
   (a) How many different ways are there of choosing the six balls?
   (b) In how many ways can a player match exactly three of the six winning numbers?
   (c) In how many ways can a player match three or more of the six winning numbers?
   (d) In addition, the machine draws a seventh ball, which is called the bonus ball. In how many ways can a player match five numbers and the bonus ball?
   (e) Construct a table of probabilities for the various winning outcomes in the lottery.

4. In how many ways can a committee consisting of five women and six men be formed from eight women and ten men?

5. From a group of seven women and six men, five persons are to be selected to form a committee so that at least three women are on it. In how many ways can it be done?

6. How many ways can twelve members of a club be formed into four committees such that committee U consists of two members, committee K consists of three members, committee M consists of five members and committee T consists of two members (assuming that each person can be on only one committee)?

7. Show that the largest entry in a row of Pascal's triangle is either the central one or one of the two central ones, depending on whether there is an odd or even number of entries in the row.

8. Prove the *hockey stick theorem*, that if $m \leq n$, then

$$\binom{n+1}{m+1} = \binom{n}{m} + \binom{n-1}{m} + \binom{n-2}{m} + \cdots + \binom{m}{m}.$$

Why does it have this name?

9. Prove that, if $m \leq n$ then

$$1 \times \binom{n}{m} + 2 \times \binom{n-1}{m} + \cdots + r \times \binom{n-r+1}{m} + \cdots + (n-m+1)\binom{m}{m} = \binom{n+2}{m+2}.$$

[BMO1 1985]

10. Isaac has a large supply of counters, and places one in each of the squares of an 8 by 8 chessboard. Each counter is either red, white or blue, A particular pattern of coloured counters is called an *arrangement*. Determine whether there are more arrangements which contain an even number of red counters or more arrangements which contain an odd number of red counters. [BMO1 2010]

HINT

3.3 Coding

As has already been mentioned, it is very common in combinatorics for two problems which look different to be completely equivalent. In the case of problems about combinations, this often reduces to showing that a new problem can be phrased in terms of cells and codes, and in this section we will look at some examples of this.

Problem 3.4

A city has streets which all run north to south and avenues which all run east to west. Each avenue meets each street. Janet starts at the corner of second street and third avenue, and wants to meet John at the corner of sixth street and ninth avenue.

How many different shortest routes could she take to meet him?

There is an unlimited number of routes Janet can use to meet John, since she might begin by going up and down the same section of road again and again, or maybe retrace the same rectangular route, avoiding John until she (or he) expires from exhaustion. However, the problem asks for the shortest route, so it is clear that she ought to go four blocks to the East and six blocks to the North, but in any order. We therefore think of this problem in terms of ten cells, which represent choices, and, in each cell, we place either E to mean that Janet goes East or N to mean that she goes North. This is what is meant by *coding*. Then a route becomes a sequence of Es and Ns, with ten in total, and exactly four Es. We now see that the solution to the problem is $\binom{10}{4}$. Alert readers might now be suspecting that there is some hidden agenda in these problems.

Problem 3.5

There are ten points arranged around a circle, and each pair is joined with a chord.

What is the maximum number of intersections of these chords?

This problem involves the geometry of a circle. Note that chords do not extend outside the circle, so we are not concerned here with 'external' intersections. We are also asking for the maximum number of intersections, so we can assume that the ten points are placed so that no three chords meet in a single point.

How do these intersecting chords work? Consider four points A, B, C and D on the circumference of the circle (figure 3.1 on the next page).

It is obvious that if we join these points in pairs, there is always going to be exactly one choice of chords which produces an intersection point inside the circle. This is, incidentally, nothing to do with the fact that two

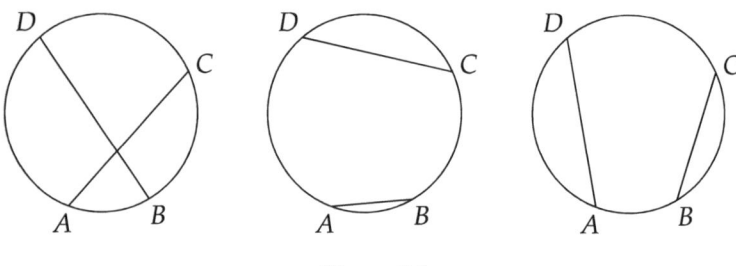

Figure 3.1

of the chords might be parallel. So the number of intersections is the same as the selection of four points out of the available ten. Once again, we have a reduction of the problem to one that has already been solved. The ten cells are the ten points and the code is simply a 1 to show that the point has been selected and a 0 to show that it has not. Since we require exactly four points to be selected, the solution to the problem is $\binom{10}{4}$.

Problem 3.6

Suppose that a, b, c, d and e are positive integers.

How many solutions are there to the equation $a + b + c + d + e = 11$?

This problem is about a *Diophantine equation*, which is one where we are only interested in integer solutions. In this case, we are looking for solutions in *positive* integers. A little thought shows that we are interested in partitioning 11 in various ways, but since the variables have names a, b, c, d and e these are ordered partitions, which are sometimes known as *compositions*. The solution $(3, 1, 2, 1, 4)$ counts as different from $(2, 4, 3, 1, 1)$. This makes the problem considerably easier than most questions in the theory of partitions.

Now consider the diagram XXXXXXXXXXX which contains eleven Xs. We can represent any solution to the equation by placing barriers in the appropriate places. For example, the solution $(a, b, c, d, e) = (3, 1, 2, 1, 4)$ is represented by XXX | X | XX | X | XXXX. It turns out, then, that the important feature is the ten gaps between the eleven Xs. We think of these gaps as ten cells and place the symbol ♦ in a cell if there is a barrier there and the symbol ✣ if there is none. Hence the solution above is coded as

♣♣♦♣♦♦♣♣♣. So a solution to the equation corresponds to a choice of four out of ten objects, and the number of solutions is $\binom{10}{4} = 210$.

Exercise 3b

A pack of cards consists of 52 cards, divided into four suits (Spades, Hearts, Diamonds and Clubs). Each suit has thirteen cards, namely (in descending order) Ace, King, Queen, Jack, Ten, Nine, Eight, Seven, Six, Five, Four, Three and Two. These values are known as denominations.

1. A bridge hand consists of 13 cards. How many bridge hands are there?

2. In how many ways can a full pack be dealt out between four players, if the order of the players matters? What if the order of the players does not matter?

3. Poker hands, which consist of five cards, are classified as follows, with the highest ranking hand appearing first. An Ace can count as either high or low, so that it can form a sequence with 5, 4, 3 and 2 as well as with 10, J, Q and K.

   Straight flush
   Five cards of the same suit in sequence.

   Four of a kind
   Four cards of the same denomination and a fifth card of another.

   Full house
   Three cards of one denomination and two of another.

   Flush
   Five cards of the same suit, but not in sequence.

   Straight
   Five cards in sequence, but not of the same suit.

   Three of a kind
   Three cards of the same denomination and two others which do not form a pair.

Two pairs
  Two cards of each of two denominations and a fifth of another.

Pair
  Two cards of the same denomination and three others which do not form a pair.

High card
  Any hand which does not satisfy any of the previous criteria.

How many hands are there of each type?

4. Twelve distinguishable books consist of three on geometry, four on number theory and five on combinatorics. In how many ways can they be arranged on a bookshelf so that books on the same topic are together? [HINT]

5. (a) How many rectangles are there in the grid shown? (Remember that a square counts as a rectangle.)

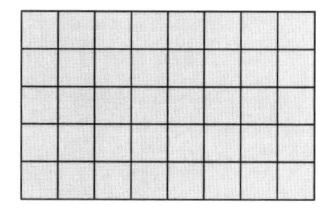

  (b) How many squares are there?

6. Prove that the maximum number of regions into which a circle is divided by chords joining two of n points on the circumference is given by the expression
$$1 + \binom{n}{2} + \binom{n}{4}.$$

[HINT]

7. Prove that the maximum number of regions into which n lines can divide a plane is $1 + n + \binom{n}{2}$.

8. How many of the permutations of the letters of the alphabet have no two vowels together? (The vowels are A, E, I, O and U.) [HINT]

Chapter 3: Choosing

9. In how many ways can three men and four women be seated at a round table with no two men next to one another?

10. Suppose that a, b, c, d and e are non-negative integers. How many solutions are there to the equation $a + b + c + d + e = 6$? [HINT]

11. Robin has five distinguishable dogs and wishes to give six identical bones to them. He is allowed to give more than one bone to any of them. In how many ways can he allocate the bones?

12. Twelve tennis players split up to play three games of doubles. In how many ways can this be done? [HINT]

13. The number 916 238 457 is an example of a nine-digit number which contains each of the digits 1 to 9 exactly once. It also has the property that the digits 1 to 5 occur in their natural order, whilst the digits 1 to 6 do not. How many such numbers are there? [BMO1 2006]

14. Adrian teaches a class of six pairs of twins. He wishes to set up teams for a quiz, but wants to avoid putting any pair of twins into the same team. Subject to this condition:
    (a) in how many ways can he split them into two teams of six?
    (b) in how many ways can he split them into three teams of four?
    [BMO1 2005]

15. Isaac attempts all six questions on an Olympiad paper in order. Each question is marked on a scale from 0 to 10. He never scores more in a later question than in any earlier question. How many different possible sequences of six marks are there? [BMO1 2009]
    [HINT]

16. Bill has sixteen books, indistinguishable in size, but otherwise distinct, which he has to parcel up into nine packages. Four of the packages are to contain one book, three of them are to contain two books and two of them are to contain three books, but there are no other restrictions on which books go into which packages. In how many ways can this be done? (The order in which he makes the packages is not important.) [HINT]

* 17. How many different 4-subsets can be chosen from {1, 2, 3, 4, 5, 6, 7, 8, 9, 10, 11, 12, 13} if no two of the numbers in the subset are consecutive?

* 18. A *binary string* is a sequence of 0s and 1s, so it is like a binary number but can begin with zeros. How many binary strings of length 9 contain exactly two occurrences of 01?

3.4 Combinations with replacement

We have now encountered permutations, in which the order in which objects are chosen matters, and combinations, in which the order does not matter. We have also allowed the same object to be chosen more than once in the case of permutations, and this is not at all difficult to analyse. How about combinations with replacement, in which we allow objects to be chosen more than once? This turns out to be harder to deal with.

Combinations without replacement are choices of r from n distinguishable objects, in which the order of selection does not matter. Since we are not allowed to choose the same object more than once, it is necessary that $r \leq n$. A useful way to visualise such a combination is to imagine a row of n cells and place one symbol into each of r cells chosen. If replacement is allowed, we still have n cells and r symbols, but now we are allowed to place more than one symbol into each cell. There is no longer a requirement that $r \leq n$, but it is still permissible to leave cells empty.

An example we have already met is problem 1.3 on page 7 about apples, oranges and pears. Apples are indistinguishable from one another, but you can tell the difference between two pieces of fruit of different varieties. Therefore we begin with a row of three cells, which represent the numbers of apples, oranges and pears, in that order, and then place four symbols in them to show how four pieces of fruit are to be chosen.

So figure 3.2 shows the case where two apples and two pears are chosen. We now represent the gaps between cells as dividers ◆, so that the choice can be coded by the pattern ❈❈◆◆❈❈.

Chapter 3: Choosing

   ┌─────┐   ┌─────┐   ┌─────┐
   │ ❖ ❖ │   │   │   │ ❖ ❖ │
   └─────┘   └─────┘   └─────┘
   Apples   Oranges   Pears

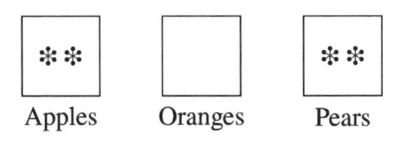

Figure 3.2

It is now clear that each arrangement can be uniquely indicated by a sequence of four ❖ symbols and two ♦ symbols and so the number of these combinations with replacement is $\binom{6}{4}$.

This is easily generalised to the case of choices of r from n distinguishable objects, where the objects are replaced after they are selected. We will have n cells and r symbols ❖, and hence we will need $n-1$ symbols ♦. The number of arrangements is therefore $\binom{n+r-1}{r}$.

It is worth using a new notation for this situation, and we will use $\left(\!\binom{n}{r}\!\right)$ to denote the number of ways of choosing r from n objects with replacement allowed. The problem just discussed would be represented by $\left(\!\binom{3}{4}\!\right)$, and the general formula for combinations with replacement is

$$\left(\!\binom{n}{r}\!\right) = \binom{n+r-1}{r} \tag{3.7}$$

In question 10 of exercise 3b we were asked to count the number of solutions to the equation $a+b+c+d+e=6$, where the variables represent non-negative integers. Now the variables can be thought of as five cells into which we place six objects, representing six units (which are indistinguishable from each other). So this is equivalent to choosing six from five objects with replacement, and is $\left(\!\binom{5}{6}\!\right) = \binom{10}{6}$. Question 11 in the same exercise is obviously the same problem.

Problem 3.6 also reduces to this problem since we begin by assigning each variable the value 1 at the start, and then it becomes a matter of 'topping them up'. This can be done in $\left(\!\binom{5}{6}\!\right)$ ways.

Problem 3.7

How many different outcomes are there if five indistinguishable dice are thrown?

In this problem the dice themselves are indistinguishable but the results when a single dice is thrown are not; they are the values 1 to 6. So these are the cells into which we now place five objects with replacement, and the answer is $\left(\!\binom{6}{5}\!\right) = \binom{10}{5} = 252$.

It is also possible to view problem 2.9, about the permutations of TUMULUS, as a question about combinations with replacement. We place the three Us first, creating four gaps into which the letters TMLS are put. We first treat these letters as indistinguishable and place markers for them in the gaps, which can be done in $\left(\!\binom{4}{4}\!\right)$ ways, which is 35. Now the sequence of markers is replaced with one of the 24 permutations of TMLS, and so the answer is 840. The key aspect of this technique is that we first create 'markers' for letters and then allocate letters to fill them. The markers are indistinguishable but the letters which will fill them are not.

Thus we have two equivalent interpretations of the symbol $\left(\!\binom{n}{r}\!\right)$, namely:

(i) the number of ways of choosing r objects from n distinguishable objects with replacement;

(ii) the number of ways of placing r indistinguishable objects into n distinguishable cells, with any number of objects allowed in each cell.

If you are puzzled in the second interpretation over what to take as cells and what to take as objects, remember that the cells are distinguishable but the objects are not.

Exercise 3c

1. How many eight-letter words have the letters in alphabetical order? (The words may contain the same letter more than once.)

2. How many non-negative integer solutions are there to the inequality $a + b + c + d + e < 12$? [HINT]

3. How many positive integer solutions are there to the inequality $a + b + c + d + e < 12$?

Chapter 3: Choosing

4. How many non-negative integer solutions are there to the inequality $a + b + c + d + e \leq 12$?

5. In how many ways can ten indistinguishable bones be given to five distinguishable dogs so that exactly two of the dogs do not get a bone?

6. In how many ways can ten indistinguishable bones be given to five distinguishable dogs so that the two biggest dogs get the same number of bones?

7. In how many ways can ten indistinguishable bones be given to five distinguishable dogs so that each dog gets a different number of bones?

8. In how many ways can five indistinguishable bones and five distinguishable bones be given to five distinguishable dogs?

9. How many permutations of BANANARAMA
   (a) have the first A before the first N?
   (b) have one of the Ns before the last A?

Chapter 4

Enumerating

4.1 Double-counting

As part of English vocabulary, the word *double-counting* is ambiguous. It is sometimes used to mean a mistake, that of counting the same items in a list more than once, and indeed it is used that way in accounting. In combinatorics, of course, accurate counting is all about avoiding this error, and we will use *overcounting* when this happens.

In what follows, double-counting is counting the same list twice, *but in a different way*, so as to produce something useful. This might be a formula, an equation or a theorem.

In the last chapter, we derived the formula for combinations by treating them as permutations from a set with repeated elements. However, we could have used the following double-counting argument.

We count the number of ways of counting permutations of r from n objects in two ways. First we select the objects one by one, ensuring that we do not select the same object twice, and this yields the familiar expression $\frac{n!}{(n-r)!}$ (see page 20). Secondly, we suppose that there are N ways of choosing a subset with r elements; it is this that we want to evaluate. These elements can now be permuted in $r!$ ways, and so, by the multiplication principle, the number of permutations is $N \times r!$. Finally we equate these expressions to obtain the equation $N \times r! = \frac{n!}{(n-r)!}$ and from this we obtain the familiar expression $\frac{n!}{(n-r)!r!}$ for $\binom{n}{r}$.

Problem 4.1

Find the value of $\binom{n}{0} + \binom{n}{1} + \cdots + \binom{n}{n}$.

Here we are asked to evaluate a sum of binomial coefficients.

We could, of course, substitute $a = b = 1$ into the expression for $(a+b)^n$ in equation (3.4) on page 33 to obtain the value 2^n. However, this is not particularly illuminating as it relies on algebraic manipulation rather than combinatorial insight.

The argument by double-counting is much more satisfactory. We are asked to sum the numbers of ways of choosing 0, 1, 2, 3, ..., n objects from n objects. This is, of course, finding the number of ways of choosing *any* number of objects out of the n objects. We now count this another way, by considering each of the n objects and deciding whether we are going to select it or not. We have two choices n times and so, by the multiplication principle, there are 2^n choices. Hence we obtain the result

$$\binom{n}{0} + \binom{n}{1} + \cdots + \binom{n}{n} = 2^n. \tag{4.1}$$

Problem 4.2

Prove that $1 + 2 + \cdots + n = \frac{1}{2}n(n+1)$.

Now we have to find a formula for the sum of the first n positive integers. We will tackle this by counting the number of dots in the array in figure 4.1 in two ways.

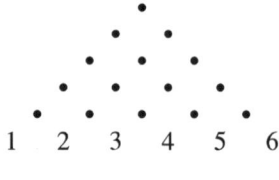

Figure 4.1

The number of dots is the sum of the numbers in each row, which is $1 + 2 + 3 + 4 + 5$. But each dot in the array can be labelled with a unique pair of different numbers in the bottom row by considering it as the intersection of two lines at 45° and 135°.

Chapter 4: Enumerating

Hence the number of dots in the array is the number of ways of choosing two of the numbers from 1 to 6, and that is $\binom{6}{2}$. Since the same argument applies for arrays of any size, we have

$$1 + 2 + \cdots + n = \binom{n+1}{2} = \tfrac{1}{2}n(n+1).$$

Problem 4.3

Denote by $p_n(k)$ the number of permutations of a set with n elements which have exactly k fixed points.

Prove that $p_n(1) + 2p_n(2) + \cdots + np_n(n) = n!$. [IMO 1987]

This problem about fixed points of permutations is from the International Mathematical Olympiad. A permutation of a set S has k fixed points if exactly k of the elements of S are unchanged by it. For example, if the set is the letters of the word WOMBAT, then the permutation BOMTAW has three fixed points, namely O, M and A. We shall call the number of fixed points the *score* of a permutation. We are required to prove that

$$p_n(1) + 2p_n(2) + \cdots + np_n(n) = n!. \tag{4.2}$$

Our method will be to count the total score of all permutations. The term $kp_n(k)$ is the total score of all permutations with exactly k fixed points, and we add these over the possible scores from 1 to k. This is one way of counting the total score. We now count this total in another way. We do this by focussing instead on the elements $\{a_1, a_2, \ldots, a_n\}$ of the set, and count how many times each a_i is fixed. If one element is fixed, then the other $n-1$ elements of the set can be permuted in any way, so each a_i is fixed $(n-1)!$ times. Since the same is true for all n elements of the set, the total score is $n!$ which is the right-hand side of equation (4.2).

This seems rather easy (and it was indeed the first question on the IMO paper) but it is important to understand what is going on. The fact that the right-hand side of equation (4.2) is $n!$ might suggest that we are counting permutations, but that is not what is happening. Let us take an example where the set is $\{1, 2, 3, 4\}$ and classify the permutations according to their score.

Four fixed points
There is one permutation 1234 and so $p_4(4) = 1$.

Exactly three fixed points
This is impossible, so $p_4(3) = 0$.

Exactly two fixed points
There are six permutations 1243, 1432, 1324, 4231, 3214, 2134 and so $p_4(2) = 6$.

Exactly one fixed point
There are eight permutations 1342, 1423, 2314, 2431, 3124, 3241, 4132, 4213 and so $p_4(1) = 8$.

No fixed points
There are nine permutations 2143, 2341, 2413, 3142, 3412, 3421, 4123, 4312, 4321 and so $p_4(0) = 9$.

Now if we were simply counting permutations, our sum would be $1 + 0 + 6 + 8 + 9 = 24 = 4!$. But what we are really doing is counting fixed points, so the calculation which appears on the left-hand side of equation (4.2) is $4 \times 1 + 3 \times 0 + 2 \times 6 + 1 \times 8 + 0 \times 9 = 24 = 4!$. On the right-hand side we are looking at how many times 1 appears in the first place in the list of permutations, and unsurprisingly this is $3! = 6$. Hence 1 is a fixed point six times, and so are 2, 3 and 4, and hence the total number of fixed points is $24 = 4!$. In fact, any attempt at a solution which depended on counting permutations would almost certainly have been incorrect.

Exercise 4a

1. Prove the identity $1^2 + 2^2 + \cdots + n^2 = \frac{1}{6}n(n+1)(2n+1)$ by counting ordered triples (r, s, k) with $0 \leq r, s < k \leq n$ from the set $\{0, 1, 2, \ldots, n\}$. [HINT]

*2. Prove the identity $1^3 + 2^3 + \cdots + n^3 = (1 + 2 + \cdots + n)^2)$ by considering lattice rectangles (as in question 5 of exercise 3b) inside a square of side n, where the top right corner of each rectangle has one coordinate equal to k and the other less than or equal to k.

Chapter 4: Enumerating

3. Prove Vandermonde's identity

$$\binom{m+n}{r} = \binom{m}{0}\binom{n}{r} + \binom{m}{1}\binom{n}{r-1} + \cdots$$
$$+ \binom{m}{k}\binom{n}{r-k} + \cdots + \binom{m}{r}\binom{n}{0},$$

where $m, n \geq 1$ and $0 \leq r \leq m+n$. (If r is greater than either m or n some terms in this expression will be zero.)

4. A club consisting of n members has to produce a quiz team, which includes a captain. It can be made up of any number of people between 1 and n.
   (a) By counting the number of such teams in two different ways, prove that

   $$\binom{n}{1} + 2\binom{n}{2} + \cdots + n\binom{n}{n} = n \times 2^{n-1}.$$

   (b) Use a similar argument to show that

   $$1 \times 0 \times \binom{n}{1} + 2 \times 1 \times \binom{n}{2} + \cdots$$
   $$+ n(n-1) \times \binom{n}{n} = n(n-1) \times 2^{n-2}.$$

5. By considering a club consisting of $2n$ people, with equal numbers of men and women, show that

   (a) $\binom{n}{0}^2 + \binom{n}{1}^2 + \cdots + \binom{n}{n}^2 = \binom{2n}{n};$

   (b) $2 \times \binom{n}{1}^2 + 4 \times \binom{n}{2}^2 + \cdots + 2n\binom{n}{n}^2 = n\binom{2n}{n};$

   (c) $1^2 \times \binom{n}{1}^2 + 2^2 \times \binom{n}{2}^2 + \cdots + n^2\binom{n}{n}^2 = n^2\binom{2(n-1)}{n-1}.$

   HINT

6. Prove that, for any $1 \leq m \leq n$

$$\binom{n}{0}\binom{n}{m} + \binom{n}{1}\binom{n-1}{m-1} + \binom{n}{2}\binom{n-2}{m-2} + \cdots$$
$$+ \binom{n}{m}\binom{n-m}{0} = 2^m \binom{n}{m}.$$

***7.** What is the total number of terms in all of the compositions (ordered partitions) of 10? [HINT]

4.2 Bijecting

In the last chapter, we solved a number of problems all of which led to the same answer $\binom{10}{4}$. In doing so, we showed that two situations, despite appearing to be about quite different things, turn out to be equivalent. For example, it turned out that the problems of counting the number of

- group hugs in a party of management trainees
- shortest routes in a city with a road network in the form of a grid
- intersections of chords inside a circle
- solutions of a Diophantine equation
- ways of allocating bones between dogs

all reduced to the question of finding the number of permutations of the word PPPPPPQQQQ. We used the word *coding* to describe the process of representing one problem by another, but now we will re-examine this using the language of set theory.

Suppose that we have two sets A and B. The obvious way of showing that the number of elements in A is the same as the number of elements in B is just to count each of them, but that may be impractical. Another way is to set up a one-to-one correspondence between the two sets, which allows us to associate with every element of A exactly one element of B. For example, the sets

$$A = \{\text{United, Kingdom, Mathematics, Trust}\}$$
$$\text{and} \quad B = \{\text{Athos, Porthos, Aramis, d'Artagnan}\}$$

can be shown to be of the same size by displaying a pairing such as

$$\text{United} \leftrightarrow \text{Porthos}$$
$$\text{Kingdom} \leftrightarrow \text{Aramis}$$
$$\text{Mathematics} \leftrightarrow \text{d'Artagnan}$$
$$\text{Trust} \leftrightarrow \text{Athos}$$

which is clearly only one of the 24 different pairings which could be used.

We will be more formal than this and talk about a *function* from one set to the other. A *bijection* (another term for a one-to-one correspondence) is a function $f: A \to B$ which has the following two properties:

(i) for any $b \in B$, there exists an $a \in A$ such that $f(a) = b$;
(ii) for any $a_1, a_2 \in A$ such that $f(a_1) = f(a_2)$, we have $a_1 = a_2$.

The first property expresses the fact that the range of f—the set of values which f takes—is the whole of B. In other words, every element of B is the image of at least one element of A. The second property says that different elements of A have different images in B. We can put these together to say that every element of B is the image of *exactly one* element of A. Because of this, it is clear that there is also an inverse function $f^{-1}: B \to A$ that reverses the effect of f. It is easy to see that the two parts of the definition of a bijection mirror exactly the two criteria for successful counting, that every case should be counted at least once, and that no case should be counted twice.

If A is a finite set with n elements, and there is a bijection between it and a set B, then B is also finite with n elements. For infinite sets, the existence of a bijection is used as the defining property of sets with the same size or *cardinality*. Interesting as this subject is, it is not the province of this book and we will not pursue it.

In the solutions to problem 3.6 on page 38 and questions 10, 11 and 17 of exercise 3b, we showed that different things could be coded using the string ✲✲◆◆✲◆◆✲✲✲, which is a permutation of a word with four letters of one kind and six of another. It was implicit in the solutions that this coding was unique and reversible, or, in other words, that it represented a bijection. Indeed, there is a second bijection here, since permutations of words made up of two distinct symbols can be thought of as combinations. In section 3.4, we identified another bijection between combinations of r objects from $n + r - 1$ objects without replacement and combinations of r objects from n objects with replacement.

Problem 4.4

Prove that $\binom{n}{0} + \binom{n}{2} + \binom{n}{4} + \cdots = \binom{n}{1} + \binom{n}{3} + \binom{n}{5} + \cdots = 2^{n-1}$.

Now we are asked to show that the sum of the odd terms in any row of Pascal's triangle is equal to the sum of the even terms. Once we know that, it is obvious from equation (4.1) that the common sum is 2^{n-1}.

Another way of phrasing this is to say that the sums of alternate entries in any row of Pascal's triangle are equal. Again, it is easy to do this by putting $a = 1$ and $b = -1$ into the binomial expression for $(a+b)^n$. For the odd rows, which contain an even number of entries, this fact is obvious from symmetry, but this argument does not help with even rows, such as

$$1 \quad 8 \quad 28 \quad 56 \quad 70 \quad 56 \quad 28 \quad 8 \quad 1$$

for which it is still true. Another approach is to use Pascal's identity (equation (3.3) on page 32) to note that the sum of the even entries in row n is the sum of all entries in row $n-1$, which is 2^{n-1}, and the same is true for the sum of the odd entries. But none of these approaches is purely combinatorial. Here is an argument which uses a bijection.

Let $n = 2m$, and consider a club with $2m$ members which decides to enter a team (of any size from zero to $2m$) into the local quiz tournament. The general knowledge mastermind Memory Mike is a member of the club. Once the team has been chosen, the following change is made. If Mike has been selected, he is dropped, and if he has not been selected, he is included. This procedure replaces every team which includes Mike with a new one which does not include him. Note also that the number of people in the team switches parity from even to odd or from odd to even.

Odd		Even
With Mike	$\longleftrightarrow$	Without Mike
Without Mike	$\longleftrightarrow$	With Mike

Table 4.1

We have now paired off teams with an even number of players with teams with an odd number of players. For example, the team consisting of Mike alone corresponds to the empty team, and the team consisting of everyone corresponds to the team containing everybody except Mike.

Hence the number of teams with an even number of members is equal to the number of teams with an odd number of members.

4.3 Partitioning

Partitions were introduced in question 5 of exercise 1a. We now look at this in more detail. (You have also met compositions, which are like partitions except that the order of parts matters. These are much easier to deal with.)

Since the order of the parts in a partition does not matter, we might as well represent it as a list of numbers in decreasing order of magnitude. For example, one of the partitions of 15 is

$$6\ 4\ 3\ 1\ 1$$

and there are many others. The numbers in the list are known as the *parts* of the partition, so this example has five parts.

A useful tool in investigating partitions is to represent them as *Ferrers diagrams*, which show the parts as left-aligned rows of dots. The Ferrers diagram for the partition above is shown in figure 4.2.

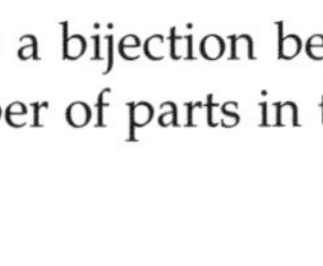

```
• • • • • •
• • • •
• • •
•
•
```

Figure 4.2

It is obvious that there is a bijection between partitions and Ferrers diagrams, and that the number of parts in the partition is the number of rows in the diagram.

Problem 4.5

Prove that the number of partitions of n into k parts is equal to the number of partitions of n with greatest part k.

We investigate this problem by the example in figure 4.2. We have, in some way, to relate it to a partition with greatest part equal to five. The diagram practically gives the game away, since it has five rows, so the longest column is of height five, and we have to produce a diagram whose longest row is of length five. If we transpose the rows and columns we obtain figure 4.3, which represents the partition

$$5\ 3\ 3\ 2\ 1\ 1,$$

a partition of 15 with greatest part equal to five.

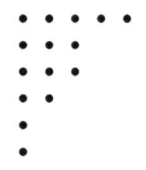

Figure 4.3

The partition is known as the *conjugate* of the first partition. Moreover, if we transpose it a second time, we are back to where we started. Hence this is a bijection between partitions with five parts and partitions with greatest part equal to five. There is, of course, nothing special about the numbers 15 and 5, which can be replaced by n and k. So we have a composition of three bijections:

partition of n with k parts $\leftrightarrow$ Ferrers diagram
$\leftrightarrow$ conjugate Ferrers diagram
$\leftrightarrow$ partition of n with greatest part k

A partition which is identical to its conjugate is known as *self-conjugate*.

Exercise 4b

1. Prove that the number of partitions of n into at most k parts is equal to the number of partitions of n with greatest part at most k. Find an explicit formula when $k = 2$.

2. Prove that the number of partitions of n into at most k parts is equal to the number of partitions of $n + k$ into exactly k parts.

Chapter 4: Enumerating

3. Prove that the number of partitions of n into even parts is equal to the number of partitions of n in which each part appears an even number of times.

4. Prove that the number of partitions of n into distinct odd parts is equal to the number of self-conjugate partitions of n. [HINT]

5. Prove that the number of partitions of n with k parts is equal to the number of partitions of $n + \binom{k}{2}$ with k distinct parts. [HINT]

* 6. Prove that the number of partitions of n into odd parts is equal to the number of partitions of n into distinct parts. [HINT]

* 7. An equilateral triangle of side length n is divided into n^2 equilateral triangles of side length 1 by drawing line segments parallel to the sides. How many parallelograms are there in this figure? [HINT]

* 8. A matrix is a rectangular array of numbers; if these are all either 0 or 1 it is known as a binary matrix. How many binary matrices, with n rows and m columns, have the property that every row and column total is odd? [HINT]

4.4 Making PIE

Problem 4.6

How many positive integers between 1 and 100 are multiples of 2 or 3?

The number of multiples of 2 is clearly 50 and the number of multiples of 3 is 33, since the smallest is 3 and the largest 99. However, the solution to this problem is not $50 + 33 = 83$, since the number 6 would have been counted twice. In fact, the numbers which have been counted twice are precisely the multiples of 6, of which there are 16. We therefore compensate for the over-counting by this number, and the correct answer is $50 + 33 - 16 = 67$.

We can think of this problem in terms of the language of set theory, and in particular Venn diagrams. If you are unfamiliar with Venn diagrams or set theory notation, you may like to look at appendix A.

Referring to figure 4.4, the set A consists of all the multiples of 2 and B of all the multiples of 3.

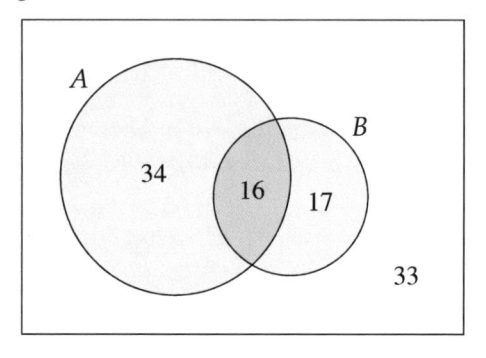

Figure 4.4

The argument above can be expressed in set notation as

$$|A \cup B| = |A| + |B| - |A \cap B|$$
$$= 50 + 33 - 16$$
$$= 67.$$

Note that we could also have deduced that $|(A \cup B)'| = 33$, counting the numbers which are multiples of neither 2 nor 3. The set $(A \cup B)'$ is the *complement* of $A \cup B$ and can also be expressed as $A' \cap B'$.

In a harder question, we might want to count the number of elements which are in at least one of the three sets A, B and C. The relevant result is that

$$|A \cup B \cup C| = |A| + |B| + |C| - |A \cap B| - |B \cap C| - |C \cap A| + |A \cap B \cap C|.$$

Figure 4.5 shows the classic Venn diagram for three sets.

What happens here is that we begin by adding the numbers of elements in the sets A, B and C separately. We have, however, counted the elements in $A \cap B$ twice, so we subtract that amount, together with the numbers in $B \cap C$ and $C \cap A$. But now we have not counted the elements in $A \cap B \cap C$

Chapter 4: Enumerating 59

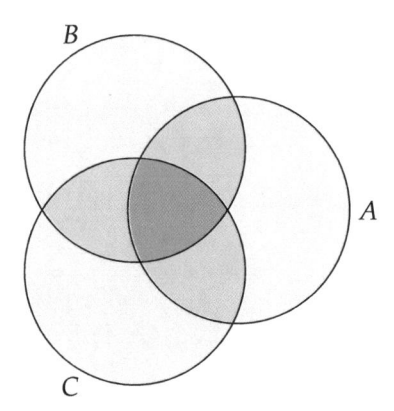

Figure 4.5

at all, so we add them back in. It is easy to check that everything in the union has been counted exactly once.

This procedure can be generalised to any number of sets. It is obvious what you have to do, but this is a situation where the notation needed is harder than the idea itself. We will write our sets as $A_1, A_2, \ldots, A_m$. The intersection of sets i and j is written A_{ij} (for $1 \leq i < j \leq m$), and similarly A_{ijk} stands for $A_i \cap A_j \cap A_k$. We also use sigma notation, which is explained in appendix B. We have

$$\left| \bigcup_i A_i \right| = \sum_i |A_i| - \sum_{i<j} |A_{ij}| + \sum_{i<j<k} |A_{ijk}| - \cdots + (-1)^n |A_{123\ldots m}|. \quad (4.3)$$

To show that this is true, it is necessary to show that every element in any of the sets is counted exactly once.

Suppose that a particular element is in exactly r of the sets. We can rename them so that it is in the sets $A_1, A_2, \ldots, A_r$. Consider the terms on the right-hand side of equation (4.3). In the first term $\sum_i |A_i|$, the element is counted r times, which is also $\binom{r}{1}$. In the second term $-\sum_{i,j} |A_{ij}|$, the element is 'uncounted' once every time that $1 \leq i < j \leq r$, that is, $\binom{r}{2}$ times. In the third term, it is counted once every time that $1 \leq i < j < k \leq r$, which is $\binom{r}{3}$ times.

Carrying on in this way, we see that it is counted exactly $\binom{r}{1} - \binom{r}{2} + \binom{r}{3} - \cdots \pm \binom{r}{r}$ times (where the final sign is $+$ if r is odd and $-$ if r is even). But, by problem 3.4, this is $\binom{r}{0}$ times, which is once, and everything in the garden is lovely.

This result is known as the *principle of inclusion and exclusion*, sometimes called the *inclusion-exclusion principle*, since it is a combination of over-generous inclusion followed by over-compensating exclusion. In order to tempt the appetite, it is often referred to as PIE.

THE INCLUSION-EXCLUSION PRINCIPLE

For sets $A_1, A_2, \ldots, A_m$,

$$\left|\bigcup_i A_i\right| = \sum_i |A_i| - \sum_{i<j} |A_{ij}| + \sum_{i<j<k} |A_{ijk}| - \cdots + (-1)^n |A_{12\ldots m}|.$$

Inclusion-exclusion is particularly useful when counting something with conditions which can overlap. The reason is that it often much easier to count an intersection than a union. In an intersection of sets which are defined by conditions, all of the conditions apply, and that usually cuts down the counting to make it manageable.

It is good practice when writing out an argument using PIE to define the sets explicitly. This focuses your mind on how the argument works and also makes it easier for the reader to understand the proof. As usual, the best way to illustrate this is to discuss some examples.

Problem 4.7

In how many ways can four couples sit in a row if no couple is sitting together?

Call the couples $A = \{A_1, A_2\}$, $B = \{B_1, B_2\}$, $C = \{C_1, C_2\}$ and $D = \{D_1, D_2\}$. Let S_A be the set of seating plans in which couple A is sitting together, and so on. The total number of arrangements is $8!$, since the eight people are distinguishable.

The set we are trying to count is $(S_A \cup S_B \cup S_C \cup S_D)'$; we do this by finding $|S_A \cup S_B \cup S_C \cup S_D|$ and subtracting the result from $8!$.

Now if couple A is together, we can treat them as a single entity and there are $7!$ permutations of seven objects, but A_1 and A_2 can be in either order, so $|S_A| = |S_B| = |S_C| = |S_D| = 2 \times 7!$. Similarly, $|S_A \cap S_B| = 2^2 \times 6!$, $|S_A \cap S_B \cap S_C| = 2^3 \times 5!$ and $|S_A \cap S_B \cap S_C \cap S_D| = 2^4 \times 4!$.

Hence, using the inclusion-exclusion principle, we get

$$|S_A \cup S_B \cup S_C \cup S_D|$$
$$= \binom{4}{1} \times 2 \times 7! - \binom{4}{2} \times 2^2 \times 6! + \binom{4}{3} \times 2^3 \times 5! - 2^4 \times 4!,$$

which is 26 496. It follows that the answer we want is 13 824.

Problem 4.8

How many five-digit numbers contain all of the digits 1, 2 and 3?

Again we start by defining our sets: S_1 as the five-digit numbers which do not contain the digit 1, and similarly S_2 and S_3. Note that it is much easier to count cases when a digit does not occur than to count cases when it does, since we do not need to worry about where it is in the number. We simply require that every digit is not, for example, 5. Again we want to count $(S_1 \cup S_2 \cup S_3)'$ and we begin by finding $|S_1 \cup S_2 \cup S_3|$. Remember that a number cannot begin with a zero. Now $|S_1| = |S_2| = |S_3| = 8 \times 9^4$, $|S_1 \cap S_2| = |S_2 \cap S_3| = |S_3 \cap S_1| = 7 \times 8^4$ and $|S_1 \cap S_2 \cap S_3| = 6 \times 7^4$.

So, from the inclusion-exclusion principle, we obtain

$$|S_1 \cup S_2 \cup S_3| = 3 \times 8 \times 9^4 - 3 \times 7 \times 8^4 + 6 \times 7^4$$
$$= 85\,854.$$

But in all there are 9×10^4 five-digit numbers, so the required answer is 4146.

4.5 Factors and multiples

This technique is often useful in questions about positive integers and their factors.

Problem 4.9

How many numbers less than 1000 are multiples of 2, 3, 5 or 7?

The sets will be multiples of 2, multiples of 3, multiples of 5 and multiples of 7; call these M_2, M_3, M_5 and M_7 respectively. We need to find the number of elements in $M_2 \cup M_3 \cup M_5 \cup M_7$. There are 999 numbers altogether, and we use the fact that multiples of any number occur at regular intervals, so we can find out how many there are by dividing. So what is $|M_2|$? Of course $999 \div 2 = 499.5$, but the answer is clearly not that but 499, since the last multiple of 2 is 998. So it will turn out to be useful to use the *floor function*, which is written $\lfloor x \rfloor$ and defined by

$\lfloor x \rfloor$ is the largest integer less than or equal to x.

With this notation, we have $|M_i| = \lfloor \frac{999}{i} \rfloor$, $|M_i \cap M_j| = \lfloor \frac{999}{ij} \rfloor$, $|M_i \cap M_j \cap M_k| = \lfloor \frac{999}{ijk} \rfloor$ and $|M_2 \cap M_3 \cap M_5 \cap M_7| = \lfloor \frac{999}{210} \rfloor$.

Therefore, using the inclusion-exclusion principle, we discover that $|M_2 \cup M_3 \cup M_5 \cup M_7|$ is equal to

$$\left\lfloor \frac{999}{2} \right\rfloor + \left\lfloor \frac{999}{3} \right\rfloor + \left\lfloor \frac{999}{5} \right\rfloor + \left\lfloor \frac{999}{7} \right\rfloor$$
$$- \left\lfloor \frac{999}{6} \right\rfloor - \left\lfloor \frac{999}{10} \right\rfloor - \left\lfloor \frac{999}{14} \right\rfloor - \left\lfloor \frac{999}{15} \right\rfloor - \left\lfloor \frac{999}{21} \right\rfloor - \left\lfloor \frac{999}{35} \right\rfloor$$
$$+ \left\lfloor \frac{999}{30} \right\rfloor + \left\lfloor \frac{999}{42} \right\rfloor + \left\lfloor \frac{999}{70} \right\rfloor + \left\lfloor \frac{999}{105} \right\rfloor - \left\lfloor \frac{999}{210} \right\rfloor$$
$$= 499 + 333 + 199 + 142$$
$$- 166 - 99 - 71 - 66 - 47 - 28 + 33 + 23 + 14 + 9 - 4$$
$$= 771.$$

The process is fairly tiresome, but not as bad as listing them all.

4.6 Primes

PIE is a *sieve method*, in that it gains information by sifting and resifting information, and the process used above is what happens in the most famous example of these, the *sieve of Eratosthenes*, which identifies prime numbers. We start with a grid of, say, the positive integers from 1 to 100. We cross out 1, since it is not a prime number.

Now the first number in the list which has not been deleted is 2 and that is a prime. Next we cross out all the multiples of 2 larger than 2 itself, and identify the next number in the grid which has not been deleted. It is 3, so that is the next prime number. Now repeat this process, deleting multiples of 3, then multiples of 5, then multiples of 7, and so on. After a while the only numbers left in the grid will be the primes less than 100. That is the situation in the grid shown in figure 4.6.

1	2	3	4	5	6	7	8	9	10
11	12	13	14	15	16	17	18	19	20
21	22	23	24	25	26	27	28	29	30
31	32	33	34	35	36	37	38	39	40
41	42	43	44	45	46	47	48	49	50
51	52	53	54	55	56	57	58	59	60
61	62	63	64	65	66	67	68	69	70
71	72	73	74	75	76	77	78	79	80
81	82	83	84	85	86	87	88	89	90
91	92	93	94	95	96	97	98	99	100

Figure 4.6

It is clear that you do not need to continue this process beyond 7. That is because the first number you cross out which has not already been deleted is the square of the prime you are working with. When you cross out the multiples of 7, you do not need to delete 14, since that has already vanished under the sweep using 2, and you do not need to delete 21 or 35 for similar reasons. Hence the first number you actually cross out is 49, the square of 7, and you will also delete 77 and 91. When it comes to 11, the first number to be affected will be the square of 11, which is 121, and it is larger than 100 and not in the grid. It follows that you can stop at the largest prime less than the square root of 100, which is 7.

At this point it is helpful to recall the Prime Factorisation Theorem, which states that any positive integer can be factorised into a product of primes in exactly one way. As it does not matter what order the primes appear in the factorisation, they are written in increasing order. The first prime number 2 is written as p_1, and similarly $p_2 = 3$, $p_3 = 5$ and p_n is the nth prime number. Then we can write

$$N = p_1^{a_1} p_2^{a_2} \cdots p_m^{a_m} = \prod_{i=1}^{m} p_i^{a_i}, \qquad (4.4)$$

where the a_i (the exponents) are non-negative integers and m is some positive integer.

This, by the way, is the reason why 1 is not considered to be a prime number, despite the fact that its only divisors are 1 and itself. If it were taken to be a prime, we could add any power of 1 to the prime factorisation of a number, and it would no longer be unique.

Now suppose that M is a factor of N. It is clear that the only primes which can divide into M are those which occur in the prime factorisation of N, and that the largest exponent of p_i which is possible is a_i. This means that $M = \prod_{i=1}^{m} p_i^{b_i}$, where $0 \leq b_i \leq a_i$. Hence there are $a_i + 1$ choices for the exponent of p_i in M, and so the number of factors of N is $\prod_{i=1}^{m}(a_i + 1)$. Note that, by taking all the b_i zero, we obtain the factor 1, and by taking $b_i = a_i$, we get the factor N.

Problem 4.10

How many of the factors of 10! are not multiples of 6, 15 or 35?

The prime factorisation of 10! is $2^8 \times 3^4 \times 5^2 \times 7^1$, so the number of its factors is $9 \times 5 \times 3 \times 2 = 270$. Now we define A_6, A_{15} and A_{35} as the sets of the factors which are multiples of 6, 15 and 35 respectively. Then we calculate $|A_6 \cup A_{15} \cup A_{35}|$ using PIE.

If a factor of 10! is also a multiple of 6, it contains at least one 2 and one 3 in its prime factorisation, so $|A_6| = 8 \times 4 \times 3 \times 2 = 192$. Similarly $|A_{15}| = 9 \times 4 \times 2 \times 2 = 144$ and $|A_{35}| = 9 \times 5 \times 2 \times 1 = 90$.

The set $A_6 \cap A_{15}$ contains multiples of 30, so $|A_6 \cap A_{15}| = 8 \times 4 \times 2 \times 2 = 128$. By the same argument $|A_6 \cap A_{35}| = 8 \times 4 \times 2 \times 1 = 64$, $|A_{15} \cap A_{35}| = 9 \times 4 \times 2 \times 1 = 72$ and $|A_6 \cap A_{15} \cap A_{35}| = 8 \times 4 \times 2 \times 1 = 64$.

Therefore, using the inclusion-exclusion principle, we obtain

$$|A_6 \cup A_{15} \cup A_{35}| = 192 + 144 + 90 - 128 - 64 - 72 + 64$$
$$= 226.$$

Hence the answer is $270 - 226 = 44$.

Exercise 4c

1. How many six-letter words begin or end with a consonant?

2. In how many ways can a bridge hand (of 13 cards) be selected from a 52 card pack if it is to contain at least one card from each suit?

3. With how many zeros does 2014! end? [HINT]

4. How many permutations of the letters of MATHEMATICS have the As between the Ms or the As between the Ts (or both)?

5. In how many ways can five distinguishable dogs be given twenty-five indistinguishable biscuits so that no dog gets more than seven biscuits?

* 6. An important concept in number theory, attributed to Euler, is the *phi function* $\phi(N)$, where N is a positive integer. It counts the number of positive integers less than N which are coprime to N. For example, $\phi(15) = 8$, since the numbers 1, 2, 4, 7, 8, 11, 13 and 14 are those (less than 15) which do not share a factor greater than 1 with 15.
Suppose that $N = p_1^{\alpha_1} p_2^{\alpha_2} \cdots p_m^{\alpha_m}$, where $p_1, \ldots, p_m$ are distinct primes and $\alpha_1, \ldots, \alpha_m$ are positive integers. Prove that

$$\phi(N) = N\left(1 - \frac{1}{p_1}\right)\left(1 - \frac{1}{p_2}\right) \cdots \left(1 - \frac{1}{p_m}\right).$$

7. In section 4.2, we gave two conditions for a function between sets to be a bijection. Splitting these up, we say that a function $f: A \to B$ is
   (i) an *injection* if, for any $a_1, a_2 \in A$ such that $f(a_1) = f(a_2)$, we have $a_1 = a_2$;
   (ii) a *surjection* if, for any $b \in B$, there exists an $a \in A$ such that $f(a) = b$.

Hence a bijection is both an injection and a surjection.
(a) How many functions are there from $\{1, 2, \ldots, m\}$ to $\{1, 2, \ldots, n\}$?
(b) If $m \leq n$, how many injections are there from $\{1, 2, \ldots, m\}$ to $\{1, 2, \ldots, n\}$?
*(c) If $m \geq n$, how many surjections are there from $\{1, 2, \ldots, m\}$ to $\{1, 2, \ldots, n\}$? HINT
(d) Hence prove that

$$n^n - \binom{n}{1}(n-1)^n + \binom{n}{2}(n-2)^n - \cdots + (-1)^n n = n!.$$

4.7 Deranging

Problem 4.11

A malevolent postman, who has to deliver six letters to six addresses in a street, is determined to do so in such a way that every letter goes to the wrong address.

In how many ways can this be done?

We can take the letters and addresses as the numbers 1 to 6, and thus solve identical questions such as finding out how many ways everyone at a meeting can take the wrong umbrella home. In the terminology of problem 4.3, the question is asking how many of the permutations of 1 2 3 4 5 6 have no fixed points. Such permutations are called *derangements*. The solution of problem 3.3 is of little help, since that involved multiplying this number by zero.

We use PIE, letting A_i be the set of permutations for which i is a fixed point, for $1 \leq i \leq 6$. Then $\bigcup_i A_i$ is the set which have at least one fixed point, which is the complement of the set we are interested in. Now $|A_i| = 5!$, since if, for example, the number 1 is fixed, then 2 3 4 5 6 can permute in any way. Similarly $|A_{ij}| = 4!$, $|A_{ijk}| = 3!$ and so on until $A_{123456} = 1$. There are $\binom{6}{2}$ ways of choosing i and j with $1 \leq i < j \leq 6$, $\binom{6}{3}$ ways of choosing i, j and k with $1 \leq i < j < k \leq 6$, and so on. So the

Chapter 4: Enumerating

calculation turns out to be

$$\left|\bigcup_i A_i\right| = \binom{6}{1} \times 5! - \binom{6}{2} \times 4! + \binom{6}{3} \times 3!$$
$$- \binom{6}{4} \times 2! + \binom{6}{5} \times 1! - \binom{6}{6} \times 0!$$

However, this is counting the non-derangements, so the number we want is

$$6! - \binom{6}{1} \times 5! + \binom{6}{2} \times 4! - \binom{6}{3} \times 3!$$
$$+ \binom{6}{4} \times 2! - \binom{6}{5} \times 1! + \binom{6}{6} \times 0!,$$

which turns out to be 265.

It is easy to generalise this to derangements of n objects. Using the symbol $!n$ for the number of derangements of n objects, we have the formula

$$!n = n! - \binom{n}{1} \times (n-1)! + \binom{n}{2} \times (n-2)! - \cdots + (-1)^n,$$

or, after the use of the formula for combinations and a little manipulation,

$$!n = n!\left(1 - \frac{1}{1!} + \frac{1}{2!} - \cdots + (-1)^n \frac{1}{n!}\right). \tag{4.5}$$

Students who are perfectly happy with PIE are often a bit worried about what is happening in this particular case. It seems that you begin with all $n!$ permutations. In the next step you get rid of $n \times (n-1)!$ of them to compensate for overcounting. But that is actually all of them—you now have none at all. What exactly is happening here? How can we recover from this desperate situation? It is worth focussing on what happens in this counting procedure, taking as an example the 24 permutations of 1234, which are listed in the first column of table 4.2 on the following page. In the second to seventh columns, we list what happens to each permutation at each stage in our sieving process.

Initially, all 24 permutations have been counted. At the first stage, when we deduct $\binom{4}{1} \times 3!$ of them, all those with at least one fixed point are deleted, but some of them are deleted more than once. The permutation

Permutation	Start	First stage	Second stage	Third stage	Fourth stage	End
1234	1	−4	+6	−4	+1	0
1243	1	−2	1			0
1324	1	−2	1			0
1342	1	−1				0
1423	1	−1				0
1432	1	−2	1			0
2134	1	−2	1			0
2143	1					1
2314	1	−1				0
2341	1					1
2413	1					1
2431	1	−1				0
3124	1	−1				0
3142	1					1
3214	1	−2	1			0
3241	1	−1				0
3412	1					1
3421	1					1
4123	1					1
4132	1	−1				0
4213	1	−1				0
4231	1	−2	1			0
4312	1					1
4321	1					1

Table 4.2

1243 is deleted twice, once since the 1 is a fixed point and again since 2 is a fixed point. So, although it appears that a total of 24 permutations are deleted, some of them have been deleted more than once. At the next stage, 12 permutations are re-instated. At this point, we are very nearly there; all of the non-derangements have been deleted apart from 1234. That has a fairly torrid time of it; it is deleted four times at the first stage, re-instated six times at the second, deleted four times at the third stage and re-instated once at the fourth, and must feel like a disreputable

Chapter 4: Enumerating

reveller who persistently re-enters a night-club only to encounter the same bouncer every time.

Each entry in the final column of the table is either 0 or 1: when the permutation is a derangement it is 1; otherwise it is 0. Therefore all the derangements have been counted once and all the rest not at all, which is how it should be.

Notice also that you can tell how many fixed points a permutation has by looking at what happens to it. A permutation with two fixed points has the history $1 - 2\ 1$, and one with one fixed point has the simpler experience $1 - 1$. You might try constructing the appropriate table with $n = 5$, but you should set aside some time if you decide to do this.

If you are familiar with the power series for e^x, you will know that

$$e^{-1} = 1 - \frac{1}{1!} + \frac{1}{2!} - \frac{1}{3!} + \cdots,$$

and so we have a limiting result

$$\lim_{n \to \infty} \frac{!n}{n!} = \frac{1}{e}, \qquad (4.6)$$

which states that the probability of a permutation being a derangement approaches $\frac{1}{e}$ as the number of objects in the permutation increases. This probability turns out to be about 37%.

Chapter 5

Forming recurrences

Now we consider in more detail some of the methods used in chapter 1 which involved tabulation, but express it in the language of sequences and iteration.

5.1 Iterating

We begin by revisiting the first problem in the book (problem 1.1 on page 1) about the number of outcomes when four coins are tossed. Having decided that the answer was 16, we claimed that this could easily be generalised to n coins to give the solution 2^n. We now examine the argument in more detail.

Let u_n stand for the number of outcomes when n coins are tossed, or, equivalently, when a single coin is tossed n times. This can be thought of as the nth term of a sequence which begins with the terms 2, 4, 8 and 16. An explicit expression for u_n in terms of n, which allows us to calculate the value easily, is known as a *closed-form formula*. Our argument in chapter 1, which relied on the multiplication principle, uses the fact that each toss has exactly two outcomes. Consequently we have to multiply 2 by itself n times, and the closed-form formula is $u_n = 2^n$.

We could, however, have proceeded in a different way. After only one toss of the coin there are only two outcomes, H or T, so $u_1 = 2$. After n tosses there are, by definition, u_n outcomes and the next toss will be either an H or a T so, again by the multiplication principle, $u_{n+1} = 2 \times u_n$. Now we have the pair of equations

$$u_{n+1} = 2u_n;$$
$$u_1 = 2. \tag{5.1}$$

From these we can find u_2, then u_3, u_4, ..., and eventually u_n for any value of n.

This is a simple case of a *recurrence relation*. Note that its statement has two parts. The first is the recurrence proper, since it describes how the $(n+1)$th term in the sequence can be calculated from previous terms. In this case, u_{n+1} depends only on u_n, but many recurrence relations will depend on more than one previous term. The second part fixes the *initial conditions*—in this case, the fact that the first term of the sequence is 2. Moving from a recurrence relation, such as recurrence 5.1, to a closed-form formula is known as *solving* the relation. In this case, it is clear that the closed form is $u_n = 2^n$.

However, there will be many recurrence relations where it is by no means obvious how to obtain a closed-form formula. In a sense, this does not matter, since even a term such as $u_{1\,000\,000}$ can easily be found using a spreadsheet. In problem 1.7 on page 15, we used a recurrence relation to find u_{10} without needing any calculation aids. So, for the time being, we will concentrate on discovering the recurrence relations rather than finding an explicit closed form solution.

The first new problem involves a romantic story invented by the mathematician Edouard Lucas to promote a game he had devised in 1883, which is nowadays called the Tower of Hanoi. It is based on an 'ancient legend'.

In the city of Benares, beneath a dome that marks the centre of the world, is a brass plate in which are set three diamond needles, each a cubit high and as thick as the body of a bee. Brahma placed sixty four discs of pure gold on one of these needles at the time of Creation. Each disc is a different size, and each is placed so that it rests on top of another disc of greater size, with the largest resting on the brass plate at the bottom and the smallest at the top. Within the temple are priests whose job it is to transfer all the gold discs from their original needle to one of the others, without ever moving more than one disc at a time. No priest can ever place any disc on top of a smaller one, or anywhere else except on one of the needles. When the task is done, and all the discs have been successfully transferred to another needle, tower, temple, and Brahmins alike will crumble into dust, and with a thunder-clap the world will vanish.

Chapter 5: Forming recurrences

Problem 5.1

If the priests manage to move one disc every second, how long have we got?

This can be tackled by constructing a recurrence relation. For the sake of argument, suppose that the discs are transferred from the first needle to the third. We shall, of course, assume that, since they are looking forward to the afterlife, the priests work in the most effective fashion, and that they will have enough discipline to complete the process when it comes to placing the final disc on the third needle rather than prevaricating because of a spiritual crisis of faith.

Let u_n be the minimum number of moves in which n discs can be transferred.

It is clear that $u_1 = 1$, since one simply picks up the disc on the first needle and places it on the third. Now suppose that there are $n+1$ discs to move. At some stage, the largest disc has to be transferred from the first needle, and this cannot be done until the other n discs have been moved from the first needle to another one. Once this is done, however, the bottom disc can be moved and then the initial sequence of moves repeated. So the most efficient system is to

(i) move the first n discs from the first onto the second needle;
(ii) move the final disc from the first needle onto the third;
(iii) then move the other n discs from the second needle to the third.

Now the number of moves needed for the second step is 1, and the number of moves for each of the first and third steps is u_n. So the total number of moves is $u_n + 1 + u_n = 2u_n + 1$. We therefore have the recurrence relation

$$u_{n+1} = 2u_n + 1;$$
$$u_1 = 1. \qquad (5.2)$$

Listing the first few values, we obtain the sequence 1, 3, 7, 15, 31, 63, ..., and conjecture that $u_n = 2^n - 1$. This fact is proved on page 105.

The end of the world will occur $2^{64} - 1$ seconds after the priests started their task. This is in the order of six hundred billion years, which is good news.

5.2 Fibonacci

In this section, we focus on a very important recurrence relation.

Problem 5.2

Sidney is standing at the top of a flight of 10 stairs and he can jump downwards either taking one stair or two stairs at a time. He might, for example, decide to descend in jumps of one stair, then two, then two, then one, then one, then two and finally one.

In how many distinct ways can he reach the bottom?

We begin with some simple cases, and will, for reasons which will become apparent, denote the number of ways Sidney can descend $n-1$ steps by F_n.

First we consider what happens when $n = 1$ and Sidney has no stairs to jump down. Disappointingly, he will need to keep still, and he can do this (from a strictly combinatorial viewpoint) in exactly one way, and we conclude that $F_1 = 1$.

When there is one stair, he has only one step to make, so $F_2 = 1$.

The first exciting case is when $n = 2$ and then he has two choices; either he can go downstairs like normal people or take the flight in one jump. Hence $F_3 = 2$.

Before we go any further, it is actually worth tabulating the results for values of n up to 6 (table 5.1).

The reason for this is that patterns might emerge, and while we cannot assume that this will continue to happen, it might give us a clue as to how to proceed. Note that, as always, the outcomes have been listed in a systematic way. Those starting with double jumps precede those with single jumps.

At this point, you might conjecture that the relevant recurrence relation is

$$F_{n+2} = F_{n+1} + F_n;$$
$$F_1 = 1,\ F_2 = 1.$$
(5.3)

This looks even more promising when F_7 turns out to be 13. However, this is just pattern-spotting and we need to look deeper. The place to look

Chapter 5: Forming recurrences

n	Stairs	Jump sizes	F_n
1	0	–	1
2	1	1	1
3	2	2	
		1 1	2
4	3	2 1	
		1 2	
		1 1 1	3
5	4	2 2	
		2 1 1	
		1 2 1	
		1 1 2	
		1 1 1 1	5
6	5	2 2 1	
		2 1 2	
		2 1 1 1	
		1 2 2	
		1 2 1 1	
		1 1 2 1	
		1 1 1 2	
		1 1 1 1 1	8

Table 5.1

is the jump patterns. They all start with a 1 or a 2, apart from the case $n = 1$ when Sidney can't do any jumping, but this is not surprising since he is restricted to jumps of one or two stairs.

When you compare each row of the table with the two which precede it, you see that earlier rows of the table 'reappear' in later ones. For example, if you look at the three outcomes for $n = 4$ and insert a ∎ symbol after the preliminary 1 or 2, you can see the outcomes for $n = 2$ and $n = 3$ (table 5.2 on the next page). If you do the same for $n = 5$, you can see the patterns for $n = 3$ and $n = 4$ (table 5.3).

```
                     2 ▮ 2
                     2 ▮ 1 1
       2 ▮ 1         1 ▮ 2 1
       1 ▮ 2         1 ▮ 1 2
       1 ▮ 1 1       1 ▮ 1 1 1

       Table 5.2     Table 5.3
```

Note that this even works for $n = 3$, where you can see the patterns for $n = 0$ and $n = 1$. This should be enough to convince you that the conjectured recurrence 5.3 is correct. We formalise this insight in a proof.

Proof

In order to jump $n + 1$ stairs, Sidney has to begin with a jump of 1 stair or 2 stairs.

If he elects to begin by jumping 1 stair, he then has n stairs to jump, and this can be done in F_{n+1} ways.

If he decides to begin with a jump of 2 stairs, he then has $n - 1$ stairs to jump, and this can be done in F_n ways.

Therefore $F_{n+2} = F_{n+1} + F_n$.

So the sequence goes 1, 1, 2, 3, 5, 8, 13, 21, 34, 55, 89 and Sidney has 89 choices.

This particularly famous sequence is named after the 12th century Italian mathematician Leonardo of Pisa, who was known as Fibonacci. It is said that he formulated the sequence in order to model the breeding behaviour of somewhat predictable rabbits. This is probably a mathematical urban myth, and it has led to a great many speculative claims about the occurrence of the sequence in both nature and art.

We could, of course, code any appropriate way for Sidney to descend his staircase by a sequence of 1s and 2s which add to 10. In doing so, we are forming a bijection between 'stair-jumping strategies' and 'compositions of 10 using only 1s and 2s', and it follows, of course, that the number of such compositions is also 89.

In this and similar problems, it is permissible to give an answer in the form of a Fibonacci number without stating an explicit formula. You will, of course, have to justify the fact that the recurrence relation 5.3 is relevant. A good approach to such problems is to begin by investigating a few small cases, in order to get a feeling for what is going on. If, after a while, you begin to suspect that Fibonacci is appropriate (but maybe with different starting values), try and spot earlier lists reappearing inside later lists, as happened with Sidney and the stairs. Once you have detected this, you need to try and identify some aspect of the problem which allows you to deduce solutions for $n = k + 2$ from the cases $n = k$ or $n = k + 1$. Equally, you might attempt to re-interpret a new problem in terms of one you have already solved, using a bijection such as the one above.

Problem 5.3

A standard set of dominoes consists of 28 thin rectangular tiles measuring one inch by two inches. They fit in four layers in a rectangular box measuring two inches by seven inches.

If we treat different dominoes as indistinguishable, in how many ways can a set be placed in its box?

Actually, this is not a problem about real dominoes, since these are distinguishable and range from the double-zero to the double-six tile, and it is not hard to check that there are indeed 28 such dominoes in a set. We are treating the dominoes as though there were no spots on them and you cannot tell which way up or which way round they are. So the problem is really about fitting 28 indistinguishable 1×2 tiles into a 2×7 box, and this does, of course, require four layers. We shall, however, continue to call them dominoes.

We focus initially on a single layer of the box which contains seven dominoes. Generalising this to n dominoes, we define a *domino box* as measuring two inches by n inches. If n is large, such an artefact would not win any design awards, but that is beside the point. Let u_n be the number of ways n tiles can fill a domino box.

Now consider any arrangement of dominoes in the box. It is obvious that dominoes can either be placed singly, with the long side parallel to the short side of the box, or in pairs, with long sides parallel to the long side of the box. It should now be clear that this situation is the same as compositions using 1s and 2s and as that in problem 5.2. Since $u_1 = 1$ and

$u_2 = 2$, we deduce that $u_n = F_{n+1}$. It follows that $u_7 = F_8 = 21$, and the solution to the problem with four layers is $21^4 = 194\,481$.

If, like real dominoes, the tiles are in fact distinguishable, it is possible to count the number of ways of fitting a double-six set into the appropriate box. We assume that all dominoes are face up. First we arrange the dominoes in order, which can be done in 28! ways. We now place these into the box, and this can be done in 21^4 ways. However, every domino apart from the seven doubles can be inserted in one of two directions, so that gives a further factor of 2^{21}. So the number of ways of packing the dominoes into the box is $21^4 \times 28! \times 2^{21}$ (or possibly half of this if the box has no markings on it so that it can be rotated through 180°). If we allow dominoes to be placed face down, there is an additional factor of 2^{28}. All of these numbers are very large, far bigger than the number of seconds which have elapsed since the Big Bang.

Incidentally, Edouard Lucas also jumped onto the bandwagon by defining the sequence which bears his name and is based on the recurrence

$$L_{n+2} = L_{n+1} + L_n;$$
$$L_1 = 1,\ L_2 = 3. \tag{5.4}$$

The first ten terms of the Lucas sequence are 1, 3, 4, 7, 11, 18, 29, 47, 76, 123.

Exercise 5a

1. Generalise problem 1.2 to n distinct letters and form a recurrence relation.

2. Produce a recurrence relation for question 2 of exercise 1b.

3. How many compositions of 10 have all parts greater than 1?

4. How many compositions of 10 are there into odd parts?

5. How many binary strings of length 10 have no consecutive 1s?

6. How many binary strings of length 10 contain the digit 1 only in consecutive groups of even length? (For instance, 1111001100 is such a string, but 1010101010 is not.)

* 7. How many binary strings of length 10 do not have an even number of consecutive 1s or consecutive 0s?

* 8. Find the number of permutations $a_1, a_2, \ldots, a_{10}$ of the numbers 1, 2, ..., 10 which have the property that $a_r < a_{r+2}$ for $1 \leq r \leq 8$ and $a_r < a_{r+3}$ for $1 \leq r \leq 7$. [BMO1 1986]

* 9. An increasing sequence of integers is said to be *alternating* if the first term is odd, the second term is even, the third term is odd, the fourth term is even, and so on. The empty sequence, with no terms, is considered to be alternating. How many alternating sequences are there involving only integers from the set $\{1, 2, \ldots, 10\}$? [BMO1 1994]

10. A set of positive integers is defined to be *wicked* if it contains no three consecutive integers. We count the empty set as a wicked set. Find the number of wicked subsets of $\{1, 2, \ldots, 10\}$. [BMO1 2003]

* 11. Find the number of permutations $j_1 j_2 j_3 j_4 j_5 j_6$ of 1 2 3 4 5 6 with the property that, for no integer r, where $1 \leq r \leq 5$, is $j_1 j_2 \ldots j_r$ a permutation of $1 2 \ldots r$. [BMO1 1991]

5.3 Counting in Catalan

Now we examine several problems which lead to the same recurrence relation.

Problem 5.4

Twelve people are seated around a circular table.

In how many ways can six pairs of people engage in handshakes so that no arms cross? (Nobody is allowed to shake hands with more than one person at once.) [BMO1 2001]

Naturally we have to make various sensible assumptions, such as the fact that nobody shakes hands with themselves or under the table. In fact, we might insist that everyone ties one hand behind their back just to avoid temptation. As usual, a good start is to simplify the problem and, in the course of doing so, generalise it to n handshakes. We will call any configuration which satisfies the conditions of the problem a *handshaking pattern* and define h_n as the number of these when there are $2n$ people.

Table 5.4 shows the first three cases.

n	Handshaking patterns	h_n
1		1
2		2
3		5

Table 5.4

Chapter 5: Forming recurrences

As always, we need to be very careful in listing cases. In order not to omit or duplicate any, we should have a system in making the list. What is then likely to happen is that we will spot a systematic way of using earlier cases to produce later ones.

It is clear that there is only one handshaking pattern with two people. The situation with four people is equally obvious, but even so we can gain some insight into the problem by examining this in more detail. Without a diagram, it might seem that person 1 has three choices for the recipient of their handshake. However, the handshake between 1 and 3 is unacceptable, since it will leave the other two people unable to shake hands without contravening the rule about arms crossing. So we have established a necessary condition for a handshake to be possible: it divides the table into two parts with an even number of people in each part.

Now we look at the diagram for six people. Again we focus on person 1. They have three choices for their handshake partner. If 1 and 2 shake hands, then the other four can shake hands in two ways. Notice that this is the case $n = 2$. If 1 and 4 shake hands, then this divides the table into two parts, each of which contain two people—and that is the case $n = 1$. If 1 and 6 shake hands, then again we have four people who can shake hands in two ways. So we have five possibilities since $5 = 2 + 1 \times 1 + 2$, noting that the middle term of this equation arises because of the multiplication principle.

It is quite useful to add the case where $n = 0$ and then define h_0 as 1. We then see that the situation when a person shakes hands with their neighbour actually divides the table into two parts, one of which contains no people. So we can refine the calculation above to say that $5 = 1 \times 2 + 1 \times 1 + 2 \times 1$, or, using the notation of the problem, $h_3 = h_0 h_2 + h_1^2 + h_2 h_0$. And we also have $h_2 = h_0 h_1 + h_1 h_0$ and even $h_1 = h_0^2$.

We have now solved the problem, or, at any rate, we have identified the crux. Jumping straight to the general case, we conjecture that h_n satisfies the recurrence relation

$$h_{n+1} = h_0 h_n + h_1 h_{n-1} + \cdots + h_n h_0;$$
$$h_0 = 1,$$

which we may write in the form (see appendix B)

$$h_{n+1} = \sum_{i=0}^{n} h_i h_{n-i};$$
$$h_0 = 1.$$

To prove this, it is enough to make the observation that person 1 shakes hands with somebody in a way which divides the remainder of the table into two even groups, one of which contains $2i$ people and the other of which contains $2(n-i)$ people. Remember that the total number is $2n+2$, so this makes sense (see figure 5.1).

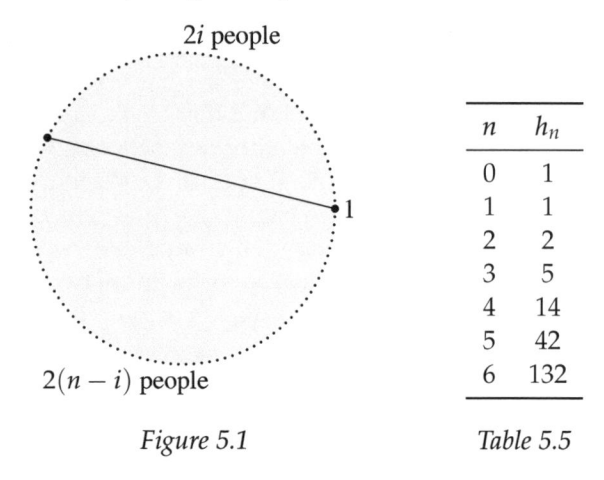

Figure 5.1

n	h_n
0	1
1	1
2	2
3	5
4	14
5	42
6	132

Table 5.5

Then we use the multiplication principle to obtain the recurrence relation.

Now we just run through the first few values of h_n to produce table 5.5 and so there are 132 ways in which the twelve people can shake hands.

Problem 5.5

A mountain profile is composed of six upstrokes and six downstrokes, starting and finishing at 'sea-level' and never going below it.

In how many ways can this be done?

We define m_n as the number of profiles using $2n$ strokes and call such a mountain profile an n-profile. Again we begin with some experimentation, as shown in table 5.6.

The fact that we see the same numbers reappearing suggests that this might be the same sequence as the handshaking patterns, but we cannot be sure unless we can prove it. The natural way to proceed is to

Chapter 5: Forming recurrences

n	Mountain profiles	m_n
1	/\	1
2	/\/\ /_/\	2
3	/\/\/\ /\/_/\ /_/\/\ /_/_/\ /__/\	5

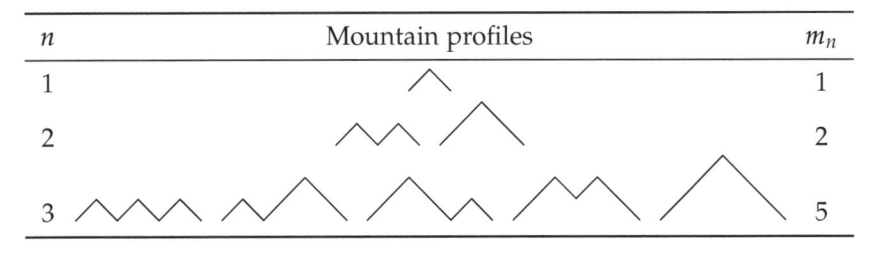

Table 5.6

attempt to form the same recurrence relation, so we require to show that $m_3 = m_0 m_2 + m_1^2 + m_2 m_0$.

This suggests that we have to use *concatenation*—forming a new profile by putting two profiles together. However, there are difficulties. The first term in this recurrence looks as though we should concatenate a 0-profile and a 2-profile to produce a 3-profile, but this simply does not work. What happens if we form a 3-profile from a 1-profile and a 2-profile? Looking at the table, this would clearly give us the first three 3-profiles, but we would not achieve the last two, which are clearly 'new' profiles. Moreover, it would produce the recurrence $m_3 = m_1 m_2 + m_2 m_1$ and the value $m_3 = 4$. How has this happened?

In fact, we are counting the first 3-profile twice, since we might concatenate 'one-peak' and a 'two-peak' or a 'two-peak' and a 'one-peak'. This gets even worse when we consider moving to 4-profiles, since the '4-peak' is counted three times. This idea, which seemed so promising at first, has the drawback that it fails the test for good counting on both criteria. It fails to count everything at least once and it counts some things more than once. We shall have to be more ingenious if we are going to make this work.

The solution is to divide the 3-profiles into two at the first place where the profile descends to sea-level. The first part can consist of either two, four or six strokes. To count the number of possible profiles for this part, allow the sea to rise so as to cover the first upstroke and the first downstroke. From the way the part was defined, what remains above the new sea-level is now a mountain profile.

Now we count. The first part may have two, four or six strokes.

Two strokes
The first part can be chosen in m_0 ways, and the profile is completed by a 2-profile, for which there are m_2 choices.

Four strokes
The first part can be chosen in m_1 ways, and the profile is completed by a 1-profile, for which there are m_1 choices.

Six strokes
The first part can be chosen in m_2 ways, and the profile is completed by a 0-profile, for which there are m_0 choices.

Note that this avoids counting the 'three-peak' profile more than once, since the first 'peak' is counted separately from the next two. As a result of this method we obtain the correct relation $m_3 = m_0 m_2 + m_1^2 + m_2 m_0$. This method clearly generalises to any profile. As a result we see that we have exactly the same recurrence relation as for handshaking patterns, and so we obtain the same sequence of numbers. There are 132 6-profiles.

The next example concerns objects called *binary family trees* which are charts displaying genealogical information. The restriction is that in these trees, parents either produce no offspring or exactly two.

To simplify matters, we will assume that all offspring are female and we will ignore the role of fathers, so that the people in the tree are just mothers and daughters. The example in figure 5.2 shows a mother A, who has daughters B and C. Then B has daughters D and E, C has daughters F and G, F has no daughters, and so on.

Note that the elder daughter always goes on the left. This means that we will not, for example, be counting reflections of the family tree in the central axis as being equivalent.

The 'objects' in this tree are known as *nodes* and lines showing the relationship between them are *branches*. There is a superfluous extra node at the top, whose only purpose is to hang the tree up; this is called the *root*. If we turned the diagram through a right-angle the tree would be familiar to those familiar with probability calculations. Nodes such as D, H and K are known as *end nodes*, since there are no branches emanating from them, and the nodes A, B, C, E and G are *source nodes*. It is essential that for each source node gives rise to exactly two branches.

Chapter 5: Forming recurrences

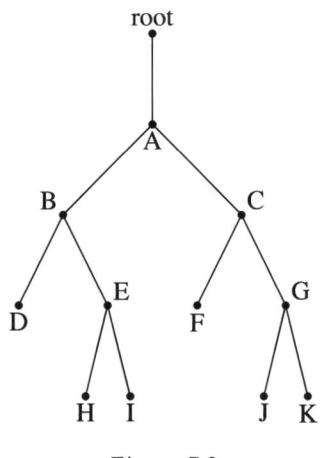

Figure 5.2

Problem 5.6

How many binary family trees are there with seven end nodes?

When we count, we are concerned only with the structure of the tree, not with names on the nodes. As has already been mentioned, we count reflected trees, such as the two in figure 5.3, as being different from one another. For convenience, we shall refer to the diagrams simply as trees.

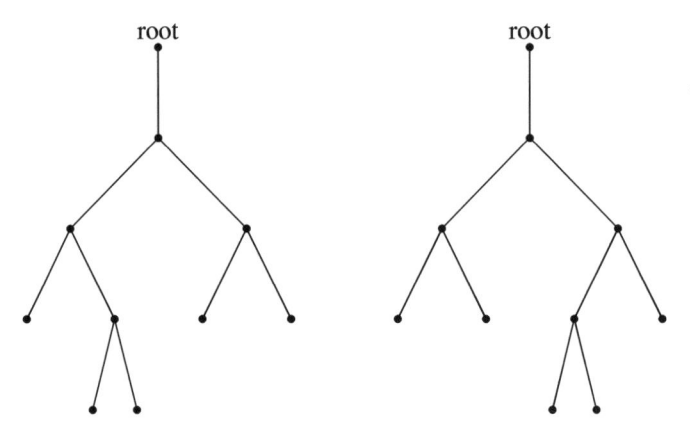

Figure 5.3

Let T_n be the number of trees with $n+1$ end nodes. Set $T_0 = 1$ and note that $T_1 = 1$ since there is only one such tree with two end nodes. Now consider a tree with $n+1$ end nodes.

At the first node after the root, the tree splits into two, one part with $k+1$ end nodes and the other with $n-k$ end nodes, for some $0 \le k \le n-1$, as shown in figure 5.4.

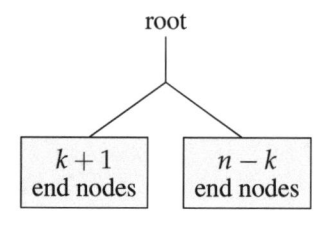

Figure 5.4

There are T_k and T_{n-k+1} ways of choosing such trees, so, summing over all k, we have

$$T_n = \sum_{k=0}^{n-1} T_k T_{n-k+1}.$$

Hence we have the same sequence of numbers and $T_6 = 132$.

The last three problems led to the same sequence of numbers. These are known as *Catalan numbers*, but not because they have anything to do with Barcelona FC. They are in fact named after the Belgian mathematician Eugène Charles Catalan, who lived from 1814 to 1894 and worked mainly in number theory. We shall therefore denote the sequence by c_n. They are defined by the recurrence relation

$$c_{n+1} = c_0 c_n + c_1 c_{n-1} + \cdots + c_{n-1} c_0;$$
$$c_0 = 1,$$
(5.5)

which may be written

$$c_{n+1} = \sum_{i=0}^{n} c_i c_{n-i};$$
$$c_0 = 1.$$

We will encounter two more examples of this sequence in exercise 5b.

Exercise 5b

1. How many ways are there of dividing an octagon into six triangles using five diagonals?

2. The expression $a \div b \div c \div d \div e \div f \div g$ is ambiguous, since it does not show the order in which the six divisions should take place. In order to resolve this ambiguity, it is necessary to insert five pairs of brackets. Two ways in which this can be done are

$$\Big(((a \div b) \div c) \div (d \div (e \div f) \div g)\Big)$$

and

$$\Big((a \div ((b \div c) \div (d \div e))) \div (f \div g)\Big)$$

and there are many others. How many different ways are there to insert five pairs of brackets into this expression? Note that we are counting the number of bracketings, not the algebraic outcomes.

5.4 Metamorphosis

We now have five different manifestations of Catalan numbers. They are

(i) handshaking patterns for n pairs of people;
(ii) mountain profiles with n upstrokes and n downstrokes;
(iii) triangulations of polygons with $n+2$ sides;
(iv) binary family trees with $n+1$ end nodes;
(v) expressions with n pairs of brackets around $n+1$ letters.

These have been shown to produce the Catalan numbers because they satisfy the same recurrence relation. In what follows, we begin with a handshaking pattern and convert it sequentially into a mountain profile, a bracketed expression, a triangulated polygon and a binary family tree before finally returning to the same handshaking pattern.

We begin with a handshaking pattern for $n = 6$, shown in the left-hand diagram of figure 5.5 on the following page. We consider each handshake to have a direction (shown by an arrow), which is from the lower number to the higher. In the process to be described, we will begin with person 1 and an outgoing handshake. As we go around the circle, the number of incoming handshakes we have encountered can never exceed the number of outgoing, although it can equal it.

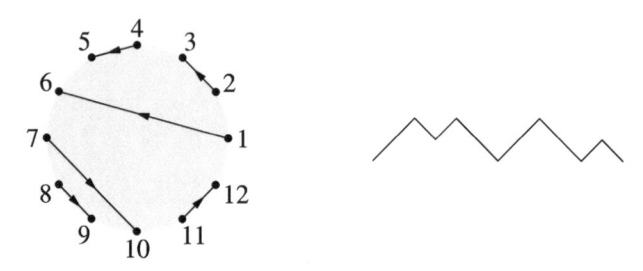

Figure 5.5

We transform the pattern into a mountain profile by carrying out the following series of steps. We start at 1 and go around the circle anticlockwise. For every outgoing handshake, we draw an upstroke. For every incoming handshake, we draw a downstroke. As a result we produce the right-hand diagram of figure 5.5.

The profile has the same number of upstrokes as downstrokes, because each handshake is between two people. Also it cannot go below sea-level, since if it did so at some stage, there would have been more incoming than outgoing handshakes. Hence we always have a valid profile. However, we also need to check that different handshaking patterns lead to different profiles. This will show that the mapping from patterns to profiles is an injection.

We label the upstrokes and downstrokes in the mountain profile in numerical order, as shown for the example above in figure 5.6.

Figure 5.6

The handshake partners can now be read off as horizontal neighbours, starting with an upstroke—1 and 6, 2 and 3, 4 and 5, 7 and 10, 8 and 9, 11 and 12. Hence the handshaking pattern can be retrieved from the mountain profile, and so each profile can only have come from one pattern.

Chapter 5: Forming recurrences 89

We now transform this profile into a way of bracketing the expression *abcdefg*, which has seven symbols. We begin on the left and move to the right, applying the following rules.

(i) An upstroke denotes a left bracket.
(ii) A downstroke denotes a new symbol.
(iii) When we reach the end of the profile, we add the *g*, which has not yet been included.
(iv) Finally we add the right brackets.

The left-hand diagram of figure 5.7 shows the mountain profile we begin with. The first three steps produce the string shown on the right of figure 5.7.

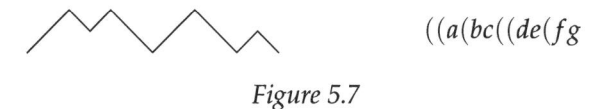

$((a(bc((de(fg$

Figure 5.7

Now we add the right brackets. It turns out that there is only one legal way to do this. It is easiest to work from the right-most uncompleted left bracket. Defining an *object* as either a letter or a completed expression, the string can only be completed by two objects and then a right bracket. Table 5.7 on the next page shows the resulting sequence of actions.

To return to the mountain profile, reverse the sequence of operations. Begin by deleting all the right brackets and the *g*, and then read from the right, replacing letters by downstrokes and left brackets by upstrokes.

Now we use the bracketed expression $((a(bc))((de)(fg)))$ to triangulate an octagon. We label the sides of an octagon with the letters *a*, *b*, *c*, *d*, *e*, *f* and *g* that are used in the expression, as shown on the left of figure 5.8.

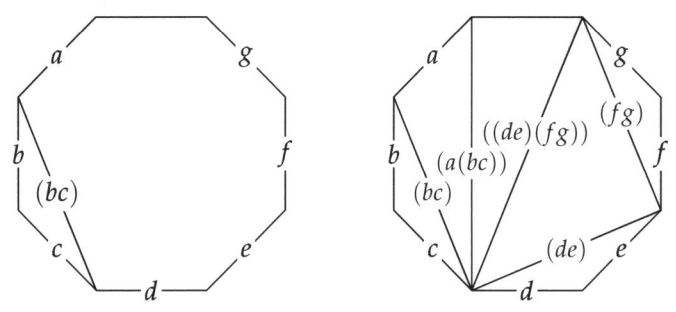

Figure 5.8

Expression	Action
$((a(bc((de(fg$	Complete the final left bracket by adding a right bracket after fg.
$((a(bc((de(fg)$	Complete the fifth left bracket by inserting a right bracket after de.
$((a(bc((de)(fg)$	Complete the fourth left bracket by adding a right bracket after $(de)(fg)$.
$((a(bc((de)(fg))$	Complete the third left bracket by inserting a right bracket after bc.
$((a(bc)((de)(fg))$	Complete the second left bracket by inserting a right bracket after $a(bc)$.
$((a(bc))((de)(fg))$	Complete the first left bracket by adding a right bracket at the end.
$((a(bc))((de)(fg)))$	

Table 5.7

We find the first completed bracket in the expression, which is (bc), and draw a diagonal to complete a triangle whose sides are the symbols involved, and label it appropriately. Thus the first chord is labelled (bc) (see the diagram on the left of figure 5.8).

Now the next completed bracket is $(a(bc))$, which corresponds to the diagonal completing the triangle with sides a and (bc).

Carrying on, we produce the triangulation shown on the right of figure 5.8. Note that the original bracketed expression would appear as the label for the side at the top.

You should take a moment to check that this process always produces a triangulation of the octagon, and that different bracketings produce different triangulations.

The next step is to use the triangulation to create a rooted binary family tree.

We begin by placing a root node above the top side of the octagon (see the diagram on the left of figure 5.9). We enter the triangle adjacent to this side, drawing a branch to a new node.

Chapter 5: Forming recurrences

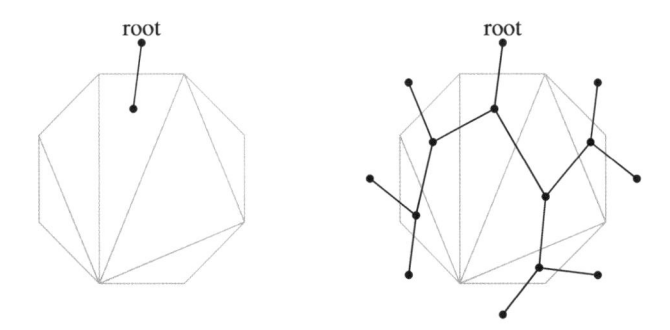

Figure 5.9

We continue this process, and whenever we are forced outside the octagon, we create an end node. Finally we end up with the diagram on the right of figure 5.9; then we lose the octagon. The result will be a rooted binary tree. Note that it has seven end nodes.

As before, you should check that this always results in a binary family tree with the right number of end nodes, and that different triangulations will result in different trees.

Assuming this to be the case, we use the tree (which has been given a good shake to make itself presentable) to create a handshaking pattern. We begin by labelling the branches in a systematic fashion.

Below the root is the first source node. We label the left branch below it as 1. If the labelled branch leads to a source node (as it does), we label the next left branch with the next digit—in this case 2. See the diagram on the left of figure 5.10 on the next page.

If the labelled branch leads to an end node (as does branch 2), we return to the previous node and label the right branch with the next digit—here 3. Continuing in this way we arrive at the diagram on the right of figure 5.10. Ardent royalists will recognise this as the system of primogeniture which determines the line of succession to the throne.

Finally we create a handshaking pattern by looking at the branching pattern. We see that branches 1 and 6 divide at the same node, and this tells us that person 1 shakes hands with person 6. In the same fashion, we see that the handshaking partners are 2 and 3, 4 and 5, 7 and 10, 8 and 9, and 11 and 12 (see figure 5.11).

As a result we are back to the original handshaking pattern. This sequence shows that $h_n \leq m_n \leq t_n \leq T_n \leq b_n \leq h_n$ and so the sequence of

Figure 5.10

Figure 5.11

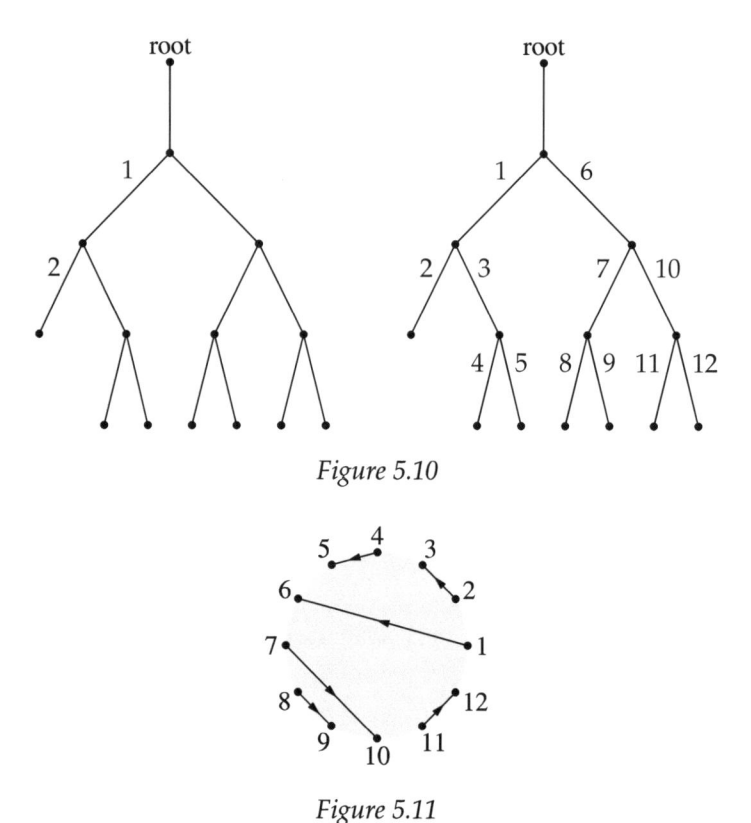

numbers determined by each scenario is the same. They are all examples of Catalan numbers and the injections turned out to be bijections.

5.5 Voting

Problem 5.7

In an election with two candidates, André polls eight votes to Bertrand's six. The polling clerk counts the ballot papers one by one in such a way that André is always ahead of his rival in the cumulative count.

In how many ways can this happen?

Chapter 5: Forming recurrences

The progress of the count can be charted on a Cartesian graph. Votes for André are shown on the y-axis and votes for his opponent on the x-axis.

A possible path which meets the conditions of the problem is illustrated in figure 5.12. In the order in which they were counted, the votes were AABAABAAABBABB.

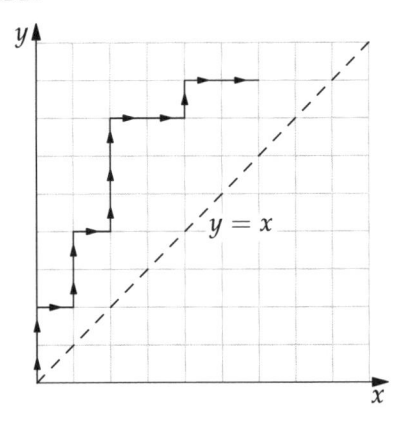

Figure 5.12

What is important is that André is always ahead. This means that the path always stays strictly above the line $y = x$.

We shall call such a path *happy*, and also generalise the problem to the case where the final outcome is (b, a), where $a > b \geq 0$ are integers. Therefore we have to count the number of happy paths from $(0,0)$ to (b, a). It is obvious that any such path begins by going to the point $(0, 1)$ and from now on we will focus our attention on counting the happy paths from $(0, 1)$ to (b, a).

We have already encountered the problem of counting all paths—happy or unhappy—from $(0, 1)$ to (b, a) since it is virtually the same as problem 3.4. By coding the path as a sequence consisting of $a - 1$ As and b Bs, we see that the answer is $\binom{a+b-1}{b}$. We now need to subtract from this the number of unhappy paths, which touch or cross the line $y = x$. In order to do this, we use a trick known as the *reflection principle*. The method is illustrated below for the case when $(b, a) = (6, 8)$.

The graph on the left of figure 5.13 on the following page shows an unhappy path which both crosses and touches the line $y = x$. Note that it first contravenes the rules of the problem at the point $(4, 4)$.

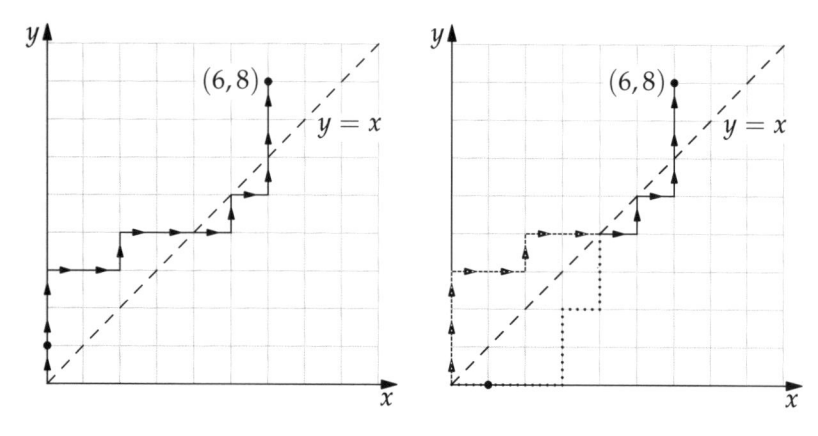

Figure 5.13

Now we take the part of the path before $(4,4)$ and reflect it in the line $y = x$. The result of concatenating this reflected path and the original path beyond $(4,4)$ is now an unhappy path from $(1,0)$ to $(6,8)$ (see the graph on the right of figure 5.13).

However, every path between these points is unhappy, since it has to cross the line in order to reach the opposite side. So these are actually all paths from $(1,0)$ to $(6,8)$.

Hence the number of unhappy paths from $(0,1)$ to (b,a) is simply the number of paths from $(1,0)$ to (b,a), and this is $\binom{a+b-1}{b-1}$.

It follows that the number of happy paths is $\binom{a+b-1}{b} - \binom{a+b-1}{b-1}$, which is easily shown to be equal to $\frac{a-b}{a}\binom{a+b-1}{b}$.

This is known as Bertrand's ballot problem, named after the French mathematician Joseph Louis François Bertrand, and the reflection idea was the brainchild of the Belgian mathematician, Desiré André. What is interesting about the solution is that ratio of happy paths to all paths is $\frac{a-b}{a}$, which depends only on the ratio $a : b$ and not on the actual values. Thus the probability of the clerk counting the votes in the specified way depends only the proportions of the final outcome.

Now we relate this to the Catalan numbers by looking at mountain profiles. The basic idea is to map the profile to a happy path on a graph. This can be done by treating upstrokes as steps in the y-direction and downstrokes as steps in the x-direction.

Chapter 5: Forming recurrences

However, a mountain profile has equal numbers of upstrokes and downstrokes, whereas a crucial feature of the voting problem is that the poll is never drawn. We therefore prevent this happening by giving André an extra vote at the beginning.

If we do this to the profile with twelve strokes shown on the left of figure 5.14 we obtain the path on the graph shown on the right.

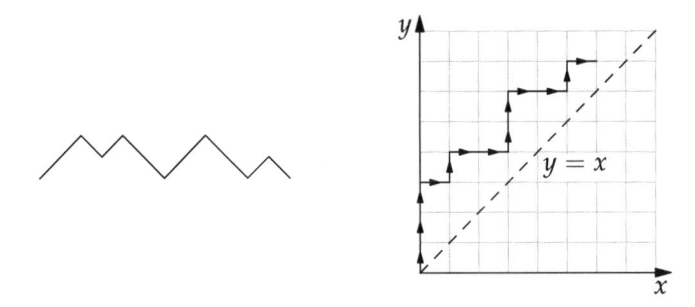

Figure 5.14

Note that the horizon at sea level is equivalent to the line $y = x + 1$ and that the finishing point is $(6,7)$. The number of such profiles is given by setting $a = 7$ and $b = 6$ to obtain $\frac{1}{7}\binom{12}{6} = 132$.

For the general Catalan number c_n, we use $a = n+1$ and $b = n$ to get

$$c_n = \frac{1}{n+1}\binom{2n}{n} \qquad (5.6)$$

This explicit formula for Catalan numbers shows that they are related to the binomial coefficients in the central spine of Pascal's triangle (figure 5.15 on the next page).

It is worth noting that equation (5.6) has an alternative formulation, namely

$$c_n = \frac{1}{2n+1}\binom{2n+1}{n} \qquad (5.7)$$

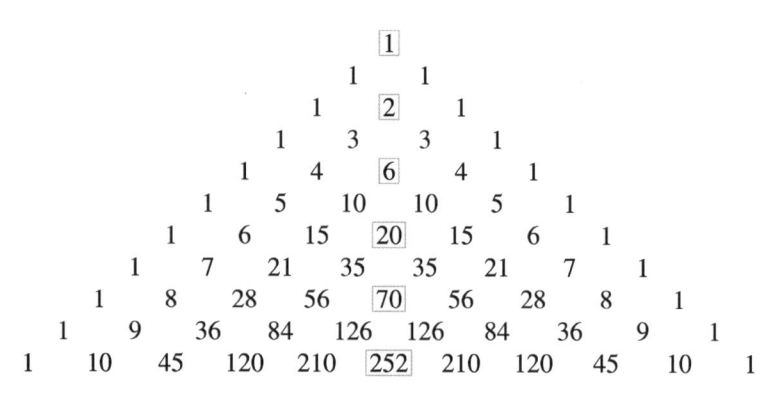

```
                    1
                  1   1
                1   2   1
              1   3   3   1
            1   4   6   4   1
          1   5  10  10   5   1
        1   6  15  20  15   6   1
      1   7  21  35  35  21   7   1
    1   8  28  56  70  56  28   8   1
  1   9  36  84 126 126  84  36   9   1
1  10  45 120 210 252 210 120  45  10   1
```
(boxed entries: 1, 2, 6, 20, 70, 252)

Figure 5.15

5.6 Going directly

What is striking about equation (5.6) is its simplicity. In fact, it is so simple that it suggests that there ought to be a direct—or intuitive—proof that Catalan numbers satisfy it.

The binomial coefficient can be interpreted as the number of ways of placing in order n upstrokes and n downstrokes. Most of these will not be mountain profiles, since they will go below sea level at least once before the end. But it suggests that we might be able to divide the set of all such paths into subsets of size $n+1$ such that each such subset contains exactly one valid mountain profile. Is it possible to do this? It turns out there are at least two proofs of this nature, but they are quite technical. In what follows we explain the ideas without giving the details. References are provided if you are interested in pursuing these.

Let us take as an example the case $n=4$. We code the path from $(0,0)$ to (n,n) by using 0 and 1 as instructions to move one unit in the positive x-direction and the positive y-direction respectively. There are 70 such permutations of the word 00001111. We will call these *strings*. The aim is divide these into 14 classes, each of which contains five strings of which exactly one represents a path which does not cross the line $y=x$, always staying above it.

Now we need to devise a way of beginning with a 'random' string, such as 10011100, and generate from it four new ones. A natural idea might be to 'cycle' the string to produce the list

10011100, 01001110, 00100111, 10010011,

Chapter 5: Forming recurrences

11001001, 11100100, 01110010, 00111001,

after which we would return to the starting point. The trouble is that this yields eight strings in the class, although it is true that exactly one of them, 11100100, is a valid profile. More seriously, if we were to begin with 10101010, there would only be two strings in the class. It is clear that this is not going to work.

However, if we introduce an extra 1 at the end of the initial string, and then cycle that, this will create nine strings consisting of four 0s and five 1s. Exactly four of these will end with a 0. We discard these, and then remove the final 1 from the other five. Let us see what happens.

Starting with 10011100, our augmented string is 100111001, and the nine cycled strings are

100111001, 001110011, 011100110, 111001100, 110011001, 100110011, 001100111, 011001110 and 110011100.

After culling these and removing final 1s, we obtain the five strings

10011100, 00111001, 11001100, 10011001 and 00110011,

which contains exactly one, 00110011, which represents a valid profile.

Now see what happens if we start with the rogue string 10101010. Our first nine strings are

101010101, 110101010, 011010101, 101101010, 010110101, 101011010, 010101101, 101010110 and 010101011,

and after omitting the ones ending in 0 and removing the 1 from the rest, we obtain

10101010, 01101010, 01011010, 01010110 and 01010101,

which are all different, and exactly one, the last, is a valid profile. Note that the extra 1 is acting as a sort of 'impurity' which prevents the duplication of strings when the cycling procedure takes place.

It can be proved that all of the strings in each class are different and that each class contains exactly one string which represents a valid profile. It follows that there are 14 mountain profiles when $n = 4$, and, as this method is generalizable, the Catalan formula is demonstrated. Details of this argument can be found in [3].

An alternative approach can be found in [4]. What makes a string a valid profile is the fact that the path on the graph never crosses the line

$y = x$, although it is allowed to touch it. If we define the *excess* as the number of 'vertical' moves that are above the line, then a valid path will have excess zero. Let us now count the excess for the strings in each of the classes above. In the first case we have table 5.8, and in the second table 5.9. Figure 5.16 shows the corresponding graphs for the first string in each table.

String	Excess
10011100	3
00111001	1
11001100	4
10011001	2
00110011	0

Table 5.8

String	Excess
10101010	4
01101010	3
01011010	2
01010110	1
01010101	0

Table 5.9

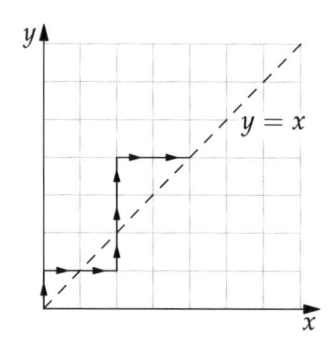

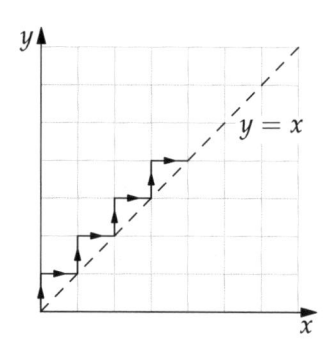

Figure 5.16

It can be shown that each class contains one string whose excess is one of the values from 0 to n. In [4] the author shows how to transform a path with excess k into another with excess $k+1$. Of course, we could now divide the set of 70 permutations into five subsets each consisting of 14 with equal excess. This might be a more natural way of viewing the process.

Chapter 6

Solving recurrences

The emphasis in the last chapter was on forming recurrence relations which would enable us to calculate a term in a sequence which was not too far from the beginning. Now we look at methods of solving recurrences, either to produce a closed-form formula or at least one which is useful for calculation. In the process we will discover some more combinatorial techniques.

6.1 Linear with constant coefficients

Given the way recurrence relations work, it is not surprising that a very useful method of proving that a formula is correct is by using mathematical induction. Details of how induction works, and how proofs by induction should be set out, may be found in appendix D.

In order to use induction, you need to know what the formula is before you prove it to be correct. This is obviously a disadvantage, but a suitable formula can often be guessed by looking at a few terms of the sequence near the start and spotting a pattern. What is clear, however, is that a recurrence relation is exactly what you need to carry out the induction step. The combinatorial insight you need to tackle a problem is effectively in the construction of the recurrence relation, not in the verification by induction that a given formula works.

For some recurrence relations, such as the following, there is a standard approach to solving them.

$$u_{n+2} = 5u_{n+1} - 6u_n;$$
$$u_1 = 2, \ u_2 = 5. \tag{6.1}$$

They are known as linear relations with constant coefficients, since the terms u_n and u_{n+1} are not squared or multiplied together, but are simply added with constant 'weights' 5 and -6. This makes u_{n+2} a linear combination of u_n and u_{n+1}. This is an example of a *second-order* recurrence relation of this type; it is possible, of course, to have linear relations of other orders.

We begin by looking at some first-order recurrence relations, generating the first few terms and seeing if we can spot a solution.

---———————————— **First-order linear** ————————————---

The relation $u_{n+1} = 2u_n$, with initial condition $u_1 = 2$, has the unique solution $u_n = 2^n$. This is obvious since we know that the first term is 2 and then every subsequent term is determined by the recurrence.

If we replace the condition $u_1 = 2$ by $u_1 = 3$, the solution is equally clearly $u_n = 3 \times 2^{n-1}$.

Changing the relation to $u_{n+1} = 2u_n + 1$, with initial condition $u_1 = 1$, we obtain the first five terms 1, 3, 7, 15, 31, ..., which suggests the solution $u_n = 2^n - 1$.

It is also clear that the last solution is unique. In fact, if we start with $u_1 = a$, we can see that the sequence starts with the terms a, $2a - 1$, $2^2a - 1$, $2^3a - 1$, ..., leading to $u_n = 2^n a - 1$.

The most important observation is that each of the solutions involves an exponential term.

We can do the same sort of investigation with second-order linear relations.

---———————————— **Second-order linear** ————————————---

The relation $u_{n+2} = 5u_{n+1} - 6u_n$, with initial conditions $u_1 = 1, u_2 = 2$, produces the sequence 1, 2, 4, 8, 16, ..., which certainly suggests that the solution is $u_n = 2^{n-1}$.

The same relation, but with $u_1 = 1$, $u_2 = 3$, produces 1, 3, 9, 27, ..., which suggests the solution $u_n = 3^{n-1}$.

Chapter 6: Solving recurrences 101

The same relation, but with $u_1 = 2$, $u_2 = 5$, produces 2, 5, 13, 43, ..., which suggests the solution $u_n = 2^{n-1} + 3^{n-1}$.

Again we have exponentials appearing, and again it would be possible to verify these solutions by induction. However, what is interesting here is the relationship between these three solutions. They all satisfy the same recurrence relation but the initial conditions differ. If we 'add' the initial condition for the first and second examples, we obtain the initial conditions for the third, and if we add the solutions for the first and second examples, we obtain the solution of the third. This suggests that the solutions of such recurrence relations have an 'additive' property.

Note also that the relation $u_{n+2} = 5u_{n+1} - 6u_n$, without any initial conditions, is satisfied by both $u_n = 2^n$ and $u_n = 3^n$, since

$$2^{n+2} = 4 \times 2^n = 10 \times 2^n - 6 \times 2^n = 5 \times 2^{n+1} - 6 \times 2^n$$

and

$$3^{n+2} = 9 \times 3^n = 15 \times 3^n - 6 \times 3^n = 5 \times 3^{n+1} - 6 \times 3^n.$$

This piece of algebra is essentially the step in an argument by induction.

This preamble suggests that it might be worth 'testing' a general exponential form $u_n = \lambda^n$ in recurrence 6.1 on page 100. We can assume that λ is not zero, since such a value would yield the 'trivial' solution $u_n = 0$, which clearly satisfies the equation $u_{n+2} = 5u_{n+1} - 6u_n$ but does not match the initial conditions of recurrence 6.1. We obtain $\lambda^{n+2} = 5\lambda^{n+1} - 6\lambda^n$ and can divide by the non-zero λ^n to obtain the quadratic

$$\lambda^2 - 5\lambda + 6 = 0,$$

which is known as the *auxiliary equation*. It has two solutions, $\lambda = 2$ and $\lambda = 3$, and so we now have exactly two candidates for a solution to recurrence 6.1, namely $u_n = 2^n$ and $u_n = 3^n$. We combine these to yield

$$u_n = A \times 2^n + B \times 3^n, \qquad (6.2)$$

where A and B are arbitrary constants, and this is also a solution to $u_{n+2} = 5u_{n+1} - 6u_n$. This is seen by substituting it into the equation; when you do so, everything vanishes. In fact, this replicates what we did above.

Now we must check that the value of u_n given by equation (6.2) satisfies the initial conditions in recurrence 6.1. We substitute for $n=1$ and $n=2$ to obtain the pair of simultaneous equations

$$2A + 3B = 2 \quad \text{and}$$
$$4A + 9B = 5,$$

which have the solution $A = \frac{1}{2}$, $B = \frac{1}{3}$. Thus the solution to recurrence 6.1 is $u_n = 2^{n-1} + 3^{n-1}$.

We can apply this method to the Fibonacci recurrence 5.3 on page 74, that is,

$$F_{n+2} = F_{n+1} + F_n;$$
$$F_1 = 1, \ F_2 = 1.$$

We obtain the auxiliary equation $\lambda^2 - \lambda - 1 = 0$, which has solutions

$$\lambda_1 = \frac{1 - \sqrt{5}}{2} \quad \text{and} \quad \lambda_2 = \frac{1 + \sqrt{5}}{2}.$$

Now the general solution is $F_n = A \times \lambda_1^n + B \times \lambda_2^n$, and from the initial conditions we obtain

$$\lambda_1 A + \lambda_2 B = 1 \quad \text{and}$$
$$\lambda_1^2 A + \lambda_2^2 B = 1.$$

But $\lambda^2 = \lambda + 1$, so, subtracting the first equation from the second, we see that $A + B = 0$. Hence

$$A = \frac{1}{\lambda_1 - \lambda_2} = -\frac{1}{\sqrt{5}} \quad \text{and} \quad B = \frac{1}{\sqrt{5}},$$

so we have

$$F_n = \frac{(1 + \sqrt{5})^n - (1 - \sqrt{5})^n}{2^n \sqrt{5}}, \qquad (6.3)$$

which is know as the *Binet formula*.

This formula is singularly unhelpful as a way of calculating the value of F_n for any $n > 2$, but it has some merits. In particular, note that for large values of n the term $\frac{(1-\sqrt{5})^n}{2^n}$ becomes very small, so that

$$F_n \approx \frac{(1 + \sqrt{5})^n}{2^n \sqrt{5}}.$$

Chapter 6: Solving recurrences 103

In turn, this means that the ratio of successive Fibonacci numbers tends to $\frac{1+\sqrt{5}}{2}$, which is the *golden ratio* and is usually represented by ϕ.

You can discover a great deal of information about this number by looking on the internet and through the literature, but you should be sceptical of many of the folkloric claims made for it. There are, however, many interesting results on relationships between terms in the Fibonacci sequence, and nearly all of these are better approached without using equation (6.3). We will not be discussing these in this book, but you might be interested to know that there is a scholarly journal, the *Fibonacci Quarterly*, devoted to the sequence.

The method shown is applicable to any recurrence relation with constant coefficients, including those which relate one term to three or more preceding ones. The trouble here is that the auxiliary equation will involve a cubic or a higher degree polynomial and it may be difficult or impossible to find the roots.

There is an awkward case when the auxiliary equation has repeated roots. Here is an example of that.

———————————— **Repeated roots** ————————————

Consider the recurrence

$$u_{n+2} = 2u_{n+1} - 1u_n;$$
$$u_1 = 1, u_2 = 3.$$

If we adopt the standard approach, the auxiliary equation is $\lambda^2 - 2\lambda + 1 = 0$, which has the repeated root $\lambda = 1$. There is not a great deal of point in testing $u_n = A \times 1^n + B \times 1^n$, since this is the same as $u_n = C$, and this cannot satisfy the initial conditions.

If we calculate the first terms of the sequence, we obtain $1, 3, 5, 7, 9, \ldots$, so it looks as if $u_n = 2n - 1$, and this can be verified as the solution by induction. So can this be fitted into the usual approach?

The correct response is to test the putative solution $u_n = (An + B) \times 1^n$, which can easily be shown to satisfy the recurrence relation, and then it turns out that we need $A = 2$ and $B = -1$ to satisfy the initial conditions.

In general, the template to use when the auxiliary equation has a repeated root is $u_n = (An + B) \times \lambda^n$.

Exercise 6a

1. Solve the recurrence relation

$$t_{n+2} = t_{n+1} + 2t_n;$$
$$t_0 = 7, \ t_1 = 8.$$

2. Solve the recurrence relation for question 2 of exercise 5a, namely

$$t_{n+2} = 2t_{n+1} + t_n;$$
$$t_1 = 3, \ t_2 = 7.$$

3. Solve the recurrence relation for the Lucas sequence described in recurrence 5.4 on page 78

$$L_{n+2} = L_{n+1} + L_n;$$
$$L_1 = 1, \ L_2 = 3.$$

4. Solve the recurrence relation

$$u_{n+3} = 2u_{n+2} + u_{n+1} - 2u_n;$$
$$u_1 = 1, \ u_2 = 2, \ u_3 = 3.$$

5. Solve the recurrence relation

$$u_{n+2} = 6u_{n+1} - 9u_n;$$
$$u_1 = 1, \ u_2 = 4.$$

Chapter 6: Solving recurrences

6.2 Non-linear

There are many problems which lead to recurrence relations which are not linear with constant coefficients. Since there is such a wide range of such recurrence relations, there are no general techniques for solving them.

In some cases, we can use an intuitive approach. An example of this is question 7 of exercise 3b, which required us to find the maximum number of regions into which n lines divide a plane. Denote this by t_n. It is clear that $t_0 = 1$. In order to achieve a maximum, we need the lines 'in general position', which means that no two are parallel and no three meet in a point. Now suppose we have n lines and t_n regions, and add another line. This will both divide the plane into two and intersect the existing lines in n points, and a little thought will show that as a result $n + 1$ new regions are created. Hence we have the recurrence relation

$$t_{n+1} = t_n + n + 1;$$
$$t_0 = 1.$$

The solution to this is clearly

$$t_n = 1 + (1 + 2 + \cdots + n)$$
$$= 1 + n + \tfrac{1}{2}n(n-1)$$
$$= 1 + n + \binom{n}{2},$$

as before.

However, one good idea is to look for a substitution which turns the given recurrence into a familiar one. For example, consider the recurrence

$$t_{n+1} = 2t_n + 1;$$
$$t_0 = 0,$$

which appeared in the context of the Tower of Hanoi on page 72. If we make the substitution $t_n = u_n + k$, then we obtain $u_{n+1} + k = 2(u_n + k) + 1$ and now we choose k to make $k = 2k + 1$, so $k = -1$. The recurrence relation now becomes

$$u_{n+1} = 2u_n;$$
$$u_0 = 1.$$

and the solution is clearly $u_n = 2^n$. Substituting back, we have $t_n = 2^n - 1$.

Another example is derangements, from problem 4.11 on page 66, which we solved using the inclusion-exclusion principle.

An alternative approach is to let d_n be the number of derangements of $12 \ldots n$. For convenience define $d_0 = 1$. We have $d_1 = 0$. For $n \geq 3$, let $a_1 a_2 \ldots a_n$ be a derangement, so $a_i \neq i$ for $1 \leq i \leq n$. Notice that since $a_1 \neq 1$ it can take $n - 1$ values, and, without loss of generality, suppose that $a_1 = 2$.

Next we look at a_2. If $a_2 = 1$ then $a_3 a_4 \ldots a_n$ is derangement of $34 \ldots n$, and there are d_{n-2} of these. So suppose that $a_2 > 2$. The next step is quite subtle. We have reached the point where $2 a_2 a_3 \ldots a_n$ is a derangement of $12 \ldots n$ where $a_2 \neq 1$ or 2. If we suppress the number 2, which is equivalent to abolishing address number 2 and the letter destined for it, we can think of $a_2 a_3 \ldots a_n$ as a derangement of $13 \ldots n$. There are d_{n-1} of these. Hence we obtain the recurrence relation

$$d_n = (n-1)(d_{n-1} + d_{n-2}) \text{ for } n \geq 2;$$
$$d_0 = 1, \ d_1 = 0. \quad (6.4)$$

and it is now easy to check that $d_6 = 265$. However, recurrence 6.4 does not have constant coefficients, so we cannot use the technique described earlier to solve it.

If we wish to find an expression for d_n just in terms of n, we need to simplify the recurrence. The crucial step is to realise that recurrence 6.4 can be rearranged as

$$d_n - n d_{n-1} = -(d_{n-1} - (n-1)d_{n-2})$$

and if we define u_n as $d_n - n d_{n-1}$ for $n \geq 2$, then this becomes $u_n = -u_{n-1}$, with $u_1 = d_1 - d_0 = -1$. Hence $u_n = (-1)^n$, which you can verify by induction if you wish, but it is obvious. Now the rest is straightforward. We have $d_n - n d_{n-1} = (-1)^n$, or, alternatively,

$$\frac{d_n}{n!} = \frac{d_{n-1}}{(n-1)!} + \frac{(-1)^n}{n!}$$
$$= \frac{d_{n-2}}{(n-2)!} + \frac{(-1)^{n-1}}{(n-1)!} + \frac{(-1)^n}{n!}$$
$$\vdots$$
$$= \frac{(-1)^0}{0!} + \frac{(-1)^1}{1!} + \cdots + \frac{(-1)^n}{n!}.$$

Therefore
$$d_n = n!\left(1 - \frac{1}{1!} + \frac{1}{2!} - \cdots + \frac{(-1)^n}{n!}\right),$$
which is the same formula as we obtained using PIE. Note that this is not a closed-form formula, unlike those we discovered for the linear recurrences discussed in section 6.1.

Exercise 6b

1. Solve the recurrence relation $t_{n+1} = t_n + 2^n$, where $t_0 = 1$.

2. Solve the recurrence relation $t_{n+1} = 2t_n + n$, where $t_1 = 2$. [HINT]

3. Solve the recurrence relation $t_{n+1} = 2t_n + 2^n$, where $t_1 = 1$. [HINT]

4. Solve the recurrence relation $(n+1)t_{n+1} = (n+2)t_n + 1$, where $t_1 = 1$. [HINT]

5. Solve the recurrence relation $t_{n+1} = (n+2)t_n + n!$, where $t_1 = 1$. [HINT]

Chapter 7

Generating

In this chapter we introduce a technique which has a wide range of applications in combinatorics. It gives us another approach to enumeration problems as well as a method for solving recurrence relations.

7.1 Generating functions

We begin by revisiting problem 3.3, which required us to find the coefficient of x^4 in the expansion of $(x+1)^{10}$. For reasons which will become clear, we will rewrite this as $(1+x)^{10}$.

This was analysed in terms of either choosing or not choosing the x term from each of the ten brackets in the expansion, yielding the binomial coefficient $\binom{10}{4}$, which is 210. Suppose that we emphasise this process of choice by writing $1+x$ as $x^0 + x^1$. Then the evaluation of the term $210x^4$ can be seen as the enumeration of 210 ordered sums consisting of six 0s and four 1s.

Suppose now that we modify this problem to that of finding the coefficient of x^4 in the expansion of $(1 + x + x^2)^{10}$. This is equivalent to finding the number of ways in which 4 can be written as an ordered sum of ten numbers which are either 0, 1 or 2. If we use six 0s and four 1s there are 210 ways, as before. If we use two 2s and eight 0s there are $\binom{10}{2} = 45$ ways, and if we use one 2, two 1s and seven 0s there are $\binom{10}{1\,2\,7} = 360$ ways. The total is 615, so that is the coefficient of x^4 in the expansion.

The coefficients in the polynomial

$$(1+x)^{10} = x^0 + 10x^1 + 45x^2 + 120x^3 + 210x^4 + 252x^5 \\ + 210x^6 + 120x^7 + 45x^8 + 10x^9 + x^{10}$$

are $\binom{10}{r}$. We can think of this polynomial as a sort of 'code' for the sequence of binomial coefficients. It is known as the *generating function* for $\binom{10}{r}$, since if we require the value of one of these, say $\binom{10}{5}$, we can just read it off by finding the coefficient of x^5 in the expansion.

In general, suppose we have a sequence $a_0, a_1, a_2, \ldots, a_n$ of real numbers (which will usually be non-negative integers). Then the generating function associated with this sequence is the polynomial

$$G(x) = a_0 + a_1 x + a_2 x^2 + \cdots + a_n x^n.$$

It is, of course, convenient that the generating function $G_{10}(x)$ can be written in the form $(1+x)^{10}$, which makes it particularly concise and easy to remember. If we write $G_1(x) = x^0 + x^1$, we see that it is the generating function for the binomial coefficients $\binom{1}{r}$ and that

$$G_{10}(x) = [G_1(x)]^{10}.$$

In the same way $H(x) = (1 + x + x^2)^{10}$ is the generating function for the sequence 1, 10, 55, 210, 615, 1452, 2850, 4740, 6765, 8350, 8953, 8350, 6765, 4740, 2850, 1452, 615, 210, 55, 10, 1, whose elements are the number of solutions to the equation $x_1 + x_2 + x_3 + \cdots + x_{10} = n$, where each x_i is either 0, 1 or 2 and $0 \leq n \leq 20$.

If, for example, $n = 10$, then we are enumerating solutions to the equation $x_1 + x_2 + x_3 + \cdots + x_{10} = 10$ using only 0, 1 and 2. An example of such a solution is $0 + 1 + 0 + 2 + 2 + 0 + 1 + 1 + 2 + 1$. This is equivalent to choosing the x^0 (or 1) term in the first, third and sixth brackets of $(1 + x + x^2)^{10}$, the x^1 (or x) term in the second, seventh, eighth and tenth brackets and the x^2 term in the fourth, fifth and ninth brackets. There is therefore a bijection between solutions to the equation and selections of terms from brackets, and it follows that the number of such solutions is the coefficient of x^{10} in the generating function, which is 8953.

It would, of course, be possible to tackle this problem by a direct approach, just as we earlier found that there were 210 solutions to $x_1 + x_2 + x_3 + \cdots + x_{10} = 4$. However, much more work would be needed to obtain 8953 as the number of solutions when $n = 10$. Using generating functions is less prone to error since, although it would take quite a long time to do it by hand, expansion of polynomials is a mechanical procedure. In fact, there are polynomial expansion calculators readily available online, one of which was used to produce the sequence of numbers above.

Generating functions were used extensively in the early nineteenth century when combinatorics was being developed as a subject. This was, of course, well before any mechanical aids to calculation were available.

Exercise 7a

Leave your solutions in factorised form.

1. A bowl contains ten apples, nine bananas and eight cherries. Find the generating function for the number of ways of choosing n pieces of fruit (for $0 \leq n \leq 27$).

2. A bowl contains ten apples, nine bananas and eight cherries. Find the generating function for the number of ways to choose n pieces of fruit (for $0 \leq n \leq 27$), if the number of apples must be even, the number of bananas must be odd and there must be at least five cherries.

3. A bowl contains ten apples, nine bananas, eight cherries and seven damsons. Find the generating function for the number of ways to choose n pieces of fruit (for $0 \leq n \leq 34$), if the number of apples and bananas must be equal and there are not more than three cherries and damsons in all.

7.2 Power series

We begin by revisiting question 3 of exercise 1b on page 16, which is repeated here for convenience.

Problem 7.1

In how many different ways is it possible to make up £1 using 1p, 2p, 5p, 10p and 50p coins?

It is clear that we never need more than 100 1p coins, 50 2p coins, and so on, so we could use the polynomial

$$G(x) = G_1(x)G_2(x)G_5(x)G_{10}(x)G_{20}(x)G_{50}(x),$$

where, for example,

$$G_{10}(x) = x^0 + x^{10} + x^{20} + x^{30} + x^{40} + x^{50} + x^{60} + x^{70} + x^{80} + x^{90} + x^{100}$$

and then we need to calculate the coefficient of x^{100} in this expression. However, this solution is somewhat unsatisfactory. The reason for this is that $G(x)$ has a term of the form kx^{213}, for example, and this does not represent the number of ways of making up £2.13, since we could achieve this by using four 50p coins and thirteen 1p coins, and $G_{50}(x) = 1 + x^{50} + x^{100}$ does not cater for this possibility. In other words, $G(x)$ works fine up to a maximum amount of £1 but fails to make sense beyond that point.

The way to avoid this dilemma is to allow generating functions to be *power series*, which look a bit like polynomials but have infinitely many terms. This would mean that the generating function for 10p coins would become

$$G_{10}(x) = x^0 + x^{10} + x^{20} + \cdots + x^{100} + \cdots$$
$$= \sum_{r=0}^{\infty} x^{10r}$$

where the sum is taken from zero to infinity. If you are unfamiliar with infinite series, you should now look at appendix E, where these are explained in sufficient detail for the purposes of this book.

Another advantage of using power series is that their sum to infinity can often be expressed in a simple way. For example, the geometric series with first term 1 and common ratio x is

$$1 + x + x^2 + \cdots + x^n + \cdots = \frac{1}{1-x}.$$

Chapter 7: Generating

This is, in fact, only true under the condition that $-1 < x < 1$. However, we will ignore matters of convergence in this chapter, since we will not actually be evaluating the power series.

In fact $G_{10}(x)$ is a geometric series with common ratio x^{10}, so it can be written in the simpler form $\frac{1}{1-x^{10}}$. This means that the generating function for the coins is

$$G(x) = \frac{1}{(1-x)(1-x^2)(1-x^5)(1-x^{10})(1-x^{20})(1-x^{50})}$$

(and it would be quite straightforward to include one pound and two pound coins as well). The solution to the problem is the coefficient of x^{100} in the expansion of $G(x)$, which, according to an online calculator, is 4562. This agrees with the solution by tabulation on page 275.

Power series can also be useful when the generating function is a polynomial, but multiplying it out would be impractical.

Problem 7.2

A pack of 32 cards has two different Jokers each of which is numbered 0. There are ten red cards numbered 1 to 10 and similarly there are 10 blue and 10 green cards. A number of cards are chosen from the pack to form a hand. The value of a card in the hand is 2^k, where k is the number on the card, and the value of the hand is the sum of the values of the cards in it. Determine the number of hands with the value 2004. [CGMO 2004]

Note first that the values of the cards range from $2^0 = 1$ for a Joker to $2^{10} = 1024$ for a Ten. The generating function for the whole pack is given by

$$G(x) = (1+x)^2(1+x^2)^3(1+x^4)^3 \cdots (1+x^{1024})^3$$
$$= (1+x)^2 \prod_{k=1}^{10} \left(1+x^{2^k}\right)^3$$

where the first bracket refers to the two Jokers, the second to the three Ones, and so on up to the final bracket which refers to the three Tens. We need to find the coefficient of x^{2004} in $G(x)$. This problem was set in an Olympiad, where web-based technology was unavailable, and it turns out that it could be solved by means of a clever trick.

Using the expression for the difference of two squares repeatedly, we have

$$1 - x^{2048} = \left(1 - x^{1024}\right)\left(1 + x^{1024}\right)$$
$$= \left(1 - x^{512}\right)\left(1 + x^{512}\right)\left(1 + x^{1024}\right)$$
$$= \left(1 - x^2\right)\prod_{k=1}^{10}\left(1 + x^{2^k}\right)$$

so $G(x) = (1+x)^2 \left(1 - x^{2048}\right)^3 \left(1 - x^2\right)^{-3}$. From appendix E, we have

$$\left(1 - x^2\right)^{-3} = 1 + 3x^2 + 6x^4 + \cdots + \binom{n+2}{2} x^{2n} + \cdots$$

and so

$$G(x) = \left(1 - x^{2048}\right)^3 \left(1 + 2x + x^2\right)\left(1 + 3x^2 + 6x^4 + \cdots \right.$$
$$\left. + \binom{n+2}{2} x^{2n} + \cdots\right).$$

To obtain the coefficient of x^{2004} in $G(x)$, we need only the 1 from the bracket $\left(1 - x^{2048}\right)^3$. In the second bracket we use only the 1 and the x^2, and it follows that the solution to the problem is the sum of the coefficients of x^{2004} and x^{2002} in the third bracket, which is $\binom{1004}{2} + \binom{1003}{3} = 1\,006\,009$.

Generating functions can also be used for partitions, but we need a more sophisticated approach.

Problem 7.3

Find a generating function for partitions into positive integers.

Let us consider first how to do this for partitioning 4. Note that these are unordered partitions, so we must be careful that 1 3 and 3 1 are not counted as two partitions in the enumeration.

The generating function turns out to be

$$P_4(x) = \left(1 + x + x^2 + x^3 + x^4\right)\left(1 + x^2 + x^4\right)\left(1 + x^3\right)\left(1 + x^4\right).$$

It becomes clear how this works if we write the indices in the rather eccentric way

$$P_4(x) = \left(1 + x^1 + x^{1+1} + x^{1+1+1} + x^{1+1+1+1}\right)$$
$$\left(1 + x^2 + x^{2+2}\right)\left(1 + x^3\right)\left(1 + x^4\right).$$

The term in x^4 arises from the products $x^4 \times 1 \times 1 \times 1$, $x^2 \times x^2 \times 1 \times 1$, $x \times 1 \times x^3 \times 1$, $1 \times x^4 \times 1 \times 1$ and $1 \times 1 \times 1 \times x^4$, so it is $5x^4$. This corresponds to the five partitions of 4, and now we can see what is going on by pairing up products and partitions as shown in table 7.1.

Product	Partition
$x^4 \times 1 \times 1 \times 1$	1 1 1 1
$x^2 \times x^2 \times 1 \times 1$	1 1 2
$x \times 1 \times x^3 \times 1$	1 3
$1 \times x^4 \times 1 \times 1$	2 2
$1 \times 1 \times 1 \times x^4$	4

Table 7.1

It is important that the second bracket only contains indices which are multiples of 2. If we mistakenly included a term x in this bracket, we would include the partition 1 1 1 1 twice, both from $x^4 \times 1 \times 1 \times 1$ and from $x \times 1 \times x^3 \times 1$. Note that this also gives the partitions of 1, 2 and 3 as coefficients of x, x^2 and x^3, but the coefficient of x^5 does not represent the partitions of 5, since, for example, the partition 1 1 1 1 1 would be omitted.

If we multiply out, we obtain

$$P(x) = 1 + x + 2x^2 + 3x^3 + 5x^4 + 5x^5 + \cdots,$$

which gives us the correct partition numbers for 0, 1, 2, 3 and 4, but not for 5. This is because we would need a bracket of the form $(1 + x^5)$ and for 6 we would also need extra terms in the second and third brackets.

The generating function for all non-negative integers requires power series, and is

$$P(x) = \left(1 + x + x^2 + \cdots\right)\left(1 + x^2 + x^4 + \cdots\right)\left(1 + x^3 + x^6 + \cdots\right)\cdots.$$

It follows that

$$P(x) = \frac{1}{(1-x)(1-x^2)(1-x^3)\cdots}$$
$$= \frac{1}{\prod_{n\geq 1}(1-x^n)}.$$

Exercise 7b

In this exercise you are asked to find generating functions for four sequences of numbers, and in each case the letter k is used to denote the position of a term in the sequence. Your final answer should not include the letter k, but may include the letters m and N where appropriate, since these represent numbers which are fixed throughout each question.

1. Find the generating function for the number of non-negative integer solutions to $x_1 + x_2 + x_3 + \cdots + x_N = k$, for $k \geq 0$, and give an interpretation of the coefficients.

2. Find the generating function for the number of positive integer solutions to $2a + 3b + 4c = k$ for $k \geq 7$.

3. Find the generating function for the number of integer solutions to $x_1 + x_2 + x_3 + \cdots + x_N = k$, where $k \geq 0$ and $0 \leq x_1 \leq x_2 \leq \cdots \leq x_N$.
   [HINT]

4. Find the generating function for the number of ways of sharing k pieces of fruit (for $k \geq 0$) from a large pile of m types of fruit between N people.

Chapter 7: Generating 117

7.3 Solving recurrences using generating functions

So far we have used generating functions as an enumerative device, and the criticism has been made several times that this is not a particularly efficient method. We now illustrate the use of generating functions to solve recurrences using the familiar example (recurrence 5.1 on page 72), in which u_n counts the number of outcomes when n coins are tossed:

$$u_{n+1} = 2u_n;$$
$$u_1 = 2.$$

The trick is to find an associated power series which will 'line up' the coefficients u_n and u_{n+1}. This can be done since

$$G(x) = 1 + u_1 x + u_2 x^2 + \cdots + u_n x^n + \cdots$$
$$xG(x) = \phantom{1+{}} x + u_1 x^2 + \cdots + u_{n-1} x^n + \cdots$$

If we multiply the second series by two and subtract it from the first, virtually everything cancels, and we obtain the formula

$$G(x) - 2xG(x) = 1,$$

so that

$$G(x) = \frac{1}{1 - 2x}$$
$$= 1 + 2x + 4x^2 + \cdots + 2^n x^n + \cdots.$$

Now we can simply read off the fact that $u_n = 2^n$. Naturally it seems rather perverse to engage in all this work to prove something which was obvious, but the point is that we can use this method for any linear recurrence with constant coefficients.

So let us consider the Fibonacci recurrence 5.3 on page 74:

$$F_{n+2} = F_{n+1} + F_n;$$
$$F_1 = 1, \; F_2 = 1.$$

This works in a similar way but we need three equations to line up.

$$G(x) = F_1 x + F_2 x^2 + F_3 x^3 + F_4 x^4 + \cdots + F_n x^n + \cdots$$
$$xG(x) = \phantom{F_1 x +{}} + F_1 x^2 + F_2 x^3 + F_3 x^4 + \cdots + F_{n-1} x^n + \cdots$$
$$x^2 G(x) = \phantom{F_1 x + F_2 x^2 +{}} + F_1 x^3 + F_2 x^4 + \cdots + F_{n-2} x^n + \cdots.$$

If we subtract the second and third equation from the first, we see that the x^2 term vanishes since $F_1 = F_2 = 1$ and all subsequent terms also vanish since $F_n = F_{n-1} + F_{n-2}$. Hence we obtain

$$(1 - x - x^2)G(x) = x,$$

and so

$$G(x) = \frac{x}{1 - x - x^2}.$$

We would like to expand this as a series, and, in particular, we would like to make use of the fact that

$$\frac{1}{1-x} = 1 + x + x^2 + \cdots + x^n + \cdots.$$

which is the geometric series on page 112. With this in mind, it seems reasonable to try and rewrite $G)x)$ as

$$\frac{x}{(1 - \alpha x)(1 - \beta x)}.$$

Expanding the denominator gives the equations $\alpha + \beta = 1$ and $\alpha\beta = -1$. We could solve these as simultaneous equations, but it turns out that we have already done the work. The values we need are the λ_1 and λ_2 already defined on page 102, namely

$$\lambda_1 = \frac{1 - \sqrt{5}}{2} \quad \text{and} \quad \lambda_2 = \frac{1 + \sqrt{5}}{2}.$$

Hence we have

$$G(x) = \frac{x}{(1 - \lambda_1 x)(1 - \lambda_2 x)}.$$

There are now two ways to proceed. One of them is to go straight to geometric series and write

$$G(x) = x(1 + \lambda_1 x + \lambda_1^2 x^2 + \cdots + \lambda_1^n x^n + \cdots)$$
$$(1 + \lambda_2 x + \lambda_2^2 x^2 + \cdots + \lambda_2^n x^n + \cdots)$$

and the coefficient of x^n in this expression is

$$\lambda_2^{n-1} + \lambda_2^{n-2}\lambda_1 + \lambda_2^{n-3}\lambda_1^2 + \cdots + \lambda_1^{n-1},$$

which is a geometric progression with sum $\frac{\lambda_2^n - \lambda_1^n}{\lambda_2 - \lambda_1}$. This produces the usual Binet formula $F_n = \frac{\lambda_2^n - \lambda_1^n}{\sqrt{5}}$.

The problem with this is that it depends on the fact that it is easy to multiply the two power series together, along with the numerator x, and simplify the resulting expression. This will not always happen, particularly if the numerator is something a little more complicated such as $3x - 7$, for example.

A second approach, which will always work, is to use a technique known as *partial fractions*. This technique has applications in many areas of mathematics, is easier to generalise our first solution and avoids the need to multiply two power series together. It involves rewriting the expression for $G(x)$ as the sum of two terms, namely

$$\frac{x}{(1-\lambda_1 x)(1-\lambda_2 x)} = \frac{A}{1-\lambda_1 x} + \frac{B}{1-\lambda_2 x},$$

where A and B are constants to be determined.

Multiplying out, we have $x = A(1 - \lambda_2 x) + B(1 - \lambda_1 x)$, so we need $A + B = 0$ and $\lambda_2 A + \lambda_1 B = -1$. These simultaneous equations yield the values

$$A = \frac{1}{\lambda_1 - \lambda_2} = -\frac{1}{\sqrt{5}} \quad \text{and} \quad B = \frac{1}{\sqrt{5}}.$$

Hence we have

$$G(x) = \frac{1}{\sqrt{5}}\left(\frac{1}{1-\lambda_2 x} - \frac{1}{1-\lambda_1 x}\right)$$

and we can expand using the geometric series and read off the coefficient of x^n to produce the Binet formula.

We now look at another example, the recurrence

$$u_{n+2} = 5u_{n+1} - 6u_n;$$
$$u_1 = 1,\ u_2 = 5.$$

Proceeding as above, we obtain

$$G(x) = \frac{2x - 5x^2}{1 - 5x + 6x^2},$$

but there is a problem here. The numerator and denominator of this expression are both quadratics, unlike the situation in the previous example where the numerator was linear and of degree less than the numerator. This is rather like the improper fraction $\frac{17}{5}$, which may be written as a mixed number $3\frac{2}{5}$. To carry out this conversion, we write 17 as a multiple of 5 plus a remainder which is less than 5. That is, we write

$$\frac{17}{5} = \frac{3 \times 5 + 2}{5}$$

and then split the fraction into two. The process with polynomials is exactly analogous.

We are faced with the fraction

$$\frac{2x - 5x^2}{1 - 5x + 6x^2}.$$

So we need to write $2x - 5x^2$ as a multiple of $1 - 5x + 6x^2$ plus a polynomial of degree less than 2. To get the x^2 terms to match, we are forced to start by writing $2x - 5x^2 = -\frac{5}{6}(1 - 5x + 6x^2)$ plus a remainder. The remainder turns out to be $\frac{1}{6}(5 - 13x)$, so we obtain

$$G(x) = -\frac{5}{6}\left(\frac{1 - 5x + 6x^2}{1 - 5x + 6x^2}\right) + \frac{1}{6}\left(\frac{5 - 13x}{1 - 5x + 6x^2}\right)$$

$$= -\frac{5}{6} + \frac{1}{6}\left(\frac{5 - 13x}{(1 - 2x)(1 - 3x)}\right).$$

Now we split the bracketed expression in the second term into partial fractions to get

$$G(x) = -\frac{5}{6} + \frac{1}{6}\left(\frac{3}{1 - 2x} + \frac{2}{1 - 3x}\right),$$

and the coefficient of x^n is easily read off as

$$\tfrac{1}{6}(2 \times 3^n + 3 \times 2^n),$$

which we may simplify to $3^{n-1} + 2^{n-1}$.

This technique of 'dividing out the denominator' should be used whenever the degree of the numerator is equal to or exceeds that of the denominator.

However, the use of generating functions is not limited to linear recurrence relations with constant coefficients. Take, for example, the Catalan recurrence 5.5 on page 86:

$$c_{n+1} = c_0 c_n + c_1 c_{n-1} + \cdots + c_{n-1} c_0;$$
$$c_0 = 1,$$

Chapter 7: Generating

The generating function is given by

$$G(x) = c_0 + c_1 x + c_2 x^2 + \cdots + c_n x^n + \cdots$$
$$= 1 + x + 2x^2 + 5x^3 + 14x^4 + 42x^5 + \cdots.$$

The key step here is to consider what happens when $G(x)$ is multiplied by itself. Doing this, we obtain

$$G(x)^2 = \left(1 + x + 2x^2 + 5x^3 + 14x^4 + 42x^5 + \cdots\right)^2$$
$$= 1 + (1 \times 1 + 1 \times 1)x + (2 \times 1 + 1 \times 1 + 1 \times 2)x^2$$
$$+ (5 \times 1 + 2 \times 1 + 1 \times 2 + 1 \times 5)x^3 + \cdots$$
$$= 1 + 2x + 5x^2 + 14x^3 + \cdots$$

and it is clear from the recurrence relation that this reproduces the Catalan sequence, omitting the first term and moving the coefficients one term forwards. Hence we have $xG(x)^2 = G(x) - 1$. Treating this as a quadratic, we obtain $G(x) = \frac{1 \pm \sqrt{1-4x}}{2x}$ and use the binomial expansion for $n = \frac{1}{2}$, giving

$$2xG(x) - 1 = \pm \left[1 - \tfrac{1}{2}(4x) - \tfrac{1}{8}(4x)^2 - \cdots \right.$$
$$\left. - \frac{1}{n \times 2^{2n-1}} \binom{2(n-1)}{n-1}(4x)^n \cdots \right].$$

We take the negative sign in front of the bracket to make the coefficients on the right positive. Finally we identify the terms in x^{n+1} on either side to obtain

$$2x c_n x^n = \frac{1}{n+1}\binom{2n}{n} 2x^{n+1},$$

from which we get the Catalan formula

$$c_n = \frac{1}{n+1}\binom{2n}{n}.$$

Exercise 7c

1. Use generating functions to solve the recurrence relation
$$t_{n+2} = 5t_{n+1} - 6t_n;$$
$$t_1 = 1, \ t_2 = 2.$$

2. Use generating functions to solve the recurrence relation
$$t_{n+2} = t_{n+1} + 2t_n;$$
$$t_0 = 7, \ t_1 = 8.$$

3. Use generating functions to solve the recurrence relation
$$t_{n+2} = 2t_{n+1} + t_n;$$
$$t_1 = 3, \ t_2 = 7.$$

4. Use generating functions to solve the recurrence relation for the Lucas sequence
$$L_{n+2} = L_{n+1} + L_n;$$
$$L_1 = 1, \ L_2 = 3.$$

5. Solve the recurrence relation $t_{n+1} = 2t_n + n$, where $t_1 = 2$.

6. Solve the recurrence relation $t_{n+1} = 2t_n + 2^n$, where $t_1 = 1$. [HINT]

7. (a) Rearrange the generating function for the Fibonacci sequence by writing $1 - x - x^2$ as $1 - x(1 + x)$ and show that
$$F_{n+1} = \binom{n}{0} + \binom{n-1}{1} + \cdots + \binom{n - \lfloor \frac{n}{2} \rfloor}{\lfloor \frac{n}{2} \rfloor}.$$
(Here $\lfloor \frac{n}{2} \rfloor$ means the largest integer less than or equal to n. In other words, if n is even it is $\frac{n}{2}$ and if n is odd it is $\frac{n-1}{2}$.)
(b) Justify this identity with reference to Pascal's identity (equation (3.3) on page 32).
(c) Justify this identity by double-counting with reference to problem 5.2 on page 74.

Chapter 8
Pigeonholing

We have spent the last few chapters addressing the fundamental question:

How many different ways are there of doing something?

Now we turn to another fundamental question:

Is something certain to happen?

8.1 The pigeonhole principle

Problem 8.1
Eight people are in a room.
Is it certain that two were born on the same day of the week?

A moment's thought is all that is needed to realise that the answer to this question is 'Yes'. There are only seven days available, and, since eight is more than seven, there is at least one day of the week on which at least two people were born.

This simple observation is an example of the pigeonhole principle, which says that if more than n pigeons are put into n pigeonholes, then at least one pigeonhole will contain more than one pigeon.

In problem 8.1, the pigeons are the eight people and the pigeonholes are the seven days of the week. The pigeons (people) are placed in the pigeonholes (days) according the day of the week on which they were born. By the pigeonhole principle, there is at least one pigeonhole which contains more than one pigeon, so there is at least one day of the week on which two people were born.

This result was first formalised by Gustav Dirichlet in 1837 and is sometimes known as *Dirichlet's principle*. Slightly more formally it says that:

> **THE PIGEONHOLE PRINCIPLE**
> If more than n objects are divided into n categories, then there is at least one category which contains more than one object.

It is worth noting that this principle does not give any hint as to which category contains multiple objects: it merely says that at least one such category exists. In the case of problem 8.1, we cannot say which people were born on the same day or which day it was. It is, of course, possible that all eight people were born on the same day. What is impossible is that all eight were born on different days.

Problem 8.2

Twelve 9-year olds are in a room.

Is it certain that two were born in the same month?

The answer to this question is fairly obviously 'No'. One child could be born in each month and no month would be used twice. In the language of the pigeonhole principle, the pigeonholes are the twelve months of the year and the pigeons are the twelve children. It is perfectly conceivable that each pigeonhole contains exactly one pigeon, so it is not certain that two of the children share a birth month.

The point here is that we really do need *more* pigeons than pigeonholes; *at least as many* simply will not do. It is also worth emphasising that the pigeonhole principle is all about certainty and not probability. If birth months were equally likely, then the chance that twelve 9-year olds all had different birth months would be $12! \div 12^{12} \approx 0.0000537$, so it might be argued that two are *almost* certain to share a birth month. For our purposes, almost certain will never be certain enough.

Problem 8.3

A large school has 2000 pupils.

Prove that at least six of them share a birthday (so, six could be born on the 15th of June, though not necessarily in the same year).

This problem invites us to consider a slight generalisation of the pigeonhole principle. Our pigeonholes will be the 366 possible days of the year, including February 29th, and our pigeons will be the 2000 pupils at the school. Certainly 2000 is more than 366 so, by the pigeonhole principle, there is a pigeonhole which contains more than one pigeon, but we can say more. If each pigeonhole contained at most five pigeons, then they would be able to house at most $5 \times 366 = 1830$ pigeons in total. 2000 is more than 1830 so one pigeonhole contains more than five pigeons. This translates to at least six pupils sharing a birthday, as required. Note that we cannot be sure that seven students share a birthday, since 366 pigeonholes, each containing at most six pigeons, could house up to $6 \times 366 = 2196$ pigeons in total. The calculations we have done could be summarised with the inequalities

$$5 \times 366 < 2000 \leq 6 \times 366.$$

More formally we have just made use of the following, more general, form of the pigeonhole principle:

THE GENERAL PIGEONHOLE PRINCIPLE

If more than nk objects are divided into n categories, then at least one category contains more than k objects.

To see that this is true, we simply observe that if n categories each contain at most k objects then they can contain at most nk objects in total.

Problem 8.4

Given fourteen integers, prove that you can always find two which differ by a multiple of 13.

This problem combines the pigeonhole principle with an important idea from number theory. Our pigeons are the fourteen numbers, and our pigeonholes are the thirteen possible remainders they leave on division by thirteen. By the pigeonhole principle, we have at least two pigeons in the same pigeonhole. This means some two of our numbers have the same remainder on division by thirteen, so their difference is a multiple of thirteen and we are done.

This solution can be concisely phrased using the language of modular arithmetic: two of the numbers are congruent modulo 13 so their difference is congruent to zero. Modular arithmetic is discussed in appendix F, and, although we will not use much of the theory of modular arithmetic in what follows, we will allow ourselves to use phrases like '20 is congruent to 7 modulo 13' or even '$20 \equiv 7 \pmod{13}$'.

We now have some idea of how to spot problems where the pigeonhole principle may be useful. Problems which involve a number of objects and ask us to prove that two or more of these objects share some property are very typical (though there are more subtle examples as we shall see later). In such problems, the objects under consideration will be our pigeons, and our task will be to define pigeonholes such that:

(i) each pigeon is in one of the pigeonholes;
(ii) a pigeonhole containing more than one pigeon corresponds to a property shared by more than one of the objects;
(iii) the number of pigeons is more than the number of pigeonholes, or possibly more than k times the number of pigeonholes for some k.

It is also worth bearing in mind that the problems need to be *existential* in nature. The pigeonhole principle does not tell us which pigeonhole contains multiple pigeons or which pigeons are in that pigeonhole, so we are looking for problems that do not ask us to specify which objects share a particular property.

In the following exercise, you should define your pigeons and pigeonholes very carefully.

Exercise 8a

1. In Mathland no person has more than 150 000 hairs on their head. In a town with 150 000 residents, is it certain that two residents have the same number of hairs on their heads?

2. A 150 001st person moves to the town in question 1. What can be said now?

3. A bag contains several red balls, several blue balls, and several yellow balls. Each day Anthony pulls out three balls one at a time, noting their colours in turn. He then returns the three balls to the bag, and does this each day for a month. Prove that there were at least two days with exactly the same outcome.

4. Prove that, among any seven square numbers, there are two which end in the same digit.

5. Prove that there are two living people whose masses are the same when measured to the nearest milligram.

6. Of 1001 positive integers how many are guaranteed to start with the same digit when written in base 10?

7. Of 1001 positive integers how many are guaranteed to start with the digit 1 when written in base 10?

8. A mathematics Olympiad is marked out of 60. If 4800 students sit the exam, how many can be guaranteed to get the same mark?

9. 49 counters, each of which can be red, blue or green, are placed into four boxes. Prove that there is a box which contains at least five counters of the same colour.

10. A small theme park has six roller coasters. If every visitor rides each roller coaster exactly once during their visit, how many visitors do there need to be to ensure that at least ten have ridden the roller coasters in the same order.

11. In Texas hold 'em poker, a hand consists of two cards drawn from a standard deck of 52. How many hands does a person need to play to be sure of being dealt the same hand three times?

12. Prove that, at a party, there are always two people who know the same number of people. (We assume that if x knows y then y knows x.)

8.2 Bounding

Problem 8.5

James is playing a game at a fair. A paddling pool contains a large number of red, blue, yellow and green rubber ducks. James is blindfolded and asked to remove ducks from the pool. He wins a prize if he takes three ducks that are all the same colour.

How many ducks does he need to remove to be certain to win?

For this problem we might be tempted to argue that, if James is extremely unlucky, then he will remove two red, two blue, two yellow and two green ducks. This is the unluckiest he can be, and if he takes one more duck he is sure to win, so he needs to take nine ducks to secure his victory.

This is the correct answer, and the game is so simple that the argument is fairly convincing. However, the logic in this 'proof' contains a subtle gap which could be fatal in a more difficult problem. The trouble lies in the statement 'This is the unluckiest he can be', so let us unpack exactly what this might mean. We can view the game as a contest between James and a mysterious evil entity called Badluck. James asks Badluck for a certain number of ducks, and Badluck is free to choose the colours of the ducks. Badluck wins if no colour is used more than twice, and we claim that if James asks Badluck for nine ducks then Badluck cannot win. This is true, but our supposed proof is questionable. It can be summarised as follows. We came up with an 'obviously good' strategy for Badluck (start by handing out two of each colour) and observed that if James asks

Badluck for a ninth duck then Badluck's strategy fails. We then, somewhat arrogantly, asserted that, because what we thought was a good strategy for Badluck fails, it follows that every possible strategy fails. Putting ourselves in Badluck's shoes we can rephrase this by saying that we tried really hard to defeat James and failed, so it is impossible to defeat James.

This kind of spurious reasoning can be very tempting, particularly as it often leads to a correct numerical answer. However, there are plenty of examples where it does not (see, for example, problem 8.18), and even if there were none, the bogus logic would still be unacceptable.

To avoid this pitfall we break the solution up into two claims and use the pigeonhole principle.

James may not win if he only takes eight ducks.
This is obvious, since he might take two of each colour.

James is sure to win if he takes nine (or more) ducks.
This is also obvious. Let the ducks be the pigeons and the colours be the pigeonholes. Since $9 > 2 \times 4$, one pigeonhole contains more than two pigeons, as required.

The two part solution is typical of problems which ask us to find the greatest or least number of objects required to make a conclusion true. An explicit example is used to show that the result may not be true for n objects, then the pigeonhole principle is used to prove the result is always true of $n+1$ objects.

Problem 8.6

What is the greatest number of numbers that can be chosen from the set $\{1, 2, \ldots, 100\}$ such that no two differ by less than 10?

Let the greatest number of numbers be k. The set $S = \{10, 20, \ldots, 100\}$ is an explicit example that shows that $k \geq 10$.

To show that $k = 10$ we need to resist the temptation to argue that taking members of S is obviously the best way to go, and no more numbers can be added to S.

Instead, we build ten pigeonholes from the numbers 1, 2, ..., 100, as follows: $\{1, 2, \ldots, 10\}$, $\{11, 12, \ldots, 20\}$, ..., $\{91, 92, \ldots, 100\}$. If we have eleven or more numbers, then two will be in the same pigeonhole and hence less than 10 apart. Therefore k is less than 11, as required.

Problem 8.7

How many numbers need to be chosen from the set $\{1, 2, \ldots, 100\}$ to ensure that some two add up to an odd number?

Let the number of numbers we need to choose be k.

The sets $E = \{2, 4, \ldots, 100\}$ and $O = \{1, 3, \ldots, 99\}$ both have the property that the sum of any two elements is even, so we know that $k > 50$.

It remains to prove that $k \leq 51$. There is more than one way to do this, but here we will aim for a solution which uses the pigeonhole principle explicitly. Our 51 numbers will be our pigeons. Now we need to divide the numbers 1 to 100 into at most fifty sets (our pigeonholes) such that two numbers in the same set correspond to a pair of numbers with odd sum. Perhaps the most natural way to split one hundred numbers into fifty sets is to use pairs of consecutive numbers, and indeed, one of the fifty pigeonholes $\{1, 2\}$, $\{3, 4\}$, ..., $\{99, 100\}$ will contain more than one pigeon. Fortunately the sum of two consecutive numbers is always odd, and so we are done.

Another possible division would be to use the pairs $\{1, 100\}$, $\{2, 99\}$, $\{3, 98\}, \ldots, \{50, 51\}$. Now we observe that more than one pigeon in a pigeonhole corresponds to a pair of numbers which add up to 101.

The remarkable thing here is that these solutions start by claiming that we have 'a consecutive pair' in the first case and 'a pair which sum to 101' in the second. Both of these claims say more than the original statement of the problem, yet somehow the stronger results turn out to be easier to prove. The moral of the story is that good problem solvers make a habit of asking the question:

> Which other result would imply what I am trying to prove?

Exercise 8b

1. I have six black socks and eight blue socks in a drawer. Socks of the same colour are indistinguishable. How many socks do I need to take from the drawer to ensure that I have a pair of the same colour?

Chapter 8: Pigeonholing

2. A restaurant menu offers a choice of three starters, four main courses and five desserts. If every diner orders a three course meal, how many diners do there need to be before we can be sure that two have ordered exactly the same meal?

3. I shuffle a standard pack of cards and turn them over one by one. How many cards do I need to turn over before I am sure of getting five from the same suit?

4. What is the greatest number of numbers that can be chosen from the set $\{1, 2, \ldots, 20\}$ such that no two differ by exactly 5?

5. Prove that, among 51 integers, you can always find two which sum to, or differ by, a multiple of 99. (Note that 0 is a multiple of 99.)

6. 55 numbers are chosen from the set $\{1, 2, \ldots, 100\}$. Prove that
   (a) some two differ by 9;
   (b) some two differ by 10;
   (c) some two differ by 12;
   (d) some two differ by 13;
   (e) it is not necessarily the case that some two differ by 11.

7. (a) There are 24 seats in a row. Prove that if 17 people sit down, then three consecutive seats will be occupied. Is this true for 16 people?
   (b) Find the maximum number of people that can be seated in a row of 25 seats without three consecutive seats being occupied.
   (c) Find the maximum number of people that can be seated in a row of 26 seats without three consecutive seats being occupied.

8. How many numbers need to be chosen from the set $\{1, 2, \ldots, 200\}$ to ensure the existence of a pair with no common factor? [HINT]

8.3 Pigeons and pigeonholes

The next few problems require a little more creativity when it comes to defining our pigeons and pigeonholes.

Problem 8.8

Five points are chosen inside an equilateral triangle of side length 2 cm.

Prove that some two of them are at most 1 cm apart.

This problem is a famous example of the pigeonhole principle being used in a geometric question. The five points will be our pigeons, so it remains for us to choose our pigeonholes wisely. The pigeonholes will be regions within the equilateral triangle, and we need to ensure that:

(i) two points in the same region are at most 1 cm apart;
(ii) the regions completely cover the equilateral triangle;
(iii) there are at most four regions.

At this point two different lines of attack are open to us. One option is to look carefully at the first requirement above and let this guide us. We want two points in the same pigeonhole to be at most 1 cm apart, so circles of diameter 1 cm seem like a good choice. It then remains to arrange four of these circles such that they completely cover our equilateral triangle, but sadly this turns out to be impossible.

A second, more fruitful, approach is to start by thinking about the number of pigeonholes we need and work from there. We are now looking for natural ways to divide our triangle into four regions. Joining the midpoints of the sides together as shown in figure 8.1 yields four equilateral triangles of side length 1 cm. Two of our five points lie in, or on the boundary of, the same small triangle, and it is now clear that these triangular pigeonholes also satisfy the first criterion. To be totally precise we should specify which pigeonhole the points actually on the dashed lines belong to. For simplicity we will say that all three of these dashed lines belong to the central triangular pigeonhole, though other conventions would work just as well.

What we learn here is that we can draw inspiration not only from the properties we would like our pigeonholes to have, but also from how

Chapter 8: Pigeonholing

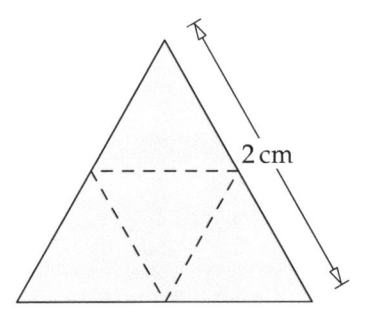

Figure 8.1

many of them we suspect there should be. The first approach failed in this example because if we are asked to think of a shape where the maximum distance between points is 1 cm, we are more likely to think of a circle with diameter 1 cm than an equilateral triangle with side length 1 cm.

Problem 8.9

A is a set of ten two-digit positive integers.

Prove that there exist two disjoint subsets of A whose members have the same sum.   [IMO 1972]

In this problem the slightly unusual thing is that the subsets of A, rather than the numbers A contains, will be our pigeons. The possible sums of their members will be the pigeonholes. If we are lucky, there will be more subsets than possible sums, so two subsets will have the same sum. Of course, the pigeonhole principle cannot guarantee that these two sets are disjoint, but if they overlap we can simply remove the numbers common to both sets to obtain disjoint sets which will still have equal sums. Now all that is needed is two easy calculations.

There are $2^{10} - 1 = 1023$ non-empty subsets of A.

Since A is a set, the numbers it contains are, by definition distinct. This means that the largest possible sum of a subset is $90 + 91 + 92 + \cdots + 99 = 945$ and the smallest possible sum is 10. So there are indeed more subsets than sums and we are done.

Problem 8.10

What is the maximum number of rooks than can be placed on an 8 × 8 chessboard such that no two rooks attack each other?

Let k be the greatest possible number of non-attacking rooks on an 8 × 8 chessboard.

Placing eight rooks on one of the long diagonals of the board (figure 8.2) is an explicit construction which shows that $k \geq 8$.

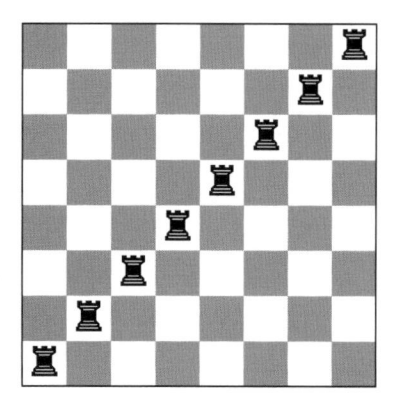

Figure 8.2

Now we want to use the pigeonhole principle to show $k < 9$, that is, that if nine rooks are placed on a chessboard, then some two will attack each other. The rooks will be the pigeons so it remains to divide the board into at most eight regions (pigeonholes) such that two pigeons in the same pigeonhole will ensure that there are two attacking rooks.

It turns out that we can use the eight rows (or columns) of the chessboard, and can therefore conclude that $k = 8$. In a full written solution we would have to avoid claiming that two rooks in the same row of a chessboard attack each other, since this is actually false. What we need is slightly more wordy. If two rooks are in the same row, then either they attack each other or there are other rooks between them. In the second case they each attack the nearest other rook in that row.

Problem 8.11

Given 101 positive integers less than 201, prove that there are two of them with the property that one divides the other.

This problem is somewhat harder than the ten which precede it.

Our instinct suggests that the 101 integers will be our pigeons. This means we need to find at most 100 pigeonholes with the property that if two numbers are in the same pigeonhole then one divides the other. We want to keep the number of pigeonholes small, so we aim to construct large sets with the required divisibility property. If the smallest member of such a set is x, the next one is $a_1 x$ for some whole number a_1 and the next one after that $a_1 a_2 x$ and so on. To keep the sets as large as possible, it makes sense to make the a_i as small as possible. In particular, if we choose all the a_i to be 2, then we get the collection of pigeonholes

$$\{1, 2, 4, 8, 16, 32, 64, 128\}, \{3, 6, 12, 24, 48, 96, 192\},$$
$$\{5, 10, 20, 40, 80, 160\}, \{7, 14, 28, 56, 112\},$$
$$\{9, 18, 36, 72, 144\}, \ldots, \{99, 198\},$$
$$\{101\}, \ldots, \{199\}.$$

There are exactly 100 pigeonholes, one for every odd number, so we are done.

It is striking that the pigeonholes are not all the same size. Also, the last fifty listed above contain only one number, so the pigeonhole which ends up containing more than one number cannot be one of these. This problem contrasts sharply with problem 8.8, in that the solution is completely focussed on properties the pigeonholes need to have, rather than the number of pigeonholes required.

Exercise 8c

1. There are 33 points inside a unit square. Prove that some three of them form a triangle with area at most $\frac{1}{32}$.

2. There are 50 points inside a unit square. Prove that the distance between some pair of them is less than $\frac{2}{9}$.

3. Points A, B, C, D and E all have integer coordinates in the two-dimensional plane. Prove that at least one of the ten line segments joining a pair of these points contains another point in the plane with integer coordinates.

4. What is the maximum number of bishops that can be placed on an 8×8 chessboard such that no two attack each other?

5. Suppose that 25 cells on an 8×8 chessboard are coloured red. Prove that we can choose 4 red squares none of which share a row or column.

6. (a) A is a set of 9 positive integers less than 61. Prove that two distinct subsets of A have the same sum.
   (b) B is a set of 8 positive integers less than 40. Prove that two distinct subsets of B have the same sum.
   (c) C is a set of 10 positive integers less that 142. Prove that two distinct subsets of C have the same sum.

7. Inside a cube of side length 15 units there are 11 000 given points. Prove that there is a sphere of unit radius which contains at least six of the given points. [BMO1 1978]

8. If ten points are within a circle of diameter 5, prove that the distance between some two of the points is less than 2. [BMO1 1983]

9. Given six points inside a 4×3 rectangle, prove that some two are at most $\sqrt{5}$ apart.

8.4 Single objects

All the problems so far have asked about the existence of two or more objects sharing some property, and we have been able to use this to guide the definitions of our pigeons and pigeonholes. The next two problems, however, do not follow this format. In particular, they ask about only one object, a number divisible by n, so we will need to be a little more ingenious in our use of the pigeonhole principle.

> **Problem 8.12**
>
> Given an integer n which is not divisible by 2 or 5, prove that one of the numbers 1, 11, 111, 1111, 11 111, ... is divisible by n.

For this problem, it is worth experimenting with some small values of n. The first three positive integers not divisible by 2 or 5 are 1, 3 and 7. The first two cases are trivial since 1 is divisible by 1, and 111 is famously divisible by 3. So our first interesting task is to show that one of the sequence of *repunits*—numbers consisting entirely of 1s—is divisible by 7.

The repunits will be our pigeons, and, taking our lead from problem 8.4, we will sort them into pigeonholes by looking at their remainders on division by 7. There are seven pigeonholes, so by the time we have looked at eight terms in the sequence, we can be sure that two have the same remainder. The difference between these repunits is a multiple of 7.

In our example it turns out that 1 and 1 111 111 are both congruent to 1 modulo 7, so 1 111 110 is congruent to 0 modulo 7.

Sadly, the difference between two repunits is not a repunit, since it consists of a string of 1s followed by a string of 0s.

However, if let s be the number of 0s (in our example $s = 1$), we can write the difference as $R \times 10^s$ where R is a repunit. Since 7 does not share any factors with 10^s, the fact that $R \times 10^s$ is a multiple of 7 implies that R is, and we are done.

Having dealt with $n = 7$, we can use exactly the same argument in the general case. We see that the condition that n is not divisible by 2 or 5 is required to ensure that it shares no factors with 10^s. We have actually proved that if n is coprime to 10, then one of the first $n + 1$ repunits is divisible by n. As in the case of problem 8.7, asking for this stronger result might have made the problem easier.

Problem 8.13

Given a positive integer n, prove that there is a multiple of n which contains exactly n 1s and no other digits apart from 0s when written in base 10.

Just as in problem 8.12, our pigeonholes will be the n possible remainders on division by n, but the choice of pigeons is not so obvious. The key observation is that the number we are trying to construct can be viewed as the sum of exactly n distinct powers of 10. There are infinitely many powers of 10, and infinity is rather more than $n(n-1)$ so, by the pigeonhole principle, there are at least n powers of 10 which are congruent to each other modulo n. If these n numbers are all congruent to r modulo n, then their sum is congruent to rn modulo n. This, in turn, is congruent to zero, so we are done.

Problem 8.14

Prove that if α is a positive real number and N is a positive integer, then there is a positive integer $q \leq N$ such that the (non-negative) difference beween $q\alpha$ and its nearest whole number is at most $\frac{1}{N-1}$.

We will need a bit of new notation for this problem. Recall from page 62 that for a real number x we write $\lfloor x \rfloor$ for the greatest integer less than or equal to x. We shall refer to $x - \lfloor x \rfloor$ as the *fractional part* of x, which we write as $\langle x \rangle$. So, for example, $\langle \frac{22}{7} \rangle$ is $\frac{1}{7}$, and $\langle -1.7 \rangle$ is 0.3.

With this in place we can proceed as follows. We consider the fractional parts of $\alpha, 2\alpha, \ldots, N\alpha$ in turn, and claim that two of them are nearly equal. We can prove this easily from the pigeonhole principle in the following way. Divide the interval from 0 to 1 into $N-1$ equal segments; these will be our pigeonholes (we make the arbitrary decision that points on the boundary between segments belong to the segment on the left). The fractional parts of the multiples of α are our pigeons so two of them, say $n\alpha$ and $m\alpha$, are in the same pigeonhole. We may assume, without loss of generality, that $n > m$. Now $(n-m)\alpha = (\lfloor n\alpha \rfloor - \lfloor m\alpha \rfloor) + (\langle n\alpha \rangle - \langle m\alpha \rangle)$. The first bracket is an integer, and the second bracket is, by our choice of m and n, between $-\frac{1}{N-1}$ and $\frac{1}{N-1}$, so we are done, by taking q as $n-m$.

By now you will probably be familiar with arguments that show that there are too many pigeons to allow single occupancy of a set of pigeonholes. An equivalent statement is to say that, if the pigeons can be accommodated singly, then there are at least as many available pigeonholes as pigeons. In other words, you should be able to understand the principle as being about both pigeons and pigeonholes.

We will keep this mind as we consider the following famous problem.

A sequence of real numbers which is strictly increasing or strictly decreasing is called *monotone*.

Problem 8.15

Prove that any sequence of $n^2 + 1$ different real numbers contains a monotone subsequence of length $n + 1$.

This problem, which is a version of the Erdős-Szekeres theorem, is arguably the most difficult problem we have met so far in this chapter. We will start with an example to get a feel for what is going on. If we take $n = 3$ we need to show that every sequence of 10 different reals has a monotone subsequence of length 4.

If we consider the sequence

$$9, 10, 5, 6, 7, 2, 3, 4, 1, 8,$$

then we see that there are many examples: 5, 6, 7, 8 and 2, 3, 4, 8 are both increasing while choosing one of 9 or 10, then one of 5, 6 or 7, then one of 2, 3, or 4 and finally 1 gives us eighteen decreasing subsequences.

We notice that even though there are lots of monotone subsequences to choose from, they all end with 1 or 8. This leads us to our key idea. Rather than focus on the subsequences themselves we will try and prove that there is always at least one member of the long sequence which is the last member of a monotone subsequence with four members.

Let us see how this strategy works on another example, namely the sequence

$$3, 2, 1, 6, 5, 9, 4, 8, 10, 7.$$

Now for each of these ten numbers we might ask ourselves whether this number is the last term in a long (that is, four term) monotone sequence, or, a little more precisely, we might ask the following two questions of each number:

(i) how long is the longest increasing subsequence ending here?
(ii) how long is the longest decreasing subsequence ending here?

This gives us a total of twenty chances to get an answer which is more than three.

If we ask these questions of a_1, which is 3, we obtain the answers one and one. For a_2, which is 2, we obtain one and two, and for a_9, which is 10, we obtain four and one. For completeness we will record the answers to all twenty questions in the following way. We label each term in the sequence with the pair (i, d) where i is the length of a longest increasing subsequence ending there and d is the length of a longest decreasing one. Our example sequence now becomes

$$3_{(1,1)},\ 2_{(1,2)},\ 1_{(1,3)},\ 6_{(2,1)},\ 5_{(2,2)},\ 9_{(3,1)},\ 4_{(2,3)},\ 8_{(3,2)},\ 10_{(4,1)},\ 7_{(3,3)}.$$

From here the next good idea is not so hard to find: we notice that all the labels are distinct. This might be a quirk of our example, but a moment's thought shows that it is true for any sequence of distinct reals. Indeed, if x is a term in the sequence with label (i, d) and y follows x in the sequence, then if $y > x$ it can extend the increasing subsequence ending with x, while if $y < x$ it can extend the decreasing subsequence. Either way, y is given a label where one of the coordinates is more than the corresponding coordinate of the label for x.

Now the end is in sight. We have ten different labels of the form (i, d) to assign, but there are only nine ordered pairs of positive whole numbers less than four, so one of the labels includes a number greater than three, as required.

The general case is identical: we assign the label (i, d) to each number as described above and observe that they are distinct. There are n^2 possible labels with i and d both less than $n + 1$, so at least one of the labels includes a number greater than n.

This is very much a pigeonhole principle proof, even though we never have a pigeonhole with more than one pigeon in it. The numbers were the pigeons, and the pigeonholes were their labels. the fact that there were $n^2 + 1$ pigeons all assigned to distinct pigeonholes implied that there were more than n^2 different pigeonholes. Hence we were using the contrapositive form of the principle, concluding that there were at least as many pigeonholes as pigeons.

Chapter 8: Pigeonholing

Exercise 8d

1. If α is a positive irrational number, prove there is a multiple of α with ten consecutive zeros immediately after the decimal point. (Recall that a number α is *irrational* if the equation $p = \alpha q$ has no integer solutions for p and q.)

2. Prove *Dirichlet's approximation theorem*, that if α is real and N is a positive integer, then there is a fraction $\frac{p}{q}$ with $q \leq N$, such that $|\alpha - \frac{p}{q}| \leq \frac{1}{q(N+1)}$.

3. Theresa has 45 mathematics problems to solve over the next 30 days. She will solve at least one a day. Prove that there is a sequence of days during which Theresa solves exactly thirteen problems. [HINT]

4. Prove that every set of n integers has a nonempty subset whose sum is divisible by n. [HINT]

*5. Prove that for every positive integer n, there is a Fibonacci number divisible by n. [HINT]

8.5 Averaging

At this point we pause to discuss a slight strengthening of the pigeonhole principle that was eloquently advocated by Dutch computer scientist Edsger W. Dijkstra. It was christened the purified pigeonhole principle by Dijkstra, but we will refer to it as the *averaging principle*.

> **The averaging principle**
> For a non-empty, finite collection of numbers, the maximum value is at least the average value.

This statement is clearly true: if the average of a collection of numbers is M, then the numbers cannot all be less than M since their sum would be small enough to ensure their average was *less* than M. The averaging principle also implies the pigeonhole principle we met earlier. Indeed, if n pigeonholes contain more than nk pigeons, then the average number of pigeons per pigeonhole is more than k, so there is a pigeonhole which contains more than k pigeons. We also note that the averaging principle deals with real numbers rather than just integers, and is therefore the most general form of the pigeonhole principle we have met so far.

Dijkstra felt that the more abstract, purified form was superior to the traditional pigeonhole principle for a number of reasons, and we will take the time to consider them, even if we do not, in the end, decide to abandon our now familiar avian friends completely.

The first objection to the traditional pigeonhole principle is that it is sometimes more natural to work with averages than totals. This certainly carries some weight, and the following problem is a case in point.

Problem 8.16

In a company there are a number of committees. Each committee contains at least half the employees.

Prove that there is an employee who is a member of at least half the committees.

The average number of committees containing a particular employee is at least half the number of committees, and the result follows.

To see this we could imagine a table with rows labelled with committees and columns labelled with employees. If employee a is in committee b, then we colour the appropriate cell in the table black. We are told that each row is at least half black, so the entire table is at least half black, so the average number of black cells per column is at least half the height of the table, as required.

This argument makes no explicit use of the number of committees or indeed the number of employees, and to introduce variables to represent these (irrelevant) numbers would be a little cumbersome.

Another observation made by Dijkstra is that the averaging principle deals only with numbers (of pigeons) while the traditional pigeonhole principle forces us to decide exactly what the pigeons are. For example, if we try to solve problem 8.16 using the traditional pigeonhole principle we run into a difficulty: what exactly are our pigeons? The context of the problem immediately suggests

$$\text{pigeonhole} = \text{committee}$$
$$\text{pigeon} = \text{employee},$$

but this tells us nothing that was not given in the question.

A closer look at the statement we are trying to prove might lead us to the less intuitive

$$\text{pigeonhole} = \text{employee}$$
$$\text{pigeon} = \text{committee containing said employee},$$

however, this also fails since now each pigeon can go into multiple pigeonholes.

In fact what we need is

$\text{pigeonhole} = \text{employee}$

$\text{pigeon} = \text{ordered pair } (a,b) \text{ where employee } a \text{ is in committee } b.$

so our pigeons are precisely the black cells in the table in our averaging principle solution.

The point here is not really that the traditional pigeonhole principle solution is much harder; indeed the correct solution uses exactly the same idea as in the averaging principle proof. However, the images of birds and boxes leads us down the wrong track initially. Also, by forcing ourselves to think about pigeons explicitly, we end up having to consider objects which feel slightly contrived, in this case the pairs (a,b). This means that, if we remove all reference to our wrong turns, our final solution looks as though it needed a superhuman level of ingenuity or perhaps just a lucky guess.

The next problem shows that we sometimes need the full generality of the phrase 'collection of numbers' rather than just 'collection of integers'.

Problem 8.17

Prove that it is impossible for all the faces of a convex polyhedron to be hexagons. [BMO1 1974]

The style of question may be unfamiliar since three-dimensional geometry has fallen out of favour with Olympiad setters in recent decades. A *polyhedron* is any three dimensional shape whose faces are polygons, and, informally, the word *convex* means the shape has no dents or holes. More formally it means that any line joining two points in the polyhedron lies completely within the polyhedron. It is also worth pointing out that the hexagons in the question do not need to be regular.

Our task is to show that a polyhedron with only hexagonal faces cannot be convex. A crucial idea, which readers unfamiliar with three dimensional geometry should take a moment to think about, is that in a convex solid the sum of the angles round any vertex is strictly less than 360°. We will also use the fact at least three faces meet at any vertex of a polyhedron. With these insights the problem is fairly straight forward.

Suppose we have a polyhedron with hexagonal faces and n vertices. We apply the averaging principle to a collection of numbers containing the sums of the angles around each vertex.

To find the total of the numbers in the collection, we count the number of faces the polyhedron has. At least three meet at each vertex, giving at least $3n$ hexagons. However, each one is counted six times, so in fact we have at least $\frac{n}{2}$ hexagons. The angles in a hexagon sum to 720°. So the total of all the angles is at least $360n°$. The averaging principle now ensures that there is a vertex whose angle sum is at least 360°, so the polyhedron cannot be convex.

Problem 8.18

Let m and n be integers greater than 1. Consider an $m \times n$ rectangular grid of points in the plane. Some k of these points are coloured red in such a way that no three red points are the vertices of a right-angled triangle two of whose sides are parallel to the sides of the grid.

Determine the greatest possible value of k. [BMO1 2002]

To find a lower bound for k, we need a good way to choose red points which avoids right angled triangles, and colouring either an entire row or an entire column red is an obvious way to do this. It is also obvious that, if we start by doing this, then any red point we add will create many right-angled triangles so the arrangement cannot be improved upon. This leads to the claim that the maximum number of points is $\max(m, n)$.

Sadly, this 'Here is a good strategy which cannot be improved.' argument has led us astray here. If we choose any point in the grid and colour all other points in its row *and* column red, while leaving the chosen point blue (figure 8.3), we obtain a set of $m + n - 2$ red points with no triangles, which is clearly better if m and n are greater than 2.

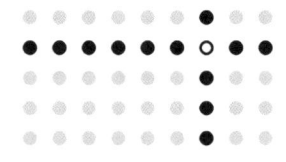

Figure 8.3

To prove that this is, in fact, the best possible bound we resist the temptation to argue that our 'good configuration' cannot be improved, and instead use the pigeonhole principle to show that any set with more red points contains a right-angled triangle.

Suppose we have at least $m + n - 1$ red points in the grid.

If a red point has another red point in its row we will say it has a *row-neighbour* and define *column-neighbour* similarly. We now claim that among any $m + n - 1$ red points there is one with both a row-neighbour and a column-neighbour. We have $m + n - 1$ points divided among m rows, so at most $m - 1$ rows contain fewer than two points. This means at least n points have a row-neighbour. Similarly, at least m points have a column-neighbour. Now each point has an average of at least $\frac{m+n}{m+n-1}$ types of neighbour (where a point with many row-neighbours but no column-neighbours has one type of neighbour). So, by the averaging principle, there is a point with more than one type of neighbour.

Therefore the maximum value of k is $m + n - 2$.

Problem 8.19

Prove that in any set of nine two-digit composite numbers, there are at least three that share a common factor.

The key insight in this problem is that if n is a composite number, then it has a prime factor which is at most $\sqrt{n}$. Since all of the numbers given in the question are less than a hundred, each has a prime factor less than ten. In particular, each of them is divisible by at least one of 2, 3, 5 and 7. There are four of these primes and we have $9 > 2 \times 4$ numbers and want three to share a factor, which is all very encouraging. With this in mind we form four pigeonholes called S_2, S_3, S_5 and S_7, and place a number into S_p if it is divisible by p.

Now we run into a potential problem: the pigeonholes overlap. In particular, all multiples of six belong to more than one pigeonhole, while numbers like 30 and 70 belong to three. Fortunately, this is not a problem at all. If we have one of these numbers we simply place a copy in each pigeonhole. This can only increase the average number of numbers per pigeonhole. Therefore the average number of numbers per pigeonhole is at least $\frac{9}{4}$, which is enough to prove the claim.

The moral of the story here is that overlapping pigeonholes are not necessarily a bad thing. In fact, they are positively beneficial in some cases. This is particularly true, if, for example, pigeonholes are chosen such that every pigeon is in at least two pigeonholes.

So Dijkstra has certainly provided us with some food for thought, and some readers will be charmed by the austere precision of his averaging principle and aim to use it exclusively. Others however, will be loath to lose the imaginary wingbeats of the Colombidae family completely, and will instead try to use whichever form of pigeonhole principle seems most appropriate to the problem at hand.

Exercise 8e

1. On any given Sunday there are thirteen football matches, each of which has three possible outcomes: home win, home loss and draw. Four friends each place a bet on the outcome of each of the games. They bet in such a way, that for each match, at least one of them is certain to win their bet on that match. Prove that at least one of the friends will win at least four of their bets.

2. There are 99 seats in a circle. Prove that if 80 people sit down, five consecutive seats will be occupied.

3. 101 boys and 101 girls stand in a circle. Prove that there is a person both of whose neighbours are girls.

4. Prove that there is an integer which can be written as the sum of four positive perfect cubes in at least 100 different ways.

8.6 Generalising

The averaging principle can be rephrased as: 'If n numbers sum to more than nk, then one of the numbers is more than k.' and this formulation invites yet another generalisation. We will call it the *inequality principle* though you should not assume this is standard terminology.

> **THE INEQUALITY PRINCIPLE**
> If $a_1 + a_2 + a_3 + \ldots + a_n > b_1 + b_2 + b_3 + \ldots + b_n$ then at least one of the a_i is greater than the corresponding b_i.

We can recover the more familiar pigeonhole principle by setting all the bs equal to k, but there are certain problems where this, most general, form is useful.

Problem 8.20

James is still at the fair. Now he is playing a game which involves throwing rings onto three pegs. Rings on the first peg are worth two points each, those on the second peg are worth three points, and those on the third are worth five. The ring scores on each peg are totalled, and James wins if there is a peg with a total which is at least ten. James is confident that he will never miss the rings entirely, but cannot be sure which peg any given ring will land on.

How many rings does he need to throw to be sure he will win?

The problem is not particularly difficult. Eight rings will not suffice since four could land on the two point peg, three on the three point peg and one on the five point peg. The inequality principle provides the analogue of the pigeonhole principle needed to prove that James is sure to win with nine rings.

Let the number of rings on the two point, three point and five point pegs be a_1, a_2 and a_3 respectively. James wins if $a_1 > 4$, $a_2 > 3$ or $a_3 > 1$. If James throws nine rings, then $a_1 + a_2 + a_3 = 9 > 4 + 3 + 1$ so one of the conditions for winning holds.

Problem 8.21

Anthony has twenty-four loose socks in his sock drawer. Six are white, six are navy, six are black and six are grey. The only time he wears white socks is while playing tennis.

How many socks does Anthony need to take from the drawer to be certain of having a matching pair of socks he can wear to the office?

Clearly nine socks may not suffice since we might have six white, one navy, one black and one grey.

To show that ten always will suffice, we argue as follows. Let the number of white, navy, black and grey socks he takes be w, n, b and g respectively. If $w + n + b + g = 10 > 6 + 1 + 1 + 1$, then either he has more than six white socks which is impossible, or he has more than one sock of another colour and can go to work.

Problem 8.22

An 8×4 chessboard is tiled by dominoes. A *cutting line* is a line which divides the board into two pieces without dividing any of the dominoes into two pieces.

Prove that every possible arrangement of the dominoes has a cutting line.

A few words of explanation are in order. Here, and throughout this chapter, a *domino* is a pair of unnumbered unit squares which share an edge. The word *tiled* means that the dominoes are placed on the board such that the two squares of the domino exactly cover two cells of the board. The dominoes may not overlap or stick out from the edge of the board.

An 8×4 grid consists of nine lines of length 4 which we will call *short* and five of length 8 which we will call *long*.

For example, the arrangement shown in figure 8.4 has two cutting lines, one short and one long.

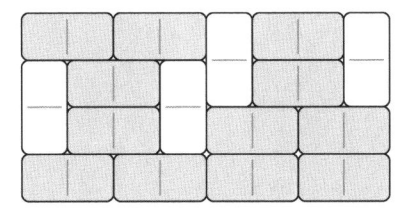

Figure 8.4

If we exclude the four lines which make up the perimeter, then we have $7 \times 4 + 3 \times 8 = 52$ internal line segments of length 1. Each domino covers exactly one of these segments, so we have $52 - 16 = 36$ uncovered segments. A cutting line consists of eight uncovered segments on a long line, or four uncovered segments on a short one.

For a given arrangement of dominoes, we let the number of uncovered segments on each of the three long lines be ℓ_1, ℓ_2 and ℓ_3 and define s_1, s_2, ..., s_7 similarly. We know that $\ell_1 + \ell_2 + \ell_3 + s_1 + s_2 + \cdots + s_7 = 36$ and would like to conclude that $\ell_i > 7$ or $s_i > 3$ for some i.

Unfortunately, $3 \times 7 + 7 \times 3$ is rather more than 36, so we appear to be stuck. The inequality principle alone is not enough to solve this problem, but it is worth seeing what can be salvaged from the wreckage.

Since 36 is greater than $3 \times 6 + 7 \times 2$, we can at least conclude that any arrangement has a long line with 7 or 8 uncovered segments or a short line with 3 or 4 uncovered segments.

If we call a line with all but one of its segments uncovered an *almost cutting* line, then the inequality principle ensures the existence of either a cutting line or an almost cutting line. Now our task is to prove that there are no almost cutting lines.

Let us suppose, for contradiction, that an almost cutting line exists. This line divides the board into two rectangular regions. The single offending domino which crosses the line covers one square in each of these regions (see figure 8.5 on the following page).

However, each of the rectangles has even area (since both 4 and 8 are even), so removing one square leaves an odd number of squares to be covered by dominoes which is clearly impossible. This observation completes the proof.

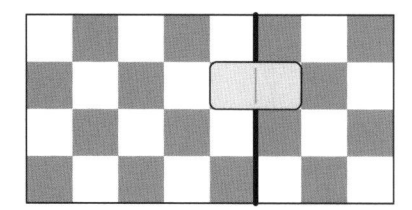

Figure 8.5

8.7 Number theory

The last three problems ask us to use the pigeonhole principle to prove some key results in elementary number theory.

It should be emphasised that all of them have standard proofs which do not use the pigeonhole principle. However, it is amazing that these results, which do not seem remotely combinatorial, can be proved simply by careful counting. The more number theoretic approach found in [2], for example, is perhaps more instructive, but the problems are included here to further illustrate the extraordinary versatility of the pigeonhole principle.

Problem 8.23

Prove Bézout's Lemma, that if a and b are coprime positive integers, then there exist integers x and y such that $ax - by = 1$.

We seek integers x and y such that $ax = by + 1$. This leads us to rephrase the claim slightly: 'If a and b are coprime, then there is a multiple of a that is congruent to 1 modulo b.'

Next we make the slightly stronger claim that the numbers $a, 2a, 3a,$ $\ldots, (b-1)a$ are all distinct modulo b. Indeed, if we suppose that $na \equiv ma$ (mod b) where $0 < m \leq n \leq b - 1$, then b divides $(n - m)a$ and, since none of the factors of b divides a, it follows that b divides $(n - m)$. Finally, since $(n - m) < b$, we see that $(n - m)$ is zero, so $n = m$, as required.

This means that if we had pigeonholes labelled with non-zero remainders on division by b, then we would have to divide the $(b - 1)$ multiples of a among the $(b - 1)$ pigeonholes with no two numbers in the same pigeonhole. This implies that each pigeonhole is occupied, including the pigeonhole labelled '1'.

Bézout's lemma is often stated as follows: 'If a and b are integers then there are integers x and y such that $ax + by = \mathrm{HCF}(a,b)$' and you are welcome to prove that this generalisation follows from the version discussed above. If you are interested in exploring an efficient method for finding x and y given a and b, then you should consult, for example, [2].

Problem 8.24

Suppose that a and b are coprime positive integers and that we are given integers r and s with $0 \leq r < a$ and $0 \leq s < b$. Suppose further that we wish to find a non-negative whole number x for which $x \equiv r \pmod{a}$ and $x \equiv s \pmod{b}$.

Prove the Chinese Remainder Theorem, that there is always a unique x less than ab with the desired properties.

More succinctly we might say, if $\mathrm{HCF}(a,b) = 1$, then the simultaneous congruences

$$x \equiv r \pmod{a}$$
$$\text{and} \quad x \equiv s \pmod{b}$$

have a unique solution modulo ab.

Our solution follows a familiar pattern.

If $n \equiv r_a \pmod{a}$ and $n \equiv r_b \pmod{b}$, then we label n with the pair (r_a, r_b) and claim that $0, 1, 2, \ldots, ab - 1$ all get different labels. There are only ab distinct labels which need to be assigned to ab distinct numbers which ensures that every label is used exactly once, as required.

To prove our claim we assume that n and m receive the same label and let d be the (positive) difference between m and n. Now d is a multiple of a which is less than ab and is divisible by b so, just as in problem 8.23, it is zero and we are done.

This proof is both charming and frustrating in that it does not tell us how to find the number with the required remainders; it merely ensures that one exists. A more constructive solution can be found using Bézout's lemma.

You might like to think about why the proof given above fails when a and b share a common factor.

The final result of this chapter has an astonishingly wide variety of proofs. The one we give here is not the shortest, but hopefully some readers will find it amusing.

Problem 8.25

Prove, using the pigeonhole principle, that there are infinitely many prime numbers.

Suppose we are given a fixed (large) integer k. We will prove that there are more than k primes. Since the choice of k is arbitrary this shows that there are infinitely many primes.

We begin by choosing a number n such that $2^n > (n+1)^k$. This can always been done, since the exponential function 2^x grows *much* faster than the polynomial function $(x+1)^k$. In particular, given a value of k, we can set $n = 2^k - 1$; then $2^n > (n+1)^k$ precisely when $2^k - 1 > k^2$, which holds for all $k > 4$.

With $2^n > (n+1)^k$ in place, we consider all the numbers less than or equal to 2^n, and suppose, for contradiction, that all of them are only divisible by the first k primes.

This assumption means that each one has a prime factorisation of the form $2^{a_1} 3^{a_2} 5^{a_3} \cdots p_k^{a_k}$, where the p_i are all prime. Since each number is at most 2^n, the exponents a_i satisfy $0 \le a_i \le n$. Now we label each number with the string of exponents $a_1, a_2, \ldots, a_k$. Clearly no two numbers receive the same label, but the number of labels available is at most $(n+1)^k$.

By construction, this is less than the number of numbers we are considering. Thus there is a number which has a prime factor which is not among the first k primes, as required. We note in passing that this proof does not use the fact that every number has a unique prime factorisation here, merely that each number has *a* factorisation, and that any given factorisation cannot represent more than one number.

Chapter 8: Pigeonholing 153

Exercise 8f

1. Ollie the octopus has four left feet and four right feet. In his cupboard he has twelve identical left shoes and nine identical right shoes. How many shoes does he need to take to ensure that he has a set of eight he can wear?

2. Ollie's friend Sammy the sinister spider has eight left feet. In his cupboard he also has twelve identical left shoes and (somewhat surprisingly) nine identical right shoes. How many shoes does he need to take to ensure he has a set he can wear?

3. Suppose p is a prime number greater than 5. Prove that $\frac{1}{p}$ is a recurring decimal. Generalise the statement.

4. Let S be a subset of the set of numbers $\{1, 2, \ldots, 2008\}$ which consists of 756 numbers. Show that there are two distinct elements a, b of S such that $a + b$ is divisible by 8. [BMO1 2007]

5. (a) Prove that among any three integers there is a subset of size 2 whose sum is divisible by 2.
   (b) Prove that among any five integers there is a subset of size 3 whose sum is divisible by 3.
   (c) Prove that among any seven integers there is a subset of size 4 whose sum is divisible by 4. [HINT]
   (d) Find a set A of ten positive integers such that no six distinct elements of A have a sum which is divisible by 6. Is it possible to find such a set if A contains eleven positive integers?
   [BMO2 2000]

6. A booking office at a railway station sells tickets to 200 destinations. One day, tickets were issued to 3800 passengers. Show that
   (a) there are (at least) six destinations at which the passenger arrival numbers are the same;
   (b) the statement in (a) becomes false if 'six' is replaced by 'seven'.
   [BMO2 1988]

7. There are 50 points in the plane, with no three collinear. Each point is coloured either red, blue, green or black. Prove that there is a colour such that at least 130 scalene triangles have three vertices of that colour. [JBMO 2007]

   HINT

8. Each one of 2009 distinct points in the plane is coloured blue or red, such that there are exactly two red points on every blue-centred unit circle. Find the greatest possible number of blue points. [JBMO 2009]

   HINT

9. Let N be a convex polygon with 1415 vertices and perimeter 2001. Prove that we can find 3 vertices of N which form a triangle of area smaller than 1. [JBMO 2001]

   HINT

Chapter 9
Tiling and colouring

9.1 Dominoes

We start this chapter with a classic brainteaser.

> **Problem 9.1**
> Two opposite corners are removed from an 8 × 8 chessboard.
> Can the remaining 62 cells be tiled with dominoes?

A few words of explanation are in order. Here, and throughout this chapter, a *domino* is a pair of unnumbered unit squares which share an edge. The word *tiled* means that the dominoes are placed on the board such that the two squares of the domino exactly cover two cells of the board. The dominoes may not overlap or stick out from the edge of the board.

Readers who are not familiar with this problem should take a moment to try it.

The right-hand diagram in figure 9.1 on the next page shows a failed attempt at covering the board shown on the left. The attempt leaves two grey cells uncovered. After a few more failed attempts we ought to become suspicious. Perhaps the task is impossible, but if so, why?

The unforgettable proof uses a *colouring argument*. A standard 8 × 8 chessboard comes equipped with the colouring shown in figure 9.2. It

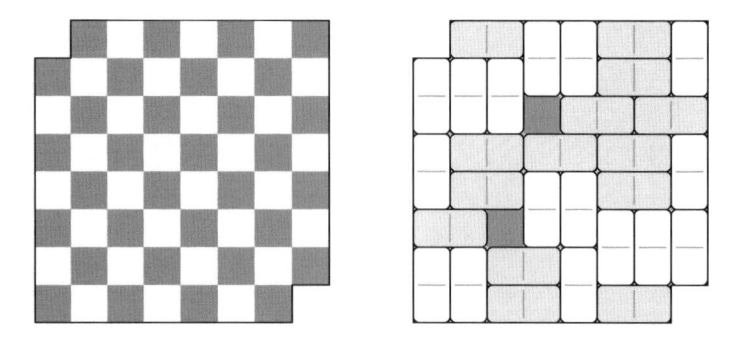

Figure 9.1

is clear that no matter where you place a domino it always covers one grey and one white cell. However, if we remove two opposite corners we remove two cells which are the same colour. Thus we have 30 cells of one colour and 32 of the other so there is no way to place 31 dominoes on the resulting figure.

Figure 9.2

Problem 9.2

Twenty-four non-overlapping dominoes are placed on a 7×7 chessboard, leaving one cell uncovered.

What are the possible positions of the uncovered cell?

Chapter 9: Tiling and colouring

Our first instinct with this problem is now to colour the chessboard and count the grey and white cells. In figure 9.3 there are 25 grey and 24 white cells. This means that the uncovered cell will certainly be grey.

Figure 9.3

However, this is not even half the battle. We have 25 grey cells, any one of which might be left over, but is it always possible to cover the 48 other cells with dominoes? It is at least conceivable that some other obstacle might prevent us from placing 24 dominoes on the board if a specific grey cell is removed.

This leaves us with 25 cases to check! Using rotations and reflections we can reduce this number to eight, but this is still extremely unappealing. More importantly, checking cases would only resolve the problem for the 7×7 board, and we would much rather prove something more general. In particular, we would like to know the answer to the following question.

Suppose that a single cell is removed from a $(2n+1) \times (2n+1)$ chessboard such that equal numbers of grey and white cells remain. Is it always possible to tile the resulting shape with dominoes?

To prove that this is indeed the case, we will repeatedly use the obvious fact that a rectangle can be tiled by dominoes if at least one of its sides has even length.

Call the removed cell C. It has the same colour as the corner cells, so the distances from the edges of C to the edges of the board are either all even or all odd. (Take a moment to convince yourself of this.)

If the distances from C to the edges of the board are all even, then we divide the board into eight rectangular regions by cutting along the extended sides of C, as shown on the left of figure 9.4 on the following page. Each of these regions has at least one even side length so can be covered by dominoes. (We note that zero is even.)

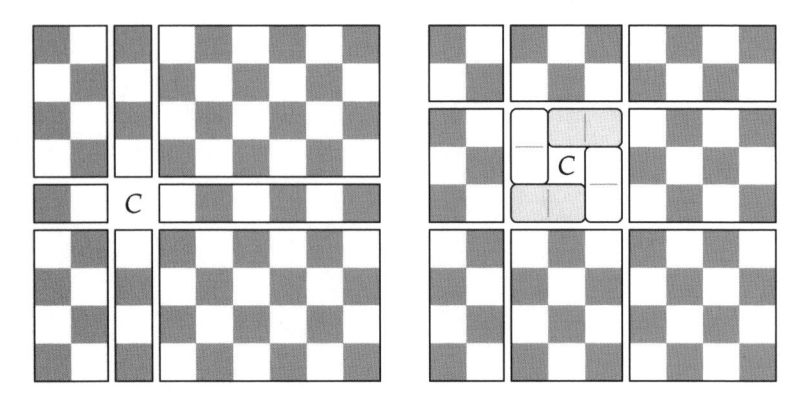

Figure 9.4

If the distances from C to edges of the board are all odd, then we can put a 3 × 3 square around C, and divide the remaining board into rectangular regions by cutting along the extended edges of this square, as shown on the right of figure 9.4. Each of these regions has at least one even side length so can be tiled. A 3 × 3 square with its centre missing can also be tiled, so the proof is complete.

Problem 9.3

Four dominoes have been placed on a 7 × 6 board as shown in figure 9.5.

Is it possible to tile the remainder of the board with dominoes?

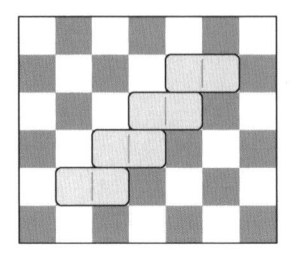

Figure 9.5

If we colour the board in the standard way, then the area we have to tile consists of 17 squares of each colour. This suggests that the tiling may be possible, but actually doing the job proves to be very troublesome. The key insight is that the dominoes already on the board very nearly divide it into two separate regions.

This leads us to focus on the top right and bottom left corners of the board. There are four different ways in which these two squares might be covered by dominoes, since each square is covered by a domino with one of two different orientations. In each of these four cases the remainder of the board is divided into two regions, and it is easy to check that none of these regions have equal numbers of grey and white squares. Therefore the task of completing the tiling is impossible.

The interesting thing about this problem is that it shows that, while every region which can be tiled with dominoes has equal numbers of grey and white squares in the standard colouring, the converse does not hold.

9.2 Trominoes and Tetrominoes

We now turn our attention to tiles made up of three unit squares which we call *trominoes* and tiles made up of four squares which we call *tetrominoes*. All tiles can be freely rotated within the plane that contains them. Sometimes we will also allow ourselves to turn tiles over, in which case we will call them *two-sided* and otherwise we will call them *one-sided*.

It is clear that there are two distinct types of tromino. Three squares in a line form a *straight tromino*, while three arranged in an L-shape form an *L-tromino*. However, as the next problem shows, the situation for tetrominoes is not quite so straightforward.

Problem 9.4

(a) Prove that there are seven distinct one-sided tetrominoes.
(b) Prove or disprove the statement: It is possible to pack all seven distinct tetrominoes into a 7 × 4 rectangle without overlapping.

[BMO1 2001]

It is not too hard to make a list of the seven different one-sided tetrominoes. They are shown in figure 9.6 on the next page. Each tetromino is referred to using a letter of the alphabet and these are also shown in the figure. The *I*-tetromino is also called a *straight* tetromino and the *O*-tetromino is also called a *square* tetromino.

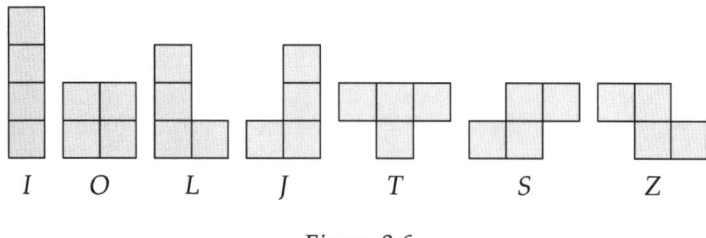

    I   O   L   J   T   S   Z

Figure 9.6

This is all very well, but it is not at all clear how best to go about proving that our list is exhaustive. It is likely that we will need to consider various cases, but we would like our method to be as clear and painless as possible.

If all four cells of a tetromino lie in a single line, then we have an *I*-tetromino. Every other tetromino contains an *L*-tromino, that is, three cells in an *L*-shape. There are seven places where a fourth cell can be joined to the *L*-tromino. Considering these in turn we obtain a complete list of all non-straight tetrominoes. We get two copies of the *T*-tetromino, and one of each of the others in our list. Figure 9.7 shows an *L*-tromino, and the letters indicate which of the seven tetrominoes is formed by replacing that letter with a cell.

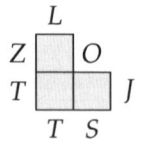

Figure 9.7

The second part of the problem asks whether a 7×4 board can be tiled with one of each of the tetrominoes. We start by colouring the board in the standard way and noting that there are equal numbers of grey and white cells. Now we look at each of the tetrominoes. The key observation is that, no matter where you place them, the *I*-, *O*-, *L*-, *J*-, *S*- and *Z*-tetrominoes all cover two cells of each colour. On the other hand, the *T*-tetromino covers either one or three grey cells depending on its position.

Chapter 9: Tiling and colouring 161

Now we can conclude by saying that our seven tetrominoes cover either 13 or 15 grey cells but not 14, so the tiling is impossible.

A neater alternative is to say that the seven tiles cover an *odd* number of grey cells between them while the board contains an even number. This is called a *parity argument* and is preferable because it is far easier to generalise. For example, an almost identical argument shows that a 7×4 rectangle cannot be tiled with seven T-tetrominoes. Indeed, the number of grey cells covered by seven Ts is the sum of seven odd numbers, and hence is an odd number.

We have shown that there are seven different one-sided tetrominoes. If we allow ourselves to turn the tiles over, then L- and J-tetrominoes become indistinguishable, as do S- and Z-tetrominoes. This leaves only five different two-sided tetrominoes, namely I, O, T, L and S. Clearly if a problem only involves T, I and O-tetrominoes, then there is no need to specify whether they are one or two-sided.

Problem 9.5

Suppose we have two copies of each of the five two-sided tetrominoes.

Can they be packed into a 10×4 rectangle?

The answer is yes. The diagram on the left of figure 9.8 shows one of the many possible tilings.

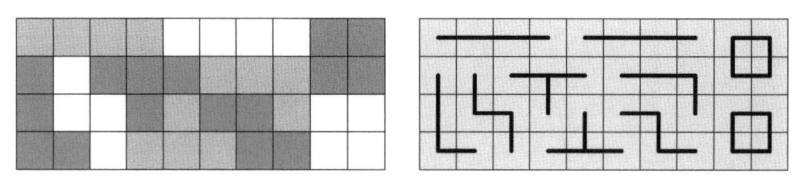

Figure 9.8

To construct our tiling we turned over one of the L-tetrominoes and one of the S-tetrominoes. Turning tiles over was explicitly permitted in this problem, but not in problem 9.4, and it is important to keep track of which convention is being used.

Note that it is quite difficult to reliably produce figures by hand like that on the left of figure 9.8. One way to deal with this is to represent each tetromino by a line which forms its *skeleton*, as shown on the right of figure 9.8.

In some ways it is disappointing that the answer to problem 9.5 is yes, particularly as there is no interesting theory behind finding a solution. However, the problem serves as a reminder that sometimes you just have to play around with a problem until you find something. In this case we might have found a legal tiling, but even in cases where the tiling is impossible, experimenting might help us find a clue as to *why* we cannot succeed.

Exercise 9a

1. A region consists of n unit squares connected by common edges. The region cannot be tiled with dominoes, but when it is coloured using the standard chessboard pattern, there are equal numbers of grey and white cells. Find the smallest possible value of n.

2. A 12×12 chessboard is given the standard colouring and one grey and one white cell are removed. Prove that it is possible to tile the remainder of the board with dominoes. [HINT]

3. Provide an alternative solution to problem 9.2 using proof by induction.

4. Consider a $2n \times n$ board. From the ith row we remove the central $2(i-1)$ unit squares. What is the maximal number of non-overlapping dominoes that can be placed within the resulting figure?   [JBMO 2006]
(The figure shows the relevant shapes for the first three values of n.)

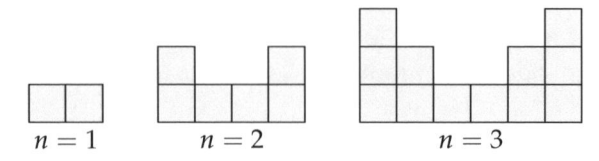

$n = 1$ $n = 2$ $n = 3$

[HINT]

Chapter 9: Tiling and colouring 163

5. Which of the following shapes can be tiled using one copy of each of the seven one-sided tetrominoes?

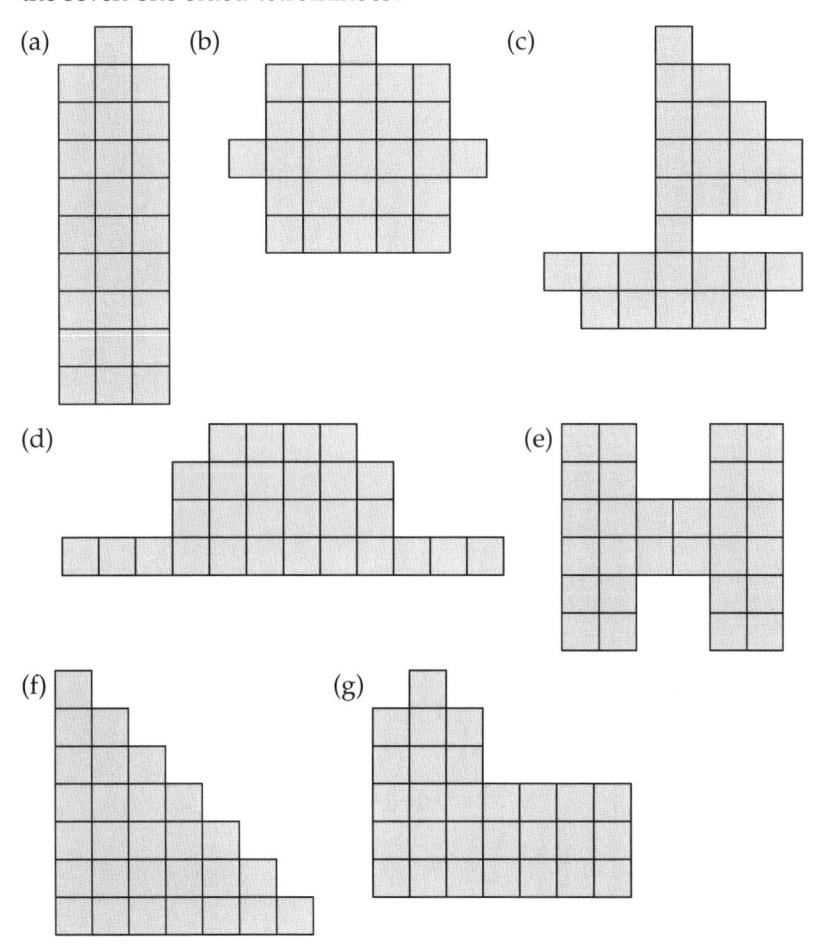

(a) (b) (c)

(d) (e)

(f) (g)

6. Can an 8×8 board be tiled with 15 T-tetrominoes and one square tetromino?

7. Suppose we have one copy of each of the five two-sided tetrominoes. Can we arrange them to form a rectangle?

8. The rectangle R has dimensions $2a \times 2b$, where a and b are integers.
   (a) Prove that R can be tiled by T-tetrominoes when both a and b are even.
   (b) Prove that R cannot be tiled by T-tetrominoes when both a and b are odd. [Maclaurin 2014]

9.3 Alternative colourings

Problem 9.6
Prove that it is impossible to tile a 10×10 chessboard with straight tetrominoes.

Our first thought here is to colour the chessboard and count the grey and white cells. The standard colouring gives 50 cells of each colour, and a straight tetromino always covers two grey and two white cells. This all seems terribly consistent with the idea that we might be able to tile the board with 25 straight tetrominoes.

In order to prove that the tiling is impossible, we will need to consider a non-standard colouring of the chessboard. There are plenty to choose from and we will take time to discuss a number of options.

The first idea is to colour the board such that a straight tetromino still always covers two grey and two white cells, but such that the chessboard no longer has 50 cells of each colour. The diagram on the left of figure 9.9 shows a possible colouring with the required properties and so gives us our first solution to the problem.

A variation on this theme is to use four different colours such that a straight tetromino always covers one cell of each colour. The condition that a straight tetromino should always cover one cell of each colour leads us to arrange these colours in diagonal stripes as shown on the right of figure 9.9. Given that we used diagonal stripes with two colours to study tiling with dominoes, this is a particularly natural colouring to try.

We should check, of course, that this colouring of the 10×10 board does not use equal numbers of squares of each colour. It does not, so we have a second solution to the problem.

Chapter 9: Tiling and colouring 165

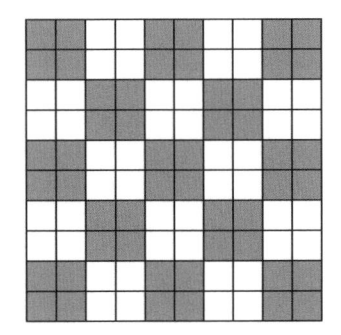

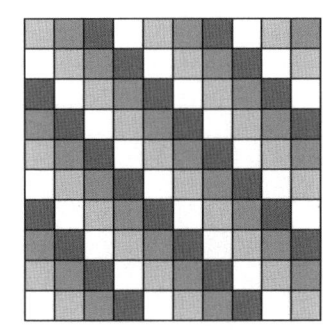

Figure 9.9

Another colouring which is sometimes useful is shown in figure 9.10. It has the property that any straight tetromino covers an *even* number of grey cells. With this colouring the 10 × 10 board has an odd number of grey cells so this gives a third way of showing that it cannot be tiled with straight tetrominoes.

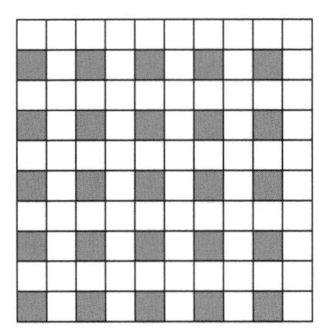

Figure 9.10

Problem 9.7

Can a 30 × 20 chessboard be tiled with two-sided tiles shaped like the one shown in figure 9.11 on the following page?

By considering the area of the shape we see that any tiling would need $\frac{20 \times 30}{8} = 75$ tiles. This is irritating since the most natural thing to do with tiles of this peculiar shape is to put pairs of them together to form 2 × 8

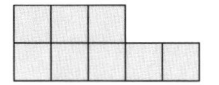

Figure 9.11

rectangles. Since 75 is odd, this pairing strategy alone will certainly not allow us to tile the whole chessboard.

Other tiling attempts also seem not to work, and at some stage we should begin to suspect that the task may be impossible.

The fact that the natural 'pair the tiles up' idea failed suggests that we may be able to prove that the tiling is impossible using some sort of parity argument. More specifically, it would be wonderful if we could find a colouring of the board with the following properties.

(i) The total number of grey cells on the board is even.
(ii) Each tile always covers an odd number of grey cells.

For any such colouring, assuming the board can be tiled, property (ii) means that the total number of grey cells is the sum of 75 odd numbers, which cannot be even, thus contradicting property (i). Fortunately, the colouring with stripes shown in figure 9.12 has both the required properties, and we conclude that the 30×20 board cannot be tiled.

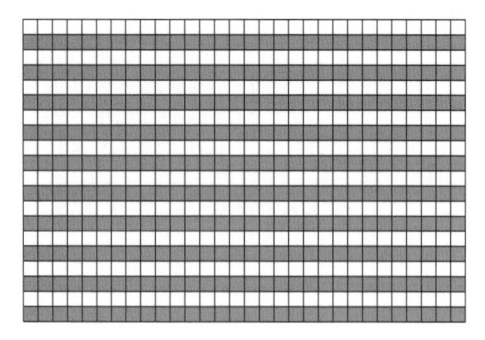

Figure 9.12

We have seen a fair number of different colouring patterns, and of course there are others, so how are we to know which one will be appropriate for a particular problem? The answer is that choosing a correct colouring requires a mixture of insight and luck. However, we can usually tell fairly quickly when a colouring is or is not likely to work. Useful colourings all have the property that something does not depend on where a particular tile is placed. It might be the number of (say) grey cells covered by the tile, or, in more sophisticated problems, the parity of the number of grey cells. If both of these seem to change when you move the tiles around, it is usually wise to look for a new colouring. To get a feel for this, it is worth thinking about why the colourings used in problem 9.6 are not appropriate for problem 9.7 and vice versa.

Problem 9.8

Suppose that a rectangular board has been tiled with rectangular tiles, each of which has at least one integer side length.

Prove that the board also has at least one integer side length.

This problem is striking because it involves tiles which may all be different, and which may have fractional, or even irrational, side lengths. It is also a famous example of a problem with many different solutions. We will give one here, and another in the following chapter, but in 1987 Stan Wagon published a paper [5] containing fourteen different proofs as well as a number of generalisations.

Our first solution to problem 9.6 used a colouring with the property that each 1×4 tile covered equal grey and white areas, but where the entire rectangle was more than half grey. This method is easily adapted to the problem at hand.

We place the bottom left corner of the board at the origin and colour it using a standard chessboard colouring except that we use cells of side length $\frac{1}{2}$, as shown on the left of figure 9.13.

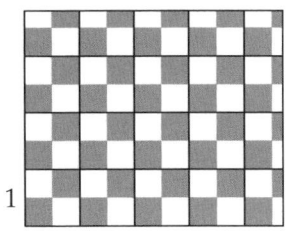

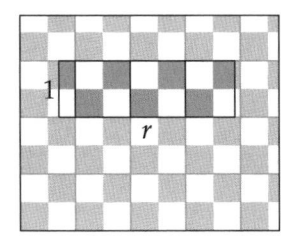

Figure 9.13

Suppose that an $r \times 1$ tile is placed on the board where r is any real number. If the y-coordinates of its corners are integers, then the colouring will naturally divide this tile into two $r \times \frac{1}{2}$ strips with opposite colouring patterns, as shown on the right of figure 9.13.

If we are not so lucky, then the colouring will divide the tile into three strips with dimensions $r \times \delta$, $r \times \frac{1}{2}$ and $r \times \left(\frac{1}{2} - \delta\right)$, as shown on the left of figure 9.14.

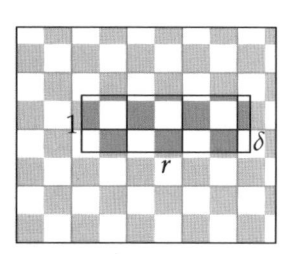

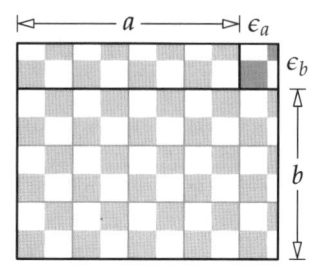

Figure 9.14

In this case the two outer strips can be placed next to each other to form a $r \times \frac{1}{2}$ strip with the opposite colour pattern to the inner strip.

Either way it is clear that an $r \times 1$ tile, and hence any tile with an integer side, always covers equal grey and white areas.

Now we suppose that the board has dimensions $(a + \epsilon_a) \times (b + \epsilon_b)$ where a, b are integers and $0 < \epsilon_a, \epsilon_b < 1$. We claim that the large rectangle is more than half grey, contradicting the fact that each tile is exactly half grey.

To see this we decompose the board into three rectangles measuring $(a + \epsilon_a) \times b$, $a \times \epsilon_b$ and $\epsilon_a \times \epsilon_b$, as shown on the right of figure 9.14. The first two have an integer side and so cover equal grey and white areas. Now we claim that the last rectangle in the top right corner is predominantly grey. If ϵ_a and ϵ_b are both at most $\frac{1}{2}$, then the entire last rectangle is grey. If, say, $\epsilon_a \leq \frac{1}{2}$ and $\frac{1}{2} < \epsilon_b < 1$, then the grey area is $\frac{1}{2}\epsilon_a$ while the white area is $\epsilon_a(1 - \epsilon_b)$ which is smaller. Finally, if $\frac{1}{2} < \epsilon_a, \epsilon_b < 1$, then the difference between the grey area and the white area is $\frac{1}{4} + (\epsilon_a - \frac{1}{2})(\epsilon_b - \frac{1}{2}) - \frac{1}{2}(\epsilon_a - \frac{1}{2}) - \frac{1}{2}(\epsilon_b - \frac{1}{2})$, which simplifies to $(1 - \epsilon_a)(1 - \epsilon_b) > 0$, as required.

Exercise 9b

1. Can a 10×10 board be tiled with two-sided L-tetrominoes? [HINT]

2. Can a 9×10 rectangle be tiled with 1×6 rectangles? [HINT]

3. Can a $10 \times 10 \times 10$ box be completely packed with $1 \times 1 \times 4$ bricks?

4. The equilateral triangle ABC has sides of integer length N. The triangle is completely divided (by drawing lines parallel to the sides of the triangle) into equilateral triangular cells of side length 1.
A continuous route is chosen, starting inside the cell with vertex A and always crossing from one cell to another through an edge shared by the two cells. No cell is visited more than once. Find, with proof, the greatest number of cells which can be visited. [BMO1 2005]
[HINT]

5. A rectangle is tiled using a combination of straight tetrominoes and square tetrominoes. One of the tiles breaks. When is it possible to rearrange the tiles and replace the broken one with a tile of the other type? [HINT]

6. An 11×11 chessboard is tiled using 1×1, 2×2 and 3×3 squares. Find the minimum possible number of 1×1 squares. [HINT]

7. A 9×7 rectangle is tiled with tiles of the two types: L-trominoes and square tetrominoes. Let $n \geq 0$ be the number of tetrominoes which can be used in such a tiling. Find all possible values of n. [JMBO 2010]
[HINT]

9.4 Tiling large boards

Problem 9.9

Prove that a $(4n+2) \times (4n+2)$ board cannot be tiled with straight tetrominoes.

This is a generalisation of problem 9.6, and the solution is essentially the same. We arrange 2×2 grey and white squares in a chessboard pattern and observe that each tetromino covers two white cells with this colouring. The only difference is that it is no longer possible to count the grey and white squares by hand since the size of the board depends on n. It is not too hard to find formulae for these numbers, but this turns out to be unnecessary. We simply note that, no matter where you place a straight tetromino, it cover exactly two white cells. Next we take the $(4n+2) \times (4n+2)$ board and split into a $(4n+2) \times 4n$ region, a $4n \times 2$ region and a 2×2 region. The first two regions can be tiled with straight tetrominoes, so they are exactly half white, while the final region is all one colour so the whole board is not half white.

Problem 9.10

For which values of m and n can an $m \times n$ rectangular chessboard be tiled with 3×5 rectangular tiles?

The first observation is that for such a tiling to exist the area of the $m \times n$ rectangle has to be divisible by 15. Therefore we may assume, without loss of generality, that m is divisible by 3. This leaves two cases: either n is divisible by 5 or m is.

In the first case we can clearly tile the board, so the only interesting case is when $m = 15k$ and we have to tile a $15k \times n$ board.

It is clear that if we can tile a $15 \times n$ board then we can tile a $15k \times n$ board by dividing it into k separate $15 \times n$ boards and tiling each of these in turn. So, for the time being, we will focus on tiling a $15 \times n$ rectangle. For $n = 3$ and $n = 5$ the tiling is easy, and we can also tile a $15 \times n$ board for any n which is a sum of threes and fives. In particular we can tile 15×8, 15×9 and 15×10 chessboards using the facts that $8 = 3+5$, $9 = 3+3+3$ and $10 = 5+5$.

However, this means we can tile a 15 × n rectangle for any $n \geq 8$ since we can simply add threes to one of 8, 9 or 10 until we reach n.

Now we know that we can tile a $15k \times n$ chessboard for any n not equal to 1, 2, 4 or 7.

The fact that we cannot immediately see how to tile a 15 × 7 board does not show that it impossible, or that tiling a 30 × 7 board, say, cannot be done. However, it is not too hard to prove that tiling these very thin boards is indeed impossible. In fact, for any $m \times 1$, $m \times 2$, $m \times 4$ or $m \times 7$ board it is clear that no legal tiling exists since we cannot even cover the first column.

At the end of this sequence of easy observations, we conclude that an $m \times n$ chessboard can be tiled with 3 × 5 rectangles provided 15 divides mn and neither dimension is equal to 1, 2, 4 or 7.

Looking back on our solution we note how useful it was to build large tilings out of smaller ones, and also that our solution did not use any colouring arguments at all.

Problem 9.11

A 1024 × 1024 chessboard is tiled using L-trominoes and a single 1 × 1 square.

Prove that the 1 × 1 square can be placed anywhere on the board.

In this problem the occurrence of the number 1024 is highly suggestive. It is equal to 2^{10} and should make us wonder whether the result is true for a $2^n \times 2^n$ board. Here we have another instance of a problem which is actually made easier by making it more general, not least because asking about a $2^n \times 2^n$ board allows us to experiment with small values of n.

The result is obvious for a 2 × 2 board.

For a 4 × 4 board we have a few cases to check. The symmetry of the situation means that we only need to consider placing the 1 × 1 tile in one of the three numbered cells shown on the left of figure 9.15 on the next page.

More to the point, if we could tile the grey L-shaped region with trominoes, then we could clearly place the 1 × 1 tile on any of the numbered cells and complete the tiling with a tromino. The diagram on the right of figure 9.15 shows that this is indeed possible.

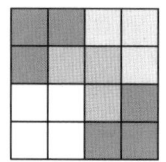

Figure 9.15

Now we would like to turn this into a proof by induction. Our claim is that if a 1×1 tile is placed anywhere on a $2^n \times 2^n$ board, then the rest of the board can be tiled with L-trominoes.

We have already discussed the base case ($n = 1$).

For the induction step we assume the result holds for $n = k$ and suppose that we have been given a $2^{k+1} \times 2^{k+1}$ board with a 1×1 tile placed on it somewhere.

If we divide board into quarters, then the 1×1 tile is in one of the quarters, so this quarter can be tiled by induction. Now we place an L-tromino in the centre of the large board so that it covers one cell in each of the remaining quarters as shown in figure 9.16. Each of these quarters can now be tiled by induction, so the proof is complete.

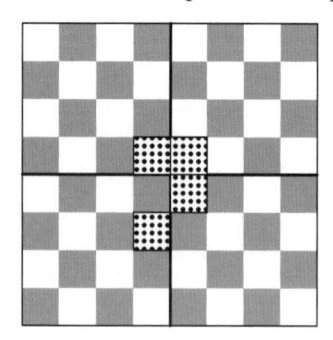

Figure 9.16

Exercise 9c

1. For which values of m and n can an $m \times n$ chessboard be tiled with:
   (a) 1×6 rectangles;
   (b) 2×3 rectangles.

2. (a) Can an 8×3 chessboard be tiled with L-tetrominoes?
   (b) For which values of m and n can an $m \times n$ rectangle be tiled with L-tetrominoes?

*3. For which n can an $n \times n$ chessboard be completely tiled with L-trominoes?

9.5 Multiple colourings

Problem 9.12

Eight straight trominoes are placed on a 5×5 square.

What are the possible positions of the uncovered cell?

Some experimenting with this problem shows that it is easy to leave the centre cell uncovered as shown in figure 9.17. However, it seems tricky to leave any other cell uncovered.

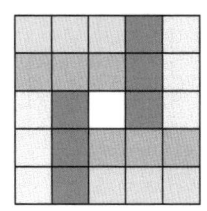

Figure 9.17

To try and prove that the centre cell is the only possible uncovered cell, we look for a colouring of the board which has nice properties when working with straight trominoes. The diagonal striped colouring with three colours (white, grey and dark grey) shown on the left of figure 9.18 seems a good choice since then every tromino covers one cell of each colour.

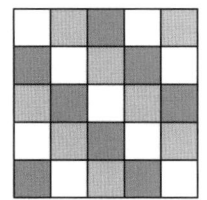

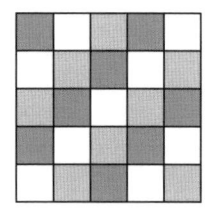

Figure 9.18

Now the number of white cells on the board is one greater than the number of grey cells, which is equal to the number of dark grey cells. Hence the uncovered cell is one of the white cells in the left-hand diagram of figure 9.18.

On its own this is unhelpful. However, we can also colour the board using stripes parallel to the other diagonal of the board. This colouring shows that the final uncovered cell is one of the white cells in the right-hand diagram of figure 9.18. By considering both colourings *at the same time*, we see that the final uncovered cell is white in both diagrams of figure 9.18, and that the centre of the board is the only cell with this property.

Problem 9.13

For which values of m and n can a $m \times n$ rectangular chessboard be tiled with 4×5 rectangular tiles?

This problem is so similar to problem 9.10 that we might be forgiven for thinking that is likely to be of a similar level of difficulty. In fact problem 9.10 is considerably easier, and was intended as something of a warm-up.

The solution begins in a similar way. By considering areas we see that 20 divides mn. From now on we will assume that 5 divides m.

If 4 divides n, then we can easily tile the board, but now, unlike problem 9.10 we have two other options to consider. Either m is in fact divisible by 20, or both n and m are divisible by 2 but not 4.

First we consider the case where m is divisible by 4, and hence is a multiple of 20. It is easy to tile 20×4 and 20×5 rectangles. Using these we can tile $20 \times n$ boards for $n = 8, 9, 10$ and $n = 12, 13, 14$ and 15. Now by adding more 20×4 rectangles we can tile any $20 \times n$ board for $n \geq 12$.

Since we can put k copies of a $20 \times n$ rectangle together we can tiles $20k \times n$ boards for all values of n except 1, 2, 3, 6, 7, and 11.

Next we show that if n is any of these six values then tiling an $n \times m$ board is impossible, regardless of the value of m. This is clear because it is impossible to cover even the first column of one of these very narrow boards.

So far everything is mirroring the solution of problem 9.10 very closely, but we have yet to consider $10a \times 2b$ boards where a and b are both odd. This means that we do not know whether or not a 10×50 board can be tiled.

It is instructive to consider this board. The only way to tile a row of ten cells is with two 5×4 rectangles. This leaves a 10×46 rectangle to cover. The same argument applies to this rectangle so any tiling reduces it to a 10×42 rectangle, then to an 10×38 rectangle and so on. This continues until a 10×2 rectangle remains which clearly cannot be covered. More generally, a $10 \times 2b$ board cannot be tiled if b is odd. Sadly there is no obvious way to extend this argument to, say, a 30×30 board.

At this point we have to consider the possibility that, if a and b are both odd, then tiling an $10a \times 2b$ board may be impossible. To test this we might turn the problem around and ask whether it is ever possible to assemble 4×5 rectangles into a larger rectangle both of whose dimensions are congruent to 2 modulo 4. If we try this it seems difficult to accomplish, but why? One reason seems to be that, when trying to build a rectangle, it is natural to use symmetric configurations. These configurations, however, use an even number of tiles. This leads to the total area of the rectangle being divisible by 8, which in turn forces one of the dimensions of the rectangle to be divisible by 4.

The experimentation has paid dividends since we can begin to devise a plan for the problem. We would like to show that if a tiled rectangle has two even sides, then it contains an even number of tiles, and thus has at least one side length divisible by four.

Having a plan is an excellent start, but how should we carry it out? We look to problems we have already solved for inspiration. Have we ever solved a problem by showing that any tiling would use an even number of tiles? Problem 9.7 followed exactly this pattern. In that problem we used a stripey colouring and argued that every tile covered an odd number of grey cells, so the total number of tiles was even.

Let us try the same approach for our current problem. The standard stripey colouring shown in figure 9.12 would give an even number of grey cells since we are assuming that the rectangle to be tiled has even sides.

A 4×5 tile covers either 8, 10 or 12 grey cells depending on its position, and all these numbers are even, which is bad news.

The trouble is that the standard stripey colouring is not really tailored to the tiles we are using. Rather than abandon stripes altogether, we try to adapt the colouring. Making every third row grey seems strange since the tiles do not suggest that the number three will be relevant. However, colouring every fourth row grey and leaving the other cells white turns out to be useful (see figure 9.19).

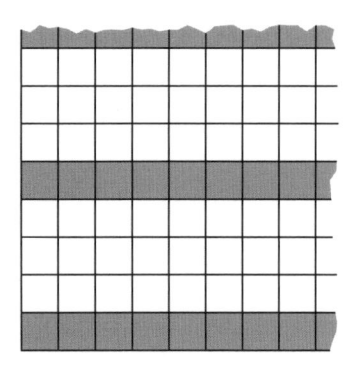

Figure 9.19

Each of our tiles now covers 4, 5 or 8 grey cells. This means that any tiling uses an even number of tiles that cover 5 grey cells. Fortunately the tiles that cover 5 grey cells are precisely the 'horizontal' or *fat* 5×4 rectangles.

Now the end is in sight. We know that any tiling uses an even number of fat tiles, but by colouring every fourth column grey we can use the same argument to show that any tiling uses an even number of *tall* 4×5 tiles.

Since the tiles are all either tall or fat, the total number of tiles is even. This shows that the total area is divisible by 8 so at least one side length is divisible by 4 as we suspected.

Finally we can summarise the solution to the problem.

An $m \times n$ rectangle can be tiled if 20 divides mn, neither dimension is 1, 2, 3, 6, 7 or 11 and at least one dimension is divisible by 4.

Finding the solution to this problem was tough going, but it would have been all but impossible if we had not been able to draw on problems 9.7 and 9.10 for inspiration. There are a number of lessons we can learn from this. The first is that experience counts for a lot in problem solving. The second is that we should make a habit of asking ourselves whether we have ever solved a problem similar to one at hand. The third is that it is wise to reflect on every problem you solve. Taking a moment to identify exactly which ideas went into a solution and why they worked makes the process of solving a problem vastly more valuable. For example, a key idea which may have gone unnoticed in our solution to problem 9.13 was that at a certain point we decided to treat different orientations of the same tile as different types of tile.

9.6 Knight's tours

We now turn to another problem where colouring is useful even though it is not a tiling problem. The problem concerns finding a sequence of moves which allow a knight to visit every cell on a given chessboard exactly once. Such a sequence of moves is called a *knight's tour*. If the knight returns to its starting position, then the tour is said to be *closed* and otherwise it is *open*.

That knight's tours exist on the standard 8×8 chessboard has been known for many centuries; indeed there are many millions of different closed tours. We will construct one such tour by breaking the problem down into smaller stages.

We start with the sequence of 8 moves shown in figure 9.20 which allows a knight to visit exactly half of the cells of a 4×4 chessboard.

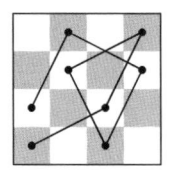

Figure 9.20

Two copies of this sequences of moves can be used to construct a closed loop which visits half the cells on a 8 × 4 board. Two possible arrangements are shown in figure 9.21.

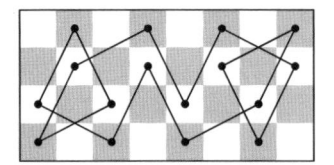

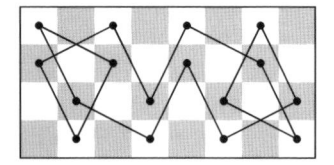

Figure 9.21

These sequences can, in turn, be used to construct an open tour on the whole 8 × 4 board. The knight simply goes around the loop shown on the left of figure 9.21 then jumps to one of the unvisited cells and goes around the loop shown on the right.

For this trick to work, the knight needs to ensure that he can still jump to some unvisited cells from the 16th cell he visits. If the 16th cell is, for example, one of the corners of the board, then he will be stuck. Fortunately, this problem is not too hard to avoid. Indeed, if we are careful about where we start, we can build an open tour of a 8 × 4 board which can be used to construct a closed tour of the whole 8 × 8 board.

The relevant open tour is shown in figure 9.22.

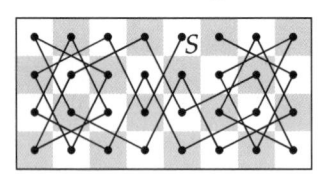

Figure 9.22

Here the knight starts on cell S, then moves anticlockwise round the loop shown on the right of figure 9.21. After fifteen moves, rather than return to S, he jumps two cells left and one cell down to join the loop shown on the left of figure 9.21, which he then follows anticlockwise. As can be seen, the knight finishes his tour on a cell directly adjacent to the starting point.

Now we are in a position to construct a closed knight's tour of an 8 × 8 chessboard without too much difficulty. We simply take a second copy of our open tour of the 8 × 4 board, rotate it by 180° and place it alongside the original 8 × 4 board, as shown in figure 9.23. Joining the end of each open tour to the start of the other gives the required closed tour of the 8 × 8 board.

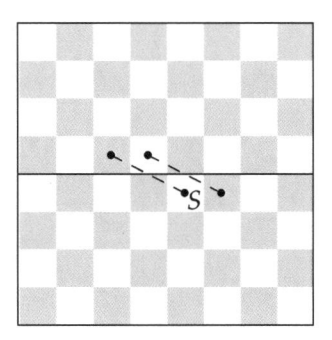

Figure 9.23

This is all very well, but having constructed an open tour on an 8 × 4 board, we might ask ourselves whether this open tour can be closed in some way. This turns out to be impossible, and we will make use of a new colouring in our proof.

Problem 9.14

Prove that there is no closed knight's tour on an 8 × 4 chessboard.

Our first thought with this problem might be to equip the 8 × 4 chessboard with the standard colouring. This colouring has the potentially useful property that the knight always alternates between grey and white cells. Unfortunately, the chessboard has an equal number of grey and white cells, so this observation alone is not enough to prove that no closed tour exists.

Our next thought might be to focus on those places where the knight's movements are most limited. For example, there are only two cells which are a knight's move away from a corner cell. This might lead us to hope for a proof that the knight cannot visit all four corners without getting stuck in one of them. However, the open tour we constructed shows that it is perfectly possible for the knight to get in and out of each corner, though it seems tricky for him to do so and finish where he started.

Keeping our attention focussed on places where the knight has a more limited number of cells he can move to, we make the following observation.

If the knight is on one of the middle two rows, then he can jump to any of the other three rows, while if he on the top or bottom row of the board, he can only jump to one of the middle two rows. This fact does not seem particularly profound, but it turns out to be the key to the problem.

We colour the board as shown in figure 9.24 and note that the knight cannot move directly from one grey cell to another.

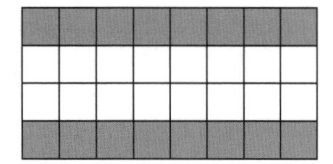

Figure 9.24

There are equal numbers of grey and white cells, so if a closed tour exists it alternates between grey and white cells in this colouring. However, it will also alternate between grey and white cells in the standard colouring. Now we consider the cells the knight reaches in odd-numbered moves. These cells are all the same colour in both colourings, but this is impossible since the colourings are different.

You should take a moment to consider why this proof does not prove that no open tour exists, and indeed why it cannot be adapted to show that no closed tour exists on an 8×8 board.

Exercise 9d

1. A $(3n+1) \times (3n+1)$ rectangle is tiled with 1×3 rectangles and a single 1×1 square. How many possible places are there for the square?

2. Prove that there is an open knight's tour on an $n \times 4$ chessboard for all $n \geq 7$.

3. A standard knight can move two cells in one direction on a chessboard and one cell in the other direction. Suppose that, rather than making standard moves, a particularly athletic knight always moves three

cells in one direction and one in the other. Prove that the athletic knight cannot conduct an open or closed tour of an 8 × 8 chessboard.

4. The figure represents fifteen cities connected by a network of roads. Is it possible to use these roads to visit each city exactly once?

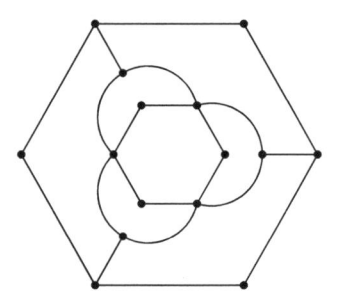

5. For which m and n can an $m \times n$ chessboard be tiled with 3×4 rectangles?

* 6. A hook is a type of hexomino shown in the figure.

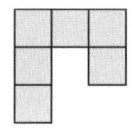

For which m and n can an $m \times n$ rectangle be tiled with hooks?

[IMO 2004]

* 7. On an infinite chessboard, a solitaire game is played as follows. At the start, we have n^2 pieces occupying a square of side n. The only allowed move is to jump over an occupied cell to an unoccupied one, and the piece which has been jumped over is removed. For which n can the game end with only one piece remaining on the board?

[IMO 1993]

* 8. We are given a positive integer r and a rectangular board $ABCD$ with dimensions $|AB| = 20$, $|BC| = 12$. The rectangle is divided into a grid of 20×12 unit cells. One can move from one cell to another only if the distance between the centers of the two cells is $\sqrt{r}$. The task is

to find a sequence of moves leading from the cell with A as a vertex to the cell with B as a vertex.

(a) Show that the task cannot be done if r is divisible by 2 or 3.
(b) Prove that the task is possible when $r = 73$.
(c) Can the task be done when r = 97?

[IMO 1996]

HINT

Chapter 10

Using invariants

In the second part of problem 9.4 on page 159 we proved that the seven distinct tetrominoes could not be used to tile a 7 × 4 chessboard. We used the standard colouring of the chessboard and noted that all the tetrominoes except the *T*-tetromino always cover two cells of each colour. We might rephrase the argument as follows.

The number of grey cells covered by the seven tiles is always odd however the tiles are rearranged. This shows that any shape with an even number of grey cells, such as a 7 × 4 chessboard, cannot be tiled.

There are many ways to arrange seven tiles, yet we managed to find a quantity which did not change between arrangements. Such quantities are called *invariants*, and finding them was the key to almost every problem in the previous chapter.

However, invariants can be used in a far broader range of contexts than just tiling problems. We investigate some of them in this chapter.

10.1 Parity

> **Problem 10.1**
>
> There are 101 circles and 101 squares drawn on a blackboard. Julia and Karthik take it in turns to erase two shapes and replace them with a single shape. If the erased shapes are the same they are replaced with a square, otherwise they are replaced with a circle. Julia wins if, after 201 turns, the final shape is a circle.
>
> (a) Can Julia win if she goes first?
> (b) Can Karthik win if he goes first?

We start by playing around with the problem to get a sense of what is going on. We will use an ordered pair (c, s) to keep track of c, the number of circles on the board and s, the number of squares. Three possible sequences of moves are:

A. $(101, 101) \to (101, 100) \to (99, 101) \to (97, 102) \to (97, 101)$;
B. $(101, 101) \to (101, 100) \to (101, 99) \to (101, 98) \to (99, 99)$;
C. $(101, 101) \to (99, 102) \to (97, 103) \to (95, 104) \to (93, 105)$.

In sequence A the move $(101, 101) \to (101, 100)$ is the result of erasing a circle and a square and replacing them with a circle, while the move $(101, 100) \to (99, 101)$ is the result of erasing two circles and replacing them with a square.

This is enough experimentation to make two important observations. The first is that the value of $c + s$ decreases by one with each move. This clearly continues, since each move reduces the number of shapes by one. Therefore, after 201 moves, there will certainly be exactly one shape left on the board. The second observation is that the number of circles always appears to be odd. In other words, the *parity* of c seems to be an invariant. It is easy to check that this is indeed the case. There are three possible moves (erase two circles, two squares or one of each) and each of these moves either does not change the value of c or reduces it by two. Initially there are an odd number of circles on the board, so when only one shape remains on the board there will still be an odd number of circles. Therefore the last shape will be a circle regardless of who goes first and regardless of the choices the players make along the way.

Chapter 10: Using invariants 185

Another way to write up essentially the same solution is to label squares with +1 and circles with −1. Now the legal moves can be reinterpreted as replacing two numbers by their product. This means the product of all the labels on the board is invariant and equal to −1.

Problem 10.2

A 6 × 6 chessboard is coloured grey and white in the standard way. A move consists of choosing any row, column or 2 × 2 square and making the grey cells in that region white and the white cells grey.

Is it possible to end up with only one grey cell?

We start by experimenting and keeping an eye out for things which do not change. We will call the operation which exchanges grey and white on a set of squares *toggling*. If we toggle the top row, the right most column and finally the top right 2 × 2 square, we obtain the sequence of colourings shown in figure 10.1.

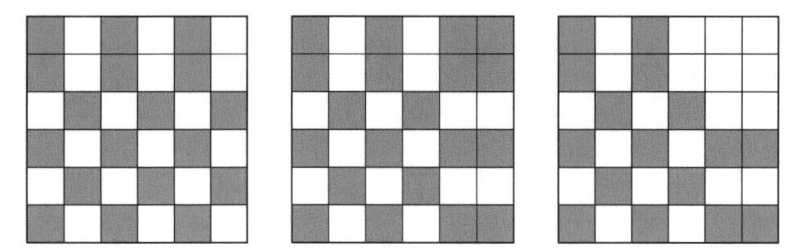

Figure 10.1

There are 18, 20 and 16 grey cells in these diagrams. The parity of the number of grey cells seems to be an invariant and checking all three legal moves confirms that this is indeed the case. There are eighteen grey cells initially, so we can never be left with just one.

Just as in problem 10.1 this solution can be rephrased using +1s and −1s rather than colours to distinguish different types of cell. As in that problem, the product of all the numbers on the chessboard is invariant under all three moves, but in this case it equals +1.

Problem 10.3

The numbers 1, 2, 3, ..., N are written in a row on a blackboard. A move consists of swapping two numbers. After n moves the numbers are back in their original order.

Prove that n is even.

Our plan for this problem is to find a quantity which in some way measures how jumbled up a list of numbers is. When the numbers are in their original order this quantity ought to be zero. We would finish our argument by saying that every swap changes the parity of this quantity, so it can only return to zero after an even number of swaps.

Our first idea for a measure of disorder might be to count how many numbers are not in the correct place in the list. This is certainly zero if and only if the numbers are in their starting order. Unfortunately, we quickly see that this measure is no use. In particular, if we have already scrambled the numbers 1, 2, 3, 4 up to get 3, 4, 1, 2, then repeatedly swapping 1 and 2 will not change our measure of disorder at all.

The measure we seek should have the property that exchanging adjacent numbers will alter it by one. With this insight, and some good fortune, we may hit upon a measure M that works: we count the number of times a number is preceded by a larger number. More precisely, for a sequence of distinct numbers $a_1, a_2, \ldots, a_N$, we let M be the number of pairs (i,j) with $i < j$ and $a_i > a_j$.

In the sequence 1, 2, 3, 4 no number is preceded by a larger number so $M = 0$. In the sequence 2, 1, 3, 4 we have $a_1 > a_2$ so $M = 1$. The sequence 4, 2, 3, 1 is more interesting and we can go along the sequence seeing how much each term contributes to the value of M.

The initial 4 is not preceded by any numbers so does not contribute to M. The 2 is preceded by 4 so it adds one to the value of M. The 3 adds one to M for the same reason, and the 1 adds three to M because it preceded by the three larger numbers 4, 2 and 3. This means that the value of M for this sequence is five. Therefore if we start with the sequence 1, 2, 3, 4 and exchange 1 and 4, then we change M by five. In particular, we change the parity of M, which is encouraging.

For the general case we suppose that we have a sequence of numbers and that we exchange the numbers x and y, where $x < y$. Now we go along the sequence and see how each term's contribution to M is affected by the swap. Clearly the contributions from terms which come before x in the original sequence are not affected. Neither is the contribution from the y (which now comes before x).

Next we consider the terms located between x and y in the original sequence. If these numbers are smaller than x or larger than y, then their contribution to M does not change. Therefore, we focus on those numbers $z_1, z_2, \ldots, z_k$ that are located between x and y and satisfy $x < z_i < y$. The contribution to M from each of these k numbers is increased by 1 by the swap, since each number is now preceded by y rather than x. Now we come to x. The swap means that x is now preceded by y and also by each of the z_i, so its contribution to M increases by $k+1$.

Numbers which come after y in the original sequence are not affected by the swap, so the total impact of the swap is to increase M by $2k+1$, which, happily, is always odd.

The case where $x > y$ is identical, except that these swaps decrease M by an odd number.

We have shown that swapping two numbers in a sequence of distinct reals always changes the parity of M, so the sequence can only return to its original order after an even number of swaps.

When we look back over this argument, it is worth noting just how useful starting with the penultimate line of the solution was. This tactic should be a familiar part of any problem solver's arsenal.

Exercise 10a

1. There are 99 squares, 100 circles and 101 triangles drawn on a blackboard. A move consists of erasing two different shapes and replacing them with a copy of the third type of shape. After 299 moves, only one shape remains. What is it?

2. The numbers 1 to 30 are written on a blackboard. Every minute two numbers are erased and replaced by the (non-negative) difference between them. Is it possible that after half an hour the final number on the board is zero?

3. The 4 × 4 board shown in the figure has fifteen white cells and one grey cell.

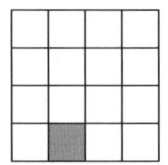

We may choose any row, column or diagonal of the board and switch the colours of its cells from grey to white and vice versa. We may also switch the colours of any set of cells whose centres lie on a line parallel to a diagonal of the board. (Note that this means we may change the colour of a single corner cell.) Is it possible to make the entire board one colour? [HINT]

4. Eight beetles sit on cells of an infinite chessboard as shown in the figure.

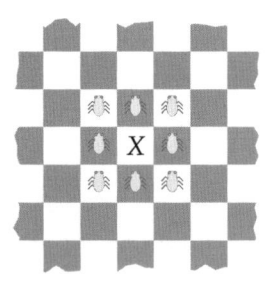

A beetle at a point P may choose a beetle at another point Q and jump over that beetle, landing at point R, where Q is the midpoint of PR. Beetles may jump diagonally, and need not be next to the beetles they are jumping over. Is it possible for a beetle to end up on the cell marked X? [HINT]

5. Initially there are m balls in one bag, and n in another, where $m, n > 0$. Two different operations are allowed:
   (i) remove an equal number of balls from each bag;
   (ii) double the number of balls in one bag.

Is it always possible to empty both bags after a finite sequence of operations?

Chapter 10: Using invariants

Operation (ii) is now replaced with

(iii) triple the number of balls in one bag.

Is it now always possible to empty both bags after a finite sequence of operations? [BMO1 2011]

10.2 Finding other invariants

In the previous section we made extensive use of parity arguments. These can be thought of as arguments which use arithmetic modulo two. The next few problems take advantage of the fact that numbers besides two also exist.

Problem 10.4

On a desert island there are seven red chameleons, eleven blue chameleons and thirteen green chameleons. If two chameleons of different colours meet, they both change to the third available colour.

(a) Is it ever possible that all the chameleons are blue?
(b) Is it ever possible that all the chameleons are red?

As always, it is worth experimenting a little. We will use the triple (r, b, g) to denote the numbers of red, blue and green chameleons respectively. One possible sequence of encounters is $(7, 11, 13) \to (9, 10, 12) \to (11, 9, 11)$. At this point if there are eleven consecutive encounters between red and green chameleons, then all the chameleons will become blue.

We have stumbled upon a solution to the first part of the problem. The key was spotting that once we had evened out the number of red and green chameleons it was easy to make them all blue.

With this in mind we attack the second part by trying to even out the number of blue and green chameleons. Put another way, we seek a sequence of encounters which makes $b - g$ equal to zero. Here, however, we run into difficulties. After a few failed attempts it is natural to consider the effects of the three types of encounter on the quantity $b - g$. This may give us a clue as to how to make this difference zero, or it may give some insight into why the task is impossible.

If a red and a green chameleon meet, then $b - g$ increases by three. If a green and a blue chameleon meet, then $b - g$ does not change. If a blue and a red chameleon meet then $b - g$ decreases by three.

This is enough to show that $b - g$ does not change modulo 3. In the initial state $(7, 11, 13)$ we have the $b - g \equiv 1 (\bmod 3)$, while in the target state $(31, 0, 0)$ we have $b - g \equiv 0 (\bmod 3)$. This proves that it is never possible for all the chameleons to be red.

Problem 10.5

The number 5^{6^7} is written on a blackboard (in base 10). The number is repeatedly erased and replaced by the sum of its digits until a single digit number remains.

What is this number?

It is well known that a number is divisible by 9 if and only if the sum of its digits is divisible by 9. It is perhaps slightly less well known that any number is congruent to the sum of its digits modulo 9. To see this suppose that '*abcd*' represents the four digit number $1000a + 100b + 10c + d$. The difference between this number and the sum of its digits is $999a + 99b + 9c$ which is clearly a multiple of nine. The general case is, of course, dealt with in the same way.

This means that if we repeatedly replace a number by the sum of its digits, then the congruence class modulo 9 is invariant. It follows that the problem is equivalent to finding 5^{6^7} modulo 9.

Now the details are straightforward. We compute the first few powers of 5 modulo 9 and hope that a pattern will emerge. We have $5^2 \equiv 7$ so $5^3 \equiv 5^2 \times 5 \equiv 8 \equiv -1$. This means $5^6 \equiv 1$ which in turn means that $5^{6^7} = (5^6)^{6^6} \equiv 1$.

Problem 10.6

Three numbers are written on a blackboard. A move consists of choosing two of them, say a and b, and replacing them with $\dfrac{12a+5b}{13}$ and $\dfrac{5a-12b}{13}$.

If the initial numbers are 3, 4, 5, can the numbers written on the board ever be 2, 4, 6?

In this problem the occurrence of the numbers 5, 12 and 13 is suggestive. We should recognise these numbers as a Pythagorean triple, and ask ourselves whether the fact that $5^2 + 12^2 = 13^2$ might be useful.

We note that

$$\left(\frac{12a+5b}{13}\right)^2 + \left(\frac{5a-12b}{13}\right)^2 = a^2 + b^2.$$

This implies that the sum of the squares of the three numbers written on the board is invariant under the move we are allowed to make. Since $3^2 + 4^2 + 5^2 = 50 \neq 2^2 + 4^2 + 6^2$ it is impossible to transform one triple into the other.

The problem is not a particularly interesting one, largely because the legal move is so evidently contrived. However, a redeeming feature is that it can easily solved by switching from an algebraic to a geometric viewpoint. If we interpret the three numbers on the board as coordinates in three dimensional space, then the move we are allowed to make corresponds to a rotation around one of the axes. Since the starting point and the target point are different distances from the origin, it is impossible to move between them.

Exercise 10b

1. There are three thousand beetles in a box. Every second two beetles fly out of the box or one beetle flies into the box. Is it possible that after an hour there is exactly one beetle left in the box?

2. A sea monster has 100 tentacles. A hobbit can cut off 4 tentacles at a time but 18 grow back; a dwarf can cut off 24 but 17 grow back; an elf can cut off 19 but 40 grow back and a wizard can cut off 48 but 13 grow back. The monster will die if it has no tentacles at any point. Can a hobbit, a dwarf, an elf and a wizard defeat the sea monster if they work together? [HINT]

3. Suppose we have five boxes, each of which contains some counters. A move consists of choosing four of the boxes and either adding a counter to each, or removing a counter from each of them. Is it possible for each box to contain two more counters than it did initially?

4. A number $N > 10$ is written on a blackboard. A move consists of splitting the base 10 representation of N into two sections representing the numbers n and m. The number N is then erased and replaced by $n + m$. For example, if $N = 115\,559\,999$ then it may be replaced by $1155 + 59\,999 = 61\,154$ or $11\,555\,999 + 9 = 11\,556\,008$.
If the first number on the board is 7^{8^9} and a sequence of moves reduces it to a ten-digit number, prove that this final number has a repeated digit.

5. The numbers 1 up to 50 are written on a blackboard. A move consists of erasing two numbers, x and y and replacing them with $xy + x + y$. After 49 moves a single number N remains. How many possible values of N are there? [HINT]

10.3 Using monovariants

We now turn our attention to quantities that are not invariant, but which have another useful property.

Problem 10.7

A chocolate bar is made up of forty small squares arranged in a 5×8 rectangle. A move consists of picking up a rectangular piece of chocolate and snapping it into two rectangles along one of the lines which border its subsquares.

What is the smallest number of moves needed to split the bar into its forty component squares?

This problem is something of a classic, largely because it is extremely simple once you see the trick, but can seem daunting if you do not. Each move increases the number of pieces of chocolate by one so, no matter what strategy you adopt, you will need exactly 39 moves.

Here the number of pieces of chocolate is not invariant, but it has the useful property that it never decreases. A quantity which never decreases or never increases is called a *monovariant*. The number of pieces of chocolate is a particularly simple example since it increases by exactly one each time a rectangle is broken. However, monovariants can be extremely useful even if their exact behaviour is more complicated.

Problem 10.8

Suppose that ten integers whose sum is zero are written on a blackboard. A move consists choosing numbers $x > 0$ and $y < 0$ on the board. These numbers are then erased and replaced by $x - 1$ and $y + 1$ respectively.

Prove that eventually all the numbers on the board will be zeros.

In this problem the sum of the numbers on the board is an obvious invariant, but this alone is not helpful. The move available seems to make the numbers on the board closer to zero, so it would be helpful to have a quantity which measured how far the numbers were from zero in some way. The sum of their absolute values seems a natural choice, and this quantity decreases by two with each move. Eventually it reaches zero, at which point all the numbers on the board are zero. Slightly more formally we might call the numbers $a_1, a_2, \ldots, a_n$ and define $T = \sum |a_i|$. The quantity T is a monovariant for the problem since it always decreases. Initially T is positive so eventually it decreases to zero as required.

Problem 10.9

Suppose that ten integers whose sum is zero are written on a blackboard. A move consists choosing numbers x and y on the board with $x > y + 1$. These numbers are then erased and replaced by $x - 1$ and $y + 1$ respectively.

Prove that eventually all the numbers on the board will be zeros.

This is a slight generalisation of the previous problem, since all the moves allowed in that problem are also permissible here. However we now have the added option of taking, say, two positive numbers and moving them closer together.

The extra freedom means that, somewhat frustratingly, $T = \sum |a_i|$ no longer decreases with every move, so we will need to find a new monovariant for the problem. The reason that $\sum |a_i|$ was an appealing first choice was that it makes no distinction between positive and negative numbers, and can only be zero when all the a_i are zero. Another natural quantity with these properties is $S = \sum a_i^2$, that is the sum of the squares of the numbers on the board. Now we suppose that x and y have been replaced with $x - 1$ and $y + 1$ and ask how this move effects the value of S. In the sum, $x^2 + y^2$ has been replaced by $(x-1)^2 + (y+1)^2 = x^2 + y^2 - 2(x - y - 1)$. Since $x > y + 1$ for the move to be legal, it is clear that each move decreases the value of S, so S eventually reaches zero as required. Considering sums of squares is an idea which crops up all over mathematics. We used the idea in problem 10.6 and will see further examples later in this chapter.

Problem 10.10

Finitely many cells on an infinite square chessboard are grey, and the remaining cells are white. Every second the entire chessboard is repainted according to the following rule. A cell in the new colouring is grey if and only if it shares an edge with at least three cells which were grey in the previous colouring.

Prove that eventually the entire chessboard will be white.

This problem would be easy if the number of grey cells always decreased, but unfortunately this need not be the case. Figure 10.2 shows an arrangement (left) where the number of grey cells increases after one repainting (right).

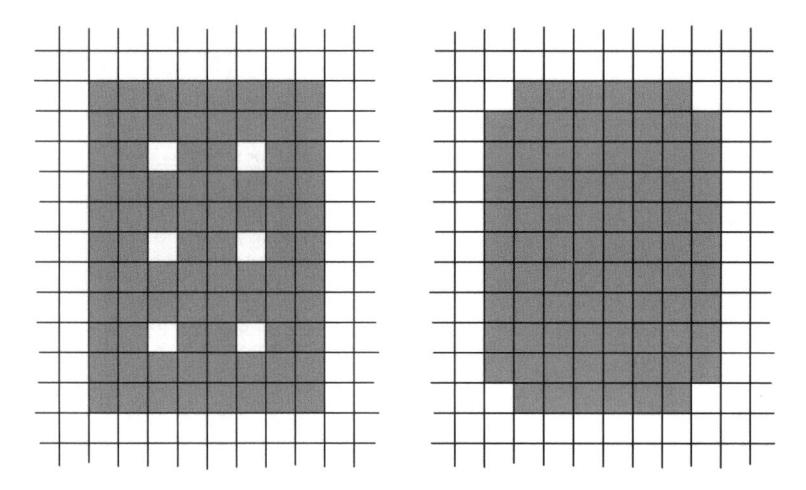

Figure 10.2

A more promising monovariant is the number of rows which contain at least one grey cell. We call this number H and note that H cannot increase since a cell in an entirely white row can never become grey. However, the problem with the monovariant H is that, while it never increases, the example in figure 10.2 shows that it need not decrease every second.

Fortunately this difficulty is not to hard to overcome. We focus on a row which is adjacent to an entirely white row (such rows exist since only finitely many cells are grey). In this row the outermost grey cells at any moment will certainly become white one second later since they have at least two white neighbours.

Therefore, any grey region in a row adjacent to an entirely white row will eventually shrink and vanish, thereby decreasing the value of H. Indeed, if we denote the maximum distance between the centres of any two grey cells in the same row by W, then H will decrease at least once every $\frac{1}{2}(W+1)$ seconds which is enough to ensure that H eventually reaches zero as required.

Problem 10.11

Some mathematicians need to be seated around a circular table at a conference. Each mathematician is friends with more than half the other mathematicians.

Prove that it is possible to seat them so that each mathematician is between two friends.

For this problem we assume, as usual, that friendship is a mutual relationship and we call mathematicians who are not friends *strangers*.

Our strategy will be to seat the mathematicians arbitrarily initially, and then to adjust the seating plan if it turns out that some neighbours are strangers.

Let S denote the number of pairs of strangers sitting next to each other. We want to show that if $S > 0$ then we can make it strictly smaller.

Let us suppose that mathematicians A and B are strangers who initially find themselves next to each other. We would like to replace B with some other mathematician C who is friends with A. However, a straight swap might, for example, leave B stranded between two strangers.

We need a way of adjusting the seating plan which makes it easy to keep track of how the quantity S is changing. The key idea is that, while swapping two guests is troublesome, if we have a sequence $A, B, \ldots, C, D$ and we reverse the order of the guests from B to C inclusive, then only two dinner-time conversations are disrupted.

In particular, if we can find two neighbours C and D such that C is friends with A and such that D is friends with B then the sequence

$$A, C \longleftarrow B, D$$

will certainly have fewer neighbouring strangers than

$$A, B \longrightarrow C, D.$$

We have been working backwards from the end of our solution, and now it is time to make use of the condition that every mathematician is friends with most of the others.

We begin by asking *A* to point out all his friends. Next we ask each of these friends whether the mathematician one space further round the table is friends with *B*. Since *A* points out more than half the guests at the conference, and less than half the guests at the conference are strangers to *B*, we are certain to find a pair of neighbours *C*, *D* where *C* is friends with *A* and *D* is friends with *B*. Reversing the order of the guests from *B* to *C* inclusive makes the value of *S* strictly smaller. Now the seating plan can be adjusted one step at a time until only friends are sat next to each other. This might disrupt the strangers, but would also provide an easy talking point for the guests, which is no bad thing at such events.

Exercise 10c

1. There are 100 competitors in a knockout tiddlywinks tournament (some players receive byes and go straight to the second round which has 64 competitors). How many matches have to be played before there is a single champion?

2. Suppose that we have a row of 200 squares, each of which can be black or white, and that initially the colours alternate along the row. A move consists of changing the colours on a set of n consecutive squares where $n \geq 1$. It is possible to make all the squares the same colour in 100 moves by changing every other square on its own. Can all the squares be made the same colour in fewer than 100 moves?

3. Brigitte and Jonathan play the following game. Jonathan chooses a positive integer N and places N counters labelled $1, 2, \ldots, N$ on the table. At each turn Brigitte may remove one counter from the game. In response Jonathan may add any number of counters to the table, provided they are all labelled with positive integers less than the label

on the counter Brigitte removed. Brigitte wishes to clear the table in a finite number of moves, and Jonathan aims to make the game last forever. Who has a winning strategy?

4. Suppose we have a row of boxes which extends infinitely in both directions. Some of these boxes contain beetles. If a box contains more than one beetle, then two beetles may move from that box to neighbouring boxes provided they move in opposite directions. Is it possible that after $n > 0$ moves the number of beetles in each box is the same as it was initially?

5. Some positive integers are written on a blackboard. A move consists of choosing two of the integers, x and y, and replacing them with $\text{LCM}(x,y)$ and $\text{HCF}(x,y)$.
   Prove that eventually the numbers on the blackboard stop changing.
   [HINT]

*6. Some pirates stand in a circle. Each one has a some gold coins. If at any point a pirate has an odd number of gold coins, the captain gives him or her another gold coin. Every time the captain's parrot squawks each pirate gives half his coins to the pirate on his or her right. Prove that, if the parrot keeps on squawking, all the pirates will eventually have the same number of gold coins.

10.4 More subtle arguments involving variation

Now we will take a moment to revisit problem 9.8 on page 167 and give another of the many possible proofs of the result.

Problem 10.12

Suppose that a rectangular board has been tiled with rectangular tiles, each of which has at least one integer side length.

Prove that the board also has at least one integer side length.

We will start by orienting the board so that its lower left corner is at the origin and its sides are parallel to the x- and y-axes. We will call points in the plane with integer coordinates *lattice points* and, if a tile has a corner which is a lattice point, we will call this point a *lattice corner*.

Since each tile has at least one integer side, it has zero, two or four lattice corners. Therefore if we count the number of lattice corners on each tile, then the sum of the results is always even. Thus the parity of this sum is an invariant for the problem.

Now we apply a double-counting argument. We count the same sum by lattice points rather than by tiles. Lattice points completely inside the board can be corners of zero, two or four tiles. Lattice points on the edge of the board can be the corners of zero or two tiles unless they are corners of the board in which case they belong to only one tile. The origin is a lattice corner which belongs to precisely one tile, so, because the sum is even, there is at least one other lattice point that is a lattice corner belonging to just one tile. This shows that at least two of the corners of the board are lattice points, so the board has an integer side length as required.

Problem 10.13

Let $\mathcal{T}$ be a set of 2005 coplanar points with no three collinear.

Show that, for any of the 2005 points, the number of triangles it lies strictly within, whose vertices are points in $\mathcal{T}$, is even. [BMO1 2005]

It is hard to know where to start with this problem, and we will give two solutions which are based on a different initial lines of attack.

We are asked to prove that something holds for every point in $\mathcal{T}$, so we might ask whether there are any points in $\mathcal{T}$ for which the conclusion is obvious. Indeed, since zero is an even number, it is reasonable to ask what points contained in no triangles look like. Evidently they should be 'near the edge of $\mathcal{T}$' in some sense. This leads to an embryonic strategy: start at the edge of $\mathcal{T}$ and work inwards.

Unfortunately, it is not at all clear how to make the notion of being 'near the edge of $\mathcal{T}$' precise. If we imagine putting a rubber band round $\mathcal{T}$, then the points which touch the rubber band do not lie in any triangles, but which points do we consider next?

The key is to introduce some movement into the way we think about the set $\mathcal{T}$. Rather than having all the points in $\mathcal{T}$ fixed we could imagine a point moving through the set $\mathcal{T}$ and ask whether it always lies in an even number of triangles.

This leads to a much better plan of attack. We choose any point P in $\mathcal{T}$ and remove it leaving 2004 other points. We then put P back on the plane a huge distance away from the rest of $\mathcal{T}$ so that it is contained in no triangles. Finally, we allow P to slide slowly back to its original position, and check that, throughout its journey, it always lies in an even number of triangles. We will need to add some other conditions to the path that P follows as the argument develops, but we are certainly making good progress.

The 2004 other points in $\mathcal{T}$ define $\binom{2004}{2}$ line segments, and we imagine that these have all been drawn on the plane. We need to check that whenever P crosses one of these segments, the parity of the number of triangles it lies does not change.

Suppose that A and B are points in $\mathcal{T}$ and that P is approaching one side of the segment AB. To make the analysis easier, we insist that P's path does not go through any points in $\mathcal{T}$ or any points where segments joining points in $\mathcal{T}$ intersect. The number of points which P needs to avoid is finite, so there is no difficulty in finding a path that works.

We assume that just before P crosses AB it is contained in an even number of triangles. Suppose that when P crosses AB it moves out of n triangles and into m new ones. It is clear that n is the number of points in $\mathcal{T}$ which are on the same side of the (extended) line AB as P was before it crossed. Similarly, m is the number of points on the side of AB which P moved into. We note that $m + n = 2002$ so n and m have the same parity. This implies that $m - n$ is even, so the parity of the number of triangles P lies in is invariant, and the proof is complete.

Our second solution to this problem does not use invariants so we will only sketch the outline. Unlike the previous argument, the mental picture can be completely static, and the guiding idea is to understand the problem for smaller sets of points and then to exploit that understanding.

(i) Check the result holds for sets of five points. That is, if $\mathcal{S}$ is a set of five points which includes a point P, then the number of triangles in $\mathcal{S}$ which contain P is even.

(ii) Choose any point P in $\mathcal{T}$ and consider all five-point subsets of $\mathcal{T}$ which contain P. Each of these sets contributes an even number of

Chapter 10: Using invariants

triangles which contain P, but each triangle will be counted many times.

(iii) Check that, in fact, every triangle containing P is counted an odd number of times in the previous step. Therefore the number of triangles is even since the total is even.

Problem 10.14

Is there a sequence of 1000 consecutive positive integers which contains exactly ten primes?

This seems like a difficult problem to play around with since asking how many primes there are in a particular sequence of numbers is a notoriously hard question. However, we can certainly begin by observing that the numbers $1, 2, \ldots, 1000$ include many more than ten primes. (In fact there are 168 primes less than 1000.)

At this point we should (briefly) entertain the possibility that *every* sequence of 1000 consecutive integers contains more than 10 primes. However, this is definitely not the case since there is a well-known construction for blocks of consecutive integers which contain no primes at all. We consider the number $N!$, which is clearly composite. Now $N! + 1$ may or may not be prime, but two divides $N! + 2$, three divides $N! + 3$, and so on. So there is a block of $N - 1$ consecutive composite numbers. In particular the 1000-term sequence $1001! + 2, 1001! + 3, \ldots, 1001! + 1001$ contains no primes.

Now we are nearly done. We consider a block of 1000 consecutive integers and imagine it moving slowly along the number line. Initially the block contains well over ten primes, but by the time its first number reaches $1001! + 2$ it does not contain any. Every time the block moves one step to the right it can gain or lose at most one prime, so the number of primes changes by either -1, 0 or 1 at each stage. This means that as the number of primes in the sequence changes from 168 to zero it passes through ten on the way.

Looking back at the solution we note that it is non-constructive: we have no idea where the sequence containing ten primes starts. It is also vaguely reminiscent of our solution to problem 10.13 since the mental picture involved gradual movement. Finally, there is a sense in which the problem is out of place in this chapter since the number of primes in a block of consecutive numbers is not technically a monovariant. However, although it can go either up or down, the way in which it changes is 'nice' enough for it to be a useful quantity.

Problem 10.15

Prove that for any positive real numbers $x_1, x_2, \ldots, x_n$ we have

$$\frac{x_1 + x_2 + \cdots + x_n}{n} \leq \sqrt{\frac{x_1^2 + x_2^2 + \cdots + x_n^2}{n}}.$$

This is a well-known inequality. The quantity on the left is called the *arithmetic mean* of the numbers, and the quantity on the right is called the *quadratic mean* or the *root mean square*. If you want to find out more about this and other inequalities you might be interested in [1].

It is clear that we have equality when all the x_i are equal. This observation will guide our solution.

The strategy is as follows. We assume the numbers are not all equal and then make them more equal without changing their sum. We then check that the quadratic mean of the numbers is decreased by this operation. If the quadratic mean can be repeatedly decreased and end up equal to the arithmetic mean, then we may conclude that it was greater than the arithmetic mean to start with.

We need a simple piece of algebra, which generalises that used in problem 10.9. Suppose that $x > y$ are real numbers and that $\epsilon < x - y$. It is clear that $(x - \epsilon) + (y + \epsilon) = x + y$. We also have that $(x - \epsilon)^2 + (y + \epsilon)^2 = x^2 + y^2 - 2\epsilon(x - y - \epsilon) < x^2 + y^2$. Therefore if we move two numbers closer together without changing their sum, then the sum of their squares, and hence their quadratic mean, decreases.

Now we consider the list $x_1, x_2, \ldots, x_n$ and call the arithmetic mean m. If all the x_i are equal to m we are done. If not, then we may choose $x_i > m$ and $x_j < m$ and replace the pair x_i, x_j with the pair $x_i + (x_j - m)$, m. Under this operation the arithmetic mean is invariant, the number of numbers equal to the arithmetic mean is strictly increasing and the quadratic mean is strictly decreasing. Eventually the numbers are all equal to m at which point the quadratic mean equals the arithmetic mean and the proof is complete.

Chapter 10: Using invariants 203

The technique we used in this problem is called *smoothing*, and it is worth noting that replacing the numbers x_i and x_j with two copies of $\frac{x_i+x_j}{2}$ fails because then the smoothing procedure may not terminate.

Problem 10.16

To each vertex of a regular pentagon an integer is assigned in such a way that the sum of all five numbers is positive. If three consecutive vertices are assigned the numbers x, y, z respectively and $y < 0$ then the following operation is allowed. The numbers x, y, z are replaced by $x + y$, $-y$, $z + y$ respectively. Such an operation is performed repeatedly as long as at least one of the five numbers is negative.

Determine whether this procedure necessarily comes to an end after a finite number of steps. [IMO 1986]

It is worth playing around with a few possible configurations to see if we can either generate larger and larger negative numbers or find a repeating cycle of states. This turns out to be difficult to accomplish, and we should get a sense that the permitted move seems to smooth out the numbers making them 'more equal' in some sense. Since the numbers have a positive sum and their sum is preserved by the operation, we begin to suspect that it may be impossible for negative numbers to last forever.

Therefore our strategy is to find a measure of how spread out the numbers are and prove that it decreases with every legal move. If our measure of spread is always a positive integer, then it can only decrease a finite number of times which would imply that any sequence of moves eventually terminates.

Problem 10.15 provides some inspiration. In that problem we smoothed out real numbers and observed that the sum of the squares always decreased. Might the same be true with our more exotic smoothing operation?

To check this we call the numbers on the pentagon v, w, x, y and z where $y < 0$ and call the sum of the squares of these numbers S. Now we apply the operation to y and call the new sum of squares S'. We hope that $S' < S$ so we compute $S' - S$ to see if it is negative. The fact that $S' - S$ can be written as a sum of differences of squares makes the calculation somewhat easier.

$$S' - S = ((x+y)^2 + (-y)^2 + (y+z)^2) - (x^2 + y^2 + z^2)$$
$$= [(x+y)^2 - x^2] + [(z+y)^2 - z^2]$$
$$= y(2x + y + 2z + y)$$
$$= 2y(x + y + z).$$

Since $y < 0$ we have $S' < S$ provided $x + y + z > 0$. This is tantalisingly close to a solution, but there is no reason why $x + y + z$ should be positive in every case. Nevertheless, considering sums of squares seems promising so we should try to adapt the idea.

A couple of quantities worth investigating are

$$(v-w)^2 + (w-x)^2 + (x-y)^2 + (y-z)^2 + (z-v)^2$$
$$\text{and} \quad (v+w)^2 + (w+x)^2 + (x+y)^2 + (y+z)^2 + (z+v)^2.$$

Unfortunately, if we investigate how the first quantity changes under our operation nothing particularly appealing emerges, as you are welcome to check. Undaunted, we turn to the second quantity and define

$$T = (v+w)^2 + (w+x)^2 + (x+y)^2 + (y+z)^2 + (z+v)^2$$
$$\text{and} \quad T' = (v+w)^2 + (w+x+y)^2 + (x+y-y)^2 + (-y+z+y)^2$$
$$+ (z+y+v)^2.$$

Now

$$T' - T = [(w+x+y)^2 - (w+x)^2] + [x^2 - (x+y)^2] + [z^2 - (y+z)^2]$$
$$+ [(z+v+y)^2 - (z+v)^2]$$
$$= y[(2w + 2x + y) + (-2x - y) + (-2z - y) + (2z + 2v + y)]$$
$$= 2y(w + v).$$

This quantity is negative provided $w + v > 0$ which on its own is just as frustrating as our first attempt. However, while $w + v$ might be negative, the question does give us that $v + w + x + y + z > 0$, and any correct solution needs to make use of this fact. To do this we simply consider the sum of S and T and note that $(S' + T') - (S + T) = 2y(v + w + x + y + z) < 0$. Hence $S + T$ is a positive integer which decreases with every move. This proves that no infinite sequence of moves exists.

Problem 10.17

Seven cells on an 8 × 8 chessboard are infected with a virus. Every second, each cell which shares a border with two or more infected cells also becomes infected. Infected cells can never be cured.

Is it possible that the entire board will become infected eventually?

Experimenting with this problem for a while should convince us that the answer might be 'No', but how should we go about proving this? The key is to look closely at the way the infection spreads.

We might rephrase the condition by saying that a cell becomes infected if at least half its perimeter is already infected. This suggests that it might be worth considering the total perimeter of the infected region. At this point the problem solves itself. Figure 10.3 shows the four ways in which an uninfected (white) cell can become infected (grey); each hatched region may be white or grey.

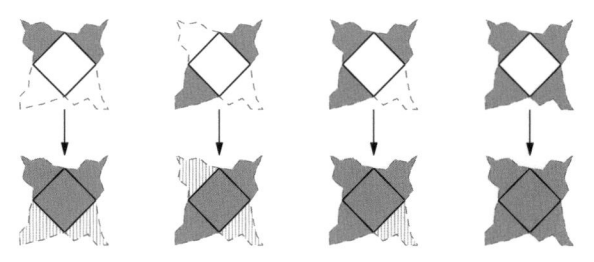

Figure 10.3

In each case it is clear that the total perimeter of the infected regions of the board does not increase. Since the total infected perimeter is at most 28 to start with and the perimeter of the board is 32, the infection cannot cover the whole board.

Exercise 10d

1. Let $x_1, x_2, \ldots, x_n$ be positive real numbers. Prove that their arithmetic mean is not less than their geometric mean. That is,
$$\frac{x_1 + x_2 + \cdots + x_n}{n} \geq (x_1 x_2 \cdots x_n)^{\frac{1}{n}}.$$
(This result is known as the *AM-GM inequality*.)

2. An n-honeycomb is defined as a hexagonal array of $3n^2 - 3n + 1$ regular hexagonal cells each of which has side length 1 unit. The figures show a 2-honeycomb and a 3-honeycomb.

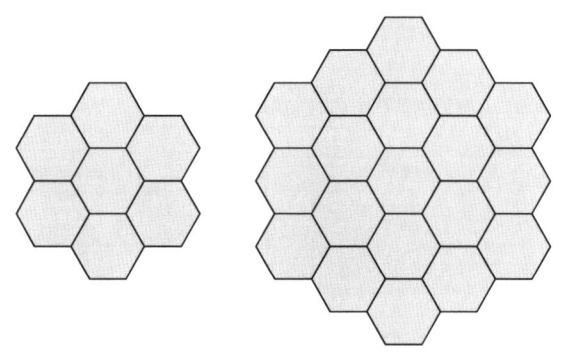

   The queen bee initially puts honey into m of the cells. Once the queen has finished, a worker bee may repeatedly choose any cell which has at least three neighbours which contain honey, and fill that cell with honey.
   Find, in terms of n, the smallest value of m for which the queen bee and the worker bee can fill an entire n-honeycomb with honey.

3. Let a, b be odd positive integers. Define the sequence (f_n) by putting $f_1 = a$, $f_2 = b$ and letting f_n for $n \geq 3$ be the greatest odd divisor of $f_{n-1} + f_{n-2}$. Show that f_n is constant for n sufficiently large and determine the eventual value as a function of a and b. [USAMO 1993]

4. Suppose that $x_1 \leq x_2 \leq \cdots \leq x_n$ and $y_1 \leq y_2 \leq \cdots \leq y_n$ are two non-decreasing sequences of real numbers. Let f be a bijection from $\{1, 2, \ldots, n\}$ to $\{1, 2, \ldots, n\}$, that is, f is a *rearrangement* of the numbers $1, 2, \ldots, n$.

Prove the *rearrangement inequality*, that

$$x_1 y_{f(1)} + x_2 y_{f(2)} + \cdots + x_n y_{f(n)} \leq x_1 y_1 + x_2 y_2 + \cdots + x_n y_n.$$

HINT

* 5. An integer is assigned to each vertex of a regular pentagon so that the sum of the five integers is 2011. A turn of a solitaire game consists of subtracting an integer m from each of the integers at two neighboring vertices and adding $2m$ to the opposite vertex, which is not adjacent to either of the first two vertices. (The amount m and the vertices chosen can vary from turn to turn.) The game is won at a certain vertex if, after some number of turns, that vertex has the number 2011 and the other four vertices have the number 0. Prove that for any choice of the initial integers, there is exactly one vertex at which the game can be won. [USAMO 2011]

* 6. Let n be a positive integer. Define a sequence by setting $a_1 = n$ and, for each $k > 1$, letting a_k be the unique integer in the range $0 \leq a_k \leq k - 1$ for which $a_1 + a_2 + \cdots + a_k$ is divisible by k. For instance, when $n = 9$ the resulting sequence is 9, 1, 2, 0, 3, 3, ... Prove that for any n the sequence $a_1, a_2, \ldots,$ eventually becomes constant. [USAMO 2007]

10.5 Solitaire games

For the next problem we require a new piece of terminology.

If we have two cells on a chessboard there is more than one way to measure the distance between them. It might be convenient to measure the distance between their centres in the traditional way, or it might be convenient to measure the shortest distance a rook would have to travel to move from one cell to the other.

This second notion of distance is called the *taxicab distance* and we will use it throughout our discussion of the next problem. For example we would say that the distance between a cell centred at $(0,0)$ and one centred at $(1,1)$ is 2 and the distance between $(0,0)$ and (x,y) is $|x| + |y|$.

Problem 10.18

Consider an infinite grid of cells, one of which, the *origin*, contains a microbe. If a microbe is ever in a cell which shares an edge with two or more empty cells, then that microbe may divide into two microbes. These microbes crawl into two of the adjacent empty cells leaving the original cell unoccupied. Divisions occur one at a time to ensure that no cell ever contains more than one microbe.

Prove that, no matter how many divisions take place, there will always be at least one microbe whose (taxicab) distance from the origin is less than 5.

The diagrams in figure 10.4 show the starting microbe and possible arrangements after one, three and six divisions. The figure illustrates that the microbes multiply so quickly that they seem to run out of space before they can move a long way from the starting cell.

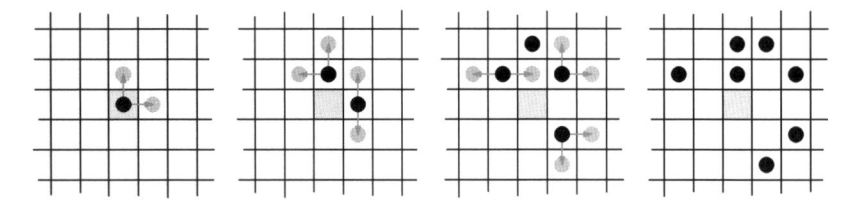

Figure 10.4

Our proof that this is indeed the case is very typical of such problems. We will assign the value 1 to the origin, and every other cell will be assigned a value depending on its (taxicab) distance from the origin. We then define the value of an arrangement of microbes to be the sum of the values of the cells which contain microbes. The values of the cells should be chosen so that a microbe dividing can never decrease the value of an arrangement. We will then argue that any arrangement of microbes all of which are more than five cells from the origin has a value less than 1 and is therefore unreachable.

When a microbe divides it might give rise to two microbes which are one cell further from the origin than their parent was. If this division is not to increase the total value of the arrangement and a cell at distance d from the start has value x, then it seems reasonable for cells at distance

Chapter 10: Using invariants

$d+1$ from the origin to have value $\frac{x}{2}$. Since the origin has value 1 this leads us to assign cells at a distance d from the origin the value $\left(\frac{1}{2}\right)^d$, as shown in figure 10.5, where the origin and the cells at a distance of 4 from the origin are highlighted.

$\frac{1}{56}$	$\frac{1}{128}$	$\frac{1}{64}$	$\frac{1}{32}$	$\frac{1}{16}$	$\frac{1}{32}$	$\frac{1}{64}$	$\frac{1}{128}$	$\frac{1}{256}$
$\frac{1}{28}$	$\frac{1}{64}$	$\frac{1}{32}$	$\frac{1}{16}$	$\frac{1}{8}$	$\frac{1}{16}$	$\frac{1}{32}$	$\frac{1}{64}$	$\frac{1}{12}$
$\frac{1}{64}$	$\frac{1}{32}$	$\frac{1}{16}$	$\frac{1}{8}$	$\frac{1}{4}$	$\frac{1}{8}$	$\frac{1}{16}$	$\frac{1}{32}$	$\frac{1}{64}$
$\frac{1}{32}$	$\frac{1}{16}$	$\frac{1}{8}$	$\frac{1}{4}$	$\frac{1}{2}$	$\frac{1}{4}$	$\frac{1}{8}$	$\frac{1}{16}$	$\frac{1}{32}$
$\frac{1}{16}$	$\frac{1}{8}$	$\frac{1}{4}$	$\frac{1}{2}$	1	$\frac{1}{2}$	$\frac{1}{4}$	$\frac{1}{8}$	$\frac{1}{16}$
$\frac{1}{32}$	$\frac{1}{16}$	$\frac{1}{8}$	$\frac{1}{4}$	$\frac{1}{2}$	$\frac{1}{4}$	$\frac{1}{8}$	$\frac{1}{16}$	$\frac{1}{32}$
$\frac{1}{64}$	$\frac{1}{32}$	$\frac{1}{16}$	$\frac{1}{8}$	$\frac{1}{4}$	$\frac{1}{8}$	$\frac{1}{16}$	$\frac{1}{32}$	$\frac{1}{64}$
$\frac{1}{128}$	$\frac{1}{64}$	$\frac{1}{32}$	$\frac{1}{16}$	$\frac{1}{8}$	$\frac{1}{16}$	$\frac{1}{32}$	$\frac{1}{64}$	$\frac{1}{12}$
$\frac{1}{}$	$\frac{1}{}$	$\frac{1}{64}$	$\frac{1}{}$	$\frac{1}{16}$	$\frac{1}{}$	$\frac{1}{}$	$\frac{1}{128}$	$\frac{1}{25}$

Figure 10.5

If a microbe at distance d from the origin divides and either of its offspring move closer to the origin, then the value of the position will increase. If both offspring move to cells at distance $d+1$ from the origin, the value of the arrangement will not change. Since the value of the arrangement is initially 1, it is clear that no subsequent arrangement can have a value less than 1. Now we need to find the total value of all the cells whose distance from the origin is 6 or more and check that it is less than 1.

We begin by finding the total value of all the cells on the chessboard. Our calculation will make frequent use of the fact that $\frac{1}{2}+\frac{1}{4}+\frac{1}{8}+\cdots=1$.

Indeed, the total value of all the cells directly above the origin is 1 and the value of the cells directly below the origin is also 1. Therefore the total value of all the cells in the column containing the origin is 3. Moving one column to the left multiplies all the values by $\frac{1}{2}$ so the contribution of all the columns to the left of the origin is $3 \times \frac{1}{2}+3 \times \frac{1}{4}+3 \times \frac{1}{8}+\cdots=3$. The columns to the right of the origin also contribute a total of 3 so the sum of all the values on the entire board is 9.

Now we add up the total value of all the cells whose distance from the origin is at most 5. This gives us $1 + 4 \times \frac{1}{2} + 8 \times \frac{1}{4} + 12 \times \frac{1}{8} + 16 \times \frac{1}{16} + 20 \times \frac{1}{32} = \frac{65}{8}$. The total value of all the cells at distance 6 or more from the origin is $9 - \frac{65}{8} = \frac{7}{8}$, which is less than 1, as required.

Problem 10.19

A solitaire game is played on an infinite triangular array of hexagonal cells, each of which may contain a counter. A move consists of jumping a counter over a counter in an adjacent cell into an unoccupied cell; the counter that was jumped over is then removed from the game. The aim of the game is to move a counter into the cell in the corner at the 'top' of the array. Figure 10.6 shows an initial arrangement of four counters which makes it possible to win the game.

Prove that every arrangement that makes it possible to win the game has at least one counter in one of the top seven rows of the board.

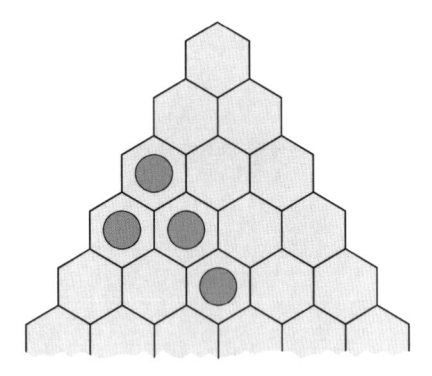

Figure 10.6

This problem is similar to the previous one, but the algebra is a little more intricate. We start by assigning values to the cells, as shown in figure 10.7 on the facing page. Here x represents a number less than one which we will choose in a moment.

We define the value of an arrangement of counters to be equal to the sum of the values assigned to the cells containing counters. Our aim is

Chapter 10: Using invariants 211

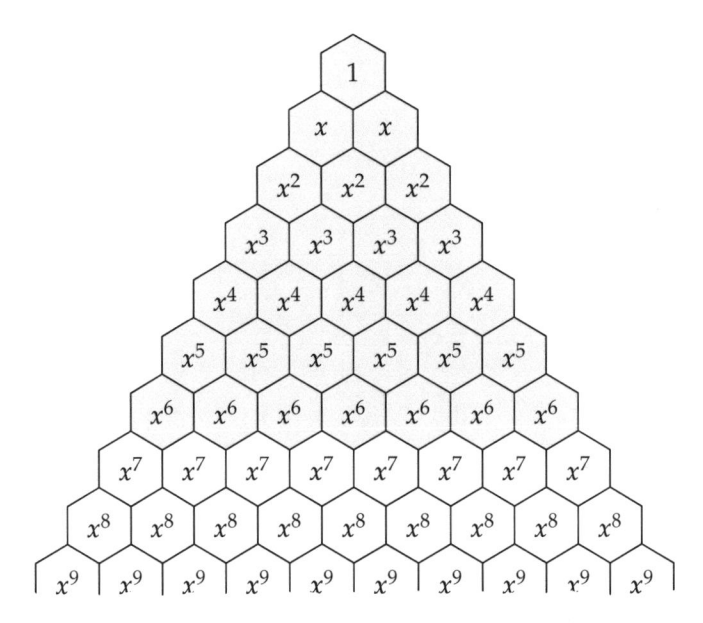

Figure 10.7

to find a number x such that no legal move can increase the value of an arrangement, and such that the total value of all the unshaded cells in figure 10.7 is less than one.

If we start in row $r+2$ and jump over a counter in row $r+1$, then we increase the total value of the arrangement by $x^r - x^{r+1} - x^{r+2}$. So we must ensure that this quantity is at most zero. Jumping horizontally or away from the top of the board can only decrease the value of the arrangement, provided $0 < x < 1$. This suggests that we should choose x such that $x^r - x^{r+1} - x^{r+2} = 0$. Dividing by x^r gives the quadratic equation $x^2 + x - 1 = 0$ which has roots $x = \frac{-1+\sqrt{5}}{2}$ and $x = \frac{-1-\sqrt{5}}{2}$. The number $\frac{-1+\sqrt{5}}{2}$ lies between 0 and 1 so is a suitable choice for x. This is the number ϕ which we met in chapter 6.

By setting x equal to ϕ we ensure that the value of an arrangement is a monovariant. If we call the value of all the unshaded cells T, then we are left with the task of checking that $T \leq 1$. The calculation will make frequent use of the fact that $1 + x + x^2 + \cdots = \frac{1}{1-x}$ provided $|x| < 1$.

If we sum the unshaded cells in lines parallel to the side of the board, then we obtain eight copies of the expression $(\phi^7 + \phi^8 + \phi^9 + \cdots)$ then one copy of each of the expressions $(\phi^8 + \phi^9 + \phi^{10} + \cdots)$, $(\phi^9 + \phi^{10} + \phi^{11} + \cdots)$, and so on. Each of these is a geometric progression so we may simplify our total to

$$T = \frac{8\phi^7}{1-\phi} + \left(\frac{\phi^8}{1-\phi} + \frac{\phi^9}{1-\phi} + \frac{\phi^{10}}{1-\phi} + \cdots\right).$$

The expression in brackets is another geometric progression, so we have

$$T = \frac{8\phi^7}{1-\phi} + \frac{\phi^8}{(1-\phi)^2}.$$

Summing the values of the cells in rows across the page, we get

$$T = 8\phi^7 + 9\phi^8 + 10\phi^9 + \cdots$$
$$= 8\phi^7(1 + \phi + \phi^2 + \cdots) + \phi^8(1 + 2\phi + 3\phi^2 + \cdots)$$
$$= \frac{8\phi^7}{1-\phi} + \frac{\phi^8}{(1-\phi)^2}.$$

Showing that $T \leq 1$ is easy with a pocket calculator, but anyone with a shred of honour will want to try the calculation by hand. The fact that $\phi^2 = 1 - \phi$ can be used repeatedly to simplify the expression systematically.

$$T = \frac{8\phi^7}{1-\phi} + \frac{\phi^8}{(1-\phi)^2}$$
$$= \frac{8\phi^7}{\phi^2} + \frac{\phi^8}{\phi^4}$$
$$= 8\phi^5 + \phi^4$$
$$= \phi^4(8\phi + 1)$$
$$= (1-\phi)^2(8\phi + 1)$$
$$= (1 - 2\phi + \phi^2)(8\phi + 1)$$
$$= (2 - 3\phi)(8\phi + 1)$$
$$= 2 + 13\phi - 24\phi^2$$
$$= -22 + 37\phi$$
$$= 1 - (23 - 37\phi)$$
$$= 1 - \tfrac{1}{2}(83 - 37\sqrt{5}).$$

Now since $83^2 = 6889 > 6845 = 5 \times 1369 = 5 \times 37^2$ the quantity being subtracted from 1 is positive, which is exactly what we needed to prove.

Exercise 10e

1. There are six counters in one cell of an infinite hexagonal grid. A move consists of choosing a non-empty cell, removing a counter from it and placing a total of three new counters into cells adjacent to the chosen cell. Prove that no matter how many moves are made, there will always be a cell with more than one counter in it.

2. A solitaire game is played on an infinite board which has a hole drilled in it at every point with integer coordinates. Some of the holes contain pegs. A move consists of jumping a peg over a directly (not diagonally) adjacent peg into an unoccupied hole; the peg that was jumped over is then removed from the game. Prove that if initially the y-coordinate of every peg is less than are equal to 0, then it is never possible to have a peg with y-coordinate equal to 5.

Chapter 11

Going to extremes

11.1 Using extremal objects

We will start by considering a problem that is so simple that many people do not even realise that it is a statement which requires a proof. Indeed we used this result without proof in our solution to problem 8.25 on page 152.

> **Problem 11.1**
> Prove that every positive integer greater than 1 can be written as a product of prime numbers.

Note that this problem does not ask us to prove that every number has a *unique* prime factorisation, merely that some factorisation exists. We will come to the issue of uniqueness in problem 11.11.

The statement seems very obvious, but obviousness is not always a reliable indicator of truth, so we should be careful. The idea behind our proof is to suppose we are given a number N which we need to factorise into primes. If the number is prime itself, then we are done, and if not, then we can break it down into two smaller factors. If these are prime, then there is nothing to do, and if they are not, then we can break them down further. If we keep factorising every factor that is not a prime, then surely we will end up with a factorisation of the original number into primes.

The argument is essentially correct, but we would like to tidy it up a little, particularly since the notion of going on and on until we can go no further and then stopping seems a little vague. With the introduction of a new idea we can sidestep this issue and, in a sense, jump straight to the finish line.

We consider all possible factorisations of N which do not include the number 1, and call the number of factors in a factorisation its *length*. We note that there are only finitely many factorisations. This is clear since a factorisation is a list of fewer than N numbers, each of which is at most N. Therefore we may focus on a *longest* factorisation. If any of the factors in this factorisation were not prime, we could split it into two factors greater than one. This would yield a longer factorisation of N which is impossible. Therefore, any longest factorisation is necessarily a factorisation into primes.

It is worth reflecting for a moment on our proof. We took a finite set of objects—in this case factorisations of N—and considered the length of each one, thereby assigning a number to each object. It then became possible to choose a longest factorisation, which served as a *maximal element* for the set. We then used proof by contradiction to show that this longest factorisation was a prime factorisation of N. The assumption that the factorisation contained a composite factor gave rise to a longer factorisation of N which contradicted the maximality of the maximal element we had chosen.

Notice that we were careful to talk about *a* longest factorisation rather than *the* longest factorisation. It is perfectly conceivable that more than one different factorisation has maximal length, but fortunately our argument works with any of them.

The next few problems all involve placing numbers on the cells of (uncoloured) chessboards. We will say that two cells are *neighbours* if they share an edge or a corner. On an infinite chessboard every cell has eight neighbours, and on a finite board edge cells have five while corner cells only have three.

Problem 11.2

A positive whole number is placed on each cell of an infinite chessboard. The number in each cell is the average of the numbers in its neighbours.

Prove that all the numbers are equal.

This is another problem with a short solution, and if we are lucky we may see the trick at once. However, if we are not so lucky, there is some good general advice we can follow.

If you don't know how to prove something, try to construct a counter-example.

This may seem like strange advice. If we wish to show that something is always the case, why would we waste time trying to exhibit a scenario where it is not the case? The reason is, that although we suspect our efforts to build a counter-example will fail, we may well gain some insight by thinking about *why* our efforts are failing.

For the current problem we might try putting a 5 and a 6 next to each other on the board. The 5 has a larger neighbour (the 6) so it also has a smaller neighbour, given the condition in the question. This number might be a 4, but, whatever it is, it has a larger neighbour (the 5) so it also has a smaller neighbour, which also has a smaller neighbour, and so on. Eventually we will be forced to use negative numbers, which are forbidden in the question.

As before, the argument is basically sound, but we would prefer one which avoided the notion of going on and on until something particular happens.

The numbers on the board are positive integers, so it makes sense to consider a smallest number on the chessboard. This number is equal to its neighbours. These in turn are equal to their neighbours and so on. Every square on the board will eventually be reached by this process, so we are done.

The solutions to the previous two problems required us to focus on a *longest* factorisation or a *smallest* positive integer. The lesson from these solutions is that focusing on an *extremal* object, that is, one which is minimal or maximal in some sense, can be a very powerful way to begin a proof. However, while the idea of taking something to an extreme value is often useful, the next problem illustrates that this idea should be used carefully.

11.2 Arranging things

Problem 11.3

A positive real number is placed on every cell of an infinite chessboard.

Prove that there is a number which is less than or equal to at least four of its neighbours.

Armed with our new idea of focus on things which are maximal or minimal, this problem seems almost trivial. We simply consider the smallest number on the board. This number is less than or equal to all its neighbours, so it is certainly less than or equal to four of them.

Sadly this 'solution' is badly flawed. The board is covered by an infinite set of positive real numbers, and an infinite set of positive reals need not have a least element. For example, the set $\left\{\frac{1}{2}, \frac{1}{3}, \frac{1}{4}, \ldots\right\}$ has no least element, nor does the set $\{x \colon x > 1\}$. Considering a smallest number on the board is not a legal opening move.

This is worrying. In fact, we might even start to doubt our previous two solutions.

Fortunately, they really do hold water. The first makes use of the fact that any *finite* set of numbers has a greatest and a least element. We applied this principle to the lengths of the factorisations of N, but it can be applied to any set of real numbers, both positive and negative. Our solution to problem 11.2 made use of the fact that any set of *positive integers* has a least member. This is fundamental to our understanding of the integers, and does not require any further justification.

Since the problem at hand deals with an infinite set of real numbers we appear to be at an impasse. However, thinking clearly about exactly what the difficulty is can give us a clue as to how to resolve it.

Our intuition suggests that we should consider a smallest number, but this is only permissible if we are dealing with a finite set of reals. Therefore we need to design a finite set of real numbers whose least element will satisfy the conditions in the problem.

Our first idea might be to focus on a small square region of the board and look at the smallest number in that region. Unfortunately, if the smallest number is in the corner of the region we are looking at, then it only has three neighbours in the region, so we cannot draw any conclusion about the neighbours which are missing.

The problem with a square grid is the corner cells, and this suggests that it might be better to remove these from a 4 × 4 region and consider the resulting shape, shown in figure 11.1.

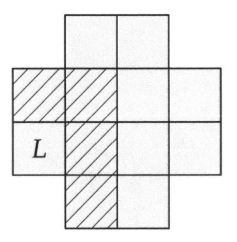

Figure 11.1

We will call this shape a *cross*. Now *every* cell in a given cross has at least four neighbouring cells also in that cross. Now we choose any cross on the board and focus on a smallest number, say L, in that cross. This number is less than or equal to at least four of its neighbours as required.

The crucial step in constructing the cross was the removal of the awkward corner cells from a 4 × 4 square. Clearly we could just as easily have removed the corner cells from any larger rectangle and the proof would have worked without alteration. You might like to consider whether it is always possible to find a number that is less than or equal to *five* or more of its neighbours.

Problem 11.4

The numbers $1, 2, \ldots, n^2$ are placed in any order on the cells of an $n \times n$ chessboard.

Prove that there are two neighbouring cells whose numbers differ by at least $n + 1$.

Let us suppose, for contradiction, that the numbers in neighbouring cells never differ by more than n. It is worth thinking informally for a moment about what this means. If we imagine going for a walk on the chessboard, it means that the numbers in the cells we are walking on cannot change too rapidly. Put another way, it means that if we go on a short walk, then the difference between our starting and finishing numbers cannot be too great. This discussion suggests a strategy for the problem. We need to find a *short* path between two *very different* numbers on the board.

At this point the details are straightforward. We consider sequences of neighbouring cells which start at the cell labelled 1 and end at the cell labelled n^2. We choose a shortest sequence. Since we may move diagonally, this sequence contains at most n cells. Therefore it contains at most $n - 1$ pairs of neighbouring cells. If neighbouring cells differed by at most n, then the maximum possible difference between the first and last cells in our sequence would be $n(n - 1)$. This is less than the actual difference of $n^2 - 1$ so we have our contradiction.

The solution is remarkably short, but that does not mean the problem is easy; finding short solutions requires luck as well as practice. It is important to bear this in mind and not to become discouraged when a problem you have been struggling with turns out to have a short solution.

Problem 11.5

At a party every guest has at most three enemies.

Prove that the guests can be divided into two rooms so that everyone has at most one enemy in the same room as them.

(We assume that if X is an enemy of Y, then Y is an enemy of X.)

In this problem we are looking for a 'friendly' division of guests, where friendly means not having too many enemies in the same room. This suggests finding some way to measure the 'friendliness' of a division and then choosing a 'friendliest' possible one.

In fact, since the condition given in the problem focuses on enemies rather than friends, we might be wise to measure the 'unfriendliness' rather than the friendliness and then minimise this. We start by trying a very simple measure of the unfriendliness of a division. We ask each guest how many of their enemies are in the same room as they are and sum the responses. We call this number that guest's *unfriendliness*. We then add up the unfriendliness of each guest and call this the *total unfriendliness* of the division.

Suppose that person P has two or three enemies in their room, and thus at most one in the other room. If P moves to the other room then the unfriendliness of at least two of P's enemies will decrease by one, and the unfriendliness of at most one of P's enemies will increase by one. P's own unfriendliness will also decrease so the total unfriendliness will certainly decrease.

Therefore in any division where the total unfriendliness is minimal, no person has more than one enemy in the same room as them. Our simple measure turns out to be perfect for the problem, which is a good advert for optimism when solving problems.

Exercise 11a

1. A class of students sit round a table. It turns out that each student's age is the average of their neighbours' ages. Prove that all the students are the same age.

2. The numbers 1, 2, ..., n^3 are placed on the $1 \times 1 \times 1$ subcubes of an $n \times n \times n$ cube. Prove that there are two neighbouring subcubes whose numbers differ by at least $n^2 + n + 1$.

3. A solitaire game is played with a deck of n cards labelled 1 to n. The cards are shuffled and placed in a stack. If the top card is labelled k, then a move consists of reversing the order of the top k cards. Prove that eventually the top card becomes (and remains) the card labelled 1.

4. At a party every pair of guests are either friends or strangers. Prove that the guests can be divided into two rooms such that each person has least half of their friends in the other room.

5. A gang of thieves has $3n$ members and each thief has stolen something from one of the other members of the gang. Prove that we can find n thieves, none of whom have stolen from each other.

6. Real numbers are placed at one degree intervals around a circle. Each number is the non-negative difference between the next two numbers on the circle going clockwise. If the sum of the numbers is 720, find the numbers.

7. In a certain country there are n cities. Between every pair of cities there is a single one-way road. Prove that there is a city which can be reached from every other city either directly, or by travelling via one other city.

*8. Suppose that n identical cars are stopped on a circular track. Together, they have enough fuel to complete one lap. Show that one of the cars can complete a lap by collecting fuel from the other cars on the way.
[HINT]

11.3 Geometrical problems

In the early 1930s, four undergraduate students at the University of Cambridge became fascinated by the following question:

Is it possible to divide a square into a finite number of smaller squares, all of which have different sizes?

Their research into the problem continued for several years and ranged across many areas of mathematics, including, somewhat surprisingly, the theory of electrical circuits. Finally they were able to answer their question in the affirmative.

Figure 11.2 shows a 112×112 square divided into 21 smaller squares. Such a diagram is called a *squared square*.

Having resolved this two-dimensional problem, we might ask whether something similar can be accomplished in three dimensions. Can we find a *cubed cube*? That is to say:

Is it possible to divide a cube into a finite number of smaller cubes, all of which have different sizes?

This is a rather daunting question. Finding a squared square took years, and all six faces of a cubed cube would need to be different squared squares of the same size. More to the point, cubing the cube might turn

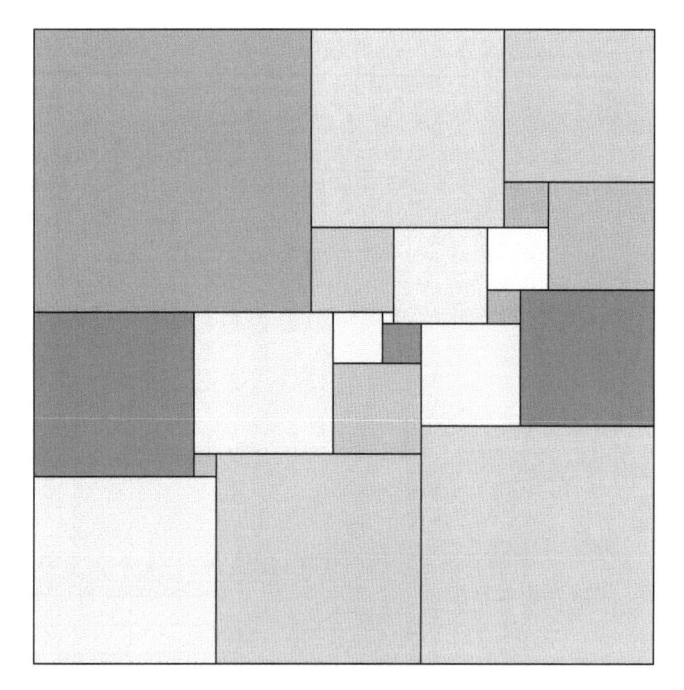

Figure 11.2

out to be impossible rather than just difficult. Even finding a good way to represent a three-dimensional arrangement of cubes is challenging. Certainly it looks as if resolving this question will be significantly harder than squaring the square.

Looks, however, can be deceiving. The solution to problem 11.6 is extremely devious, but it is also short, relatively easy to understand, and more or less impossible to forget.

Problem 11.6

Prove that a cube cannot be split into a finite number of cubes of different sizes.

Let us suppose that a cubed cube exists, and try to prove that it cannot be made up of a finite number of subcubes. The bottom face of the original cube will be a squared square. The key idea is to focus on the *smallest* square in this squared square. A moment's careful thought shows that, since the other squares are all larger and could not fit round it, the smallest square cannot be in a corner or on an edge of the large squared square.

Back in three dimensions this smallest square is the bottom face of a cube which we will call C_1. Now we consider the top face of C_1. Since the cubes touching the sides of C_1 are larger than it, they 'tower over it' providing four 'walls' around the top face. Therefore the top face of C_1 is covered by other cubes which fit within the walls. They cannot be the same size as C_1, so are smaller. This shows that the top face of C_1 is another squared square.

Now we focus on the smallest square in this squared square. That is, we focus on the smallest cube touching the top face of C_1 and call this cube C_2. Exactly the same argument shows that the top face of C_2 is another squared square. Just as before, we focus on the smallest cube touching the top face of C_2 and call this cube C_3. This process can be continued indefinitely, which is impossible. If follows that the original assumption is false, and no decomposition into a finite number of cubes exists.

Problem 11.7

Prove that no right-angled isosceles triangle has integer side lengths.

Let us call isosceles right-angled triangles with integer side lengths *nasty*. We are asked to show that no nasty triangles exist. It is worth noting that, since the ratio of the hypotenuse of a nasty triangle to another of its sides is $\sqrt{2}$, we are essentially being asked to provide a geometrical proof that $\sqrt{2}$ cannot be written as the ratio of two integers.

Let us imagine that we have some evil adversary who has provided us with a triangle which he claims is nasty, and let us also suppose that this triangle is the *smallest* possible nasty triangle, in the sense that it has the smallest possible hypotenuse. Our task is now to use this triangle, shown in the left-hand diagram of figure 11.3 on the next page, to construct a smaller triangle which is also nasty. This will contradict the minimality of the triangle and lead us to conclude that no nasty triangles exist.

There is more than one approach, but one involves adding a line DE perpendicular to AC as shown in the right-hand diagram of figure 11.3 in the hope that the isosceles right-angled triangle ADE turns out to be nasty.

Figure 11.3

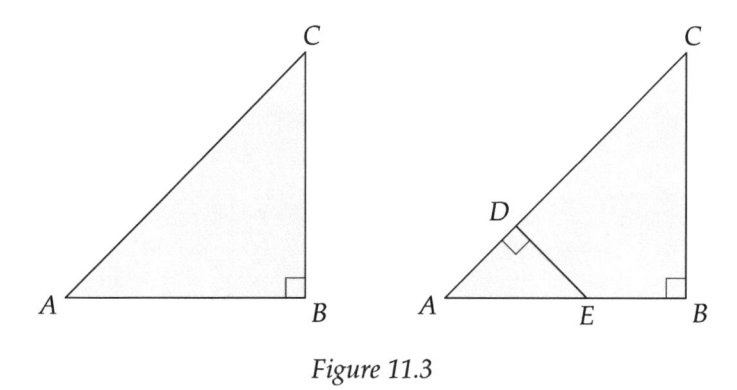

For this to work we need to ensure that AD and AE are both integers.

Since AC is an integer, AD will be an integer provided CD is. This in turn will show that $DE = AD$ is an integer.

To make sure AE is an integer it is enough to ensure that EB is an integer, since AB is an integer.

We are getting close. We choose D such that CD and CB are equal. This is appealing because it ensures that triangles CDE and CBE are congruent. Now $EB = DE = AD$ and all three are integers as required.

Therefore triangle ADE has integer side lengths so is a smaller nasty triangle than the smallest one. This is exactly the contradiction we were looking for and the proof is complete.

Problem 11.8

Suppose we are given n points in the plane.

Prove that there is a polygon which has these points as its vertices and does not intersect itself.

Time spent studying the simplest case of the problem is seldom time wasted, so we take a moment to consider $n = 4$. Suppose we are given four points A, B, C and D. We might join them up using the circuit $ABCD$. If we are lucky, then this circuit will not intersect itself and we will have found the required polygon. If we are less lucky, then two of the lines may cross as in figure 11.4 on the following page, in which case the circuit does not satisify the requirements of the problem.

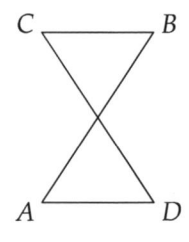

Figure 11.4

This is not too hard to resolve, we can simply 'untwist' the circuit by replacing it with the circuit *ACBD*.

We can now form an initial plan of attack for the general problem. We could start by taking any circuit round the n points. If this happens to intersect itself, we could try to untwist the circuit, removing one crossing point at a time until we end up with a polygon. One difficulty is that it may not be easy to describe the desired untwisting process in general. Another, more pressing, problem is that untwisting one crossing point might create other new crossing points in a sufficiently complex circuit.

Let us refine our plan of attack in light of these anticipated difficulties. Our first idea involved untwisting again and again until we could untwist no further. This is reminiscent of factoring again and again until we can factor no further. This, in turn, suggests that we may be able to jump straight to the finish line by maximising or minimising some quantity associated with the circuit we are considering. Thinking carefully about the $n = 4$ case provides us with the necessary clue. The untwisting manoeuvre reduces the total length of the circuit.

Now we can present an almost instant solution to the problem. Consider a shortest circuit round the n points. This certainly exists since there are only finitely many possible circuits. Suppose for contradiction that two segments AB and CD intersect at X (such as on the left of figure 11.5).

We now construct a shorter circuit (see the right of figure 11.5) as follows:

(i) Start at A and go straight to C.
(ii) Use the original sequence from B to C in reverse order.
(iii) Go from B to D.
(iv) Complete the circuit with the original sequence which joined D to A.

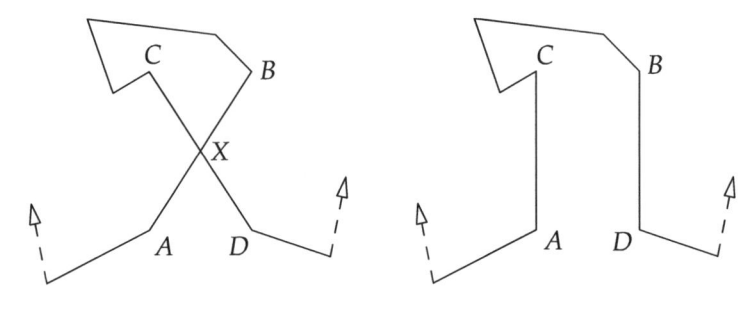

Figure 11.5

The line segments used are the same except that AC and BD have replaced AB and CD. Now $AB + CD = (AX + XC) + (BX + XD)$, which is clearly greater than $AC + BD$ by the triangle inequality, which says that two sides of a triangle always sum to more than the third side. This is impossible since the original circuit was a shortest one. Therefore the assumption that there was a shortest circuit which intersected itself was false.

One nice feature of this proof is that it effortlessly avoids the problem that an untwisting move might create new crossing points since we are not focussing on the number of crossing points at any stage.

Problem 11.9

Suppose that n people stand in a field such that the distances between pairs of people are all distinct. At a signal, everyone shoots his nearest neighbour.

(a) Prove that at least one person survives if n is odd.
(b) Prove that nobody is shot by more than 5 people.

(a) To get a feel for the problem, we consider the simplest possible case, namely when $n = 3$. The three people are the vertices of a scalene triangle, and the two at the ends of the shortest side will certainly shoot each other. The last person will shoot at one of the first two and survive. If we reflect on this tragic little episode, we notice that at least one person survives provided at least one other person receives more than one bullet.

For the general case, we first note that the number of deaths is the same as the number of bullets. We then consider the shortest distance between two people. These two people, whom we may call P and Q, will shoot each other. Now if another person shoots either P or Q we are done, by considering the number of bullets.

If, on the other hand, nobody else fires at P or Q, then we can simply ignore P and Q altogether and repeat the preceding argument on the remaining people.

Since the original number of people is odd, we cannot pair off all the shooters. Eventually we will find someone who is shot more than once, so someone else is bound to survive.

(b) We suppose for contradiction that T is shot by six people $A, B, \ldots, F$ and consider the six angles BTA, CTB, $\ldots$, ATF (see figure 11.6).

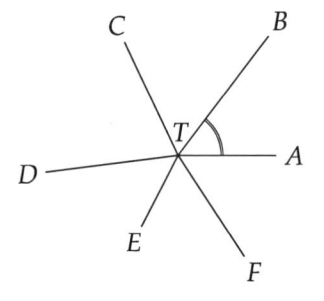

Figure 11.6

These sum to 360° so, by the averaging principle, one of them is at least 60°. We suppose, renaming the people if necessary, that $\angle BTA \geq 60°$ and claim that this means T cannot have been shot by both A and B. Indeed, T will only be shot by both A and B if AB is the longest side in the triangle TAB. However, in any triangle, the longest side is opposite the largest angle. Therefore if T is shot by both A and B, then all the angles in triangle TAB are at most 60°. This is only possible if the triangle is equilateral, but the question specifies that the distances between shooters are all distinct, so we have a contradiction.

Chapter 11: Going to extremes

Exercise 11b

1. Prove that no equilateral triangle has integer sides and integer height.

2. $2n$ points are given in the plane with no three collinear. Half are coloured red and half blue. Each blue point is joined to exactly one red point with a straight line. Prove that it is possible to do this in such a way that none of the lines cross. [Putnam 1979]

3. Suppose that n coins of different sizes are placed on a table. Prove that one coin is touching at most 5 others.

4. By choosing a suitable direction to be the downward direction, and then considering the lowest point in each region, prove that n lines divide the plane into at most $\binom{n}{2} + n + 1$ regions. (This is question 7 of exercise 3b on page 40.)

11.4 Number theory

Next we will consider a few problems from number theory which further illustrate the power of focusing on a minimal object.

Problem 11.10

Prove that there is no positive integer n such that $\sqrt{6n}$ is an integer.

This problem is less geometrical than the previous one, but the overall strategy is similar.

We will call positive integers n with the property that $\sqrt{6n}$ is also an integer *nefarious* integers.

To show that no nefarious integers exist we will consider a hypothetical smallest nefarious integer and then construct a smaller nefarious integer.

Let the smallest nefarious integer be N.

The key step in this problem, which we will discuss in a moment, is to consider $M = (\sqrt{6} - 2)N$. We claim that M is a smaller nefarious integer than N.

There are three conditions we need to check.

The first condition is that $0 < M < N$. This follows from the fact that $3 > \sqrt{6} > 2$ so M is obtained by multiplying N by a number between 0 and 1.

The second condition is that M is an integer. This is true because $M = \sqrt{6}N - 2N$ and both $\sqrt{6}N$ and $2N$ are integers by the definition of N.

The final condition is that $\sqrt{6}M$ is an integer. This is clear since $\sqrt{6}M = 6N - 2\sqrt{6}N$ which is the difference between two integers.

Having a smaller nefarious integer than the smallest one is absurd, so the assumption that there are any nefarious integers at all is false.

The solution is quick and elegant, but where did the magical idea of considering $(\sqrt{6} - 2)N$ come from? The answer is that it came from a careful consideration of problem 11.7. The claim that there is no isosceles right-angled triangle is a geometrical way of asserting that there is no positive integer n such that $\sqrt{2}n$ is also an integer. The solution to that problem started with an integer a, supposed to be the smallest possible side length of a nasty triangle, and constructed a second integer $b - a$ which turned out to be the side of a smaller nasty triangle. Since $b = \sqrt{2}a$, we have that $b - a = a \times (\sqrt{2} - 1)$. In light of this discussion, multiplying N by $(\sqrt{6} - 2)$ looks clever, but not inhumanly so.

Problem 11.11

Prove that every integer greater than one has a unique prime factorisation if the primes are written in ascending order of size.

We suppose that $N = p_1 p_2 \cdots p_n$ and $N = q_1 q_2 \cdots q_m$, where the p_i and the q_i are all prime and we have $p_i \leq p_{i+1}$ and $q_i \leq q_{i+1}$. For contradiction, we suppose further that the two factorisations are not identical and that N is the least integer which has two different prime factorisations. Our task is now to construct a smaller integer with two different factorisations.

We begin by observing that none of the primes p_i is equal any of the q_j since if this were the case we could divide N by p_i and obtain a smaller number with distinct factorisations. Therefore we may assume, without loss of generality, that $p_1 > q_1$.

The key step is ingenious. We consider $M = (p_1 - q_1)p_2 p_3 \cdots p_n$ which is clearly less than N.

If we factorise the number $p_1 - q_1$ into primes we obtain a factorisation of M. This factorisation *does not* use the prime q_1 since if q_1 divided $(p_1 - q_1)$ it would be a factor of p_1 which is impossible.

Now note that

$$M = p_1 p_2 \cdots p_n - q_1 p_2 p_3 \cdots p_n$$
$$= q_1 q_2 \cdots q_m - q_1 p_2 p_3 \cdots p_n.$$

Since q_1 is a common factor of the last expression, this gives a factorisation of M which *does* use the prime q_1.

Thus M is an integer less than N with two different prime factorisations. This contradiction completes the proof.

Problem 11.12

Prove that there are no positive integer solutions to the equation $a^2 + b^2 = 3(c^2 + d^2)$.

An idea which is often helpful with problems of this type is to consider the equation modulo some small number. For example, to see that the equation $x^2 = 4y^2 + 2$ has no integer solutions, we can consider it modulo four. Checking the four possible values of x modulo four shows that the left hand side is either congruent to 0 or 1, while the right hand side is always congruent to 2, so there can be no solution.

For the problem at hand it seems sensible to consider the equation modulo three as this makes the right hand side congruent to 0. A quick check shows that all squares are either 0 or 1 modulo three, so the only way to have $a^2 + b^2 \equiv 0 (\bmod 3)$ is to have $a \equiv b \equiv 0 (\bmod 3)$. Unlike the equation $x^2 = 4y^2 + 2$, we do not immediately reach a contradiction, but we learn that if there are any solutions at all then $a = 3e$ and $b = 3f$ for some integers e and f. Substituting this back into the original equation, we have $(3e)^2 + (3f)^2 = 3(c^2 + d^2)$ which simplifies to $3e^2 + 3f^2 = c^2 + d^2$. This looks suspiciously like the original problem and at this point there are a number of similar ways to turn the work we have done into a proof that the equation has no solutions. One option is to suppose, for contradiction, that the equation has solutions and to focus on a solution (a,b,c,d) where the value of a^2+b^2 is as small as possible. We have already seen that $(c,d,\frac{a}{3},\frac{b}{3})$ is another solution to the equation and it is clear that $c^2+d^2 < a^2+b^2$ so we have found a smaller solution than the smallest one which is impossible.

11.5 Harder geometrical problems

All the solutions in this chapter can be described as having a two part structure. The first step is to find a suitable mathematical object to minimise or maximise, and the second is to use this extremal object to solve the problem, often by deriving a contradiction. In most of the problems we have seen so far, most of the insight has been needed in the first step, after which things have been fairly straightforward. We now consider three problems where concluding once we have chosen an extremal object is rather more intricate.

Problem 11.13

A strip of width w is the set of all points which lie on, or between, two parallel lines distance w apart.

Let S be a set of n points on the plane, where $n \geq 3$, such that any three different points of S can be covered by a strip of width 1.

Prove that S can be covered by a strip of width 2. [Balkan MO 2010]

This is a hard problem, not least because the condition that any three points are covered by a strip of width 1 does not seem familiar. We need to focus on this condition and see what we can extract from it.

Trying to find equivalent reformulations of a problem is often very useful, since new perspectives can bring new insights with them. We might rephrase the condition as follows.

If we take any triangle with vertices in S, then one of its three possible heights is at most 1.

Chapter 11: Going to extremes

To put it another way, if P, Q and R are points in $\mathcal{S}$, then one of the following holds.

I. The distance from R to PQ is at most 1.
II. The distance from Q to RP is at most 1.
III. The distance from P to QR is at most 1.

This is rather wordy, but it also something we can start to work with. In particular, if we focus on two points P and Q, there are three regions where another point R might be situated, shown in figure 11.7.

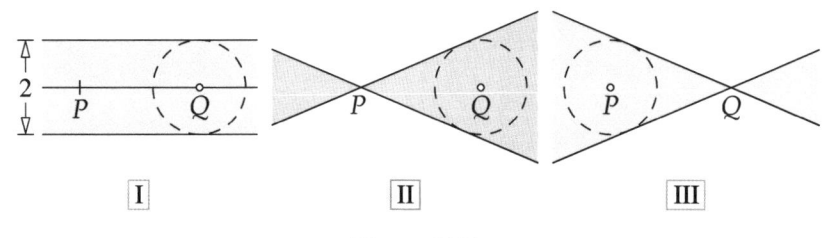

Figure 11.7

For any points P and Q, all other points in $\mathcal{S}$ are in the union of these regions, shown on the left in figure 11.8.

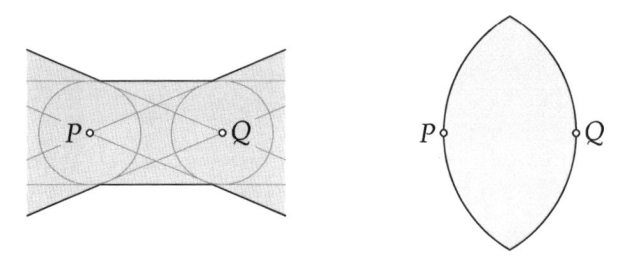

Figure 11.8

We have turned the condition in the question into something we can visualise. For every pair of points P and Q in $\mathcal{S}$ we have a region where all other points in $\mathcal{S}$ lie. If this region were a strip of width two, we would be done. Sadly it is not. Indeed, as we move further and further away from the points P and Q, the region where another point might be fails more and more spectacularly to be a strip. This is discouraging, but, if we stay calm, dealing with this failure will lead us to the crux of this problem.

The region we would like to be a strip gets too wide if we are far away from P and Q, so we need to ensure that no points in $\mathcal{S}$ are too far away from P and Q. We can achieve this by focusing on an extremal pair of points.

We choose the points P and Q such that the distance between them is maximal in S. This means that every point in S also lies in the region shown on the right in figure 11.8.

The solution is now within our grasp. We need to show that the intersection of the two regions in figure 11.8 is completely within a strip of width 2. The crucial piece of geometry is shown in figure 11.9.

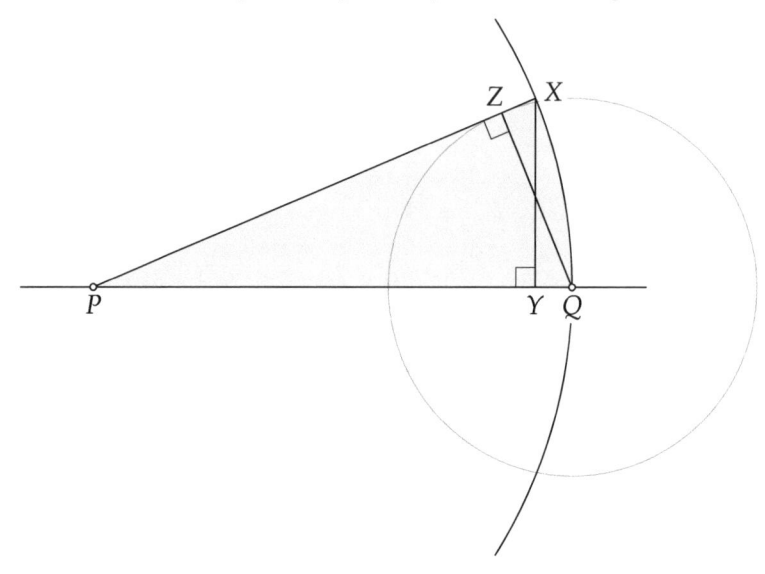

Figure 11.9

By symmetry we need only focus on clause II of our reformulation of the condition. That is, we want the distance between Q and RP to be at most 1. With this in mind we choose PX to be tangent to a unit circle around Q at the point Z. Now the point R lies on or below the line PX.

We observe that the triangles PYX and PZQ are right-angled, share an angle at P and have hypotenuses $PQ = PX$. This means they are congruent so $XY = QZ = 1$.

Now we have finished. The region on the left of figure 11.8 includes many points that are more than 1 unit away from the line PQ. However, we have shown that none of these troublesome points lie within the region shown on the right of figure 11.8. Therefore all points in S are at most 1 unit away from the line PQ as required.

Problem 11.14

A convex pentagon has rational sides and equal angles.

Prove that the pentagon is regular. [Balkan MO 2001]

Let us call irregular pentagons with equal angles and integer sides *naughty* pentagons.

If there is an irregular pentagon with rational sides and equal angles, it can be enlarged to form a naughty pentagon. So it is enough to prove that there are no naughty pentagons.

As in problem 11.7 we will focus on a (hypothetical) smallest naughty pentagon and try to construct a smaller one. We should be careful to state that by smallest we mean a pentagon of minimal perimeter.

Let us suppose that our evil adversary has provided us with a naughty pentagon $ABCDE$. We need to build a smaller pentagon with equal angles, so our strategy will be to remove a slice of $ABCDE$ using a cut parallel to one of its sides. This cut will reduce the length of two of the sides, and increase the length of a third. Fortunately the two lengths we lose and the length we gain form a triangle, so overall the perimeter is certain to decrease.

Now we must decide where to make our cut. A lesson we can learn from problem 11.7 is that it is a good idea to try and create symmetry in the diagram.

This leads us to a key idea, which is illustrated in figure 11.10. The pentagon $ABCDE$ has been reflected in the perpendicular bisector of CD to form an identical pentagon $A'B'DCE'$ and another pentagon $XE'CDE$.

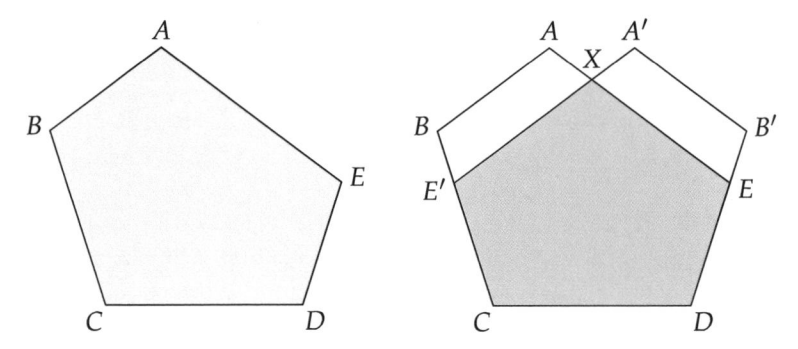

Figure 11.10

Our hope is that $XE'CDE$ will be a smaller naughty pentagon. This will complete the solution.

It is easy to see that $XE'CDE$ has equal angles.

Checking it has integer sides is also fairly straightforward. The sides CD and DE are sides of the original pentagon so are integers. CE' is equal to DE by construction, and the sides $E'X$ and EX are both equal to $AE - (BC - ED)$ which is an integer. The last relation holds since $E'BAX$ is an isosceles trapezium so $BE'=AX$.

We appear to be doing very well.

However, we would be wise to be cautious, particularly as this problem is from a relatively recent International competition so is likely to contain some subtleties.

With this in mind we look carefully at all the conditions $XE'CDE$ needs to satisfy if it is to be our desired smaller naughty pentagon:

(i) equal angles;
(ii) integer sides;
(iii) strictly smaller perimeter than $ABCDE$;
(iv) not regular.

We have already checked the first two conditions but have not yet considered the last two.

Figure 11.10 includes an implicit assumption that ED is the shortest side of $ABCDE$. By renaming the vertices if necessary, we are free to assume this, but the proof might still fail if $BC = ED$, since then $XE'CDE$ will not be smaller than $ABCDE$. If this disaster occurs we may be able to rescue the situation by reflecting $ABCDE$ in the perpendicular bisector of AE rather than CD. However, we will be in real trouble if AB and BC are both equal in length to the shortest side ED.

Fortunately, it turns out that a naughty pentagon cannot have two shortest sides next to each other.

To see this, suppose that $CD = ED$ are shortest sides of $ABCDE$. There is a unique regular pentagon with vertices C, D and E, say $PQCDE$ (see figure 11.11).

Since $ABCDE$ has equal angles AB is parallel to PQ. The minimality of CD means that $CB \geq CD$. If $CB = CD$, then $ABCDE$ is regular not naughty, and if $CB > CD$, then $AB < PQ$, which is equal to CD, contradicting the minimality of CD.

This result ensures that we are able to satisfy condition (iii) in our list. In fact, it also ensures we can satisfy condition (iv) since it implies that

Chapter 11: Going to extremes

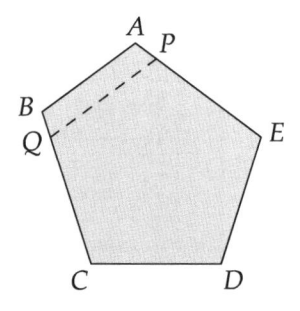

Figure 11.11

ED is shorter than both *CD* and *AE* and one of these sides will belong to the smaller naughty pentagon we construct.

After a good deal of careful checking we see that there is a smaller naughty pentagon than the smallest one. This contradiction completes the proof.

Having proved in problem 11.1 that every integer greater than one can be written as a product of primes, we now turn to the rather more substantial claim that this factorisation is unique. This is known as the *fundamental theorem of arithmetic* and is a cornerstone of elementary number theory. The traditional proof of this result uses Bezout's lemma (problem 8.23 on page 150) and probably gives a clearer sense of *why* the theorem is true. However, the proof we give here does serve as another illustration of the power of considering a minimal object.

Problem 11.15

Suppose that a finite set *S* of points in the plane has the property that any line through two of them passes through a third.

Prove that all the points lie on a single line.

This problem was posed by James Sylvester in 1893 and remained unsolved for some forty years. The first proofs of the result used techniques from an area of mathematics called projective geometry and are fairly subtle.

We present a solution published by Leroy Kelly in 1958. The fact that this elegant argument was discovered more than sixty years after the problem was first posed provides further evidence that having a good idea is not always easy, and that a simple proof may be hard to find.

Let us suppose that not all the points in S lie on the same straight line. This means there are a number of distinct lines $\mathcal{L}_i$ which connect points in the set S, and that for each of these lines, there are points in S which are not on that line.

Now for any line $\mathcal{L}$, we might ask how close the points in S are to $\mathcal{L}$. More precisely, we consider the perpendicular distances from $\mathcal{L}$ to points not on $\mathcal{L}$.

We focus on the line $\mathcal{L}_0$ and the point P_0 such that the distance d_0 from P_0 to $\mathcal{L}_0$ is the least among all possible choices of lines and points.

Our aim is to find P_1 in S and $\mathcal{L}_1$ joining two points in S such the distance from P_1 to $\mathcal{L}_1$ is smaller than d_0. This will contradict the choice of P_0 and $\mathcal{L}_0$ and force us to conclude that there is no way to choose any line $\mathcal{L}$ with a point P not on $\mathcal{L}$.

Of course, our proof will need to use the condition given in the statement of the theorem, namely that each line $\mathcal{L}$ has at least three points from S on it.

The left-hand diagram of figure 11.12 shows P_0, $\mathcal{L}_0$ and the foot of the perpendicular from P_0 to $\mathcal{L}_0$ which has been labelled Q.

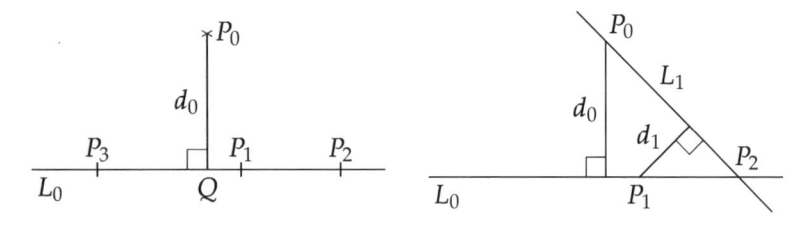

Figure 11.12

Now, there are at least three points in S which lie on $\mathcal{L}_0$, thus at least two lie on the same side of Q. In the diagram these two points have been labelled P_1 and P_2. It is worth mentioning that P_1 might coincide with Q, but that this would not affect the argument.

The right-hand diagram of figure 11.12 shows that if we choose $\mathcal{L}_1$ to be the line joining P_0 and P_2 then the distance between P_1 and $\mathcal{L}_1$ is less than d_0 which is exactly the contradiction we were hoping to reach.

The final exercise of the chapter contains a mixture of existence and non-existence results.

Exercise 11c

1. Prove that if k is an integer, then $\sqrt{k}$ is either an integer or irrational.

2. Prove that there are no integer solutions to the equation $x^3 + 2y^3 + 4z^3 = 0$ apart from $(x, y, z) = (0, 0, 0)$.

3. Suppose that n points are given such that the area of every triangle is at most 1. Prove that all the points are contained in a triangle of area at most 4. [KMO 1995]

4. Prove that every convex polyhedron has two faces with the same number sides.

5. Given a set of non-collinear points in the plane, prove that there is a line passing through exactly two of the points.

Appendices

Appendix A

Sets

A *set* is a collection of objects, which are known as *elements*. If a is an element of a set A, we write $a \in A$. Similarly, $a \notin A$ indicates the fact that a does not belong to A.

One way of showing the members of a set is to list them inside curly brackets. For example, $S = \{2, 3, 5, 7, 11, 13, 17, 19\}$ is the set of prime numbers smaller than 20.

An alternative way of indicating this set is to use set-builder notation

$$S = \{x : x \text{ is a natural number, } x \text{ is prime and } x < 20\},$$

which is read as 'the set of x such that x is a natural number, x is prime and x is smaller than 20'.

If every element of a set A is an element of a set B, then we say that A is a *subset* of B and write $A \subset B$.

Of course, sets need not be sets of numbers; we might define a set to be all the pupils in a school, and then subsets could be pupils in the same year group, all the girls in the school or members of the chess team.

It is also necessary to define an empty set $\emptyset$ which has no members. Alternatively, $\emptyset = \{\}$.

It is important to distinguish between A and the set $\{A\}$, which is the set consisting of A alone. It is true that $A \in \{A\}$, but false that $A \in A$.

Given sets A and B we can define new sets such as

- the *union* $A \cup B$, which consists of all elements either in A or B or both,
- the *intersection* $A \cap B$, which consists of all element in both A and B, and

- the *complement* A' which consists of all elements not in A.

A useful way of representing sets is to use *Venn diagrams*, in which the sets A, B and C are shown as closed curves, with intersections and unions being shown in the obvious way.

For example, the shaded region on the left of figure A.1 represents the set $B \cap C$. The shaded region shown on the right of figure A.1 is a bit more complicated. It represents the set $A' \cap B \cap C$.

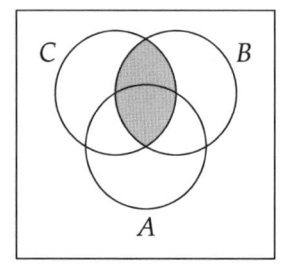

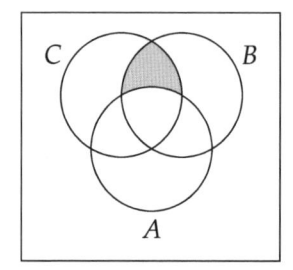

Figure A.1

Venn diagrams are useful for demonstrating that two sets which look different in set notation are in fact the same. For example, we can show that $(A \cup B)' = A' \cap B'$.

Begin with the union $A \cup B$ of the sets A and B, shown on the left of figure A.2. Switch to $(A \cup B)'$, the complement of $A \cup B$, shown on the right of figure A.2.

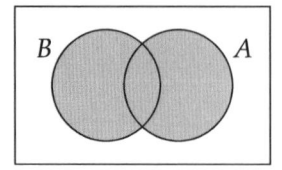

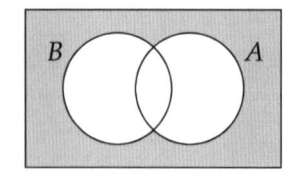

Figure A.2

The figure on the left of figure A.3 shows the set A', the complement of A. Intersect it with B', the complement of B, as shown on the right of figure A.3.

Since the Venn diagrams are the same, we conclude that $(A \cup B)' = A' \cap B'$. This method should be employed in exercise A.

Appendix A: Sets 245

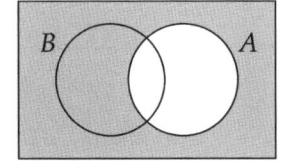

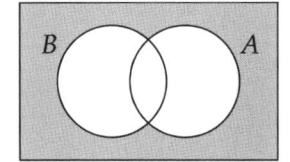

Figure A.3

The notation $|A|$ is used to mean the number of elements in set A. (An alternative is $n(A)$ but this will not be used.) In section 4.4, this is used extensively as a means of counting.

One way of showing how many elements there are in a set is to place numbers inside the regions of the Venn diagram. For example, in figure A.4 we see that $|A \cap B \cap C| = 4$.

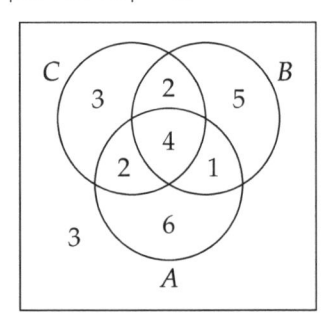

Figure A.4

Unfortunately this is sometimes used to mean that $A \cap B \cap C = \{4\}$, the set consisting of just one element, the number 4. This ambiguity should not arise if the context is clear.

A subset of a set consisting of exactly k elements is called a k-set. These are mentioned in the discussion about multinomial coefficients in section 3.2.

Note that sets may not contain repeated elements and that the order of elements in the listing does not matter. Thus the set written as $\{a, b, b, c, b, d, d, d\}$ is exactly the same as the set $\{a, b, c, d\}$.

Exercise A

1. Prove that $(A \cap B)' = A' \cup B'$.

2. Prove that $A \cap (B \cup C) = (A \cap B) \cup (A \cap C)$.

3. Prove that $|A \cup B| = |A| + |B| - |A \cap B|$.

Appendix B

Sigma notation

It is often necessary to write down the sum of a finite or infinite sequence of terms, and there is a useful notation for doing this.

A simple example is the sum of the squares of the first 100 natural numbers, $1^2 + 2^2 + \cdots + 100^2$. Here we have used the three dots $\cdots$ (technically known as an *ellipsis*) to indicate the missing numbers. In sigma notation, we represent this sum by

$$\sum_{i=1}^{100} i^2.$$

The upper case Greek letter sigma, which is equivalent to the English S, stands for sum. Above and below the $\sum$ we show the *range* of the summation, and in this case we begin when $i = 1$ and finish when $i = 100$. Finally i^2, which is known as the *summand*, tells us what terms we have to add. In this case, we have to add the squares of all the numbers from 1 to 100.

Here are some more examples of this notation:

$$\sum_{i=1}^{20} i = 1 + 2 + \cdots + 20;$$

$$\sum_{i=0}^{50} (2i + 1) = 1 + 3 + 5 + \cdots + 101;$$

$$\sum_{i=5}^{10} \frac{i}{i+1} = \frac{5}{6} + \frac{6}{7} + \frac{7}{8} + \frac{8}{9} + \frac{9}{10} + \frac{10}{11};$$

$$\sum_{i=1}^{5} i \times 2^i = 1 \times 2 + 2 \times 4 + 3 \times 8 + 4 \times 16 + 5 \times 32;$$

$$\sum_{i=1}^{50} (-1)^i i = (-1) + 2 + (-3) + \cdots + 50.$$

Notice the use of $(-1)^i$ in the final example, which allows us to add a series of terms with alternating plus and minus signs.

In all of these cases, it would have been theoretically possible to write down all the terms in the summation. However, if we want to write down the sum of the first n positive integers, there is no way of doing this without using an ellipsis. But writing down the sum is straightforward using sigma notation, since the sum is represented by $\sum_{i=1}^{n} i$.

This representation is not unique, and you should check that all the following are alternative ways of showing the same thing as $\sum_{i=1}^{n} i$.

$$\sum_{r=0}^{n} r \qquad \sum_{r=1}^{n} r \qquad \sum_{i=0}^{n-1} (i+1) \qquad \sum_{k=0}^{n} (n-k)$$

It is also permissible to use shorthand notation such as $\sum_{1}^{n} i$ or even $\sum i$ when there is no ambiguity about the range.

The variable i can be any symbol, which effectively 'disappears' when the summation is carried out. For this reason it is called a *dummy variable*. Note that the notation $\sum_{0}^{r} r$ is meaningless, since we are effectively requiring r to be a variable and a constant at the same time.

An example that is easy to misinterpret is $\sum_{i=1}^{n} 1$. Here all the terms are the same, and you have to add n terms, each of which is equal to 1. It turns out that this is a rather eccentric way of writing n.

The variable i can also function as an *index* of summation. If we define a sequence by the formula $a_i = \frac{i}{i+1}$, then we can represent the sum

$$\frac{5}{6} + \frac{6}{7} + \frac{7}{8} + \frac{8}{9} + \frac{9}{10} + \frac{10}{11}$$

by $\sum_{i=5}^{10} a_i$.

Another variation is to denote the range as a set. If we define $S = \{3, 4, 5, 6, 7\}$, then

$$\sum_{i \in S} i^2$$

Appendix B: Sigma notation

represents the squares of the numbers in S, namely $3^2 + 4^2 + 5^2 + 6^2 + 7^2$. Alternatively, we could write this as

$$\sum_{3 \leq i \leq 7} i^2,$$

with an interval below the sigma, or even

$$\sum_{3 \leq i \leq 7} b_i,$$

where $b_i = i^2$. It should be clear that sigma notation is very flexible and allows you to express the same thing in many different ways.

There are fairly obvious 'identities', which are known as the rules of sigma algebra, including:

(i) if k is constant, then $\sum k a_i = k \sum a_i$;
(ii) $\sum (a_i + b_i) = \sum a_i + \sum b_i$;
(iii) $\sum_{i=1}^{n} a_i = \sum_{i=k+1}^{k+n} a_{i-k}$;
(iv) $\sum_{i=1}^{k} a_i + \sum_{i=k+1}^{n} a_i = \sum_{i=1}^{n} a_i$.

The sum $\sum_{i=1}^{5}(3i + 1)$ is $4 + 7 + 10 + 13 + 16$, which is 50. Using the rules above, this can be evaluated as $3 \sum_{i=1}^{5} i + \sum_{i=1}^{5} 1 = 3(1 + 2 + 3 + 4 + 5) + 5 = 50$. Do not make the mistake of thinking that $\sum_{i=1}^{5} 1 = 1$.

Another situation which avoids the use of an ellipsis is when writing infinite sums. For example, the sum to infinity of the geometric series with first term 1 and common ratio $\frac{1}{2}$ is written

$$\sum_{k=0}^{\infty} (\tfrac{1}{2})^k,$$

and, as will be seen in appendix E, this is equal to 2.

There is an analogous notation for the *product* of terms of a sequence, which works in exactly the same way but uses $\prod$ instead of $\sum$. Here the upper case Greek letter pi is equivalent the English P, so this is called pi notation. In addition, a similar notation is used with unions and intersections of sets, and there is plenty of flexibility to represent various useful expressions. Here are some examples:

$$\prod_{i=1}^{n} i = 1 \times 2 \times 3 \times \cdots \times n = n!;$$

$$\prod_{i=2}^{9} \frac{i+1}{i-1} = \frac{3}{1} \times \frac{4}{2} \times \frac{5}{3} \times \frac{6}{4} \times \frac{7}{5} \times \frac{8}{6} \times \frac{9}{7} \times \frac{10}{8} = 45;$$

$$\bigcup_{1 \leq i \leq 5} A_i = A_1 \cup A_2 \cup A_3 \cup A_4 \cup A_5;$$

$$\sum_{1 \leq i < j \leq 4} |A_i \cap A_j| = |A_1 \cap A_2| + |A_1 \cap A_3| + |A_1 \cap A_4| \\ + |A_2 \cap A_3| + |A_2 \cap A_4| + |A_3 \cap A_4|.$$

Note the use of the inequality below the sigma in the final example to indicate that we want to add six expressions each of which depends on a different choice of two sets from four.

Exercise B

1. Find the value of
   (a) $\sum_{k=1}^{7} k^2$;

   (b) $\sum_{i=2}^{8} 2^{i-2}$;

   (c) $\sum_{r=1}^{6} \frac{1}{2}r(r+1)$;

   (d) $\sum_{i=1}^{1000} (-1)^i$;

   (e) $\sum_{k=1}^{4} p_k^k$ where p_k is the kth prime number.

2. Use sigma or pi notation to express
   (a) the binomial theorem, equation (3.4);
   (b) the hockey stick theorem in question 8 of exercise 3a;
   (c) the binomial sum in question 6 of exercise 4a;
   (d) the multinomial coefficient, equation (3.6).

Appendix C

Polynomials

A *polynomial* is an algebraic expression such as $5x^2 - 2x^3 + \sqrt{2}x^2 + 3x - 1.234$, which consists of the *terms* $5x^2$, $-2x^3$, $\sqrt{2}x^2$, $3x$ and -1.234 added together. Each term is made up of a non-negative integer power of x, such as x^3, multiplied by a number (possibly zero) which is known as the *coefficient*. For example, the coefficient of x^3 in the example is -2 and the coefficient of x^4 is 0. The terms are usually arranged in decreasing order of the powers and the first term (with a non-zero coefficient) is known as the *leading term*. The *degree* of a polynomial is the power of its leading term. The example has degree 5 and is a *quintic*, and polynomials of degree 4, 3, and 2 are known respectively as *quartics*, *cubics* and *quadratics*. A linear polynomial is of degree 1 and a non-zero constant polynomial is of degree 0.

When several linear polynomials are multiplied together, the result is a polynomial of higher degree. For example, the result of multiplying out the three brackets $(x+2)(x+3)(2x+1)$ is a cubic. One way of doing this is to begin with $(x+3)(2x+1)$ to obtain $2x^2 + x + 6x + 3$. When like terms are collected together this becomes $2x^2 + 7x + 3$. It is then multiplied by $x+2$ to obtain

$$(x+2)(2x^2 + 7x + 3) = 2x^3 + 7x^2 + 3x + 4x^2 + 14x + 6,$$

which in turn becomes $2x^3 + 11x^2 + 17x + 6$.

An alternative approach, which involves combinatorial methods, is to examine the expression $(x+2)(x+3)(2x+1)$ and work out each of the coefficients directly. Let us focus on the term in x^2. This can be produced in three different ways. We might multiply the x in the first bracket by the x in the second bracket by the 1 in the third bracket and obtain x^2. Alternatively we might multiply the x in the first bracket by the 3 in the second bracket by the $2x$ in the third bracket and get $6x^2$. Finally we could multiply the 2 in the first bracket by the x in the second bracket by the $2x$ in the third bracket to obtain $4x^2$. Gathering these three terms together we obtain the $11x^2$ in the final expression. With practice this process becomes quite straightforward, so long as there are not too many brackets to multiply.

The reverse process, expressing $2x^3 + 11x^2 + 17x + 6$ as $(x+2)(x+3)(2x+1)$, is known as factorising and is much harder to do.

Exercise C

Write each of the following as single polynomials with powers in decreasing order.

1. $(x-1)(x+4)(x-2)$.

2. $(x-1)(x^3 + x^2 + x + 1)$.

3. $(x+2)(x^4 - 2x^3 + 4x^2 - 8x + 16)$.

4. $(x^2 - 2x + 3)(x^2 + x - 5)$.

5. $(3x-1)(4x+3) - (x-3)(x+2) - (2x-1)(x+5)$.

Appendix D

Mathematical induction

Suppose you wish to prove that something is true for all natural numbers. This may seem like a daunting task, as there are infinitely many cases to check, one for each such number. A useful tool for doing this is the technique of *mathematical induction*. It formalises the obvious fact that every natural number can be reached by starting at 1 and repeatedly adding 1.

Mathematical induction (or, loosely, induction) uses the fact that the natural numbers behave like a step-ladder. If we want to reach any point on the ladder then

(i) we must be able to get onto the ladder;
(ii) we must have a method for moving from one rung to the next.

We use induction to prove propositions about natural numbers. We call the proposition to be proved the *inductive hypothesis*, the first step the *base* of the induction and the process of moving from $n = k$ to $n = k+1$ the *step*. It is important to set proofs by induction out properly so that the logic of the process is explicit.

For example, let us use mathematical induction to prove that $\sum_{i=1}^{n} i = \frac{1}{2}n(n+1)$.

Inductive hypothesis
$\sum_{i=1}^{n} i = \frac{1}{2}n(n+1)$.

Base
If $n = 1$, the left-hand side is 1 and the right-hand side is $\frac{1}{2} \times 1 \times 2$, which also equals 1.

Step

We assume the inductive hypothesis for $n = k$, namely that $\sum_{i=1}^{k} i = \frac{1}{2}k(k+1)$. Then we consider the sum $\sum_{i=1}^{k+1} i$. This can be written as $(k+1) + \sum_{i=1}^{k} i$ which, by the inductive hypothesis, is equal to

$$\frac{1}{2}k(k+1) + (k+1) = \frac{1}{2}(k+1)(k+2)$$
$$= \frac{1}{2}(k+1)((k+1)+1).$$

We have shown that the inductive hypothesis for $n = k$ implies the corresponding result for $n = k+1$.

Conclusion

It follows by induction that $\sum_{i=1}^{n} i = \frac{1}{2}n(n+1)$ for all $n \geq 1$.

If you are setting this out, be careful to use k for the particular integer in the step and to reserve n for a general integer.

Although induction is a very powerful method, there are some drawbacks. One is that you cannot proceed unless you have an inductive hypothesis, so it is necessary to 'guess' the result you are trying to prove. This could be done by drawing up a sequence of values and conjecturing a general result. If this seems a dubious way to proceed, there is actually nothing to worry about. You cannot use induction to prove things which are not true.

A weightier objection to the method is that, although it is very effective as a proof technique, it is not especially illuminating as to *why* a particular result should be true. In the course of this book we have said several times that combinatorial methods are preferable in proving combinatorial facts. Indeed, problem 4.2 was about a combinatorial proof of the result we have just shown by induction. Since it is really an algebraic result, this is not so important, but while it is quite possible to prove many combinatorial identities, such as Pascal's identity (equation (3.3) on page 32), using induction, it is preferable to use more appropriate methods to show why they are true. All the same, there are some areas of the subject where the method is widely used. It will often turn out that the step involves real combinatorial insights, so the general criticism is perhaps not so pertinent. It is also clear that induction is particularly suitable for arguments about recursion, and it can, of course, be used to solve recurrence relations, so long as we can guess the form of the general term of the sequence. Some of the questions in exercise D also appear in exercise 6b of the main text where induction is avoided.

Appendix D: Mathematical induction

The method of induction can be extended in various ways. The base case could, of course, be $n = 0$ or any integer (including negative ones, if it makes sense). We can also use a form where the base case is $n = 1$ and $n = 2$ and the step assumes the proposition for $n = k$ and $n = k+1$ and deduces it for $n = k+2$. This is particularly appropriate for second-order linear recurrences with constant coefficients.

Exercise D

1. For each of the following recurrence relations, conjecture the form of the solution and use mathematical induction to verify your conjecture.
   (a) $t_{n+1} = 2t_n + n$; $t_1 = 2$.
   (b) $t_{n+1} = 2t_n + 2^n$; $t_1 = 1$.
   (c) $t_{n+2} = t_{n+1} + 2t_n$; $t_0 = 7$, $t_1 = 8$.

2. Prove by induction that
$$\sum_{i=1}^{n} \frac{1}{i(i+1)} = \frac{n}{n+1}$$
   for $n \geq 1$.

3. Prove by induction that $2^n < n!$ for $n \geq 4$.

4. Prove that any postage over 43p can be made up using only 5p and 12p stamps.

5. Let S be a finite set of natural numbers. Criticise these alleged proofs of the proposition that all the elements of S are equal.
   (a) We use induction on $|S|$. If $|S| = 1$, it only has one element and the proposition is trivially true. Suppose now that we have proved the result for $|S| = k$. Consider now a set S of $k+1$ elements. Let S_1 be the subset of S consisting of its first k elements and let S_2 be the subset of S consisting of its last k elements. Since $|S_1| = k = |S_2|$, all elements of these two sets are equal. However,

the two sets overlap, so it follows that all elements of S are equal. The result follows by induction.

(b) We use induction on the largest element of S. If this is 1, then all elements of S are 1 and the base of the induction is established. Suppose that the proposition is true for all sets with largest element k. Let S be a set with largest element $k+1$. Reduce all the elements of S by 1 to produce a set S^* with largest element k. By the inductive hypothesis all elements of S^* are equal. Now we simply add 1 to every element in S^* to reproduce the original S with all its elements equal. The result follows by induction.

Appendix E

Finite and infinite series

The following results on sums of integer powers are worth knowing. Combinatorial proofs of them can be found in chapter 4, and they can also be tackled by induction.

$$\sum_{i=1}^{n} i = \tfrac{1}{2}n(n+1);$$

$$\sum_{i=1}^{n} i^2 = \tfrac{1}{6}n(n+1)(2n+1);$$

$$\sum_{i=1}^{n} i^3 = \tfrac{1}{4}n^2(n+1)^2$$

$$= \left(\sum_{i=1}^{n} i\right)^2.$$

In addition, it is worthwhile knowing how to sum the terms of a *geometric progression*. This sequence is defined by means of the recurrence relation

$$u_{n+1} = r u_n;$$
$$u_1 = a.$$

The obvious solution is $u_n = ar^{n-1}$.

In general, the result of summing terms of a sequence (u_n) is called a *series*. If the number of terms of the series is finite, we define the *partial sum* of the series as $S_n = \sum_{i=1}^{n} u_i$.

The sum to n terms of the geometric progression is $S_n = \sum_{i=1}^{n} ar^{n-1}$. If $r = 1$ it is obvious that $S_n = an$. If $r \neq 1$ then we can proceed as follows. Writing out the sum 'in full' gives

$$S_n = a + ar + \cdots + ar^{n-1}.$$

Now we multiply both sides by r to produce

$$rS_n = ar + ar^2 + \cdots + ar^n.$$

Comparing this with S_n, we see that

$$rS_n = S_n + a(r^n - 1),$$

so that

$$S_n = \frac{a(r^n - 1)}{r - 1}.$$

Note that we need $r \neq 1$ to avoid dividing by zero.

Now we consider what happens as $n \to \infty$.

If $r > 1$ or $r < -1$, then the term r^n grows in magnitude without limit, meaning that its sum is not finite, and we say that the series is *divergent*. In the special case when $r = -1$, where the sum oscillates between a and $-a$, the series is also said to be divergent.

If $-1 < r < 1$, then the term r^n becomes arbitrarily small as n increases, and we say that the series is *convergent* with *sum to infinity*

$$S = \frac{1}{1 - r}.$$

Another important series is given by the general binomial theorem, which states that, for any rational number r that is not a positive integer,

$$(1 + x)^r = 1 + rx + \frac{r(r - 1)}{2!}x^2 + \cdots + \frac{r(r - 1) \cdots (r - n + 1)}{n!}x^n + \cdots.$$

This infinite series is valid only if $-1 < x < 1$.

It is worth listing some special cases of the binomial series which crop up in the book.

$r = -1$
$$(1 + x)^{-1} = 1 - x + x^2 - x^3 + \cdots + (-1)^n x^n + \cdots.$$

$r = -2$
$$(1 + x)^{-2} = 1 - 2x + 3x^2 - 4x^3 + \cdots + (-1)^n (n + 1) x^n + \cdots.$$

$r = -3$
$$(1+x)^{-3} = 1 - 3x + 6x^2 - 10x^3 + \cdots + (-1)^n \binom{n+2}{2} x^n + \cdots.$$
$r = \frac{1}{2}$
$$(1+x)^{\frac{1}{2}} = 1 + \frac{1}{2}x - \frac{1}{8}x^2 + \frac{1}{16}x^3 + \cdots + \frac{(-1)^{n-1}}{n \times 2^{2n-1}} \binom{2n-2}{n-1} x^n + \cdots.$$

Exercise E

1. Prove that $\sum_{i=1}^{n}(2i-1) = n^2$ for $n \geq 1$, by using sigma algebra and the formula for $\sum_{i=1}^{n} i$.

2. Prove that $\sum_{i=1}^{n} i^2 = \frac{1}{6}n(n+1)(2n+1)$ for $n \geq 1$
   (a) by induction;
   (b) by considering the expression $\sum_{i=1}^{n} i^3 - \sum_{i=1}^{n}(i-1)^3$.

3. Prove that $\sum_{i=1}^{n} i^3 = \frac{1}{4}n^2(n+1)^2$ for $n \geq 1$
   (a) by induction;
   (b) in a way analogous to question 2(b).

4. Evaluate $\sum_{i=1}^{n} ir^i$ by multiplying the series by $(1-r)^2$, and find the sum to infinity under conditions to be stated.

5. Evaluate $\sum_{i=1}^{n} i^2 r^i$ by a similar method to question 4, and find the sum to infinity under conditions to be stated.

Appendix F

Congruences

The idea of dividing one integer by another and obtaining a remainder is a familiar one. For example, if 27 is divided by 4 the remainder is 3 since $27 = 6 \times 4 + 3$.

It is often useful to focus on remainders, and there is specific notation for doing so. To express the fact that 27 leaves remainder 3 on division by 4 we write $27 \equiv 3 \pmod{4}$, and say '27 is *congruent* to 3 *modulo* 4'.

To allow ourselves a little more flexibility, we also say that two numbers are congruent modulo n if they leave the same remainder on division by n. Thus the statements $27 \equiv 11 \pmod{4}$ and $27 \equiv -1 \pmod{4}$ are also true. (When teaching division with remainder, few primary school teachers would ask students what -1 divided by 4 is, but the correct answer is -1 with a remainder of 3.) In fact there are infinitely many integers, positive and negative, which are congruent to 27 modulo 4. The following congruences are also all true, and you should take a moment to check them:

$$12 \equiv 2 \pmod{10};$$
$$35 \equiv 0 \pmod{7};$$
$$23 \equiv 47 \pmod{12};$$
$$7 + 8 \equiv 4 \pmod{11};$$
$$7 \times 8 \equiv 1 \pmod{11}.$$

Thinking of congruence only in terms of remainders is a little clumsy, but fortunately there are many equivalent ways to define the concept. It is worth keeping the following two in mind:

(i) $x \equiv y \pmod{n}$ if $x - y$ is a multiple of n;
(ii) $x \equiv y \pmod{n}$ if there is a whole number k such that $x = y + nk$.

Either definition can be used to show that, for example, $-18 \equiv -25 \pmod{7}$.

We can use definition (ii) to prove an important result about modular arithmetic:

if $a_1 \equiv a_2 \pmod{n}$ and $b_1 \equiv b_2 \pmod{n}$, then

$$a_1 + b_1 \equiv a_2 + b_2 \pmod{n}$$

and

$$a_1 b_1 \equiv a_2 b_2 \pmod{n}.$$

The proof is straightforward. We are given that $a_1 = a_2 + nj$ and $b_1 = b_2 + nk$ for some integers j and k. Therefore $a_1 + b_1 = a_2 + nj + b_2 + nk = (a_2 + b_2) + n(j + k)$ and $a_1 b_1 = (a_2 + nj)(b_2 + nk) = a_2 b_2 + n(jb_2 + ka_2 + njk)$.

The point of this result is that in a calculation where we only care about the result modulo n, we can change the numbers to smaller ones before performing the calculation.

For example, to find $89 + 68 \pmod{11}$ we note that $89 \equiv 1 \pmod{11}$ and $68 \equiv 2 \pmod{11}$ so the answer is 3. This saves the hassle of actually computing $89 + 68 = 157$ and then subtracting 154. Moreover, $89 \times 68 \equiv 1 \times 2 \pmod{11}$ and calculating 1×2 is rather more appealing than calculating 89×68. Similarly, to compute the remainder when 167^2 is divided by 17, we need not actually square 167. Instead we note that $167^2 \equiv (-3)^2 \equiv 9 \pmod{17}$.

Modular arithmetic is a large subject in its own right, but for our purposes it is enough to be familiar with the $x \equiv y \pmod{n}$ notation.

Appendix F: Congruences

Exercise F

1. In each case find an integer between 0 and $n-1$ inclusive which is congruent to x modulo n.
   (a) $x = 169 + 489$, $n = 16$.
   (b) $x = 57 \times 73$, $n = 8$.
   (c) $x = 1542^2$, $n = 10$.
   (d) $x = 599 \times 1512$, $n = 15$.
   (e) $x = 13^8$, $n = 17$.

2. Which of the following statements are true?
   (a) $3^6 \equiv 1 \pmod{7}$.
   (b) $x^6 \equiv 1 \pmod{7}$ for all integers x.
   (c) If $x \equiv 1 \pmod{6}$, then $x \equiv 1 \pmod{3}$.
   (d) If $x \equiv 2 \pmod{3}$, then $x^2 \equiv 1 \pmod{3}$.
   (e) If $x \equiv 2 \pmod{3}$, then $x^2 \equiv 4 \pmod{9}$.
   (f) If $x^2 \equiv 1 \pmod{8}$, then $x \equiv \pm 1 \pmod{8}$.
   (g) If $x^2 \equiv 5 \pmod{11}$, then $x \equiv \pm 4 \pmod{11}$.
   (h) If a, b and c are integers with no common factor and $a^2 = b^2 + c^2$, then a is an odd number.

Hints

Hints for some of the questions in some of the exercises.

1b 3. Partitions are hard enough to begin with, but when they involve stipulated (and arbitrary) parts, the only sensible way to proceed is to draw up a table. In this case, it is sensible to tabulate the number of ways in which particular amounts can be split up with the largest denomination of coin specified.

1b 4. Consider suspending the cube from A.

2a 5(a). Distinguish between the cases where the first digit is even or odd.

2b 2(g). Does it matter how close together the Ns are?

2b 5. Start with a letter which is not repeated.

3a 10. Calculate the difference between the numbers of arrangements with even and odd numbers of red counters.

3b 4. Use glue.

3b 6. The question asks for the 'maximum' number. Does this say something about how the lines are drawn? Now draw the lines one by one, ensuring that no possible region is omitted.

3b 8. Begin with the consonants.

3b 10. Is it possible to reduce this to problem 3.6?

3b 12. Think carefully about what makes two arrangements of players into pairs different.

3b 15. Try drawing a statistical chart to show Isaac's performance.

3b 16. Label each book with its destination parcel.

3c 2. Make the inequality into an equation.

4a 1. Treat separately the cases where r and s are equal and unequal.

4a 5. Choose a quiz team which reflects the make-up of the club, and later think about issues of leadership.

4a 7. Write the compositions as sums, such as $2 + 3 + 1 + 2 + 1 + 1$.

4b 4. Can you tell that a partition is self-conjugate by examining the Ferrers diagram?

4b 5. What is another way of writing $\binom{n}{2}$? Add this number of dots to the Ferrers diagram.

4b 6. Begin with a partition of n into odd parts. Let these parts be $k_1, k_1, \ldots, k_1, k_2, \ldots, k_2, \ldots, k_r, \ldots, k_r$, so that k_i occurs n_i times with $\sum n_i k_i = n$. Split up the numbers $n_i k_i$ in such a way that the resulting numbers are all distinct, and that you have created a bijection between partitions of odd parts and partitions with distinct parts.

4b 7. Add a line parallel to the base of the triangle and one unit below it, and 'extend' the diagram to meet the new line.

4b 8. If the row and column sums are odd, what can you say about n and m?

4c 3. What determines how many zeros there are as a result of a multiplication?

4c 7(c). What is true about the sequence of images of the elements 1, 2, $\ldots, m$?

6b 2. Use a substitution of the form $t_n = u_n + an + b$.

6b 3. Use a substitution of the form $t_n = a \times 2^n u_n$.

6b 4. Find a recurrence relation for $u_n = t_{n+1} - t_n$.

Hints

6b 5. Use the substitution $t_n = n! \times u_n$.

7b 3. Replace x_1 by y_1, x_2 by $y_1 + y_2$, and so on.

7c 6. In calculating $G(x)$, divide out the expression on the right-hand side before dividing through by $1 - 2x$.

8b 8. Take another look at the solution to problem 8.7.

8d 3. Let a_n be the number of problems she has solved up to and including day n so that $a_{30} = 45$. Now let $b_n = a_n + 13$ and prove that $a_i = b_j$ for some i and j.

8d 4. If you consider the special case where the n numbers are the first n powers of 10, you obtain a question very similar to problem 8.12 on page 137.

8d 5. Work modulo n. If you know two consecutive terms in the sequence, you can find the *previous* term as well as the next one.

8f 5(c). First prove that there are three pairs with even sum.

8f 7. You can turn any set of triangles into a set of scalene triangles by removing all the isosceles triangles.

8f 8. It might be easier to find the smallest possible number of red points.

8f 9. Look for a triangle with two short sides.

9a 2. Try to adapt the solution to problem 9.2.

9a 4. This is somewhat similar to problem 9.3.

9b 1. We have already met a colouring that works.

9b 2. Invent a new colouring based on one used in problem 9.6.

9b 4. Find a triangular analogue to the standard chessboard colouring.

9b 5. We have already met a colouring that works.

9b 6. We have already met a colouring that works.

9b 7. We have already met a colouring that works.

9d 8. The moves available feel similar to knight's moves. Try adapting the colouring used in problem 9.14.

10a 3. Rather than focus on the whole board, ignore some of the squares entirely.

10a 4. Set up a coordinate system with the origin at X.

10b 2. Find a common feature of $(-4+18), (-24+17), (-19+40)$ and $(-48+13)$.

10b 5. Note that $xy + x + y = (x+1)(y+1) - 1$.

10c 5. Write the numbers in prime factorised form, and focus on the exponents.

10d 4. Use induction.

11a 8. Consider a graph of fuel available against distance travelled.

Solutions

Solutions to every question in all the exercises.

Exercise 1a

1. There are 24 possible menus, shown in table 1a.A.

APX	APY	AQX	AQY	ARX	ARY	ASX	ASY
BPX	BPY	BQX	BQY	BRX	BRY	BSX	BSY
CPX	CPY	CQX	CQY	CRX	CRY	CSX	CSY

   Table 1a.A

2. There are 30 permutations, shown in table 1a.B.

ACCOO	ACOCO	ACOOC	AOCCO	AOCOC	AOOCC
CACOO	CAOCO	CAOOC	CCAOO	CCOAO	CCOOA
COACO	COAOC	COCAO	COCOA	COOAC	COOCA
OACCO	OACOC	OAOCC	OCACO	OCAOC	OCCAO
OCCOA	OCOAC	OCOCA	OOACC	OOCAC	OOCCA

   Table 1a.B

3. (a) There are 56 outcomes, shown in table 1a.C on the following page.
   (b) Now there are six outcomes for the red die, six for the white die and six for the blue die, so, as in question 1, there are $6^3 = 216$ outcomes, rather too many to list!

4. There are 13 lines with a length of six *moras*, shown in table 1a.D on the next page.

111	112	113	114	115	116	122	123
124	125	126	133	134	135	136	144
145	146	155	156	166	222	223	224
225	226	233	234	235	236	244	245
246	255	256	266	333	334	335	336
344	345	346	355	356	366	444	445
446	455	456	466	555	556	566	666

Table 1a.C

HHH HHLL HLHL HLLH HLLLL
LHHL LHLH LHLLL LLHH
LLHLL LLLHL LLLLH LLLLLL

Table 1a.D

5. There are 11 partitions, shown in table 1a.E.

111111 21111 2211 222
3111 321 33 411 42 51 6

Table 1a.E

6. For the alphabetical ordering, the result of converting to binary codes is shown in table 1a.F.

00111	01011	10011	01101	10101
11001	01110	10110	11010	11100

Table 1a.F

For the colex ordering, we have table 1a.G, which is in increasing alphabetical ordering of the binary numbers. It will therefore turn out that ranking and unranking is more straightforward for the colex ordering.

00111	01011	01101	01110	10011
10101	10110	11001	11010	11100

Table 1a.G

7. (a) 90 (b) THHHTTHH

8. (a) 229 (b) YMNODA
9. (a) 44
   (b) CTY
10. The following method is due to the mathematician Narayana Pandit, who flourished in India in the fourteenth century. We describe the method for N numbers and denote the number in position k by $a(k)$.
    (i) Find the largest k such that $a(k) < a(k+1)$ and then the largest ℓ such that $a(k) < a(\ell)$.
    (ii) Swap $a(k)$ and $a(\ell)$.
    (iii) Reverse all the numbers from $a(k+1)$ to $a(N)$.

    Let us see how this works. We begin with the permutation 1234. The first k is 3 and the first ℓ is 4, so we swap 3 and 4. Now $k+1 = 4$ and there is nothing to reverse. This produces the second permutation 1243.

    Next, we see that $k = 2$ and $\ell = 3$, so we swap 2 and 3 to produce 1342. Next we reverse the sequence 42 to give 24, and so the third permutation is 1324.

    Now $k = 2$ and $\ell = 4$, so we swap 4 and 2 to produce 1342. Again there is nothing to reverse, so this is the fourth permutation.

    You should check that the algorithm works to produce the whole of the alphabetical ordering.

Exercise 1b

1. (a) A shortest path from left to right involves five hexagons. It is clearly impossible to reach the other side using only four hexagons and there are many ways of achieving this limit with five. We can enumerate them in exactly the same way as we did for problem 1.4 on page 8 (see the diagram on the left of figure 1b.A on the following page).

   Hence there are 45 shortest paths from the left to the right.

   (b) We may repeat the process in the other direction (see the diagram on the right of figure 1b.A).

   If we are in the second or fourth columns, there is no reason to switch to an adjacent column, since that would increase the

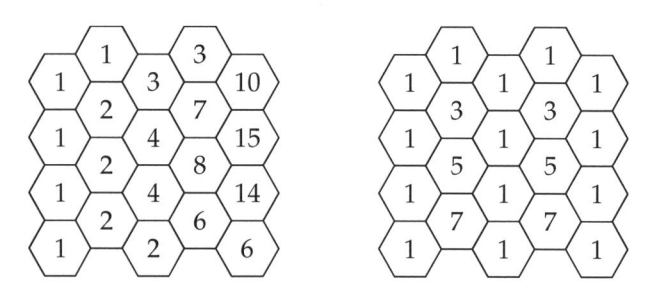

Figure 1b.A

length of the path. In the other three columns, it is permissible to switch. Hence the odd-numbered columns consist entirely of 1s, whereas the even-numbered columns increase in value.

Hence there are 17 shortest paths from the top to the bottom.

2. The reason why this approach is appropriate is that we can think of the series of days in terms of a 'flow diagram'. S is a day spent surfing, W one spent water-skiing and X is a rest day.

   (i) S can be followed by S or X
   (ii) W can be followed by W or X
   (iii) X can be followed by S, W or X

Table 1b.A is constructed in the following way. The columns stand for the numbers of days, and the entry in the table is the number of ways to have a sequence ending in S, X or W.

The first day can be S, X or W, so all the entries in the first column are 1. Suppose we have constructed the table up to a certain column. To get the entry in the S row and the next column, add the values for S and X in the previous column. Do the same thing for the W row. However, with the X row, add all three entries in the previous column.

Activity	1	2	3	4	5	6	7	8	9
S	1	2	5	12	29	70	169	408	985
X	1	3	7	17	41	99	239	577	1393
W	1	2	5	12	29	70	169	408	985

Table 1b.A

Solutions

The solution to the problem is the sum of the entries in the ninth column, so there are 3363 different ways Isaac can organise his holiday.

3. Table 1b.B shows the number of ways in which particular amounts can be split up with the largest denomination of coin specified.

Amount (p)	\multicolumn{5}{c}{Largest coin used (p)}
	1	2	5	10	20	50
5	1	2	1	0	0	0
10	1	5	4	1	0	0
15	1	7	10	4	0	0
20	1	10	18	11	1	0
25	1	12	29	22	4	0
30	1	15	42	40	11	0
35	1	17	58	64	22	0
40	1	20	76	98	41	0
45	1	22	97	140	68	0
50	1	25	120	195	109	1
55	1	27	146	260	162	4
60	1	30	174	341	236	11
65	1	32	205	434	328	22
70	1	35	238	546	450	41
75	1	37	274	672	596	68
80	1	40	312	820	782	109
85	1	42	353	984	1000	162
90	1	45	396	1173	1270	236
95	1	47	442	1380	1580	328
100	1	50	490	1615	1955	451

Table 1b.B

The second column simply says that any amount made up of 1p coins can only be split up in one way. The third column relies on the fact that a partition depends only the number of 2p coins used. This can be any number between 1 and half the amount (ignoring any remainder). All the other entries in the grid are calculated in the following way. As an example, consider the entry corresponding to (75, 20). We know that there is a 20p coin used, so what remains is 55p to be divided into parts which are at most 20. But this is the sum of the grid entries in the cells $(55, 20)$, $(55, 10)$, $(55, 5)$, $(55, 2)$ and $(55, 1)$, namely 596.

Now the solution is the sum of the entries in the 100p row, which is 4562.

4. With the cube suspended from A, allowable routes travel downwards from A to B because each route is made up of six unit segments in directions parallel to the edges of the cube.

The diagrams in figure 1b.B show the number of routes from A to other points on the surface of the cube.

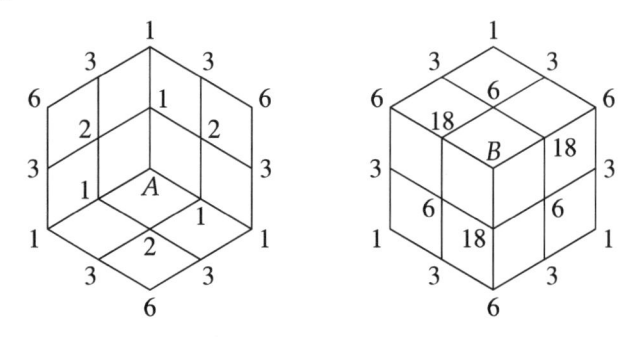

Figure 1b.B

Hence there are $18 + 18 + 18 = 54$ routes from A to B.

5. The reason for the elaborate story is to make it clear that the recipient of the gift is able to take any cube and look at it in any position. In addition, the order in which the three cubes are taken from the bag makes no difference.

If, on a particular cube, the number of faces painted green is zero, one, five or six, there is only one cube which can result. If two faces are painted green, then these might be opposite or adjacent faces, so there are two possible cubes. If three faces are painted green, then they might form a 'collar' (with two opposite faces and one other) or a 'cap' (with no opposite faces) and so again there are two possible cubes. The reader should visualise the effect of rotating these to clarify that all collars are the same and all caps are the same.

Now we consider the distribution of faces between the three cubes in the bag, in each case counting the number of possible gifts. In table 1b.C, the first three columns are the number of faces painted green, so it is clear that the remaining faces are yellow. Since the order of cubes is not important, we can label them A, B and C so that the number of green faces in A is greater than or equal to the number in B which is, in turn, greater than or equal to the number in C.

Cube A	Cube B	Cube C	Gifts
6	3	0	$1 \times 2 \times 1 = 2$
6	2	1	$1 \times 2 \times 1 = 2$
5	4	0	$1 \times 2 \times 1 = 2$
5	3	1	$1 \times 2 \times 1 = 2$
5	2	2	3
4	4	1	3
4	3	2	$2 \times 2 \times 2 = 8$
3	3	3	4

Table 1b.C

In the first row, the cubes are distinguishable, and so the calculation in the third column is based on the fact that there is one possible cube with 6 green faces, two with 3 and one with 0. The same logic applies to the next three rows and the seventh. In the fifth row, cubes B and C might be two opposites, two adjacents or one of each, so there are three different gifts possible. In the sixth row, the argument is the same but applied to collars and caps for cubes A and B. In the final row, the cubes are all either collars or caps; they might be all collars, two collars and a cap, one collar and two caps or all three caps, so there are four different gifts. Adding up the numbers in the final column, we see that the solution is 26.

6. Note first that in any rotation or reflection adjacent faces remain adjacent and opposite faces remain opposite. Hence faces 1 and 2 are always adjacent. Without loss of generality we can take face 1 as the base. The top face can be 3, 4, 5 or 6. Call the four faces making the sides a 'ring' and note that ordering the numbers clockwise or anticlockwise makes no difference since numberings are indistinguishable under reflection.

Top face 3
   The ring is formed by 2, 4, 5 and 6, with 5 adjacent to 4 and 6

and opposite to 2. There is only one such cube possible, since the ring is 2 4 5 6.

Top face 4

The ring is formed by 2, 3, 5 and 6, with 2 and 3 adjacent and 5 and 6 adjacent. There are two such cubes since 2 can be opposite to 5 or 6.

Top face 5

The ring is formed by 2, 3, 4 and 6, with 2, 3 and 4 adjacent. There is one such cube since 3 is opposite to 6.

Top face 6

The ring is formed by 2, 3, 4 and 5 in order, so there is one such cube.

Hence there are five distinct numberings of the cube.

In the real world, numbered cubes can be rotated about axes but cannot be reflected in a plane of symmetry without becoming a new cube. This situation is explored in the following question.

7. Place the die with the 1 on the bottom. There are 5 choices for the number on the top face. After choosing that, place the smallest remaining number on the front face. Then there are $3! = 6$ ways of placing the last three numbers. Hence altogether there are $5 \times 6 = 30$ ways to number the die.

Exercise 2a

1. (a) If we label each activity by its initial letter, we see that this problem is about permutations of ROCKY, and there are $5! = 120$ of these.
   (b) Now there are 5 choices for the first day's activity and then 4 choices for each subsequent day, so the number of schedules is $5 \times 4^4 = 1280$. This is a permutation with replacement under the condition that consecutive choices are different.
   (c) Of the 120 permutations of ROCKY, half will have R before C and half will have C before R, so there are 60 choices of the first type.
   (d) Of the 60 permutations with R before C, half will have Y before O, so there are 30 choices of this type. Alternatively, there are six ways in which ROCY can be arranged, namely RCOY, ROCY, ROYC, OYRC, ORYC and OCRY, and now the K can be introduced into any one of these five places.

2. These are just the 1320 permutations of 3 objects from 12.

3. The black square can be chosen in 32 ways. Once this is chosen, the row and column in which it lies are eliminated, and now there are 24 choices for the white square. Hence there are 768 ways in which the two squares can be chosen.

4. In the top row, there are eight squares for the first rook. Now there are only seven squares available in the second row, six in the third, and so on, so the answer is $8! = 40\,320$.

5. (a) If the first digit is even, it cannot be 0, so there are $4 \times 5^6 = 62\,500$ such numbers. If, however, the first digit is odd, there are $5^7 = 78\,125$ numbers. The total is $140\,625$.
   (b) If the last digit is even, it is 0, and if odd it is 5. So we count the choices by looking at the digits in the reverse order and there are $2 \times 5 \times 4 \times 4 \times 3 \times 3 \times 2 = 2880$ numbers

6. We have to omit one of the digits, but, as the number which results has to be divisible by 3, this has to be the 3, since otherwise the digit sum is not divisible by 3. This leaves us with 1, 2, 4 and 5. The last digit has to be even, so we choose the digits from the right to the left, and there are $2 \times 3! = 12$ ways of doing this.

7. The total number of numbers between 1000 and 9999 is $9 \times 10^3 = 9000$ (which is obvious anyway) and there are $9 \times 9 \times 8 \times 7 = 4536$ without a repeated digit, so the number with a repeated digit is 4464.

8. James can choose any of three colours to go in the first, second, third and fourth places. This yields $3^4 = 81$ arrangements. However, he cannot choose four blue balls, since he only has three. This is the only arrangement he cannot make, and so the solution to the problem is 80.

9. Start by seating couple X, so as to establish a fixed point; now the other three couples can be arranged in 3! ways. Next the individual in each couple can be arranged in $2^4 = 16$ ways, and so the solution to the problem is 96.

10. (a) Assuming that the fans are distinguishable as human beings, the solution is $8! = 40\,320$.
    (b) By the same argument as question 9, the solution is $2! \times 4! \times 3! \times 2! = 576$.

Exercise 2b

1. Abbreviating the titles as N, I and C, we need the permutations of NNNIIIICCCCC, and there are $\binom{12}{3\,4\,5} = 27\,720$ ways of arranging this collection, which clearly belongs to a discriminating bibliophile.

2. (a) This is the easiest question in the book, since there is only one such permutation.
   (b) Think of AAAAA as a single letter; we now have a permutation of B, N, N, R, M and the megaA, and there are $\frac{6!}{2} = 360$ permutations of these letters.
   (c) Now think of BNNRM as being a single letter. We now have six letters consisting of this and the five As, and there are 6 ways of arranging these. Now allow the letters of BNNRM to permute amongst themselves; there are $\frac{5!}{2} = 60$ ways of doing this, and so the answer is 360.
   (d) If the Ns are together, then there are $\binom{9}{5\,1\,1\,1\,1} = 3024$ permutations; hence there are $15\,120 - 3024 = 12\,096$ permutations with

Solutions

the Ns separated.

(e) Now the answer is $360 - 5! = 240$.

(f) First place the As and Ns as AAAAANN. Now insert the B; this can be done in 8 ways. Next the R can be inserted in 9 ways and then the M in 10 ways. Hence the answer is $8 \times 9 \times 10 = 720$ ways.

(g) If the resulting word includes the sequence ANANA, then it is a permutation of B, R, M, A, A and ANANA, and there are $\frac{6!}{2}$ of these. If it contains the two sequences ANA and ANA, then it is permutation of B, R, M, A, ANA and ANA, and again there are $\frac{6!}{2}$. So the total is 720.

3. We begin by arranging the letters of UCCE; there are $\frac{4!}{2} = 12$ ways of doing this. Now there are five 'gaps' for the Ss to be placed, including a space at the start and one at the end. Distinguishing the Ss, there are $5 \times 4 \times 3 = 60$ ways of placing them, but then when the subscripts are removed, there are only 10 ways. So the answer is 120.

4. If the three letters are all different there are $5 \times 4 \times 3 = 60$ possible permutations.

If one letter is repeated exactly twice then the permutation is of the form XXY, XYX or YXX, where X is A or N, and Y is one of the four remaining letters. This gives $3 \times 2 \times 4 = 24$ permutations.

Finally there is the permutation AAA.

Hence the total number of permutations is 85.

You have to be careful about arguments of this type. It is tempting to argue as follows. Place subscripts to make all the letters distinguishable, consider the $10 \times 9 \times 8 = 720$ permutations of three of these and then divide by some cleverly chosen number to deal with the overcounting. Unfortunately this approach, which worked well when finding ten-letter permutations of BANANARAMA, fails here. The reason is that the overcounting is not uniform when dealing with three-letter permutations. A list of the 10! permutations of $BA_1N_1A_2N_2A_3RA_4MA_5$ contains every permutation of BANANARAMA exactly $5! \times 2!$ times. On the other hand, a list of the 720 three-letter permutations contains BRM only once but ANA $5 \times 2 \times 4 = 40$ times.

5. Choose one of the distinguishable letters, for example B, to be at the head of the table and count the remainder clockwise. The result is

a permutation of ANANARAMA and there are $\binom{9}{5\,2\,1\,1\,1} = 1512$ of these.

Exercise 3a

1. This is $\binom{12}{6} = 924$.

2. Since the teams are distinguishable, this is $\binom{15}{6} \times \binom{9}{6} = 420\,420$.

3. (a) There are $\binom{49}{6} = 13\,983\,816$, almost 14 million, different ways.
   (b) The player must not only choose 3 of the 6 winning numbers but also 3 of the 43 losing numbers. The number of ways of doing this is $\binom{6}{3} \times \binom{43}{3} = 246\,820$.
   (c) Using the same argument as above, this is $\binom{6}{3} \times \binom{43}{3} + \binom{6}{4} \times \binom{43}{2} + \binom{6}{5} \times 43 + 1$, which is $260\,624$.
   (d) This is obviously 6.
   (e) The probabilities are shown in table 3a.A.

Winning numbers	Probability (to 3 sf)
3	0.0177
4	0.000969
5	0.0000184
5 and bonus	0.000000429
6	0.0000000715
Any win	0.0187

   Table 3a.A

4. This is $\binom{8}{5} \times \binom{10}{6} = 11\,760$.

5. There are either three, four or five women, and so the answer is $\binom{7}{3} \times \binom{6}{2} + \binom{7}{4} \times \binom{6}{1} + \binom{7}{5} = 756$.

   If you begin by choosing three women, which can be done in $\binom{7}{3}$ ways, and then pick two of the remaining ten people in $\binom{10}{2}$ ways, you obtain an answer of 1575. This tempting argument is incorrect, because you have counted some possibilities more than once. For example, you might choose Gertie from the women and then Mabel from the remaining people, or you might choose Mabel from the women and Gertie from the rest. Thus the committee with both Gertie and Mabel has been counted at least twice. There is no 'quick fix' to this mistake; you cannot just divide 1575 by a convenient integer to obtain the correct answer.

6. This is the multinomial coefficient $\binom{12}{2\;3\;5\;2}$, which equals 166 320.

7. Either work with algebraic inequalities or, much better, use Pascal's identity (equation (3.3) on page 32), referring each row to the one above it. Since we begin with 1 on its own, the symmetry follows.

8. Now $\binom{n+1}{m+1}$ is the number of subsets of $\{1, 2, \ldots, n+1\}$ with $m+1$ members. We can count these subsets another way by focussing on their largest element. If the largest element is $n+1$, then the remaining m numbers need to be chosen from the numbers less than $n+1$, which can be done in $\binom{n}{m}$ ways. More generally, if the largest element is $n+1-r$, then the remaining m elements need to be chosen from the numbers less than $n+1-r$, which can be done in $\binom{n-r}{m}$ ways. Summing these expressions gives the required result. If we highlight the appropriate terms in Pascal's triangle, then we get something which looks like a hockey stick. We could, of course, just use the Portkey argument repeatedly.

9. Now $\binom{n+2}{m+2}$ is the number of $m+2$ element subsets of $\{1, 2, \ldots, n+2\}$. We use a similar approach to question 8 but count the subsets by their second largest elements. If the second largest element in $n+1$, then the largest element is the only number greater than $n+1$ and the other m elements need to be chosen from the numbers less than $n+1$, which can be done in $\binom{n}{m}$ ways. More generally, if the second largest element is $n+2-r$, then the largest element needs to be chosen from the r numbers greater than $n+2-r$ and the remaining m numbers need to be chosen from the $n-r+1$ numbers less than $n+2-r$. Hence, by the multiplication principle, the number of subsets with second greatest element $n+2-r$ is $r \times \binom{n-r+1}{r}$ and summing these expressions gives the required result.

10. The number of ways of placing r red counters is $\binom{64}{r} 2^{64-r}$ since all the other squares are filled with either white or blue counters. Denote the number of arrangements with an even number of red counters by E and the number with an odd number by O. Then

$$E - O = \binom{64}{0} 2^{64} - \binom{64}{1} 2^{63} + \binom{64}{2} 2^{62} - \cdots - \binom{64}{63} 2^1 + \binom{64}{64} 2^0$$
$$= (2-1)^{64}$$
$$= 1$$

and so E exceeds O by 1.

Exercise 3b

1. This is $\binom{52}{13}$, which is approximately 6.35×10^{11}.

2. If the order of the players matters, then the first hand can be chosen in $\binom{52}{13}$ ways, the second in $\binom{39}{13}$, and the third in $\binom{26}{13}$, after which the fourth is determined. So the answer is

$$\binom{52}{13} \times \binom{39}{13} \times \binom{26}{13} \approx 5.36 \times 10^{28}.$$

   If the order of the players does not matter, we divide by 4! to produce roughly 2.24×10^{27}.

3. The number of possible poker hands is $\binom{52}{5} = 2\,598\,960$.

   Straight flush
   There are ten such hands in each suit (headed by an Ace down to a Five) and so there are 40 altogether.

   Four of a kind
   There are 13 possible denominations and, for each of these, 48 ways to complete the hand, so the answer is 624.

   Full house
   There are 13 ways to choose the denomination for the three cards and 12 ways to choose the denomination for the pair. There are four ways of choosing three suits from four and six ways of choosing two suits from four, so the number of full houses is 3744.

   Flush
   There are four possible suits, and for each these there are $\binom{13}{5} = 1287$ ways of choosing five cards, but ten of them will be straight flushes. So the answer is $4 \times (1287 - 10) = 5108$.

   Straight
   The straight can be headed by any card from Ace to Five, and there are 4^5 choices for suits. However, 40 of these are straight flushes, so the answer is $10 \times 4^5 - 40 = 10\,200$.

Three of a kind
> There are 13 choices for the denomination of the three cards and 4 choices for the suits. Now there are 48 choices for the fourth and 44 choices for the fifth card, but it does not matter what order these are chosen. So there are 54 912 such hands.

Two pairs
> The first pair can be chosen in $13 \times 6 = 78$ ways and the second in $12 \times 6 = 72$ ways, but it does not matter which order the two pairs are chosen, so we must divide by 2. Now the hand can be completed in 44 ways, so there are 123 552 such hands.

Pair
> The pair can be chosen in 78 ways, and the three cards to complete the hand in 48, 44 and 40 ways. But the order in which these three cards are picked does not matter, so we must divide by 6, and the final answer is 1 098 240.

High card
> So far, we have accounted for 1 296 420 hands so, by subtraction, the number remaining is 1 302 540.

Notice that, as we go down the classification, the different types of hand become more common. For example, hands which count as *Two pairs* are more common than *Three of a kind*, which are in turn more common than *Pairs*. Hands which only qualify as *High card* are the most common of all, since more than half of all possible hands are of this type. Indeed, it makes perfect sense for a rare hand to 'score more' than a common one, although poker, being a gambling game in which nobody can see anyone else's hand, is actually more complicated than that.

It might seem interesting to liven up the game by allowing wild cards which can take any value. These might be existing cards in the pack or extra cards, which are known as Jokers. In mathematical terms, this is not recommended, since even the addition of a single Joker produces some unexpected consequences.

Suppose, for example, that you are dealt a hand consisting of two 5s, one 7, one King and a Joker. You have two sensible options; the first is to count the Joker as a third 5 and the second is to count it as a second K. (Note that there is no possibility of achieving a *Flush*, since the 5s are of different suits.)

If *Three of a kind* ranks above *Two pairs* you will naturally choose the first option. Let us now count how many hands there are in each of the two categories. Since only natural occurrences will count as such, the number of *Two pairs* hands is still 123 552. However, the 54 912 natural occurrences of *Three of a kind* are supplemented by $13 \times \binom{4}{2} \times 48 \times 44 \div 2 = 82\,368$ hands of the type XXYZJ, giving a total of 137 280 hands in this category. We conclude that *Three of a kind* is more common than *Two pairs*, but it outranks it.

Suppose instead we decide that *Two pairs* will beat *Three of a kind*. Now the 82 368 hands with a Joker will be considered as *Two pairs*, giving a total of 205 920 in that category, as against the 54 912 natural occurences of *Three of a kind*. So it is even more absurd for *Two pairs* to outrank *Three of a kind*.

Indeed, unless you construct a complex categorisation which treats various combinations of a Joker with other cards differently from hands without a Joker, there is no way around this dilemma.

The situation is only exacerbated by having more than one Joker, or letting other cards, such as 2s, act as wild cards. This phenomenon is sufficiently well known to have a name, the *wild card poker paradox*.

4. We begin by gluing the books together to produce three mega-books, which can be arranged in six ways on the shelf. Now we unglue them and multiply by 3!, 4! and 5!, so there are 103 680 ways to arrange the books.

5. (a) Think of the bottom edge and the left-hand edge of the grid as an x-axis and a y-axis. A rectangle is defined by two diagonally opposite vertices, and these in turn are determined by two grid points on the axes. The x-axis has nine grid points and the y-axis six, so there are $\binom{9}{2} \times \binom{6}{2} = 540$ rectangles.

   (b) The approach we used in (a) for rectangles will not work, since there is a dependency between the choices on the two axes. In fact, this is a good example of a problem which is not about combinations. It is best to split it into cases.

   The biggest square you can achieve has side length 5, and it is defined by its top left-hand corner, which can be in 4 places. The next biggest square has length 4 and its top left-hand corner can be in 10 places. The same argument for squares of side 3, 2 and 1 shows that there are 18, 28 and 40 of them, and so there are

100 squares in total.

6. We will achieve the maximum number of regions if no three chords pass through a single point and no two chords are parallel. Before any chords are drawn, there is 1 region consisting of the whole circle, and drawing new chords creates extra regions. Each new chord creates one more region than the number of old chords it crosses. We see, then, that new regions arise in two ways. A region will be created for each chord drawn, and, as there are $\binom{n}{2}$ chords in total joining n points on the circumference, they give rise to $\binom{n}{2}$ extra regions. In addition, a region will be created for each intersection of two chords, and, by the argument of problem 3.5 on page 37, there are $\binom{n}{4}$ such intersections from n points on the circumference. This proves the result. The expression can be multiplied out to produce the quartic expression $\frac{1}{24}(n^4 - 6n^3 + 23n^2 - 18n + 24)$.

It is worth listing the first few terms of this sequence, since it turns out that the number of regions for 1, 2, 3, 4 and 5 points is 1, 2, 4, 8 and 16, and it is very tempting to conjecture that there are 32 regions with 6 points. Careful drawing will show that there are only 31. A little thought shows that it is impossible for the number of regions to double every time, since every new chord would have to intersect every existing region, and that will not happen. As we have seen the correct analysis yields a quartic in n. This is an excellent example of the danger of *pattern-spotting* in mathematics.

7. The approach is the same as in the previous question. Before any lines are drawn, there is one region. Each new line gives rise to a new region, and every intersection with existing lines also creates a new region. Hence the number of regions is

$$1 + \text{the number of lines} + \text{the number of intersections}$$

and this yields the expression $1 + n + \binom{n}{2}$. Note that this is also the maximum number of regions inside a circle created by n chords if they need not pass through fixed points on the circumference, since you can increase the radius of the circle (or alternatively shrink the configuration of lines) until all the intersections are inside it.

Readers who are unhappy with the 'informal' nature of these last two solutions will find further discussion of this question in chapters 6 and 10.

8. First place the 21 consonants in some order; there are 21! ways of doing this. There are now 22 gaps in which the vowels can be placed, and we have to choose five of these; this can be done in $\binom{22}{5}$ ways. Finally, there are 5! ways to arrange the vowels in order, so the final answer is $21! \times \binom{22}{5} \times 5!$, which is approximately 1.61×10^{26}.

9. First place one woman at the 'head' of the table and then arrange the other three women in six ways. There are now four gaps for the men, of which three must be chosen, and then six ways of arranging the men in the spaces. So the answer is 144.

10. Let $a^* = 1+a, b^* = 1+b, c^* = 1+c, d^* = 1+d$ and $e^* = 1+e$. Then $a^*, \ldots, e^*$ are positive integers and $a^* + b^* + c^* + d^* + e^* = 11$. So we are back to problem 3.6 on page 38 and the answer is $\binom{10}{4} = 210$. Alternatively, we can tackle this directly. Consider a solution such as $2, 0, 1, 0, 3$. Code this as a sequence of symbols ✾✾◆◆✾◆◆✾✾✾, where the symbol ✾ represents a unit and the four symbols ◆ divide the sequence into five parts. Note that any sequence of six symbols ✾ and four symbols ◆ would constitute a solution to the equation, and any solution to the equation can be coded as a sequence of six symbols ✾ and four symbols ◆. The answer is therefore $\binom{10}{4} = 210$.

11. This is the same as the last problem, but this time interpret a symbol ✾ as a bone and the symbol ◆ as a space between two dogs.

12. It is important to understand what are to be counted as different arrangements. It matters who your partner is and which two players are your opponents, but which court you are on or which side of the court you begin the set do not matter.

One approach is to select the three fours first. This can be done in $\frac{1}{3!} \times \binom{12}{4} \times \binom{8}{4}$ ways, since it does not matter which order the fours are chosen. Now each four can be split into pairs of opponents in $\frac{1}{2}\binom{4}{2}$ ways; again it does not matter in which order the pairs are chosen. Hence the answer is

$$\frac{1}{3!} \times \binom{12}{4} \times \binom{8}{4} \times \left(\frac{1}{2}\binom{4}{2}\right)^3,$$

which is 155 925.

Another approach is to select one of the players, choose their partner in 11 ways, and then their opponents in $\binom{10}{2}$ ways. Now choose one of the eight remaining players, choose their partner in 7 ways and their opponents in $\binom{6}{2}$ ways. There are four players left; again select one of them and choose their partner in 3 ways. This gives

$$11 \times \binom{10}{2} \times 7 \times \binom{6}{2} \times 3 = 155\,925,$$

which is definitely easier, particularly as there is no possibility of counting the same split twice.

13. First place the digits 1 to 5 in their correct order, and consider the gaps between them including a gap at the beginning and one at the end. There are therefore six places for extra digits to go. Now place the 6 into an appropriate space; since it cannot go after the 5, there are five places where it can go. Now there are seven places for new digits, and the 7 can go into any one of them. Argue similarly for the 8 and the 9 and you will see that there are $5 \times 7 \times 8 \times 9 = 2520$ such numbers.

14. (a) Call the teams A and B. For each pair of twins, Adrian must allocate them between the teams, and there are clearly 26 ways of doing this. But now, since we do not care which team is A and which is B, we have counted every possibility twice, so we must divide by two to achieve the answer 32.

    (b) Call the teams A, B and C. When Adrian picks team A, he has 12 choices for the first member, 10 for the second (since he cannot pick the twin of his first choice), 8 for the third and 6 for the fourth, so this means that he has $12 \times 10 \times 8 \times 6 = 5760$ choices. However, it does not matter which order the team is filled, so we must divide by 24 to give 240. Adrian now thinks about team B. There are two remaining pairs of twins, and he must pick one member from each pair, which is 4 choices, and then he must fill up the team from the remaining four people, which can be done in $\binom{4}{2} = 6$ ways. That gives 24 ways of picking team B and team C is then determined. Again the team names are arbitrary, so the final answer is $\frac{240 \times 24}{6} = 960$.

15. Summarise Isaac's performance in a bar chart, with marks on the y-axis and questions on the x-axis. The example shown in figure 3b.A represents marks of 8, 6, 3, 3, 2 and 1.

    As he works through the paper, the scores either stay the same or decrease, so the profile of the chart from the point A to the point

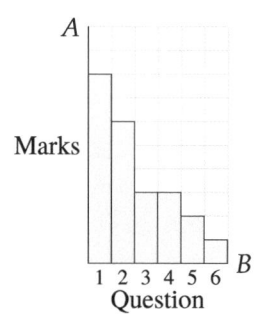

Figure 3b.A

B consists of segments which either go to the right or downwards. We can therefore code the chart using D for down and R for right; this example will code as DDRDDRDDDRRDRDRD. Note that there are 16 cells and 6 Rs, so the number of ways Isaac can score is $\binom{16}{6} = 8008$.

16. Consider the books as 16 cells, and number the parcels so that packages 1 to 4 contain one book, packages 5 to 7 contain two books and packages 8 to 9 contain three books. Now assign the books to packages by writing the number of the package in the appropriate cell.

    The result is a permutation of the numbers 1234556677888999 and there are $\binom{16}{1\,1\,1\,1\,2\,2\,2\,3\,3}$ of these. However, the packages are not in fact numbered, and you cannot distinguish the four which contain one book, the three which contain two books and the two which contain three books. We must therefore divide by 4! × 3! × 2!. The result is

    $$\frac{16!}{(2!)^3(3!)^2 4!3!2!} = 252\,252\,000.$$

17. We can code any such subset by a sequence such as ✣✣♦♦✣✣♦✣✣✣. Now we interpret the symbol ✣ as an instruction 'do not select the element' and the symbol ♦ as 'select the element and omit the next one'. So the sequence in question would omit 1 and 2, choose 3 and omit 4, choose 5 and omit 6, omit 7, choose 8 and omit 9, choose 10 and omit 11, and then omit the rest. So the result is the subset {3, 5, 8, 10}. Notice that we have included a 'ghost' 14 in the set, but that is never selected. This is necessary as it allows us to select 13.

So again the answer is $\binom{10}{4} = 210$.

18. Look at the eight gaps between digits. We are interested in the gaps where 0 is followed by 1 or when 1 is followed by 0. There will be exactly two gaps of the first type, and between these there will be one gap of the second type. This suggests that the answer might be $\binom{8}{3}$, since we can interpret from a pattern such as ✽◆✽✽◆✽◆✽ by treating ✽ as an instruction 'no change' and ◆ as 'change'. This particular pattern would yield the sequence 001110011 which does indeed satisfy the requirements of the problem. Unfortunately, if we begin with a 1, the same pattern yields the complementary sequence 110001100 which does not work. To make matters worse, there are sequences which satisfy the condition, such as 001110010, which would be coded by the pattern ✽◆✽✽◆✽◆◆ and this has four of the eight cells filled with the symbol ◆. So we are disobeying the two principal tenets of correct enumeration; we are counting some occurrences twice and we are not counting others at all.

The two problems with this approach are that we do not know either the first digit of the sequence or the number of changes of digit. We can fix this by appending a 1 at the left of the sequence and a 0 at the right, which has the effect of ensuring that there are an odd number of changes of digit and thus of the symbol ◆. Now the sequence 001110011 becomes 10011100110 and is coded as ◆✽◆✽✽◆✽◆✽◆, where there are ten cells with five ◆ symbols. The second sequence 110001100, which does not satisfy the criterion, becomes 11100011000 and is coded as ✽✽◆✽✽◆✽◆✽✽. Now there are only three ◆ symbols so this will not be counted. The sequence 001110010 becomes 10011100100 and is coded as ◆✽◆✽✽◆✽◆◆✽ and here five of the ten cells are filled with ◆ symbols. When we decode, we always begin with a 1, which is discarded along with the final digit.

It is now clear that there are $\binom{10}{5} = 252$ sequences with exactly two occurrences of 01.

Solutions

Exercise 3c

1. The letters of the alphabet are distinguishable, so they are 26 cells in alphabetical order, and we have to place eight markers in them to indicate how many of each are chosen. The answer is therefore $\left(\!\binom{26}{8}\!\right) = \binom{33}{8}$, which is 13 884 156.
   Only one of these words is meaningful in English (although it is actually a Latin word). AEGILOPS is the name for a species of goatgrass and it is also used for a stye in the corner of the eye. It is the longest English word with letters in alphabetical order.

2. Rephrase the question as $a + b + c + d + e \leq 11$ and introduce a sixth variable f which makes the sum 11. We are now counting non-negative integer solutions to $a + b + c + d + e + f = 11$. There are six cells representing the variables and we place eleven markers into them. Hence the number of solutions is $\left(\!\binom{6}{11}\!\right) = \binom{16}{11}$, which is 4368.

3. As for question 2, replace the inequality by $a + b + c + d + e \leq 11$ and add a sixth variable (which could take the value zero). Place one marker in each of the first five cells of six cells to avoid zero values for a, b, c, d or e. Now we place six more markers in the six cells. This can be done in $\left(\!\binom{6}{6}\!\right) = \binom{11}{6}$ ways, so there are 462 solutions to the inequality.

4. The number of non-negative integer solutions to $a + b + c + d + e = 12$ is $\left(\!\binom{5}{12}\!\right) = \binom{16}{12} = 1820$, so, adding the 4368 from question 2, we obtain 6188.

5. First we choose the two unfortunate dogs; there are $\binom{5}{2} = 10$ ways of doing this. Give each of the remaining three dogs a bone, to make sure that none of them go hungry. Now we must allocate seven bones between three dogs, and there are $\left(\!\binom{3}{7}\!\right) = \binom{9}{7} = 36$ ways to do this, so the answer is 360.

6. The biggest dogs get either 0, 1, 2, 3, 4 or 5 bones each, and the remaining bones are distributed amongst the other three dogs. So

the answer is

$$\left(\!\binom{3}{10}\!\right) + \left(\!\binom{3}{8}\!\right) + \left(\!\binom{3}{6}\!\right) + \left(\!\binom{3}{4}\!\right) + \left(\!\binom{3}{2}\!\right) + \left(\!\binom{3}{0}\!\right)$$
$$= \binom{12}{10} + \binom{10}{8} + \binom{8}{6} + \binom{6}{4} + \binom{4}{2} + \binom{2}{0},$$

which is 161.

7. There is only one way of partitioning 10 into five non-negative integers, namely 0 1 2 3 4. So this is just a permutation of 5 objects and the answer is $5! = 120$.

8. The indistinguishable bones can be allocated in $\left(\!\binom{5}{5}\!\right) = \binom{9}{5} = 126$ ways, and now each of the other bones can be allocated to any dog, so this is a permutation with replacement, and there are $5^5 = 3125$ of these. The answer is 393750.

9. (a) Begin by placing the first A, and two Ns to produce ANN. Now insert the other four As anywhere after the first A. This is a combination of four from three spaces with replacement, so there are $\left(\!\binom{3}{4}\!\right) = \binom{6}{4}$ ways of doing this. (Alternatively, start off with five As and insert two Ns into the five spaces with replacement in $\left(\!\binom{5}{2}\!\right) = \binom{6}{2}$ ways.)

   Now the B, R and M can be placed anywhere (in sequence) and this can happen in $8 \times 9 \times 10$ ways. The answer is 10800.

   (b) Place the five As and then insert the Ns into the six spaces with replacement in $\left(\!\binom{6}{2}\!\right) = \binom{7}{2}$ ways. Of these, the one where both Ns follow the As is inadmissible, so there are 20 ways of arranging the Ns and As. Now the B, R and M can be inserted in $8 \times 9 \times 10$ ways, so the answer is 14400.

Exercise 4a

1. For each value of k, there are k^2 ways to choose r and s from $\{0, 1, 2, \ldots, k-1\}$, and so one expression is $1^2 + 2^2 + \cdots + k^2$. Now treat separately the case where r and s are equal and the case where they are unequal. When $r = s$, then we have $0 \leq r = s < k \leq n$ and there are $\binom{n+1}{2}$ choices. When $r < s$, then $0 \leq r < s < k \leq n$ and there are $\binom{n+1}{3}$ choices, and similarly when $r > s$. So in all the number of choices is

$$\binom{n+1}{2} + 2\binom{n+1}{3} = \tfrac{1}{2}n(n+1) + \tfrac{1}{3}(n-1)n(n+1)$$
$$= \tfrac{1}{6}n(n+1)(2n+1).$$

2. As already established, there are $\binom{n+1}{2}^2$ rectangles within a square grid of side n, and this is $(1 + 2 + \cdots + n)^2$. Call a rectangle 'special' if its top-right corner lies on one or both of the lines $x = k$ or $y = k$. We show that there are k^3 special rectangles.

   Consider the square of points (x, y) with $0 \leq x, y \leq k$. A special rectangle either has two vertices on the top edge of this square or two vertices on the rightmost edge of the square. The first type will include rectangles with a vertex at (k, k). To choose a rectangle of the first type we choose two x-coordinates from the set $\{0, 1, \ldots, k\}$ in $\binom{k+2}{2}$ ways, and then choose the height of the rectangle in k ways. To choose a rectangle of the second type we choose two y-coordinates from the set $\{0, 1, \ldots, k-1\}$ in $\binom{k}{2}$ ways, and then choose a width for the rectangle in k ways. Thus the number of special rectangles is $\tfrac{1}{2}k(k+1) \times k + \tfrac{1}{2}(k-1)k \times k = k^3$, as required.

3. Count the number of ways of choosing r objects from $m + n$ objects. This, by definition, is $\binom{m+n}{r}$. Alternatively, we could choose k objects from the first m and $r - k$ from the remaining n for each k with $0 \leq k \leq r$. Summing these yields the right-hand side.

4. (a) A team consisting of k members can be chosen in $\binom{n}{k}$ ways, and then there are k choices for the captain, so, summing over values of k between 1 and n, we obtain the left-hand side of the desired result. Alternatively, the club could choose the captain first, in n ways, and then the captain could choose the remainder of the team, with between 0 and $n - 1$ members, which can be

done in 2^{n-1} ways by the result of problem 4.1. This yields the expression on the right-hand side.

This can also be proved by starting with the binomial expansion for $(x+1)^n$, differentiating and setting $x = 1$, but surely the combinatorial argument is more satisfying.

(b) Do the same but choose a captain and a vice-captain. The algebraic proof involves differentiating, multiplying both sides by x and differentiating a second time.

5. (a) We count the number of ways of producing a quiz team with equal numbers of men and women involving between 0 and $2n$ members. The number of ways of choosing k men is $\binom{n}{k}$, and this also applies to choosing k women, so this yields the left-hand side of the result. Alternatively, suppose you just choose n out of the $2n$ members. Suppose that this consists of m men and w women, with $m + w = n$. Replace such a selection by a team consisting of the m men chosen and the $m = n - w$ women not chosen. This process will result in every possible team with equal numbers of men and women, and so the right-hand side of the result is $\binom{2n}{n}$.

An algebraic method is to notice that $(x+1)^n \times (x+1)^n = (x+1)^{2n}$ and calculate the coefficient of x^n on both sides.

(b) Do the same thing but also choose a captain. The left-hand side counts the number of ways of choosing a team of k men and k women and electing a captain, summed over all values of k in the range $1 \leq k \leq n$. The right-hand side counts the number of ways of first selecting a team of equal numbers of men and women as in (a) and then choosing the captain.

(c) Now we choose a team consisting of equal numbers of men and women but with two captains, one of each sex, in order to avoid disputes. Choose k men in $\binom{n}{k}$ ways and a male captain in k ways and then do the same for the women. Then, summing over k for $1 \leq k \leq n$, the left-hand side of the result represents the number of balanced teams with a male and a female captain. Alternatively, choose the two captains in n^2 ways and then make up the rest of the team with between 0 and $n-1$ of each sex, which, by part (a), can happen in $\binom{2(n-1)}{n-1}$ ways. This gives the right-hand side of the result.

Solutions

6. Consider a club consisting of n members, and pick a first and a second team with a total of m members. You are allowed to put everyone into the first team or the second team (which does not seem sporting, but it solves the problem). How many ways can this be done? By considering all partitions of m and summing, we obtain the left-hand side of the result. Alternatively, you could just select the members and then allocate them either to the first and second team, and this yields the right-hand side of the result.

7. We write the compositions as sums, such as $2+3+1+2+1+1$. This one has six numbers and five occurrences of the symbol $+$. The number of compositions with six numbers is therefore the number of ways of choosing five gaps between ten units in which to place the $+$ symbols, and that is $\binom{9}{5}$. Hence the total number of terms in compositions with six numbers is $6 \times \binom{9}{5}$ and the number of terms in all the compositions is

$$1 \times \binom{9}{0} + 2 \times \binom{9}{1} + 3 \times \binom{9}{2} + \cdots + 10 \times \binom{9}{9}.$$

But this is found by combining the results of equation (3.1) on page 30 and question 4(a) to yield $2^9 + 9 \times 2^8$, which equals 11×2^8. In general we obtain $(n+1)2^{n-2}$ for the number of terms in all compositions of n.

Exercise 4b

1. Either use the result of problem 3.5 on page 37 and add the cases for $1, 2, \ldots, k$ together, or use conjugates directly. When $k = 2$, we are asking for the number of partitions of n into 1s and 2s. This is clearly determined by the number of 2s in the partition. When $n = 2m$ or $n = 2m+1$, this is anything between 0 and m, so it is $m+1$. Using the floor function notation, we can write it as $\lfloor \frac{1}{2}n \rfloor + 1$.

2. Take the Ferrers diagram for n, add one dot to every row, and then add rows consisting of a single dot until the total number of rows is k. Check that this is a bijection by beginning with a partition of $n + k$ into k parts and deleting one dot from each row.

3. Draw the Ferrers diagram and take its conjugate.

4. The Ferrers diagram of a self-conjugate partition has symmetry about the leading diagonal. Hence it is possible to 'peel off' L-shaped regions from the 'outside' which contain an odd number of dots. These can be reassembled to produce a Ferrers diagram where each row is odd.

Figure 4b.A

For example, the diagram on the left of figure 4b.A can be converted to that on the right by dividing it into three L-shapes, one with eleven dots, one with five dots and one with a single dot. This operation can be reversed so we have the necessary bijection.

5. Working from the bottom row of the Ferrers diagram upwards, add $0, 1, 2, \ldots, k-1$ dots to each row. This process can be reversed so it is a bijection.

6. Write each n_i in binary and thus express it as a sum of distinct powers of 2. Now split $n_i k_i$ up by multiplying k_i by each of these powers. The result is that the sum of the new numbers is still n and they are all distinct, so it is a partition of the desired form. This process can be reversed since we can write each part m_i as $2^{t_i} t_i$, with t_i odd, and then add all the parts involving t_i.

For example, suppose we have partitioned 92 as

7 7 7 7 7 5 5 5 5 5 5 5 3 3 3 3 3 3 1 1 1 1.

This partition consists of five 7s, seven 5s, six 3s and four 1s. The partition 7 7 7 7 7 is replaced by 28 7, using the fact that 5 in binary is $4 + 1$. Similarly 5 5 5 5 5 5 5 is replaced by 20 10 5, since 7 is $4 + 2 + 1$. In the same way we replace 3 3 3 3 3 3 by 12 6 and 1 1 1 1 by 4. Now we have the partition 28 20 12 10 7 6 5 4 of 92, which has distinct parts. If we were to begin with 28 20 12 10 7 6 5 4, we would write $28 = 4 \times 7$ and $7 = 1 \times 7$ and so produce five 7s, and so on; different partitions would produce different results since binary representation is unique.

7. Figure 4b.B illustrates this in the case $n = 4$.

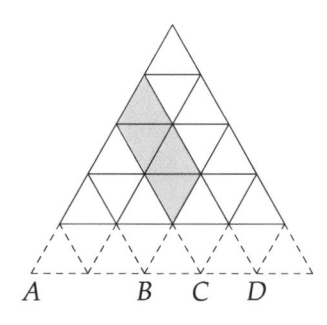

Figure 4b.B

There are three different orientations of the parallelogram in the figure, since any two of the three sides of the triangle can be used as directions. Figure 4b.B shows the case n = 4, and a parallelogram with sides parallel to the 'left' and 'right' sides of the triangle. We add a line parallel to the base as shown.

The sides of the parallelogram, when extended, meet the line at four points A, B, C and D. Note that the two sides orientated 'left' give rise to A and B, and those orientated 'right' give C and D. Note that this process is reversible, so different quadruples of points will correspond to different parallelograms

This is a bijection between parallelograms in the triangle and quadruples of points on the appropriate line.

Since there are six possible points on the line, there are $\binom{6}{4}$ ways of choosing these points, so there are $3 \times \binom{6}{4}$ parallellograms. In general, the number will be $3 \times \binom{n+2}{4}$.

8. We deal first with the special case where there is one row or one column, when it is clear that all the entries are 1, so there is only one such matrix. In order for an $n \times m$ binary matrix to have the property of odd row and column sums, n and m need to have the same parity. This is because the total of the row sums is equal to the total of the column sums, and as both of these are odd, then we cannot have one of n and m odd and the other even. So we assume that this is the case.

We set up a bijection between $n \times m$ binary matrices with odd row and column sums and $(n-1) \times (m-1)$ binary matrices with no restrictions. Clearly we can peel off the right-most column and bottom row to produce a binary matrix. Suppose now that we have an arbitrary $(n-1) \times (m-1)$ binary matrix. For each row we add one more number at the right to make the row sum odd, and similarly for the columns; this can only be done in one way. Now we need to fill in the cell in the nth row and mth column to make these two have an odd sum. This can be done in only one way.

So the number of $n \times m$ binary matrices with the odd sum property is equal to the total number of all $(n-1) \times (m-1)$ binary matrices, which is 2^{n+m-2}.

Exercise 4c

1. Let the sets of words which begin and end with a consonant be B and E respectively. Then $|B| = |E| = 21 \times 26^5$ and $|B \cap E| = 21^2 \times 26^4$, so $|B \cup E| = 2 \times 21 \times 26^5 - 21^2 \times 26^4$, which is approximately 2.97×10^8.

2. Let A_S be the set of hands containing no Spade, and define A_H, A_D and A_C similarly. Then

$$|A_S| = |A_H| = |A_D| = |A_C| = \binom{39}{13}$$
$$|A_S \cap A_H| = |A_S \cap A_D| = |A_S \cap A_C|$$
$$= |A_H \cap A_D| = |A_H \cap A_C| = |A_D \cap A_C| = \binom{26}{13}$$
$$|A_S \cap A_H \cap A_D| = |A_S \cap A_H \cap A_C|$$
$$= |A_S \cap A_D \cap A_C| = |A_H \cap A_D \cap A_C| = 1$$
$$|A_S \cap A_H \cap A_D \cap A_C| = 0.$$

Hence $|A_S \cup A_H \cup A_D \cup A_C| = 4 \times \binom{39}{13} - 6 \times \binom{26}{13} + 4 \times 1$, and we want the number of hands in the complement of this set, which is approximately 6.03×10^{11}, about 95% of all hands.

3. The number of zeros at the end of a number depends on the powers of 2 and 5 in its prime factorisation. In 2014!, there is clearly no shortage of 2s, so what we must do is determine the largest power of 5 which is a factor of this number. This in turn depends only on the multiples of 5 which appear in the set $S = \{1, 2, 3, \ldots, 2014\}$. We

begin by calculating how many of the numbers in S divide by 5; this is $\lfloor \frac{2014}{5} \rfloor = 402$. But the multiples of 25 will each contribute 5^2 to the total, and so they need to be counted twice; we can achieve that by adding a further $\lfloor \frac{2014}{25} \rfloor = 80$. Continuing in this vein, the number of zeros is

$$\left\lfloor \frac{2014}{5} \right\rfloor + \left\lfloor \frac{2014}{25} \right\rfloor + \left\lfloor \frac{2014}{125} \right\rfloor + \left\lfloor \frac{2014}{625} \right\rfloor = 402 + 80 + 16 + 3$$
$$= 501.$$

This is not so much the inclusion-exclusion principle as the inclusion-inclusion principle.

4. First we count the ways in which the As are between the Ms. These have to be in the order MAAM, and there are five gaps in which we insert seven markers; this can be done in $\left(\!\binom{5}{7}\!\right)$ ways, as these are combinations with replacement. We now insert a permutation of TTHEICS at the markers, and there are $\frac{1}{2} \times 7!$ ways of doing this. So there are $\left(\!\binom{5}{7}\!\right) \times \frac{7!}{2}$ such permutations, and clearly the same number with the As between the Ts. We now have to subtract the permutations with the As between both the Ms and the Ts. The As are flanked by one of the four permutations MTMT, MTTM, TMMT and TMTM. Now there are seven gaps and five markers, and the five letters in HEICS to place at the markers, so the number of these permutations is $4 \times \left(\!\binom{7}{5}\!\right) \times 5!$. Hence the answer is

$$2 \times \left(\!\binom{5}{7}\!\right) \times \frac{7!}{2} - 4 \times \left(\!\binom{7}{5}\!\right) \times 5!,$$

which equals 1 441 440.

5. Call the dogs A, B, C, D and E. Twenty-five biscuits can be distributed between the dogs in $\left(\!\binom{5}{25}\!\right)$ ways, since these are combinations with replacement. Now let S_A, S_B, S_C, S_D and S_E be the sets of distributions in which A, B, C, D and E respectively obtain at least eight biscuits.

To calculate $|S_A|$, we give dog A eight biscuits to be getting on with, and distribute the remaining seventeen biscuits in $\left(\!\binom{5}{17}\!\right)$ ways. We must remember to allow the possibility that dog A gets more than eight biscuits.

To calculate $|S_A \cap S_B|$, adopt the same strategy; give the first two dogs eight biscuits each and distribute the remaining nine in $\left(\!\binom{5}{9}\!\right)$ ways.

The number of ways in which three dogs can exceed their quota is $\left(\!\binom{5}{1}\!\right)$, which is just 5, of course. Note that it is impossible for four dogs to have eight or more biscuits.

So the answer to the problem is

$$\left(\!\binom{5}{25}\!\right) - \binom{5}{1} \times \left(\!\binom{5}{17}\!\right) + \binom{5}{2} \times \left(\!\binom{5}{9}\!\right) - \binom{5}{3} \times 5,$$

which is 926. It is encouraging, particularly if you are a dog, to realise how useful mathematics can be for resolving such pressing issues.

6. We begin by listing all the numbers less than or equal to N, and then eliminate those which share a factor with N. We shall use the notation $n \mid m$ to mean that n is a factor of m.

We apply PIE to the sets $A_i = \{M \leq N : p_i \mid M\}$. Thus A_1 is the set of numbers less than or equal to N which have a prime factor p_1, and so on. Then $|A_i| = \frac{N}{p_i}$, since A_i is the set $\{p_i, 2p_i, 3p_i, \ldots, \frac{N}{p_i} p_i\}$, and for exactly the same reason $|A_{ij}| = \frac{N}{p_i p_j}$. Now we have

$$\left|\bigcup_i A_i\right| = \sum_i \frac{N}{p_i} - \sum_{i,j} \frac{N}{p_i p_j} + \cdots - (-1)^m \frac{N}{\prod_{i=1}^m p_i}$$

and so

$$\phi(N) = N - \sum_i \frac{N}{p_i} + \sum_{i,j} \frac{N}{p_i p_j} - \sum_{i,j,k} \frac{N}{p_i p_j p_k} + \cdots + (-1)^m \frac{N}{\prod_{i=1}^m p_i}.$$

If you look at the rather alarming expression on the right-hand side in special cases, you will see that it factorises as

$$N\left(1 - \frac{1}{p_1}\right)\left(1 - \frac{1}{p_2}\right) \cdots \left(1 - \frac{1}{p_m}\right),$$

which is what is required.

7. (a) n^m.
   (b) $_nP_m$ (and $n!$ if $n = m$, when they are bijections).
   (c) Unlike the first two parts, this is not easy. Any function from $\{1,2,\ldots,m\}$ can be represented as a sequence of m images (or values in the codomain), and so becomes a permutation of m elements with replacement from the set $\{1,2,\ldots,n\}$. In order to be a surjection, we require that each value in the codomain appears at least once. Now let S_1 be the set of permutations which do not contain the value 1, and so on up to S_n. We need to calculate the number of elements in the complement of $S_1 \cup S_2 \cup \ldots \cup S_n$. The total number of permutations is n^m. Also

$$|S_i| = (n-1)^m \quad \text{for } 1 \leq i \leq n,$$
$$|S_i \cap S_j| = (n-2)^m \quad \text{for } 1 \leq i < j \leq n,$$
$$|S_i \cap S_j \cap S_k| = (n-3)^m \quad \text{for } 1 \leq i < j < k \leq n,$$

and so on, so using PIE and subtracting the result from the total, we have the solution

$$n^m - \binom{n}{1}(n-1)^m + \binom{n}{2}(n-2)^m - \cdots$$
$$+ (-1)^{n-1}\binom{n}{n-1} \times 1^m.$$

   (d) Set $n = m$. The surjections are bijections and the result follows from double-counting.

Exercise 5a

1. Let u_n be the number of permutations of n objects. Then the recurrence relation

$$u_{n+1} = (n+1)u_n;$$
$$u_1 = 1$$

   follows directly from the multiplication principle.

2. One way of doing this is to define s_n, w_n and x_n as the number of ways Isaac can schedule a holiday of n days and spend the last day respectively surfing, water-skiing or resting. Then

$$s_{n+1} = s_n + x_n;$$
$$w_{n+1} = w_n + x_n;$$
$$x_{n+1} = s_n + w_n + x_n;$$
$$s_1 = w_1 = x_1 = 1,$$

   which involves three simultaneous recurrences. We can replace s_n and w_n with a single variable y_n and then have

$$x_{n+1} = x_n + y_n;$$
$$y_{n+1} = 2x_n + y_n;$$
$$x_1 = 1;$$
$$y_1 = 2,$$

   which has only two variables.

   In fact, we can do better than that and avoid the simultaneous equations, since

$$\begin{aligned}x_{n+2} &= x_{n+1} + y_{n+1} \\ &= x_{n+1} + 2x_n + y_n \\ &= x_{n+1} + 2x_n + x_{n+1} - x_n \\ &= 2x_{n+1} + x_n\end{aligned}$$

   and, in the same way, $y_{n+2} = 2y_{n+1} + y_n$. Note that the initial conditions the last two sequences are different.

As the problem asks for the total number of days scheduled, we can define $t_n = x_n + y_n$, and now we have the simplest form of the recurrence, namely

$$t_{n+2} = 2t_{n+1} + t_n;$$
$$t_1 = 3, \ t_2 = 7.$$

3. Let u_n be the number of compositions of n without using 1. Clearly $n > 1$ for this to make sense, and $u_2 = u_3 = 1$. Consider such compositions of $n + 2$. If the first part is 2, then the composition can be completed in u_n ways. If it is greater than 2, then we can just add 1 to the first part of a composition of $n + 1$, and there are u_{n+1} ways of doing that. Hence $u_{n+2} = u_{n+1} + u_n$, and so we have $u_n = F_{n-1}$ and in particular $u_{10} = F_9 = 34$.

4. Let u_n be the number of compositions of n into odd parts. Then $u_1 = u_2 = 1$. Now consider any such composition of $n + 2$. If it begins with a 1, then it can be completed in u_{n+1} ways. If not, then add 2 to the first part of any composition of n, so there are u_n of these. It follows that $u_{n+2} = u_{n+1} + u_n$, and so we have $u_n = F_n$ and in particular $u_{10} = F_{10} = 55$.

5. Call such a string *good*, and let u_n be the number of good strings of length n. For $n = 1$ both strings 0 and 1 are good, so $u_1 = 2$. For $n = 2$ there are three good strings, 00, 01 and 10, so $u_2 = 3$. A string of length $n + 2$ either begins with a 0 followed by a good string of length $n + 1$, and there are u_{n+1} of these, or with a 10 followed by a good string of length n, and there are u_n of these. Hence $u_{n+2} = u_{n+1} + u_n$, and the sequence is Fibonacci but begins with 2 and 3. Hence $u_n = F_{n+2}$ and in particular $u_{10} = F_{12} = 144$.

We can also approach this problem using combinations. Begin with a row of k 0s, where $k \leq 10$, and insert $(10 - k)$ 1s so as to produce a good string. The places where a 1 can go are the gaps between the 0s and the spaces at the beginning and end, and we cannot insert two 1s into the same place. This can be done in $\binom{k+1}{10-k}$ ways. The minimum value of k is 5, since the sequence 1010101010 is possible, but it is impossible to create a good string with four 0s and six 1s. So the solution is

$$\binom{6}{5} + \binom{7}{4} + \binom{8}{3} + \binom{9}{2} + \binom{10}{1} + \binom{11}{0} = 144.$$

This occurrence of Fibonacci numbers as sums of diagonals in Pascal's triangle is revisited in exercise 7c on page 122.

6. Call such a string *bad*, and let u_n be the number of bad strings of length n. For $n = 1$ only string 0 is bad, so $u_1 = 1$. For $n = 2$ there are two bad strings, 00 and 11, so $u_2 = 2$. A bad string of length $n + 2$ either begins with a 0 followed by a bad string of length $n + 1$, and there are u_{n+1} of these, or with a 11 followed by a bad string of length n (since it has to start with an even number, including zero, of 1s and then continue to be bad) and there are u_n of these. Hence $u_{n+2} = u_{n+1} + u_n$, and the sequence is Fibonacci but begins with 1 and 2. Hence $u_n = F_{n+1}$ and in particular $u_{10} = F_{11} = 89$.

7. Call such a string *ugly*. Note that if a string S is ugly, the string $\bar{S}$ formed from S by replacing each 0 by 1 and each 1 by 0 is also ugly. Let u_n be the number of such strings of length n which begin with 0. There will also be u_n ugly strings which begin with 1. For $n = 1$ the string 0 is ugly, so $u_1 = 1$. For $n = 2$ the only ugly string starting with 0 is 01, so $u_2 = 1$.

Now we count the number of ugly strings of length $n + 2$ beginning with 0. If the string begins 00, it will be followed by an ugly string of length n beginning with 0, and there are u_n of these. If it begins 01, it can be thought of as 0 followed by an ugly string of length $n + 1$ beginning with 1, and there are u_{n+1} of these. Again $u_{n+2} = u_{n+1} + u_n$, and the sequence is Fibonacci, beginning with 1 and 1, so $u_n = F_n$. So the total number of ugly strings is $2F_n$ and in particular this is 110 when $n = 10$.

This is a more subtle argument than for the previous two questions, and it might be helpful for readers to see table 5a.A, which shows how the recursion works, involving both columns.

8. Let u_n be the number of such permutations of $12\ldots n$. The conditions do not apply for $n = 1$ or 2, so $u_1 = 1$ and $u_2 = 2$. For $n = 3$, the first condition applies; there are three suitable permutations 123, 132 and 213 and so $u_3 = 3$. Beyond this, both conditions apply. We have $a_n > a_{n-3} > a_{n-5} > \cdots$ and $a_n > a_{n-2} > a_{n-4} > \cdots$, so it is clear that a_n is either $n - 1$ or n. If it is n, there are u_{n-1} ways of permuting the remaining numbers $12\ldots(n-1)$. If it is $n-1$, there are u_{n-2} ways of permuting the remaining numbers $12\ldots(n-2)\,n$. It follows that $u_n = u_{n-1} + u_{n-2}$, so the sequence

n	Start with 0	Start with 1
1	0	1
2	01	10
3	00∥0 = 000 0∥10 = 010	11∥1 = 111 1∥01 = 101
4	00∥01 = 0001 0∥111 = 0111 0∥101 = 0101	11∥10 = 1110 1∥000 = 1000 1∥010 = 1010
5	00∥000 = 00000 00∥010 = 00010 0∥1110 = 01110 0∥1000 = 01000 0∥1010 = 01010	11∥111 = 11111 11∥101 = 11101 1∥0001 = 10001 1∥0111 = 10111 1∥0101 = 10101

Table 5a.A

is Fibonacci, beginning with 1 and 2, and so $u_n = F_{n+1}$ and in particular $u_{10} = F_{11} = 89$.

9. Let the number of alternating sequences from the set $\{1, 2, \ldots, n\}$ be u_n. We have table 5a.B.

n	Alternating sequences	u_n
1	∅ 1	2
2	∅ 1 12	3
3	∅ 1 12 123 3	5
4	∅ 1 12 123 1234 14 3 34	8

Table 5a.B

Note that every alternating sequence apart from the empty one begins with either 1 or an odd number greater than 1. Now let us look at alternating sequences from the set $\{1, 2, \ldots, n\}$.

If such a sequence begins with 1 and has more than one term, then the subsequent terms alternate between even and odd. This means that you can subtract 1 from each term and obtain an alternating sequence from the set $\{1, 2, \ldots, n-1\}$. If the sequence is simply

1 on its own, we can think of the remaining terms as the empty sequence. We have now formed a bijection between the set of alternating sequences from $\{1, 2, \ldots, n\}$ beginning with 1 and the set of alternating sequences from $\{1, 2, \ldots, n-1\}$, and so the number of these is u_{n-1}.

If such a sequence begins with 3 or more, we can subtract 2 from each term to produce an alternating sequence from $\{1, 2, \ldots, n-2\}$. If we begin with the empty sequence, we leave it alone. We now have a bijection between the set of alternating sequences which are either empty or do not begin with 1 and the set of alternating sequences from $\{1, 2, \ldots, n-2\}$, and so the number of these is u_{n-2}.

Again we have $u_n = u_{n-1} + u_{n-2}$ and the sequence is Fibonacci, beginning with 2 and 3, so $u_n = F_{n+2}$ and in particular $u_{10} = F_{12} = 144$. Note that it is essential to include the empty sequence as alternating for this method to work.

10. Let w_n be the number of wicked subsets of $\{1, 2, \ldots, n\}$. Then $w_0 = 1$, $w_1 = 2$ and $w_2 = 4$ as in these cases every subset, including the empty set, is wicked. If a wicked subset does not contain n, it is a wicked subset of $\{1, 2, \ldots, n-1\}$, and there are w_{n-1} of these. If it contains n but not $n-1$, then it is completed by a wicked subset of $\{1, 2, \ldots, n-2\}$, and there are w_{n-2} of these. If it contains both n and $n-1$, then it cannot contain $n-2$, and so it is completed by a wicked subset of $\{1, 2, \ldots, n-3\}$, and there are w_{n-3} of these. Note that for this argument to work it is essential that we include the empty set as wicked, so we can count the wicked set $\{n-1, n\}$.

Hence $w_n = w_{n-1} + w_{n-2} + w_{n-3}$, which is not the Fibonacci recurrence relation, although it is similar. Then, by working our way up from the beginning, we find that $w_{10} = 504$.

11. Call permutations which satisfy the condition *acceptable* and those which contravene it *excluded*. As we are going to form a recurrence relation, we generalise the problem to permutations of $12 \ldots n$. We shall denote the numbers of acceptable and excluded permutations by t_n and s_n, noting that $t_n + s_n = n!$.

The condition is inapplicable for $n = 1$ so we shall set $s_1 = 0$ and $t_1 = 1$. When $n = 2$, the permutation 12 is excluded (since 1 is a permutation of 1) and 21 is acceptable, so $s_2 = t_2 = 1$.

Solutions

Next we look at the permutations of 123, where we must check two things. We truncate each permutation at the first digit and check that what results is not a permutation of 1. This means that the first digit cannot be 1, so we exclude the 2! permutations 123 and 132. Now we truncate each permutation at the second digit, and check that what results is not a permutation of 12. This means that the permutation cannot begin with 12 or 21, so 213 is also excluded.

It is worth re-interpreting these findings in terms of earlier stages of the recursion. When $n = 1$, the permutation 1 is acceptable, so the number of exclusions at the first digit is $2! \times t_1$. When $n = 2$, the permutation 21 is acceptable, so the number of further exclusions at the second digit is $1! \times t_2$. Thus we can write $s_3 = 2! \times t_1 + 1! \times t_2$ and $t_3 = 3! - 2! \times t_1 - 1! \times t_2$. The excluded permutations for $n = 3$ depend on acceptable permutations for $n = 1$ and $n = 2$. The acceptable permutations are 231, 312 and 321.

You should check that an analogous argument can be applied to the case where $n = 4$, so that the calculation is $t_4 = 4! - 3! \times t_1 - 2! \times t_2 - 1! \times t_3$. We can now draw up table 5a.C.

Length	Total	Exclude	Result
1	1	0	1
2	2	1	1
3	6	2 1	3
4	24	6 2 3	13
5	120	24 6 6 13	71
6	720	120 24 18 26 71	461

Table 5a.C

Hence we have $t_6 = 461$.

Exercise 5b

1. Let t_n be the number of ways of triangulating a polygon with $n+2$ sides into n triangles using $n-1$ diagonals. Set $t_0 = 1$ and note that $t_1 = 1$ since a triangle can only be triangulated in one way.

   Figure 5b.A and the argument below relate to an octagon, which is the case $n = 6$.

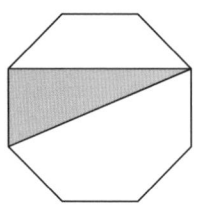

   Figure 5b.A

   Fix one side of the octagon, which is part of exactly one triangle in any triangulation. When this triangle is completed using the vertex shown, it creates a 4-gon and a 5-gon which can be further triangulated in $t_2 t_3$ ways, and summing over all vertices we have

   $$t_6 = \sum_{k=0}^{5} t_k t_{5-k}.$$

   This argument can easily be generalised, and we obtain the usual recurrence relation

   $$t_n = \sum_{k=0}^{n-1} t_k t_{n-k-1}.$$

   Consequently we have the same sequence of numbers and $t_6 = 132$.

2. Let b_n be the number of ways of bracketing an expression containing $n+1$ symbols. Then the outermost bracket associates the results of previously bracketing $k+1$ symbols and $n-k$ symbols, for $0 \leq k \leq n-1$. This would produce $b_k b_{n-k-1}$ different bracketings and by summing over all possible k, we obtain

   $$b_n = \sum_{k=0}^{n-1} b_k b_{n-k-1}.$$

   Hence we have the same sequence of numbers and $b_6 = 132$.

Exercise 6a

1. The auxiliary equation is $\lambda^2 - \lambda - 2 = 0$, which has roots $\lambda = -1$ and $\lambda = 2$ so $t_n = A \times (-1)^n + B \times 2^n$. We have $A + B = 7$ and $-A + 2B = 8$, so $A = 2$ and $B = 5$. Hence $t_n = 5 \times 2^n + 2 \times (-1)^n$.

2. The auxiliary equation is $\lambda^2 - 2\lambda - 1 = 0$ which has roots $\lambda_1 = 1 + \sqrt{2}$ and $\lambda_2 = 1 - \sqrt{2}$. Hence $t_n = A\lambda_1^n + B\lambda_2^n$, with $3 = A\lambda_1 + B\lambda_2$ and $7 = A\lambda_1^2 + B\lambda_2^2$. The solutions are $A = \frac{1}{2}\lambda_1$ and $B = \frac{1}{2}\lambda_2$ so $t_n = \frac{1}{2}(\lambda_1^{n+1} + \lambda_2^{n+1})$.

3. Most of the work for the Fibonacci sequence carries over, so it is only the initial conditions which need adjusting. Again with $\lambda_1 = \frac{1-\sqrt{5}}{2}$ and $\lambda_2 = \frac{1+\sqrt{5}}{2}$, we have $L_n = A\lambda_1^n + B\lambda_2^n$ and now

$$\lambda_1 A + \lambda_2 B = 1$$
$$\lambda_1^2 A + \lambda_2^2 B = 3,$$

so using $\lambda^2 = \lambda + 1$, we get $A + B = 2$. This yields $A = B = 1$ and we obtain $L_n = \lambda_1^n + \lambda_2^n$.

4. The auxiliary equation is $\lambda^3 - 2\lambda^2 - \lambda + 2 = 0$, which has roots 1, -1 and 2, so the formula is $u_n = A + B \times (-1)^n + C \times 2^n$, and it is easy to check that $A = \frac{1}{2}$, $B = \frac{1}{6}$ and $C = \frac{1}{3}$. Hence we obtain $u_n = \frac{1}{6}(3 + (-1)^n + 2^{n+1})$.

5. The auxiliary equation is $\lambda^2 - 6\lambda + 9 = 0$, which has repeated root 3, so the formula is $u_n = (A + Bn) \times 3^n$, and then we find that $A = \frac{2}{9}$ and $B = \frac{1}{9}$. Hence we obtain $u_n = (2+n) \times 3^{n-2}$.

Exercise 6b

1. Clearly $t_{n+1} = t_0 + (1 + 2 + 2^2 + \cdots + 2^n) = 2^{n+1}$.

2. With $t_n = u_n + an + b$ we obtain

$$u_{n+1} + an + a + b = 2u_n + (2a+1)n + 2b.$$

Now we choose a and b by requiring that $a = 2a + 1$ and $a + b = 2b$, so $a = b = -1$. Hence $u_{n+1} = 2u_n$ and $u_1 = 4$, so $u_n = 2^{n+1}$ and $t_n = 2^{n+1} - n - 1$.

3. With $t_n = a \times 2^n u_n$ we obtain $2au_{n+1} = 2au_n + 1$ (after dividing through by 2^n), and if we choose $a = \frac{1}{2}$ we have $u_{n+1} = u_n + 1$ with $u_1 = 1$. Hence $u_n = n$ and $t_n = n \times 2^{n-1}$.

4. We have
$$(n+1)t_{n+1} = (n+2)t_n + 1$$
$$\text{and} \quad (n+2)t_{n+2} = (n+3)t_{n+1} + 1.$$

   Subtracting, rearranging and letting $u_n = t_{n+1} - t_n$, we obtain $u_{n+1} = u_n$ and so $u_n = 1$. Hence $t_n = n$.

5. Using $t_n = n! \times u_n$, we obtain $(n+1)u_{n+1} = (n+2)u_n + 1$ with $u_1 = 1$, so from question 4 we have $u_n = n$, and thus $t_n = n \times n!$.

Exercise 7a

1. For the apples alone, the generating function is

$$G_a(x) = 1 + x + x^2 + \cdots + x^{10},$$

and there are similar expressions for $G_b(x)$ and $G_c(x)$. Hence the generating function for all the fruit is the product $G_a(x)G_b(x)G_c(x)$, namely

$$\left(1 + x + x^2 + \cdots + x^{10}\right)\left(1 + x + x^2 + \cdots + x^9\right)\left(1 + x + x^2 + \cdots + x^8\right)$$

and the coefficients of this polynomial are the numbers of ways of selecting up to 27 pieces of fruit.

2. Now we have

$$G_a(x) = 1 + x^2 + x^4 + x^6 + x^8 + x^{10},$$
$$G_b(x) = x + x^3 + x^5 + x^7 + x^9,$$
$$G_c(x) = x^5 + x^6 + x^7 + x^8$$

and $G(x) = G_a(x)G_b(x)G_c(x)$.

3. Since there are equal numbers of apples and bananas, we use a single generating function for these two kinds of fruit, namely

$$G_1(x) = 1 + x^2 + x^4 + \cdots + x^{18}.$$

For the cherries and damsons, the possibilities for their numbers are $(0,0)$, $(1,0)$, $(0,1)$, $(2,0)$, $(1,1)$, $(0,2)$, $(3,0)$, $(2,1)$, $(1,2)$ and $(0,3)$, and so the generating function is $G_2(x) = 1 + 2x + 3x^2 + 4x^3$. Hence $G(x) = G_1(x)G_2(x)$.

Exercise 7b

1. The variable x_1 can take non-negative values so has generating function
$$G_1(x) = 1 + x + x^2 + \cdots + x^n + \cdots = \frac{1}{1-x}.$$
Hence the generating function for the sum is
$$G(x) = \frac{1}{(1-x)^N}.$$
Each solution to the equation corresponds to a combination of N objects from k with replacement, and so the coefficients are the values of $\left(\!\binom{k}{N}\!\right)$. It follows that
$$(1-x)^{-N} = \sum_{k=0}^{\infty} \left(\!\binom{k}{N}\!\right) x^k = \sum_{k=0}^{\infty} \binom{N+k-1}{N} x^k,$$
which generalises the expansion of $(1+x)^{-3}$ in appendix E.

2. Since zero solutions are not allowed, the generating function is
$$G(x) = \frac{x^{12}}{(1-x^3)(1-x^4)(1-x^5)}.$$

3. With the substitution suggested in the hint, we have
$$Ny_1 + (N-1)y_2 + \cdots + y_N = k,$$
with non-negative integer solutions, so the generating function is
$$G(x) = \frac{1}{(1-x)(1-x^2)(1-x^3)\cdots(1-x^N)}.$$

4. This is combinations with replacement but with Nm categories, so the generating function is
$$G(x) = \frac{1}{(1-x)^{Nm}}.$$

Exercise 7c

1. We have
$$G(x) = t_1 x + t_2 x^2 + t_3 x^3 + \cdots + t_n x^n + \cdots$$
$$-5x G(x) = -5t_1 x^2 - 5t_2 x^3 - \cdots - 5t_{n-1} x^n + \cdots$$
$$6x^2 G(x) = 6t_1 x^3 + \cdots + 6t_{n-2} x^n + \cdots$$

and, after adding, we obtain $(1 - 5x + 6x^2)G(x) = x - 3x^2$. Cancelling the common factor $1 - 3x$ we see that
$$G(x) = \frac{x}{1 - 2x}$$
$$= x(1 + 2x + 4x^2 + \cdots + 2^n x^n + \cdots).$$
It follows that $t_n = 2^{n-1}$.

2. Let $G(x) = t_0 + t_1 x + t_2 x^2 + t_3 x^3 + \cdots + t_n x^n$. Then
$$(1 - x - 2x^2)G(x) = t_0 + (t_1 - t_0)x + (t_2 - t_1 - 2t_0)x^2 + \cdots$$
$$+ (t_n - t_{n-1} - 2t_{n-2})x^n + \cdots$$
$$= 7 + x$$
so
$$G(x) = \frac{7 + x}{(1 + x)(1 - 2x)}$$
$$= \frac{2}{1 + x} + \frac{5}{1 - 2x}.$$
Using the binomial expansion for $(1 - 2x)^{-1}$, the coefficient of x^n is $5 \times 2^n + 2(-1)^n$ and so this is the formula for t_n.

3. By a similar argument to question 2, the generating function is given by $(1 - 2x - x^2)G(x) = 3x + x^2$ so
$$G(x) = \frac{3x + x^2}{1 - 2x - x^2}$$
$$= -1 + \frac{x + 1}{(\lambda_1 + x)(\lambda_2 + x)},$$

where $\lambda_1 = 1 + \sqrt{2}$ and $\lambda_2 = 1 - \sqrt{2}$. In partial fractions, this is

$$G(x) = -1 + \frac{1}{2\sqrt{2}}\left(\frac{\lambda_2 - 1}{\lambda_2 + x} - \frac{\lambda_1 - 1}{\lambda_1 + x}\right)$$

$$= -1 + \frac{1}{2\sqrt{2}}\left(\frac{1 + \lambda_1}{1 - \lambda_1 x} - \frac{1 + \lambda_2}{1 - \lambda_2 x}\right)$$

and the coefficient of x^n is $t_n = \frac{1}{2\sqrt{2}}((1 + \lambda_1)\lambda_1^n - (1 + \lambda_2)\lambda_2^n)$, but since $1 + \lambda = \lambda\sqrt{2}$ this is the same as $t_n = \frac{1}{2}(\lambda_1^{n+1} + \lambda_2^{n+1})$.

4. The argument mirrors that for the Fibonacci sequence, apart from the initial conditions. We have

$$G(x) = \frac{x(1 + 2x)}{1 - x - x^2}$$

$$= \frac{x(1 + 2x)}{(1 - \lambda_1 x)(1 - \lambda_2 x)},$$

where $\lambda_1 = \frac{1-\sqrt{5}}{2}$ and $\lambda_2 = \frac{1+\sqrt{5}}{2}$. After some manipulation using $\lambda_1\lambda_2 = -1$ and $\lambda_1 + \lambda_2 = 1$, this simplifies to

$$G(x) = x\left(\frac{\lambda_1}{1 - \lambda_1 x} + \frac{\lambda_2}{1 - \lambda_2 x}\right)$$

and the coefficient of x^n is $\lambda_1^n + \lambda_2^n$.

5. Let $G(x) = t_1 x + t_2 x^2 + \cdots$ with $t_1 = 2$. Then we have

$$G(x) = t_1 x + t_2 x^2 + t_3 x^3 + \cdots \quad + t_n x^n + \cdots$$
$$2xG(x) = \quad 2t_1 x^2 + 2t_2 x^3 + \cdots + 2t_{n-1} x^n + \cdots$$

and $t_{n+1} - 2t_n = n$, so

$$(1 - 2x)G(x) = 2x + x^2 + 2x^3 + 3x^4 + \cdots + (n-1)x^n + \cdots.$$

But

$$x + x^2 + 2x^3 + 3x^4 + \cdots + (n-1)x^n + \cdots = \frac{x^2}{(1-x)^2}$$

$$= 1 + \frac{2x - 1}{(1-x)^2}$$

Solutions

and so
$$(1-2x)G(x) = 2x + 1 + \frac{2x-1}{(1-x)^2}.$$
Hence
$$G(x) = 1 + \frac{2}{1-2x} - \frac{1}{(1-x)^2}.$$
Now, using the binomial expansions for $(1-2x)^{-1}$ and $(1-x)^{-2}$, we get $t_n = 2^{n+1} - (n+1)$.

6. Let $G(x) = t_1 x + t_2 x^2 + \cdots$. Then we have
$$\begin{aligned} G(x) &= t_1 x + t_2 x^2 + t_3 x^3 + \cdots + t_n x^n + \cdots \\ 2xG(x) &= \quad\quad 2t_1 x^2 + 2t_2 x^3 + \cdots + 2t_{n-1} x^n + \cdots \\ S &= \quad\quad 2x^2 + 2^2 x^3 + \cdots + 2^{n-1} x^n + \cdots, \end{aligned}$$
so $(1-2x)G(x) - S(x) = x$ and $S(x) = \dfrac{2x^2}{1-2x}$. Hence
$$(1-2x)G(x) = x + \frac{2x^2}{1-2x}$$
$$= \frac{x}{1-2x},$$
so
$$G(x) = \frac{x}{(1-2x)^2}.$$
Now, using the binomial expansion for $(1-2x)^{-2}$, we obtain $t_n = n \times 2^{n-1}$.

7. (a) Write the generating function as
$$G(x) = \frac{x}{1 - x(1+x)}$$
$$= x\big(x(1+x) + x^2(1+x)^2 + x^3(1+x)^3 + \cdots\big).$$
Now F_{n+1} is the coefficient of x^n in the expression inside the bracket. This coefficient is the sum of contributions from the terms $x^r (1+x)^{n-r}$ in the range $0 \le r \le \tfrac{1}{2}n$, each being the binomial coefficient $\binom{n-r}{r}$, which is the required expression.

(b) In Pascal's triangle, the entries representing binomial coefficients of the required type form 'shallow diagonals'. The first seven

1
1 1
1 2 1
1 3 3 1
1 4 6 4 1
1 5 10 10 5 1
1 6 15 20 15 6 1
1 7 21 35 35 21 7 1

Figure 7c.A

shallow diagonals are highlighted in figure 7c.A.

The first, second and third shallow diagonals have sums 1, 1 and 2, and it is clear from Pascal's identity that, for $n \geq 4$, the sum of the nth shallow diagonal is found by adding the sums of the $(n-1)$th and $(n-2)$th diagonals.

(c) We count the number of ways in which Sidney can descend n stairs in two ways. By the recursive argument, this is F_{n+1}. Alternatively, we count the number of ways by specifying the number of double jumps used. If Sidney uses no double jump, then he has to choose none of n moves. If he uses exactly 1, then there are $n-1$ moves and he chooses one of them as the double jump. If he uses exactly 2, there are $n-2$ moves and he chooses two of them as the double jump. Hence we obtain the right-hand side of the identity.

Solutions

Exercise 8a

1. No it is not certain. If we take people as pigeons and number of hairs they have as pigeonholes, then we do not have *more* pigeons than pigeonholes, so cannot conclude that two pigeons are in the same pigeonhole.

2. It is still not certain that two people have the same number of hairs, since one of the residents might be completely bald. Thus the number of available pigeonholes is in fact 150 001. We can say that either two people have the same number, possibly zero, of hairs, or there is exactly one person with every possible number of hairs.

3. The outcomes are permutations with replacement from the set {R, B, Y}. Let the outcomes each day be the pigeons, and the possible outcomes be the pigeonholes. There are 27 pigeonholes and every month has more than 27 days so the result follows.

4. Let the seven square numbers be the pigeons, and their final digits be the pigeonholes. All square numbers end in one of the digits 0, 1, 4, 5, 6 and 9. Thus there are only six pigeonholes and the result follows. To prove that the list of possible last digits is indeed exhaustive, we can either expand $(10n)^2$, $(10n \pm 1)^2$, $(10n \pm 2)^2$, $(10n \pm 3)^2$, $(10n \pm 4)^2$ and $(10n + 5)^2$, or, equivalently, use arithmetic modulo ten.

5. Let the people in the world be the pigeons and their possible masses, measured to the nearest milligram, be the pigeonholes. Although we do not know exactly how many pigeons there are, or indeed, how many pigeonholes, we can make some crude estimates. In particular, no living person has a mass of more than 1000 kg, and there are 1 000 000 milligrams in a kilogram, so we have at most 1 000 000 000 pigeonholes. This is one (US) billion, and there are more than a billion people in the world, so we are done.

6. Answer: 112. Let the numbers be the pigeons and their first digits be the pigeonholes. There are nine pigeonholes (0 is not a possible first digit) and $9 \times 111 < 1001 \leq 9 \times 112$ so we can be sure that more than 111 pigeons are in the same pigeonhole, but cannot guarantee that more than 112 are.

7. Answer: none. The point here is that there is no reason why pigeons need to be evenly distributed among pigeonholes. All the numbers could start with, say, a 2.

8. Answer: 79. Let the students be the pigeons and the possible scores be the pigeonholes. There are sixty-one possible scores since both zero and sixty are possible. We have $78 \times 61 < 4800 \leq 79 \times 61$, so we are done.

9. One solution uses the general pigeonhole principle twice. First note that since $49 > 4 \times 12$ there is a box which contains at least 13 counters. Now take these counters and place them in pigeonholes according to their colour. There are three available colours and $13 > 4 \times 3$ so one colour is represented more than four times as required.

   An alternative solution starts by building pigeonholes labelled with a box number and a colour. There are twelve such pigeonholes, namely (1, Red), (1, Blue), (1, Green), (2, Red) and so on. But $49 > 4 \times 12$, so the result follows directly from the pigeonhole principle.

10. Answer: 6481. Let the visitors be the pigeons, and the possible permutations of the six roller coasters be the pigeonholes. There are $6! = 720$ pigeonholes and $6481 = 9 \times 6! + 1$ so at least one pigeonhole contains more than nine pigeons.

11. Answer: 2653. Let the possible hands be the pigeonholes. These are combinations of two cards chosen from fifty-two so there are $\binom{52}{2} = 1326$ of them. If the hands the player is dealt are the pigeons, then we can guarantee three pigeons in a pigeonhole provided we have at least $2 \times 1326 + 1 = 2653$ pigeons.

12. Suppose there are n people at the party. Let the people be the pigeons and the number of people they know be the pigeonholes. We now consider two cases.

    Case I

    If someone at the party knows everyone, then every guest knows at least one other person. The pigeonholes can therefore be labelled as $1, 2, \ldots, n-1$. There are more pigeons than pigeonholes so the result follows.

    Case II

    If nobody at the party knows everyone else, then the greatest number of people a guest can know is $n - 2$ so the pigeonholes are now $0, 1, \ldots, n - 2$ and the result follows as before.

Exercise 8b

1. Three socks will always suffice since they could be different colours. There are two pigeonholes, Black and Blue, and the socks we choose are the pigeons. Of three pigeons, two will be in the same pigeonhole and hence of the same colour. Clearly two socks may not suffice. The number of blue and black socks available is almost completely irrelevant. All we are using is that there are at least three in total and at least one of each.

2. Answer: 61. Let the diners be the pigeons and the possible meals be the pigeonholes. There are $3 \times 4 \times 5 = 60$ pigeonholes by the Multiplication Principle so we need more than sixty diners to ensure at least two have the same meal. Clearly sixty diners may not suffice.

3. Answer: 17. Let the cards be the pigeons and the suits be the pigeonholes. There are four pigeonholes, so, using the general pigeonhole principle, we can be sure that more than four pigeons are in the same pigeonhole provided the number of pigeons is more than 4×4. Sixteen cards may not suffice.

4. Answer: 10. The set $\{1, 2, 3, 4, 5, 11, 12, 13, 14, 15\}$ shows that ten numbers can be chosen. To prove that among eleven or more numbers there are always two that differ by 5, we use the pairs $\{1, 6\}$, $\{2, 7\}, \ldots, \{5, 10\}, \{11, 16\}, \ldots, \{15, 20\}$ as pigeonholes. There are ten pigeonholes so we are done.

5. Here we need to divide the integers into at most 50 pigeonholes. Two numbers (pigeons) in the same pigeonhole should either be congruent modulo 99, in which case their difference is a multiple of 99, or one should be congruent to minus the other, in which case their sum is congruent to zero. So the pigeonholes are $\{\pm 1 \pmod{99}\}$, $\{\pm 2 \pmod{99}\}, \ldots, \{\pm 49 \pmod{99}\}$ and finally $\{0 \pmod{99}\}$.

6. In each part of this question we need to divide the set $\{1, 2, \ldots, 100\}$ into at most 54 sets which we will use as pigeonholes. The 55 numbers will be our pigeons, so one of our sets will contain more

than one number.

The key insight is that $2n$ consecutive numbers can be divided into n pairs of numbers which differ by n, namely $\{1, n+1\}, \{2, n+2\}, \ldots, \{n, 2n\}$.

(a) By taking $m = 5$ and $n = 9$, we divide the numbers 1 to 90 into 45 pairs that differ by 9.
Add the pair set $\{91, 100\}$ and the singletons $\{92\}, \{93\}, \ldots, \{99\}$ to obtain a total of 54 sets. One of these sets is bound to contain more than one of the 55 numbers, but the only sets for which this is possible is the pairs. Therefore we will certainly have a pair of numbers which differ by exactly nine.

(b) By taking $m = 10$ and $n = 5$, we divide the numbers 1 to 100 into 50 pairs that differ by 10.

(c) By taking $m = 4$ and $n = 12$, we divide the numbers from 1 to 96 into 48 pairs that differ by 12. Adding the 4 remaining singletons gives 52 pigeonholes.

(d) By taking $m = 4$ and $n = 13$, we divide the numbers from 1 to 104 into 52 pairs that differ by 13. Removing the numbers greater than 100 still gives 52 pigeonholes: 48 pairs and 4 singletons.

(e) By taking $m = 4$ and $n = 11$, we divide the numbers 1 to 88 into 44 pairs that differ by 11. If we take the smallest number from each of these pairs, together with the numbers from 89 to 99, we obtain a set of 55 numbers such that no two differ by 11, namely

$$\{1, \ldots, 11, 23, \ldots, 33, 45, \ldots, 55, 67, \ldots, 77, 89, \ldots, 99\}.$$

7. (a) We divide the 24 seats into eight blocks of three consecutive seats which we use as pigeonholes. Since $17 > 2 \times 8$, one pigeonhole contains more than two pigeons (people) and we are done.
If we only had 16 people, then we could number the seats 1, 2, $\ldots$, 24 and seat people in all the seats whose numbers are not divisible by three, that is 1, 2, 4, 5, 7, $\ldots$. This arrangement does not have three consecutive seats occupied.

(b) Answer: 17. We can seat 17 people by placing them in seats whose numbers are not divisible by three. If we had more than 17 people, then we would have more than 16 sitting in the first 24 seats. In this case part (a) ensures the existence of three consecutive occupied seats.

(c) Answer: 18. The solution is identical to the previous part. There are 18 seats whose numbers are not divisible by three, and more than 18 people means more than 16 in the first 24 seats.

8. Answer: 101. The set $\{2, 4, \ldots, 200\}$ shows that 100 numbers may not suffice. To show that 101 numbers always will, we proceed as in problem 8.7 on page 130 and prove that if we have 101 numbers, then some two are consecutive. Consecutive numbers cannot share a common factor so we are done.

Exercise 8c

1. The points will be our pigeons. We let the fact that there are 33 of them guide our choice of pigeonholes. We want three pigeons to end up in the same pigeonhole, so we want at most 16 pigeonholes. This prompts us to divide the square into 16 equal squares as shown on the left of figure 8c.A.

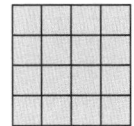

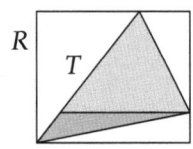

Figure 8c.A

We now have 16 pigeonholes so there will be three points which lie in (or on the boundary of) the same $\frac{1}{4} \times \frac{1}{4}$ square.

We claim that these three points form a triangle with area at most $\frac{1}{32}$. This completes the proof.

To sketch a proof of this (obvious) claim, let the triangle be called T and let the smallest rectangle which contains T and has sides parallel to those of the square be called R. Since R fits completely inside the $\frac{1}{4} \times \frac{1}{4}$ square, we need to show that the area of T is at most half the area of R.

If two vertices of T are on the top or bottom edge of R, then the height of T equals the height of R and the base of T is at most the width of R, so the result follows from the formula for the area of a triangle.

If T has a vertex which is not on the top or bottom edge of R, then we draw a line through this vertex parallel to the bottom of R, as shown on the right of figure 8c.A, dividing T into two triangles. The sum of their heights is the height of R and their (common) base is at most the width of R so the result follows as before.

2. The points will be our pigeons. We have 50 of them and want a pair in the same pigeonhole which suggests looking for 49 pigeonholes. Figure 8c.B shows the square divided into 49 subsquares in the obvious way. Now the pigeonhole principle implies that there are two points in, or on the boundary of, the same small square. These points are at most $\frac{1}{7}\sqrt{2}$ apart.

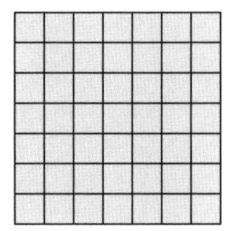

Figure 8c.B

It remains to check that $\frac{1}{7}\sqrt{2} < \frac{2}{9}$ which follows from the observation that $(\frac{1}{7}\sqrt{2})^2 = \frac{4}{98} < (\frac{2}{9})^2$.

3. We have five points (pigeons), so we are looking for four pigeonholes. If we consider the parity of each of the coordinates of a point, we have four options to use as pigeonholes: (even, even), (even, odd), (odd, even), (odd, odd). It is also clear that if two points are in the same pigeonhole, then their midpoint has integer coordinates.

4. First we observe that placing a bishop on every cell in the top row and the middle six cells in the bottom row (the left-hand diagram in figure 8c.C) yields an arrangement of fourteen non-attacking bishops.

   It remains to use the pigeonhole principle to show that among fifteen bishops some two attack each other. We divide the white squares on the board into seven pigeonholes as shown on the right of figure 8c.C and divide the black squares into seven pigeonholes in a similar way. This gives a total of fourteen pigeonholes and we can now conclude the question as in problem 8.10 on page 134.

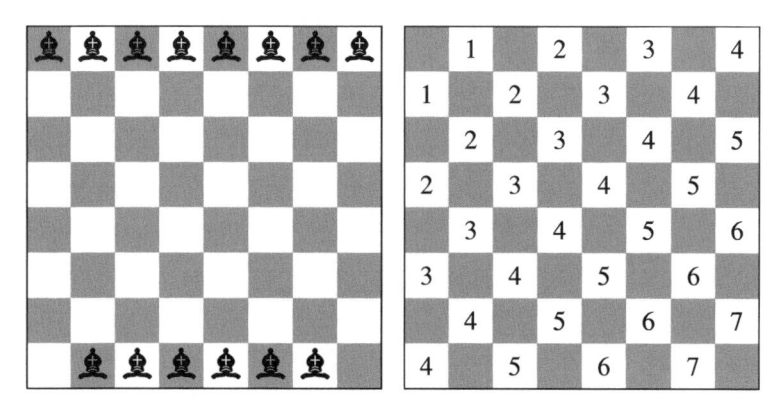

Figure 8c.C

5. We divide the board into 8 'diagonal' pigeonholes as shown in figure 8c.D.

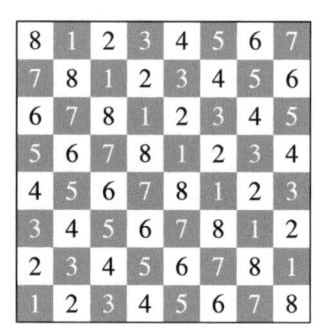

Figure 8c.D

Since $25 > 8 \times 3$ there is a pigeonhole which contains at least four red squares and none of these are in the same row or column.

6. (a) Let the non-empty subsets be the pigeons. There are $2^9 - 1 = 511$ of them. Now we let the possible sums of their elements be the pigeonholes. Each sum is an integer between 1 and $60 + 59 + \cdots + 52 = 504$ inclusive. So there is a sum which is represented by more than one subset, as required.

    (b) An exact replica of the argument used in part a) fails here, since $2^8 - 1 < 39 + 38 + \cdots + 32$. However, if we exclude the subset with eight members then we still have $2^8 - 2 = 254$ subsets with between one and seven members, but now the possible sums vary between 1 and $39 + 38 + \cdots + 33 = 252$, so we can complete the solution as above.

(c) In part (b) the key idea was that excluding the largest possible subset decreased the number of available sums more than it decreased the number subsets. We can extract more from this idea by excluding more large subsets as follows:

Let the subsets of C with at most seven members be the pigeons, and the possible sums be the pigeonholes. There are $141 + 140 + \cdots + 135 = 966$ pigeonholes, so it remains to count the pigeons. We start with 1023 non empty subsets and subtract one of size 10, ten of size 9 and forty-five of size 8 to obtain 967 subsets.

7. We wish to divide the cube into fewer than $11\,000 \div 5 = 2200$ pigeonholes. The most natural way to subdivide a cube is into smaller cubes. Now $14^3 > 2200 > 13^3$, so we try $13^3 = 2197$ small cubes of side length $\frac{15}{13}$. Certainly one such cube contains at least 6 points inside it (or on its boundary), and that cube has diagonal of length $\frac{15}{13}\sqrt{3}$. Therefore the sphere through the corners of that cube has radius $\frac{15}{26}\sqrt{3}$. But

$$\left(\frac{15}{26}\sqrt{3}\right)^2 = \frac{675}{676} < 1,$$

so the cube, including its corners, fits completely *inside* a unit sphere. This completes the proof.

8. We want to divide the circle into nine pigeonholes such that the distance between any two points in a pigeonhole is less than two.

The division into nine equal sectors fails spectacularly, so we are forced into considering pigeonholes which are not all identical. We start by placing a circle of diameter 2 at the centre of the given circle and taking its interior as our first pigeonhole. This leaves a ring or *annulus* whose internal and external radii are 1 and $\frac{5}{2}$ respectively. We divide this ring into eight identical pieces, as shown in figure 8c.E on the facing page.

Now it remains to check that the distances AB and AC are both less than two. These are the only possible candidates for a maximal length in the region, since any other length can be increased by sliding one of the endpoints along the boundary of the pigeonhole.

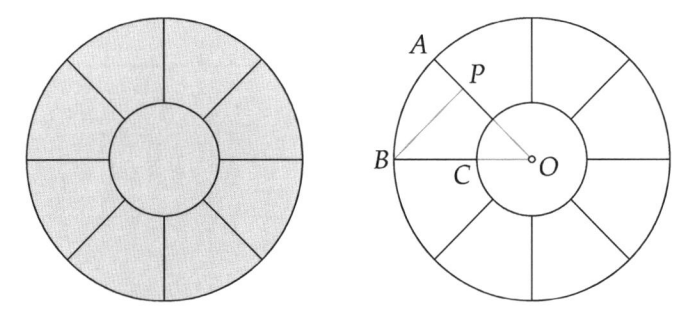

Figure 8c.E

We call the centre of the circles O and use P to denote the foot of the perpendicular from B to OA. Now triangle BOP is isosceles and right-angled and ABP is also right-angled. A careful application of Pythagoras' Theorem gives $AB^2 = \frac{25}{4}(2 - \sqrt{2})$. Since $\sqrt{2} > 1.4$ we have $AB^2 < \frac{15}{4} < 4$, as required.

If we draw the perpendicular from C to OA, then a similar argument gives $AC^2 = \frac{29 - 10\sqrt{2}}{4}$. Once again the approximation $\sqrt{2} > 1.4$ gives $AC^2 < 4$, as required.

9. Divide the rectangle into the five pigeonholes shown in figure 8c.F.

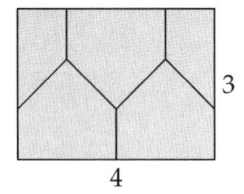

Figure 8c.F

The maximum distance between two points in, or on the boundary of, the same pigeonhole is $\sqrt{5}$ as required.

Exercise 8d

1. Using problem 8.14 on page 138 we can find an integer q such that $q\alpha$ is within 10^{-12} of an integer, so the fractional part either has 10 zeros or 10 nines after the decimal point. In the first case we are done. In the second case we have $q\alpha = n - \epsilon$ where $0 < \epsilon < 10^{-12}$ and n is a whole number.

   The key idea is as follows. Since $q\alpha = n - \epsilon$, we have $2q\alpha = 2n - 2\epsilon$ and, more generally, $kq\alpha = kn - k\epsilon$. These all seem to be a little less than an integer. However, if we take k large enough so that $k\epsilon$ is nearly one, then $kq\alpha$ will be just a little more than the integer $kn - 1$. Now it remains to write this argument up a little more formally.

   Let $m\epsilon$ be the largest multiple of ϵ which is less than 1, then $m\epsilon = 1 - \delta$ where $\delta \leq \epsilon < 10^{-12}$. Now $mq\alpha = mn - m\epsilon = (mn - 1) + \delta$ which has ten zeros after the decimal point, as required.

2. This is a strengthened version of problem 8.14 on page 138. As before, we take the fractional parts of $\alpha, 2\alpha, \ldots, N\alpha$ as pigeons, but we also add 0 to give a total of $N + 1$ pigeons. Now, letting the form of what we need to prove guide us, we divide the interval between 0 and 1 into $N + 1$ equal segments to use as pigeonholes. If two of our numbers are in (or on the boundary of) the same segment we can conclude as before. Otherwise there is exactly one number in each segment, including the last one. So there is a q such that $\frac{N}{N+1} \leq \langle q\alpha \rangle < 1$. Thus $q\alpha$ is at most $\frac{1}{N+1}$ away from some whole number p and the result follows.

3. Using the notation given in the hint, we note that the a_i and the b_j are all between 1 and 58. There are 60 of them in total, so some two of them are equal. However, the a_i are all distinct, as are the b_j. Therefore $a_i = b_j$ for some choice of i and j, as required.

4. Let the members of the set be $a_1, a_2, \ldots, a_n$. Taking our lead from problem 8.12 on page 137, we use the sums $a_1, a_1 + a_2, a_1 + a_2 + a_3, \ldots,$ and $a_1 + a_2 + \cdots + a_n$ as our pigeons. The pigeonholes are the possible remainders on division by n. If the pigeonhole labelled '0' is occupied we are done, and if not then two of the sums leave the same remainder on division by n. Their difference is a multiple of n and is the sum of the members of a subset, as required.

5. We use consecutive pairs of terms as our pigeons, and corresponding pairs of remainders on division by n as pigeonholes. There are infinitely many pigeons and only n^2 pigeonholes so a pair of remainders comes up more than once. However, any pair of remainders completely determines the remainders of the terms that follow and *precede* it. This means that the sequence of remainders is completely periodic. In particular, since the sequence begins 1, 1, there is a $k > 1$ such that $F_k \equiv F_{k+1} \equiv 1 \pmod{n}$. We now observe that F_{k-1} is a multiple of n, as required.

Exercise 8e

1. The average number of bets won is at least $\frac{13}{4} > 3$ so the result follows from the averaging principle. This question contains some 'noise', that is, extra information which is irrelevant to the solution. In particular, we make no use of the fact that a football match can have three outcomes. Redundant information is not usually given in Olympiad problems, and the question 'Have I used everything given in the question?' is, generally, one problem solvers should ask themselves. However, this question serves as a warning that not every number need be relevant to a solution.

2. For each seat define a pigeonhole consisting of that seat, its neighbours and their neighbours. This gives 99 pigeonholes of five seats each. Each person sits in five such pigeonholes, so the average number of people per pigeonhole is $(5 \times 80) \div 99 > 4$. So, by the averaging principle, there is a pigeonhole with more than four pigeons in it, as required.

3. Number the positions in the circle 1, 2, ..., 202, and label each child with the number of their place. Either more than 50 girls have odd numbers, or more than 50 have even numbers. We suppose, without loss of generality, that more than 50 of the girls are even numbered. For each even place define a pigeonhole consisting of that place and the place two to the right. Each even numbered girl belongs to two such pigeonholes, so the average number of girls in such a pigeonhole is at least $(2 \times 51) \div 101 > 1$. By the averaging principle, this means two girls occupy consecutive even numbered positions.

4. The key idea in this problem is that the number of ways of choosing four cubes less than some specified number eventually becomes far larger than the number of different sums those four cubes might have. Therefore the average number of ways to write a number as the sum of four cubes tends to infinity; in particular it passes a hundred at some stage.

More explicitly, if we consider the first n cubes, then there are $\binom{n}{4}$ ways to choose four of them. Every sum of four cubes chosen from among the first n cubes is less than $4n^3$. Therefore the average number of ways to express a number less than $4n^3$ as the sum of four cubes is more than

$$\frac{\binom{n}{4}}{4n^3} = \frac{n(n-1)(n-2)(n-3)}{4! \times 4n^3}$$

$$= \frac{(n-1)(n-2)(n-3)}{96n^2}$$

$$= \frac{n-6}{96} + \frac{11n-6}{96n^2},$$

which is clearly larger than 100 if $n \geq 9606$. The result now follows from the averaging principle.

Exercise 8f

1. Answer: 16. Fifteen may not suffice since Ollie might take twelve left shoes and only three right shoes. To show that sixteen will suffice we need to take care to avoid a fallacious 'This is as bad as it could be' type of argument.

   Suppose he takes sixteen shoes. We denote the number of left shoes by L and the number of right shoes by R. If $L \leq 3$, then $R \geq 13$ which is impossible. So $L \geq 4$. Similarly, $R \geq 4$ so we are done.

2. Answer: 17. We denote the number of left shoes by L and the number of right shoes by R. Sixteen might not suffice since we could have $R = 9$ and $L = 7$. On the other hand, if $R + L \geq 17$ and $L \leq 7$ then $R \geq 10$ which is impossible. Therefore seventeen shoes always suffice.

3. If we actually perform the division, we see that the decimal expansion will recur as soon as a remainder in the division process is repeated. There are p possible remainders, so the decimal recurs with a repeating block of length at most p. More generally, $\frac{m}{n}$ recurs for all n provided we consider terminating decimals like $\frac{1}{2} = 0.5$ to have recurring zeros. If we exclude such fractions, then we need to exclude $\frac{m}{n}$ for all n of the form $2^a 5^b$.

4. We present two solutions.

   Divide S into sets S_0, S_1, S_2, S_3 and S_4, where S_i contains those numbers which are congruent to $\pm i$ modulo 8. Setting $a_i = |S_i|$ we have $756 = a_0 + a_1 + a_2 + a_3 + a_4 > 1 + 251 + 251 + 251 + 1$. If $a_0 > 1$ we have two multiples of 8 so we are done, and if $a_4 > 1$ we have two odd multiples of four so we are done. Otherwise we have $a_j > 251$ where j is 1, 2 or 3. This S_j contains 251 numbers which leave remainder j, and 251 which leave remainder $-j$. Therefore we have at least one of each remainder and we are done.

   A second, more elegant, solution uses only the classic version of the pigeonhole principle. We put all the multiples of 8 in one pigeonhole, and the remaining multiples of 4 in another. We then divide the remaining 1506 numbers into 753 pairs which sum to 2008. We have a total of 755 pigeonholes, so at least one contains two numbers and we are done.

5. (a) The numbers are the pigeons, and the two pigeonholes are called 'Even' and 'Odd'.
   (b) Now the pigeonholes are the remainders on division by 3. However, the argument is more subtle than just an application of the pigeonhole principle. If all three pigeonholes contain at least one number we are done. If this does not happen, then only two pigeonholes are used, in which case one contains at least three numbers which also meets the requirements of the problem.
   (c) Take a pair with even sum. (Part (a) ensures this is possible since $7 \geq 3$.) Five numbers are left so we can take another pair with even sum. This leaves three numbers, so we can take another pair with even sum. So we have $x_1 + x_2 = 2s_1$, $x_3 + x_4 = 2s_2$ and $x_5 + x_6 = 2s_3$. Now focus on the three numbers s_1, s_2 and s_3. Some pair of these have even sum, so we can choose four

numbers that add up to twice an even number, as required.

(d) If we work modulo six, we may take any set consisting of five numbers congruent to zero and five numbers congruent to one. A subset of size six contains between one and five numbers congruent to one, so the sum cannot be a multiple of 6.

The answer to the second part is 'No'. If we have a set of eleven integers we can choose five pairs with even sums (as is part (c)). From these five sums we can choose three which add up to a multiple of three by using part (b). This gives us a set of six numbers with the required property.

These problems are special cases of a more general theorem, that every set of $2n - 1$ integers has a subset of size n whose elements sum to a multiple of n. However, the proof of this statement, while not totally inaccessible, is beyond the scope of this book.

6. (a) We will call an arrangement of arrival numbers at the 200 stations a *good* arrangement if no six stations have the same arrival number.

The idea in the problem is that the 'best possible' good arrangement is (probably) to have five stations with no arrivals, five with one, five with two all the way up to five with thirty-nine. This arrangements requires a total of $5(0 + 1 + 2 + \cdots + 30) = 3900$ tickets, and it seems unlikely that a good arrangement with fewer tickets is possible. However, turning this into a watertight argument is tricky.

We want to show that any good arrangement requires more than 3800 tickets. It is crucial that the claims we make about such an arrangement are easy to justify. In particular, we should avoid making the argument that it would obviously be mad not to have as many stations as possible with small numbers of arrivals.

An elegant approach is to count the number of tickets in a good arrangement in a different order. It is not a good idea to take the number of stations with one arrival, add twice the number with two arrivals, then three times the number with three arrivals, and so on. Instead, take the number of stations with *at least* one arrival, then add the number of stations with at least two arrivals, then add the number with at least three, and so on. It is clear that a station with k arrivals is counted exactly k times by this method.

Now we can appeal to the pigeonhole principle and argue that, for any i, there needs to be at least $200 - 5i$ stations with at least i arrivals. If there were not, there would be more than $5i$ stations with arrival numbers in the set $\{0, 1, \ldots, i-1\}$ and so one arrival number would occur more than five times.

Therefore the total number of tickets needed in a good arrangement is at least $195 + 190 + 185 + \cdots + 5 = 3900$. Our intuition was correct, and the problem is solved.

This technique could be described as 'changing the order of summation' and has many applications throughout mathematics.

(b) The arrangement with six stations with no arrivals, six with one, six with two, and so on, requires 3234 tickets. The remaining 566 passengers can all be sent to, for example, the last station on the list.

7. By the pigeonhole principle, there are at least thirteen points which are the same colour. Since no three points are collinear there are $\binom{13}{3} = 286$ triangles with three vertices of that colour. We now need to show that not too many of these can be isosceles. (Note that equilateral triangles are isosceles.) There are $\binom{13}{2} = 78$ pairs of points. Each of these pairs can be the base of at most two isosceles triangles since otherwise there would be three points on the same line. Thus the number of isosceles triangles is at most $2 \times 78 = 156$, and the result follows.

8. Let the number of red points be R. We will show that R cannot be too small. Indeed, given any pair of red points less than 2 units apart, there are exactly two places where a blue point could go. They are the other two vertices of the unit rhombus that has the red points at opposite vertices.

This means $2\binom{R}{2} \geq 2009 - R$ or $R^2 \geq 2009$ so $R > 44$.

To show that R can equal 45 we simply place 45 red points on a line of length less than 2 units. There are $2\binom{45}{2} = 1980$ possible sites for a blue point and we need only use 1964 of them. So the maximum number of blue points is 1964.

9. We label each of the vertices with the sum of the lengths of the two edges which meet there. The sum of these labels is twice the perimeter, so the average label is $\frac{4002}{1415}$. Therefore there are vertices v_{i-1}, v_i and v_{i+1} such that the edges $v_{i-1}v_i$ and v_iv_{i+1} have lengths

x and y where $x + y \leq \frac{4002}{1415}$.

We claim that the area A of triangle $v_{i-1}v_iv_{i+1}$ is less than 1.
Now $A = \frac{1}{2}xy\sin(\theta)$ for some θ, so $A \leq \frac{xy}{2}$.
Also, $xy = (\frac{x+y}{2})^2 - (\frac{x-y}{2})^2$ so $xy \leq (\frac{x+y}{2})^2$, a result known as the *AM-GM inequality*.
So we have $A \leq \frac{1}{2}(\frac{2001}{1415})^2 = \frac{1}{2} \times \frac{4\,004\,001}{2\,002\,225} < 1$, as required.

Exercise 9a

1. The smallest possible value of n is 6. It is clear that n is even and that the L, I, O and S-tetrominoes can all be tiled with dominoes. Figure 9a.A shows an arrangement of six cells. To see that this region cannot be tiled with dominoes, we note that the domino that covers the marked cell always isolates at least one single cell.

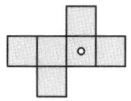

Figure 9a.A

2. We start by considering the rectangular region of the board which has the removed cells at opposite corners. Since these cells are different colours, the region has one even dimension e and one odd dimension o. Now divide the remainder of the 12×12 board into rectangles each of which has at least one even dimension. One possible division is shown in figure 9a.B. Each of the seven rectangles has at least one even (possibly zero) dimension.

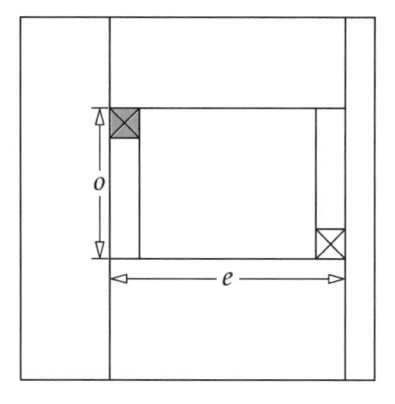

Figure 9a.B

3. We claim that if a single cell is removed from a $(2n+1) \times (2n+1)$ chessboard such that equal numbers of grey and white cells remain, then it is possible to tile the resulting shape with dominoes.

Base case: $n = 1$

Using the rotational symmetry, there are only two cases to consider for the 3×3 square; the removed cell might be in the centre or a corner of the board. In both cases the rest of the board can be tiled as shown in figure 9a.C.

Figure 9a.C

Induction step

Assume the result holds for $n = k$ and consider a board of size

$$\bigl(2(k+1)+1\bigr) \times \bigl(2(k+1)+1\bigr)$$

with one cell removed.

There is at least one $(2k+1) \times (2k+1)$ sub-board which contains both the removed cell and one of the corners of the original board. By the induction hypothesis, this board can be tiled, and the remaining L-shape has width two, so can also be tiled, as shown in figure 9a.D.

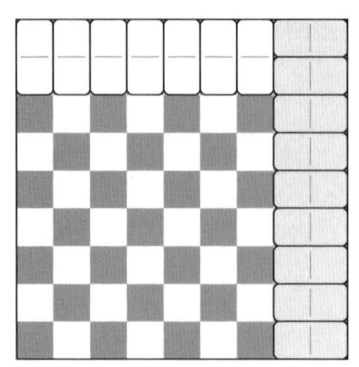

Figure 9a.D

4. We consider two cases depending on whether or not there is a domino in the middle of the bottom row of the figure. If there

is, then the maximum number of dominoes is one plus twice the maximum number that can be packed into the *truncated staircase* shown on the left of figure 9a.E. Otherwise, the maximum number of dominoes is twice the number that can be packed into the *staircase* shown on the right of figure 9a.E.

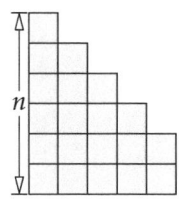

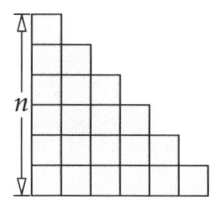

Figure 9a.E

If we pack dominoes into the truncated staircase in the manner shown in figure 9a.F, then all the uncovered cells are the same colour in the standard chessboard colouring.

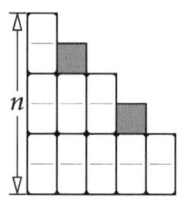

Figure 9a.F

This shows that it is impossible to pack in more dominoes even if we rearrange them. It also shows that it is never possible to pack more dominoes into a staircase than a truncated staircase.

Therefore, if we can pack m dominoes into a truncated staircase of height n, then the answer to the question will be $2m + 1$.

The expression for m depends on the parity of n and it would be reasonable to split the solution into two subcases. However, it turns out that $m = \lfloor \frac{n}{2} \rfloor \times \lceil \frac{n}{2} \rceil$, where $\lceil x \rceil$ denotes the least integer greater than or equal to x. This can be verified by a routine induction, so the final answer to the question is $2\lfloor \frac{n}{2} \rfloor \times \lceil \frac{n}{2} \rceil + 1$.

5. (a) The shape can be tiled, as shown in figure 9a.G on the next page.

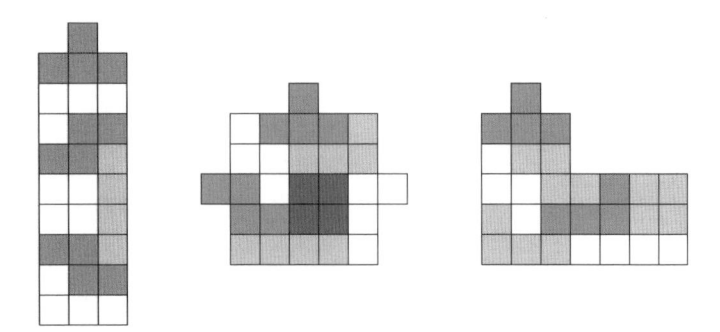

Figure 9a.G

- (b) The shape can be tiled, as shown in figure 9a.G.
- (c) The shape consists of only 27 cells so cannot be tiled.
- (d) It is impossible to cover both ends of the bottom row of the shape, so it cannot be tiled.
- (e) If we colour the shape with the standard chessboard pattern, then it has equal numbers of black and white cells, so it cannot be tiled.
- (f) If we colour the shape with the standard pattern, then the difference between the number of black and white cells is three. For any arrangement of the seven tetrominoes this difference is two, so the shape cannot be tiled.
- (g) The shape can be tiled, as shown in figure 9a.G.

6. The board cannot be tiled. The square tetromino covers two white squares while the 15 T-tetrominoes cover an odd number of white squares between them. Therefore they cannot be used to cover any board with an even number of white squares.

7. No such arrangement is possible. The only possible rectangles with area 20 are the 1×20, 2×10 and 4×5 rectangles. Each of these has exactly 10 white squares in the standard colouring, while the five tetrominoes always cover and odd number of white squares between them.

8. (a) This follows easily from the fact that a 4×4 square can be tiled as shown in figure 9a.H on the facing page.
   (b) If we colour the board in the usual way, it contains $2ab$ black cells. However, the number of black cells covered by ab non-

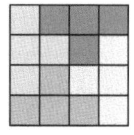

Figure 9a.H

overlapping T tetrominoes is a sum of an odd number of odd numbers so is odd.

Exercise 9b

1. No. If we colour the board with alternating red and white stripes, we have 50 cells of each colour. However, each L tetromino covers an odd number of red cells so 25 L tetrominoes always cover an odd number of red cells.

2. No. We adapt the colouring shown on the left in figure 9.9 on page 165 by using 3×3 grey and white squares arranged in a chessboard pattern. Each tile is exactly half white, but the whole board is not.

    Alternatively, we adapt the colouring shown on the right in figure 9.9 on page 165 by using diagonal stripes of six different colours. Each tile now covers one cell of each colour, but the board does not have equal numbers of each type.

    A third solution adapts the colouring shown in figure 9.10 on page 165. We position the board on the x-y plane so that the co-ordinates of the centres of cells are integers with $0 \leq x \leq 8$ and $0 \leq y \leq 9$. Then we colour grey the cells whose centres have both coordinates congruent to 1 modulo 3. Each tile now covers an even number of grey squares while the entire board has nine grey squares.

    Finally, we can also deduce this result from problem 9.8 on page 167. If we shrink the tiles by a factor of six, then they become $1 \times \frac{1}{6}$ rectangles. Each of these has an integer side, so if we arrange any number of them into a rectangle, this rectangle must also have an integer side. However, if we shrink an 8×9 board by a factor of 6, neither dimension is an integer, so the tiling is impossible.

3. No. The arguments are similar to those used in the previous question, but we need to extend our colourings to three dimensions. We can arrange $2 \times 2 \times 2$ grey and white cubes in the obvious 3D analogue of a chessboard pattern. Each brick is exactly half white, but the entire box is not. (To see this note that a $10 \times 10 \times 8$ cuboid is exactly half white, while the remaining $10 \times 10 \times 2$ layer is predominantly the colour of the corner cells.)

To adapt the solution based on diagonal stripes we use four colours called 0, 1, 2 and 3. We assume the centres of the small cubical cells have integer coordinates between zero and nine and assign the cube centred at (x, y, z) colour $x + y + z$ where the sum is taken modulo four. Each brick now fills one small cube of each colour.

Checking that this colouring does not use each colour equally often is quite subtle. We note that it is possible to pack 248 bricks into the box leaving only a $2 \times 2 \times 2$ cubical region unfilled. By the design of the colouring, any region filled by bricks will contain equal numbers of cells of each colour, but the $2 \times 2 \times 2$ cube left over does not.

Finally, we can colour the cells whose centres have three even coordinates grey and the others white. Each brick now covers an even number of grey cells, while the whole box contains 125 grey cells.

4. The large triangle is made up of N^2 small triangles. Exactly $\frac{N(N+1)}{2}$ of these point 'up' and the other $\frac{N(N-1)}{2}$ point 'down'. A route through the triangle alternates between triangles of each type so there can be no path longer than $2 \times \frac{N(N-1)}{2} + 1$. (The $+1$ comes from the fact that the route may both start and end in an 'up' triangle.)

There are a number of different paths which show that this bound can in fact be attained, such as that shown in figure 9b.A, so the answer is $N^2 - N + 1$.

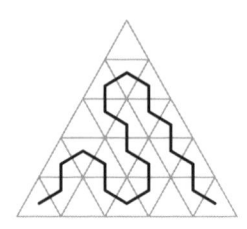

Figure 9b.A

5. It is never possible. We colour every other cell in every other row grey as in figure 9b.B. Now every straight tetromino covers an even number of grey cells while every square tetromino covers exactly one.

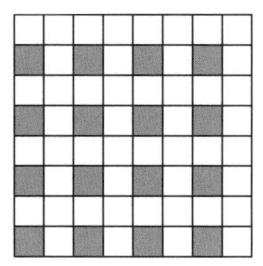

Figure 9b.B

6. If we place a 1×1 tile in the centre of the board, then we can divide the remaining area into four 5×6 rectangles each of which can be covered with two 3×3 tiles and three 2×2 squares.

   Now we claim that it is impossible to tile the board with only 2×2 and 3×3 tiles. To prove this we colour the board with red and white stripes and note that the difference between the number of red cells and the number of white cells is eleven. However, if a region is covered by 3×3 tiles then the difference between the number of red and white cells is always a multiple of three and adding 2×2 tiles cannot change this difference.

7. The possible values of n are 0 and 3.

   Colour the board as shown in the left-hand diagram of figure 9b.C.

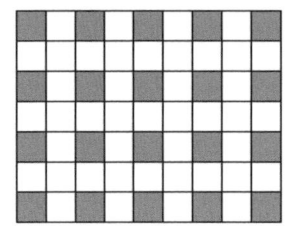

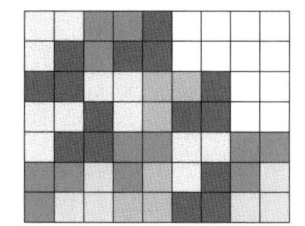

   Figure 9b.C

   Suppose we have m trominoes and n squares. By considering areas we see that $3m + 4n = 63$ which implies that n is a multiple of three. However, each tile can only cover one grey cell so we have $m + n \geq 20$. This implies that $3m + 3n \geq 60$ so $n \leq 3$.

The right-hand diagram of figure 9b.C shows a board partially tiled with L-trominoes. The untiled area can be filled with either four more trominoes or three squares, so $n = 0$ and $n = 3$ are both possible.

Exercise 9c

1. (a) Either m or n needs to be divisible by six. This is clearly sufficient. To show that is necessary we argue as in question 2 of exercise 9b.
   (b) The area mn needs to be divisible by six and we also need $m, n > 1$. The tiling is easy if one of the sides is divisible by two and the other by three. The other case is a $6a \times b$ board, which we may cover by tiling a copies of a $6 \times b$ board. If b is two or three the tiling is easy, and if $b > 3$ we can simply tile 6×2 subsections of the board until either a 6×2 or 6×3 rectangle remains.

2. (a) Yes; one such tiling is shown in figure 9c.A.

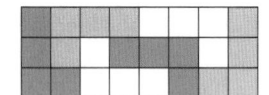

   Figure 9c.A

   (b) The area mn needs to be divisible by eight and we also need $m, n > 1$. To show that we may not have $mn = 4a$ where a is odd, we colour the board with alternating red and white stripes such that it has $2a$ red cells. Each of the L-tetrominoes now covers an odd number of red cells, and the sum of a odd numbers is odd so cannot be $2a$.

   It remains to check that the board can be tiled if eight divides mn. Since a 4×2 rectangle can be tiled it is easy to tile a $4p \times 2q$ board. To tile a board of size $8p \times q$ we split it into p separate $8 \times q$ boards and cover each with a combination of 8×2 and 8×3 rectangles.

3. The board can be tiled if n is multiple of three and $n \geq 6$. The area of the board has to be divisible by three, so n also needs to be divisible by three.

   Since a 2×3 rectangle can be tiled, part (b) of question 1 implies that a $6a \times 6a$ square can be tiled. We prove that all $(6a+3) \times (6a+3)$ boards can be tiled by induction.

   Figure 9c.B shows a tiling of a 9×9 board which is the base case for the induction.

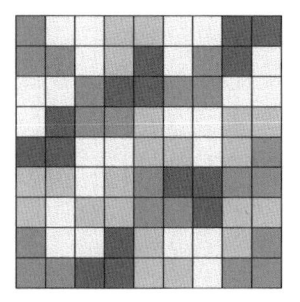

   Figure 9c.B

   Given a $(6k+9) \times (6k+9)$ board, the $(6k+3) \times (6k+3)$ square in the lower left corner can be tiled by the induction hypothesis. The remaining large L shape can be split into a 6×6 square in the top right corner of the board and two $6 \times (6k+3)$ rectangles. All three of these regions can be tiled, which completes the induction step.

   This induction proof differs from those we have met so far in that the base case is not entirely straightforward.

Exercise 9d

1. There are $(n+1)^2$ possible places for the square. The same argument as used in problem 9.12 on page 173 shows that the square is one of the grey cells indicated for a 7×7 board in figure 9d.A on the following page.

   To check that the square can indeed be any of these we adapt the argument used in the second solution to problem 9.2 on page 156. We extend the edges of the square tile until they meet the edges of the board. This divides the board into eight rectangular regions each

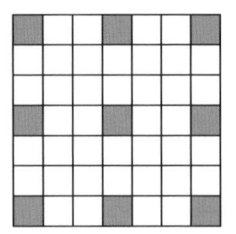

Figure 9d.A

of which has at least one dimension which is a multiple of three. All these regions can be tiled with straight trominoes.

2. To construct an open tour we construct a loop which visits half the cells on the $n \times 4$ boards. Then we reflect this loop in the longer center line of the board to construct another loop which visits the remaining cells. The knight can go round one loop and then jump onto the other loop to complete the open tour. The relevant loops for even and odd values of n are shown in figure 9d.B.

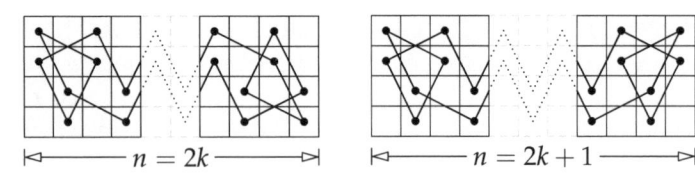

$n = 2k$ $n = 2k + 1$

Figure 9d.B

3. If we give the chessboard the standard colouring, then the athletic knight can only visit cells of one colour.

4. We colour six of the cities white and nine of them black as shown in figure 9d.C.

   A journey on the road network alternates between the colours, so any journey visiting all nine black cities visits at least one white city more than once.

5. An $m \times n$ rectangle can be tiled if:

   (i) 12 divides mn;
   (ii) neither dimension is 1, 2 or 5; and

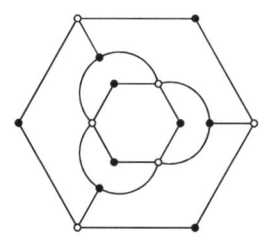

Figure 9d.C

(iii) at least one dimension is divisible by 4.

The solution is almost identical to the one given to problem 9.13 on page 174.

We need to prove that we cannot have both dimensions congruent to 2 modulo 4. Call a 4×3 tile *fat* and a 3×4 tile *tall*. Colour every fourth row of the rectangle red. Then a tall tile always covers three red cells and a fat tile always covers an even number. The total number of red cells is even so the number of tall tiles is even. A similar argument shows that the number of fat tiles is even, so the area of the rectangle is divisible by 24 which implies that one of the sides is divisible by 4.

6. An $m \times n$ rectangle can be tiled if:

   (i) 12 divides mn;
   (ii) neither dimension is 1, 2 or 5; and
   (iii) at least one dimension is divisible by 4.

The previous question implies that all such rectangles can be tiled since two hooks can be arranged to form a 3×4 rectangle. It is also clear that $m \times 1$ and $m \times 2$ boards cannot contain even one hook and that it is impossible to cover all four corners of an $m \times 5$ board. It remains to check that the condition that 12 divides mn is in fact necessary, and that it is impossible for both dimensions to be congruent to 2 modulo 4.

If we consider the hook shape we see that there is one cell outside the hook which shares an edge with three of the cells which make up the hook. We will call this cell the *centre* of the hook. If we have a hook A in any tiling, then the centre of A will be covered by another hook B. There are only two ways to do this and in each case the centre of B is covered by the original hook A. This means that, in any tiling, hooks always come in pairs so the condition that 12 divides mn is needed. In fact, tiling with hooks is equivalent to tiling with the shapes shown in figure 9d.D.

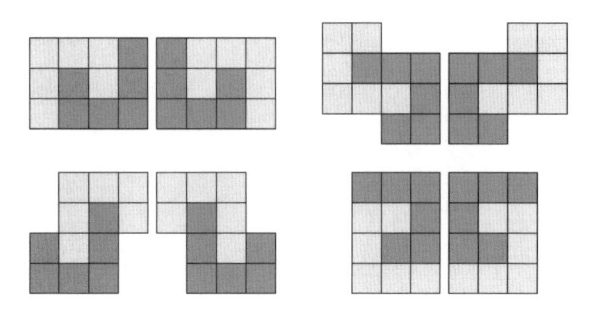

Figure 9d.D

We call those in the top row *fat* pairs and those in the bottom row *tall* pairs. Now we suppose that both m and n are even and colour every fourth row of the rectangle red. The number of red cells covered by a fat pair is always even, and the number covered by a tall pair is always three. This implies that there are an even number of tall pairs. A similar argument shows there are an even number of fat pairs. Thus the area of the rectangle is divisible by 24, so at least one side is divisible by 4.

7. We call ending the game with one piece on the board *winning*. The game can be won if and only if n is not a multiple of three. We show it can be won if n is congruent to 1 or 2 modulo 3 by induction. There are two base cases: $n = 1$ and $n = 2$. In the first case the game is already won and in the second it is easy. For the induction step it suffices to show that a $(k+3) \times (k+3)$ square of pieces can be reduced to a $k \times k$ square.

The first four diagrams in figure 9d.E show a sequence of moves which removes a line of three pieces from the board.

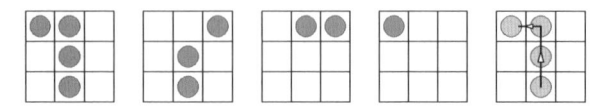

Figure 9d.E

We will indicate this sequence of moves by the arrow shown in the last diagram in this figure. Figure 9d.F shows how this sequence can be used to reduce a $(k+3) \times (k+3)$ square to a $k \times k$ square as required.

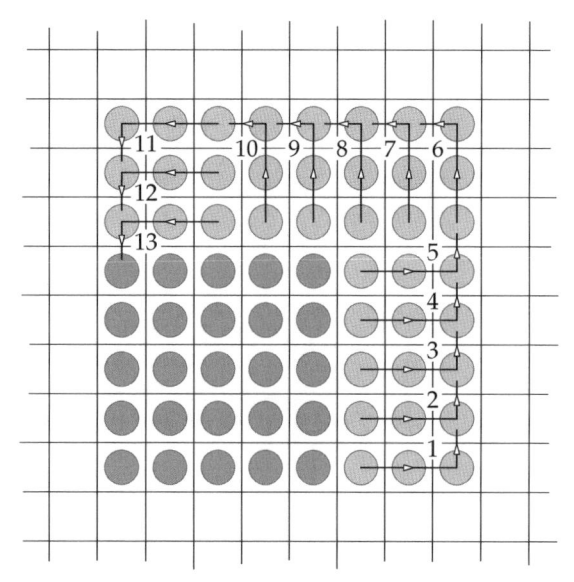

Figure 9d.F

To show that the game cannot be won if $n = 3k$ we colour the board as shown in figure 9d.G.

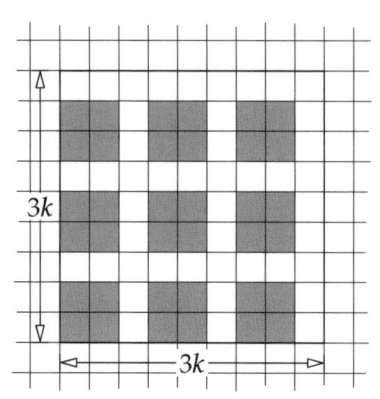

Figure 9d.G

This colouring has the property that the number of grey cells with pieces on them is always even. Therefore, if one piece remains at the end of the game, then it cannot be on a grey cell. However, there are four equivalent versions of this colouring, each of which makes a different corner of the original $3k \times 3k$ square grey. Considering these four colourings simultaneously shows that if there is only one piece on the board, then there are no places where it can be.

8. For this problem it will be convenient to assume the centres of the cells have coordinates (x, y) where x and y are integers satisfying $0 \leq x \leq 19$ and $0 \leq y \leq 11$. The task then becomes finding a sequence of moves from $(0,0)$ to $(19,0)$. We also note that a move is given by a vector of the form $\binom{a}{b}$, where a, b are integers with $a^2 + b^2 = r^2$.

   (a) If r is even, then a and b have the same parity. This means that if we colour the board with a standard chessboard colouring, then it is impossible to change colour. However $(0,0)$ and $(19,0)$ have different colours in this colouring.

   If r is a multiple of three, then $a^2 + b^2 \equiv 0$ modulo 3. The only solution to this congruence is $a \equiv b \equiv 0$ modulo 3. Therefore we can only reach points where both coordinates are multiples of three since we start at a point where both coordinates are multiples of three.

   (b) We observe that $a = 8$, $b = 3$ is a solution to $a^2 + b^2 = 73$. Now we make the following sequence of moves. $(0,0) \rightarrow (8,3) \rightarrow (0,6) \rightarrow (8,9)$ then $(5,1) \rightarrow (13,4) \rightarrow (5,7) \rightarrow (13,10)$ then $(16,2) \rightarrow (8,5) \rightarrow (16,8)$ then finally $(19,0)$ as required.

   (c) The only integer solutions to $a^2 + b^2 = 97$ are $a, b = \pm 9, \pm 4$ (in either order), so the possible moves are given by the vectors

   $$\begin{pmatrix} \pm 9 \\ \pm 4 \end{pmatrix} \text{ and } \begin{pmatrix} \pm 4 \\ \pm 9 \end{pmatrix}.$$

   By considering the parity of the coordinates, we see that any sequence of moves from $(0,0)$ to $(19,0)$ will contain an odd number of moves of the first form and an even number of the second form.

   Now we colour the board as shown in figure 9d.H on the facing page.

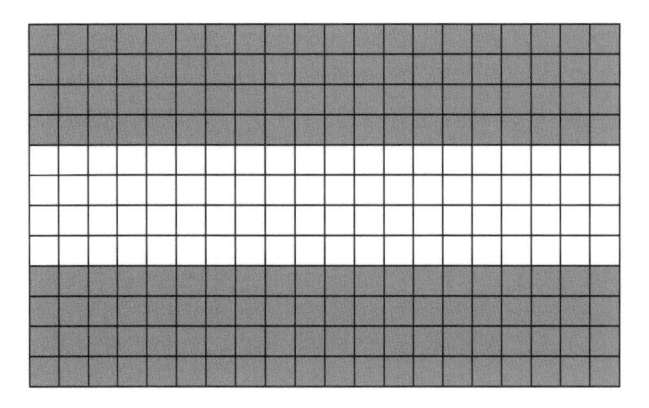

Figure 9d.H

With this colouring moves of the first form go from grey to white cells or vice versa, while moves of the second form only go between grey cells. Since $(0,0)$ and $(19,0)$ have the same colour, any journey between them will change colour an even number of times, which is a contradiction.

Exercise 10a

1. A circle. The difference between the number of squares and the number of triangles is always even so if one shape remains it cannot be a triangle or a square.

2. No. Replacing the x and y by $|x-y|$ changes the sum of all the numbers on the board by an even amount (either $2x$ or $2y$) so the parity of this sum is an invariant. The sum $1+2+\cdots+30$ contains an odd number of odd numbers so is odd, while zero is even.

3. No. Consider the eight cells marked in figure 10a.A. The number of these cells which are grey is always odd.

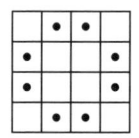

Figure 10a.A

4. No. Suppose the centre of the cell marked X is the origin and that the beetles are initially in cells with centres (x,y) where $x,y \in \{-1,0,1\}$. We classify points according to the parity of their coordinates. There are four categories: (odd, odd), (odd, even), (even, odd) and (even, even). When a beetle jumps the category of the cell it lands on is the same as the category of the cell it jumps from. Since none of the beetles are initially in the (even, even) category, there can never be a beetle at the origin.

5. We use the ordered pair (r,s) to denote the numbers of counters in the bags.

    Operations (i) and (ii)
    Yes. The starting state is (m,n), where, without loss of generality, we may assume that $m \geq n$. First we remove $n-1$ counters from each bag to reach the state $(m-n+1,1)$. By doubling the number of counters in the second bag and then removing one counter from each bag, we effectively remove one counter from the first bag. We do this repeatedly until the state $(1,1)$ is reached. Finally, we remove these two counters.

Solutions 351

Operations (i) and (iii)
No. The parity of $r - s$ does not change under either operation. If this difference is odd initially, then the bags can never both be empty. (If the difference is even, then both bags can be emptied but this is not part of the problem.)

Exercise 10b

1. No. We consider the number of beetles modulo 3. This quantity follows the sequence 0, 1, 2, 0, 1, 2, ..., so after 3600 seconds the number of beetles is divisible by three.

2. No. Let N be the number of tentacles modulo 7. Initially N is 2. If the monster survives an attack, then the number of tentacles which grow back always ensures that N returns to 2. The monster could be killed if it ever had 4, 24, 19 or 48 tentacles but none of these are congruent to 2 modulo 7 so the monster is sure to survive.

3. No it is not possible. The total number of counters considered modulo 4 is an invariant, so this quantity can never be increased by ten.

4. Consider the two numbers on the board before and after a move. These numbers are always congruent modulo 9. For example, the number $1\,000\,000a + 100\,000b + 10\,000c + 1000d + 100e + 10f + g$ may be replaced by, say, $(100a + 10b + c) + (1000d + 100e + 10f + g)$; the difference between these numbers is a multiple of 9. A similar argument can be applied to any move.

   Suppose that after some moves a ten-digit number with no repeated digits is written on the board. The sum of the digits of this number is $9 + 8 + \cdots + 1 + 0 = 45$ which shows that the number is congruent to 0 modulo 9. However, the number 7^{8^9} has no threes among its prime factors, so is not a multiple of nine.

5. One. Suppose the numbers $a_1, a_2, \ldots, a_n$ are on the board and let $Q = (a_1 + 1)(a_2 + 1) \cdots (a_n + 1) - 1$. A move consists of replacing a_i and a_j by $(a_i + 1)(a_j + 1) - 1$. This does not change the value of Q so the final number is always $50! - 1$.

Exercise 10c

1. 99. Each match reduces the number of competitors left in the tournament by one.

2. No. Let N be the number of straight lines separating a black region and a white region. Initially $N = 199$ and each move reduces N by at most 2.

3. Brigitte can win by always removing a counter with the highest available number. The highest available number cannot increase and will always decrease after finitely many moves. Therefore it will reach 1 eventually, at which point the number of counters on the table becomes strictly decreasing.

   The interesting feature of this game is that, while it always ends after a finite number of moves, it is impossible give an upper bound for the number of moves it will take.

4. No. Suppose the boxes are centred at $(x, 0)$ where x is an integer. A move consists of replacing two beetles at $(x, 0)$ with one at $(x + 1, 0)$ and one at $(x - 1, 0)$. We observe that

   $$(x+1)^2 + (x-1)^2 = x^2 + x^2 + 2.$$

   This shows that the sum of the squares of the x-coordinates of the beetles increases with every move so can never return to its starting value.

5. We represent each number using the sequence of exponents which occur in its prime factorisation. For example, we would represent the number $44 = 2^4 \times 3^0 \times 5^0 \times 7^0 \times 11^1$ by the quintuple $2, 0, 0, 0, 1$.

   We will also imagine that the sequences of exponents are written in a single row and that whenever we make a move we place the LCM on the right and the HCF on the left.

   With these conventions in place we can see when we apply the operation to the example numbers $492\,800 = 2^8 \times 3^0 \times 5^2 \times 7^1 \times 11^1$ and $8\,083\,152 = 2^4 \times 3^8 \times 5^0 \times 7^1 \times 11^1$.

   The quintuples $8, 0, 2, 1, 1$ and $4, 8, 0, 1, 1$ are replaced with $4, 0, 0, 1, 1$ and $8, 8, 2, 1, 1$ in that order.

   If we focus on the exponents of a particular prime, then the moves we can make are simply sorting these exponents in increasing order.

Eventually the exponents will be perfectly sorted for each prime and the numbers will stop changing.

If we wanted to write the solution up more formally, then we would need to use a monovariant that measured how nearly sorted the exponents were for each prime. However, letting this monovariant do its work in the background makes the proof easier to understand.

6. We call the combination of the parrot squawking and the captain distributing extra coins a move. After every move all the pirates have an even number of coins. Now we focus on the poorest pirates. Any poorest pirate standing to the right of a richer pirate will have more coins after the next move, while any poorest pirate standing to the right of another poorest pirate will have the same number of coins after the next move.

Now we ask how many of the poorest pirates are standing to the right of another poorest pirate.

None
   If none of them are, then the minimum wealth of a pirate will increase.

Some
   If some but not all of them are, then the number of poorest pirates will decrease.

All
   If all of them are, then all the pirates are equally wealthy.

We note that the wealth of a richest pirate can never be increased by a move. This implies that the first case happens finitely often, and occurrences of this case are separated by finitely many occurrences of the second case, so the third case will eventually occur.

Exercise 10d

1. If we have $x > y$ and $0 < \epsilon < x - y$, then $(x - \epsilon) + (y + \epsilon) = x + y$ and $(x - \epsilon)(y + \epsilon) = xy + \epsilon(x - y - \epsilon) > xy$. This shows that making two numbers more equal without changing their sum increases their product. This in turn increases the geometric mean of any set containing them. Now we argue as in problem 10.15, making the x_i equal to the arithmetic mean one at a time.

2. The smallest value of m is $2n - 1$. The total infected perimeter can never increase, as in problem 10.17. The perimeter of an n-honeycomb is $6(2n - 1)$, which shows that at least $2n - 1$ cells are needed.

Figure 10d.A shows an initial configuration for a 4-honeycomb with 7 cells containing honey. This can easily be extended to the general case, showing that the task is possible when $m = 2n - 1$.

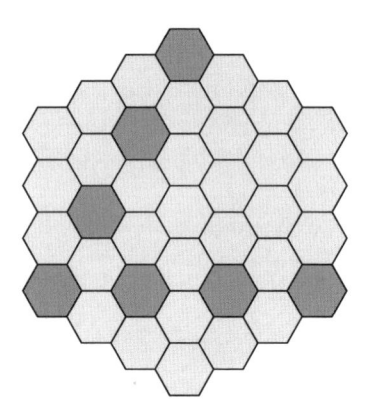

Figure 10d.A

3. For all sufficiently large n we have $f_n = \text{HCF}(a, b)$.

It is clear that if any two adjacent terms in the sequence are equal, then the sequence will be constant from then on. The sequence is not a strictly decreasing one, as shown by the example 9, 1, 5, 3, 1, 1, ... However, if $f_{n-1} \neq f_n$, then $f_{n+1} \leq \frac{1}{2}(f_{n-1} + f_n) < \max(f_{n-1}, f_n)$. Similarly, if $f_n \neq f_{n+1}$, then $f_{n+2} < \max(f_n, f_{n+1}) \leq \max(f_{n-1}, f_n)$. This implies that, if we define $g_n = \max(f_{2n-1}, f_{2n})$, then (g_n) is a sequence which decreases unless (f_n) becomes constant. The terms in (g_n) cannot decrease infinitely often since they are all positive integers so (f_n) is eventually always equal to some number ℓ.

We note that, if some odd number d divides two consecutive terms in the sequence (f_n), then it divides the subsequent term and therefore all subsequent terms. This shows that $\text{HCF}(a, b)$ divides ℓ. Similarly, if some odd number d divides two consecutive terms of (f_n), then it divides the previous term and therefore all previous terms. This shows that ℓ divides $\text{HCF}(a, b)$ and hence that $\ell = \text{HCF}(a, b)$.

4. To prove the result when $n = 2$, we note that
$$(x_1y_1 + x_2y_2) - (x_1y_2 + x_2y_1) = (x_2 - x_1)(y_2 - y_1),$$
which is positive since $x_1 < x_2$ and $y_1 < y_2$.

We prove the general case by induction on n. Suppose the result holds for $n = k$ and that we are given
$$A = x_1 y_{f(1)} + x_2 y_{f(2)} + \cdots + x_{k+1} y_{f(k+1)}.$$
Let B denote
$$x_1 y_1 + x_2 y_2 + \cdots + x_{k+1} y_{k+1}.$$
We aim to show that $A \leq B$.

If $f(k+1) = k+1$, then there is nothing to prove since
$$A - x_{k+1} y_{k+1} \leq B - x_{k+1} y_{k+1}$$
by the induction hypothesis. If $f(k+1) \neq k+1$, then we can exchange the places of $y_{f(k+1)}$ and y_{k+1} in the expression for A and call the new expression A'. The result for $n = 2$ ensures that $A \leq A'$, and the induction hypothesis ensures that $A' \leq B$.

5. Let the vertices of the pentagon be A, B, C, D and E, and let the integers written at these vertices be a, b, c, d and e respectively (see figure 10d.B).

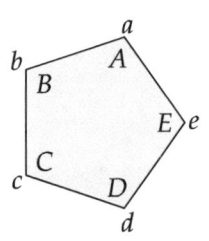

Figure 10d.B

We associate an invariant with each vertex as follows:
$$T_A \equiv b + 2c + 3d + 4e \pmod{5};$$
$$T_B \equiv c + 2d + 3e + 4a \pmod{5};$$
$$T_C \equiv d + 2e + 3a + 4b \pmod{5};$$
$$T_D \equiv e + 2a + 3b + 4c \pmod{5};$$
$$T_E \equiv a + 2b + 3c + 4d \pmod{5}.$$

It is easy to check that all five quantities are invariant under any legal move. We also note that $T_A - T_B \equiv a+b+c+d+e \equiv 1$ modulo 5. Indeed, the difference between the T values associated with neighbouring vertices is always 1 modulo 5. This implies that exactly one of these T values is congruent to zero. If the game can be won at any vertex, then the T value associated with that vertex will be zero, so the game can be won at at most one vertex.

Now we suppose, without loss of generality, that $T_A \equiv 0$ modulo 5 and make the sequence of three moves illustrated in figure 10d.C.

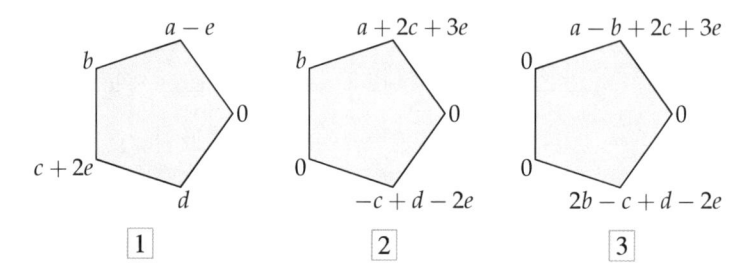

Figure 10d.C

At this point we use the condition that $T_A \equiv 0$ modulo 5, which implies that $2b - c + d - 2e = 5k$ for some integer k. Now we make the sequence of moves illustrated in figure 10d.D, so that we can then win the game at vertex A.

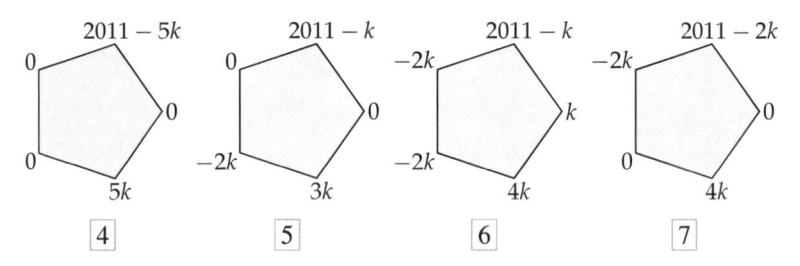

Figure 10d.D

6. The condition in the question ensures that $a_1 + a_2 + \cdots + a_k = kb_k$ for some integer b_k. We have $(k+1)b_{k+1} - kb_k = a_{k+1} \leq k$. Hence

$$b_{k+1} \leq \frac{k}{k+1}(b_k + 1) < b_k + 1,$$

Solutions

so (b_k) is a non-increasing sequence of positive integers. This sequence can only decrease finitely many times, so eventually it is equal to some limit ℓ. Now, if $b_k = b_{k+1} = \ell$, then we have $a_{k+1} = (k+1)b_{k+1} - kb_k = \ell$. Therefore eventually the sequence (a_n) is constant.

Exercise 10e

1. We assign a value to each cell, as shown in figure 10e.A.

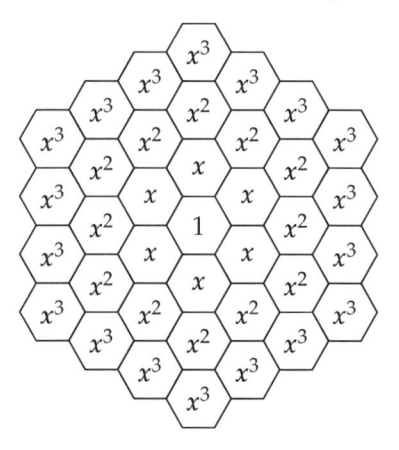

Figure 10e.A

Let the value of an arrangement of counters be the sum of the values of the occupied cells, and note that, if $x = \frac{1}{3}$, then no move can decrease the value of any arrangement. Also, the value of the initial arrangement is six.

Now the value of the arrangement with one counter in each cell is

$$1 + 6x + 12x^2 + 18x^3 + \cdots = 1 + 6x(1 + 2x + 3x^2 + \cdots)$$
$$= 1 + \frac{6x}{(1-x)^2}.$$

Putting $x = \frac{1}{3}$, we obtain $1 + \frac{9}{2}$, which is less than six, so we are done.

2. We call the point $(0,5)$ the *target*, and assign the value x^d to points that are at (taxicab) distance d from the target. The total value of all the points on or below the x-axis is

$$x^5 + 3x^6 + 5x^7 + \cdots = x^5(1 + 2x + 3x^2 + \cdots)$$
$$+ x^6(1 + 2x^2 + 3x^3 + \cdots)$$
$$= \frac{x^5 + x^6}{(1-x)^2}.$$

Now we set $x = \phi$ as we did in problem 10.19, which ensures that no move can increase the value of an arrangement. Then the total value of any finite number of pegs on or below the x-axis is less than

$$\frac{\phi^5 + \phi^6}{(1-\phi)^2}.$$

Using the fact that $1 - \phi = \phi^2$, we obtain

$$\frac{\phi^5 + \phi^6}{(1-\phi)^2} = \frac{\phi^5 + \phi^6}{\phi^4}$$
$$= \phi + \phi^2$$
$$= 1.$$

But the target has value 1, so the target cannot be reached.

This game was invented by the Princeton mathematician John Horton Conway, and is therefore known as *Conway's soldiers*.

Exercise 11a

1. Focus on a youngest (or oldest) student and the result follows.

2. The solution is almost identical to the one given for problem 11.4.

3. Suppose, for contradiction, that the game continues forever without 1 being seen. There are some labels which are seen infinitely often. We focus on M, the largest of these infinitely recurring labels. Since all labels greater than M occur finitely often, there comes a point after which no label greater than M is ever seen. Once this point is reached we wait for the next time M is seen. The card labelled M moves to a position M below the top card, but now no card with a label less than M can even make the card labelled M move again. Since all cards greater than M have already had their last turn on the top, we conclude that M is never seen again, contradicting the assumption that it is seen infinitely often.

   This argument breaks down if M is 1 since then reversing the order of the first M cards does not change the top card.

4. Let a person's *score* be the number of friends they have in the other room and choose a separation into two rooms that maximises the total score. If a person had x friends in their room and y in the other room with $x > y$, then they could swap rooms and increase the total score which is impossible. (The total score would go up by $2x - 2y$.)

5. Choose a largest possible group of thieves who have not stolen from each other. Suppose this group contains $k < n$ thieves, leaving $3n - k$ others. Each of the k thieves has stolen from one of the others and been stolen from one of them. These $2k$ crimes have at most $2k$ different victims, none of whom can join the group we choose originally. However, this leaves at least $3n - 3k > 0$ thieves, any one of whom could join the group. Since the original group was as large as possible, this is a contradiction.

6. The condition given in the question implies that none of the numbers are negative. We choose a largest number x and call the two numbers to its right y and z. Now the difference between y and z is x, but neither y nor z can be larger than x. It follows that one of them is zero and the other is equal to x. Thus the arrangement is either $x, x, 0$ or $x, 0, x$. Either way we can now work round the circle

anticlockwise and see that the 360 numbers consist of 240 copies of x and 120 zeros. Therefore $x = 3$ and we are done.

7. Let us suppose that no city has more than m roads leading into it. We call a city with a maximal number of roads leading to it C_0 and label the other cities $C_1, C_2, \ldots, C_{n-1}$ such that the roads $C_0C_1, C_0C_2, \ldots, C_0C_m$ all lead to C_0. Now suppose, for contradiction, that there is another city C_* which does not have a road leading to any of $C_1, C_2, \ldots, C_m$. This means all m roads $C_*C_1, C_*C_2, \ldots, C_*C_m$ all lead to C_*. However, C_0C_* also leads to C_* (since C_* is not in the first m cities) so $m + 1$ roads lead to C_* which is impossible.

8. This question is a classic. The solution is easy to follow, but extremely hard to come up with.

   We imagine that a friendly passer-by offers to loan the cars some fuel to help them complete their circuit. Car 1 borrows a large amount of extra fuel so it has more than enough to get round. It then sets off and every time it passes a car it takes all of that car's fuel. Since the amount of fuel used equals the total amount the n cars had before the friendly passer-by appeared, car 1 can complete a lap and return the borrowed amount of fuel to the lender.

   Now we consider the fuel gauge in car 1 as it goes round the track. The gauge goes down steadily until car 1 meets car 2, at which point it jumps up by some amount before beginning to go down steadily again. This means a graph of fuel against distance travelled for car 1 will have a saw-tooth shape like the one shown in figure 11a.A on the facing page.

   A tooth on the saw occurs whenever car 1 meets another car. Now focus on a lowest point on the fuel graph (labelled X in the figure.) This occurs at some particular car called car m. A moment's thought is all that is needed to realise that car m could have completed a circuit of the track even if no one had been available to lend the cars any fuel.

Solutions

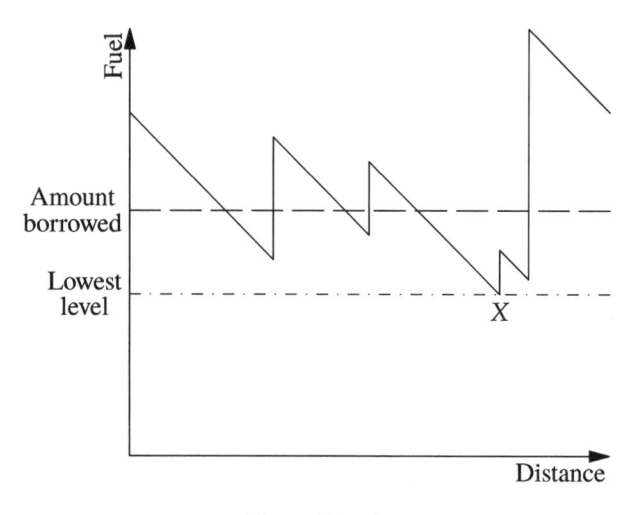

Figure 11a.A

Exercise 11b

1. Suppose that an equilateral triangle has side length s and height h where s and h are integers. We note that s is even since $(\frac{s}{2})^2 = s^2 - h^2$.

   Now we can focus on half equilateral triangles, that is right-angled triangles with one side equal to half the hypotenuse. We consider a (hypothetical) smallest half equilateral triangle with integer sides and mimic the construction in problem 11.7 to build a smaller one. The analogy is almost exact. It is clear that AD is an integer. This means that $AE = 2AD$ is an integer. Thus $EB = AB - AE$ is an integer which makes $ED = EB$ an integer.

2. Call the red and blue points $R_1, R_2, \ldots, R_n$ and $B_1, B_2, \ldots, B_n$ respectively. Join R_i to B_j such that the total length of the lines R_iB_j is minimal. Now argue as in problem 11.8.

3. This is very similar to part (b) of problem 11.9. Focus on the smallest coin. Call its centre C_0 and suppose, for contradiction, that coins with centres $C_1, C_2, \ldots, C_6$ all touch it. Using the averaging principle, and relabelling if necessary, we may assume that the angle $\angle C_1C_0C_2$ is at most $60°$. This contradicts the fact that in triangle $C_1C_0C_2$ the longest side is C_1C_2.

4. We begin by choosing a direction which we will consider to be the downward direction. If we choose this direction so that none of the lines are perpendicular to it, then each of the $\binom{n}{2}$ points of intersections formed by the lines is the lowest point of exactly one region.

This accounts for the $\binom{n}{2}$ term and also suggests where the $n+1$ term might come from. Although every point of intersection is the lowest point of some region, it is not the case that every region has a lowest point. Some regions are what we might call *infinitely descending*, and we would like to show that there are exactly $n+1$ such regions.

To count these infinitely descending regions, we imagine adding a new line which is below all the points of intersection formed by the first n lines and which is perpendicular to the downward direction. Since the new line is below all the 'action', it passes through each of the infinitely descending regions exactly once. Also, since none of the n lines is horizontal, each of them crosses the new line. Thus the new line has n intersection points on it, meaning it passes through $n+1$ regions as required.

Exercise 11c

1. This generalises 11.10. Suppose that $\sqrt{k}$ is not an integer. If it is rational, then there is a smallest positive integer M such that $\sqrt{k}M$ is an integer. Now we consider $N = (\sqrt{k} - \lfloor\sqrt{k}\rfloor)M$. Since N is obtained by multiplying M by a number between 0 and 1, we have $0 < N < M$. Now $N = \sqrt{k}M - \lfloor\sqrt{k}\rfloor M$, so N is the difference between two integers and is therefore an integer. Similarly, $\sqrt{k}N = kM - \lfloor\sqrt{k}\rfloor(\sqrt{k}M)$ is an integer, so we are done.

   The reason that this proof does not show that, for example, $\sqrt{4}$ is irrational is that if a positive integer is multiplied by $(\sqrt{4} - \lfloor\sqrt{4}\rfloor)$ the result is not a positive integer.

2. Suppose there are solutions and choose one where $|x| + |y| + |z| > 0$ is minimal. Since zero is an even number, we see that x is even so $x = 2a$ for some integer a. This gives $8a^3 + 2y^3 + 4z^3 = 0$, so if (x, y, z) is a solution to the original equation then so is $(y, z, \frac{x}{2})$. This almost contradicts the fact that $|x| + |y| + |z|$ is minimal, except that

Solutions

x might equal zero. To deal with this we repeat the argument on the solution $(y, z, \frac{x}{2})$ to obtain first the solution $(z, \frac{x}{2}, \frac{y}{2})$ and then the solution $(\frac{x}{2}, \frac{y}{2}, \frac{z}{2})$ which really does contradict the minimality of $|x| + |y| + |z|$.

3. Here we focus on a largest triangle $P_0 P_1 P_2$. Through each vertex of the triangle we draw a line parallel to the other side. These form the large triangle $Q_0 Q_1 Q_2$ as shown on the left of figure 11c.A.

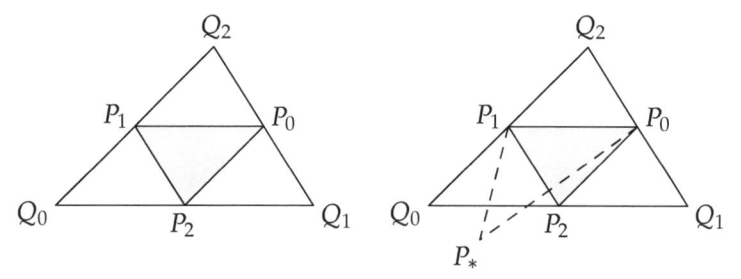

Figure 11c.A

We claim that all n points lie within this larger triangle. Suppose, for contradiction, that a point P_* lies on the other side of line $Q_i Q_j$ (see the right-hand diagram of figure 11c.A). The triangle $P_i P_j P_*$ has a larger area than the triangle $P_0 P_1 P_2$ since it has the same base and a larger height. This contradiction completes the proof.

4. Suppose that the maximum number of sides any face has is n and consider a face with n sides. Each of its n neighbouring faces has between 3 and n sides, so, by the pigeonhole principle, two of these faces have the same number of sides.

It is worth noting that this argument breaks down if the polyhedron is not convex since then it is possible for two faces to share more than one side, so an n-sided face may have fewer then n- neighbouring faces. In fact the claim does not hold for non-convex polyhedra, though constructing a counterexample is a delicate task.

5. This is a trick question. It is exactly equivalent to problem 11.15.

Exercise A

1. The shared Venn diagram is shown in figure A.1.

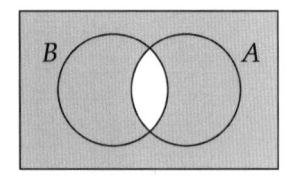

   Figure A.1

2. Both Venn diagrams look like figure A.2.

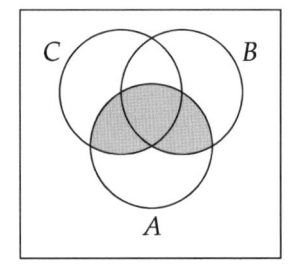

   Figure A.2

3. The left-hand expression $|A \cup B|$ is the number of elements in set A or in set B or in both. When the number of elements in set A is added to the number of elements in set B, any element that is in both sets is counted twice. Therefore the number of elements in both sets, which is $|A \cap B|$, needs to be subtracted.

Exercise B

1. (a) 140;
   (b) 127;
   (c) 56;
   (d) 0;
   (e) 2537.

2. (a) $(x+y)^n = \sum_{k=0}^{n} \binom{n}{k} x^k y^{n-k}$;

   (b) $\binom{n+1}{m} = \sum_{k=m}^{n} \binom{k}{m}$ for $m \leq n$;

   (c) $2^m \binom{n}{m} = \sum_{k=0}^{m} \binom{n}{k}\binom{n-k}{m-k}$ for $1 \leq m \leq n$;

   (d) $\binom{n}{r_1 \, r_2 \, \ldots \, r_k} = \prod_{i=1}^{k} \binom{n - \sum_{j=0}^{i-1} r_j}{r_i}$, where $n = \sum_{j=0}^{k} r_j$ and $r_0 = 0$.

Exercise C

1. $x^3 + x^2 - 10x + 8$.
2. $x^4 - 1$.
3. $x^5 + 32$.
4. $x^4 - x^3 - 4x^2 + 13x - 15$.
5. $9x^2 - 3x + 8$.

Exercise D

1. (a) The inductive hypothesis has that $t_n = 2^{n+1} - (n+1)$. The base is true since $2^2 - 2 = 2 = t_1$. Suppose that $t_k = 2^{k+1} - (k+1)$; then $t_{k+1} = 2(2^{k+1} - (k+1)) + k = 2^{k+2} - (k+2)$, which is the inductive hypothesis with $n = k+1$. The result follows by induction.
   (b) The inductive hypothesis is that $t_n = n \times 2^{n-1}$. The base is true since $2 \times 2^0 = 2 = t_1$. Suppose that $t_k = k \times 2^{k-1}$; then $t_{k+1} = 2(k \times 2^{k-1}) + 2^k = (k+1) \times 2^k$, which is the inductive hypothesis with $n = k+1$. The result follows by induction.
   (c) The inductive hypothesis is that $t_n = 5 \times 2^n + 2 \times (-1)^n$. The base consists of $n = 0$ and $n = 1$ and is easily checked. Suppose that $t_k = 5 \times 2^k + 2 \times (-1)^k$ and $t_{k+1} = 5 \times 2^{k+1} + 2 \times (-1)^{k+1}$; then $t_{k+2} = (5 \times 2^{k+1} + 2 \times (-1)^{k+1}) + 2(5 \times 2^k + 2 \times (-1)^k) = 5 \times 2^{k+2} + 2 \times (-1)^{k+2}$, which is the inductive hypothesis with $n = k+2$. The result follows by induction.

2. The base is trivial. Suppose that the inductive hypothesis is true for $n = k$. Then

$$\sum_{i=1}^{k+1} \frac{1}{i(i+1)} = \frac{k}{k+1} + \frac{1}{(k+1)(k+2)}$$

$$= \frac{k^2 + 2k + 1}{(k+1)(k+2)}$$

$$= \frac{k+1}{k+2},$$

which is the inductive hypothesis with $n = k+1$. The result follows by induction.

3. The base is true since $2^4 = 16 < 24 = 4!$. Suppose that the inductive hypothesis is true for $n = k \geq 4$.
   Then $2^{k+1} = 2 \times 2^k < 2 \times k! < (k+1)!$, which is the inductive hypothesis with $n = k+1$. The result follows by induction.
   Note that the result is false for $n = 3$.

4. Table D.1 on the next page shows how to make various postage amounts using the available stamps.

Postage	Stamps
44p	four 5p and two 12p
45p	nine 5p
46p	two 5p and three 12p
47p	seven 5p and one 12p
48p	four 12p

Table D.1

We now have five consecutive postages which are available, and clearly we can supplement these using 5p stamps alone to create all larger totals. This can be written formally as an induction with five base cases and a hypothesis for $n = k, k+1, k+2, k+3$ and $k+4$.

Note that 43p is impossible.

You might like to generalise this problem for other values (or numbers) of stamps.

5. (a) The step works for all values of k greater than 2, but it does not work for 2 itself. For example, if $S = \{3, 79\}$ then $S_1 = \{3\}$ and $S_2 = \{79\}$ and there is no overlap.
   (b) The reason why the base works is that natural numbers cannot be less than 1. However, if $1 \in S$ then $0 \in S^*$ and the induction hypothesis does not apply to S^*.

It is quite comforting to know that not all numbers are equal.

Exercise E

1. $\sum_{i=1}^{n}(2i-1) = 2\sum_{i=1}^{n}i - \sum_{i=1}^{n}1$
$= n(n-1) + n$
$= n^2.$

2. (a) For the base, both sides are equal to 1. The induction hypothesis is that the formula is true for $n = k$. Now

$$\sum_{i=1}^{k+1} i^2 = \sum_{i=1}^{k} i^2 + (k+1)^2$$
$$= \tfrac{1}{6}k(k+1)(2k+1) + (k+1)^2$$
$$= \tfrac{1}{6}(k+1)(2k^2 + k + 6k + 6)$$
$$= \tfrac{1}{6}(k+1)(2k^2 + 7k + 6)$$
$$= \tfrac{1}{6}(k+1)(k+2)(2k+3),$$

which is the formula for $n = k+1$.

(b) First we note that

$$\sum_{i=1}^{n} i^3 - \sum_{i=1}^{n}(i-1)^3 = (1^3 + 2^3 + \cdots + n^3)$$
$$- (0^3 + 1^3 + \cdots + (n-1)^3)$$
$$= n^3.$$

Now by sigma algebra

$$\sum_{i=1}^{n} i^3 - \sum_{i=1}^{n}(i-1)^3 = 3\sum_{i=1}^{n} i^2 - 3\sum_{i=1}^{n} i + \sum_{i=1}^{n} 1.$$

Equating the two expressions, and using $\sum_{i=1}^{n} i = \tfrac{1}{2}n(n+1)$, we have $n^3 = 3\sum_{i=1}^{n} i^2 - \tfrac{3}{2}n(n+1) + n$ and now we can rearrange and factorise to obtain the desired expression for $\sum_{i=1}^{n} i^2$.

3. (a) The crucial part of the step is that $\frac{1}{4}k^2(k+1)^2 + (k+1)^3 = \frac{1}{4}(k+1)^2(k^2+4k+4)$.
   (b) We have
   $$n^4 = \sum_{i=1}^{n} i^4 - \sum_{i=1}^{n}(i-1)^4$$
   $$= 4\sum_{i=1}^{n} i^3 - 6\sum_{i=1}^{n} i^2 + 4\sum_{i=1}^{n} i - n$$
   and the result follows by rearranging and factorising.

4. Writing S_n for $\sum_{i=1}^{n} ir^i$, we have $(1-r)^2 S_n = r - (n+1)r^{n+1} + nr^{n+2}$, noting that all the coefficients of terms from r^2 to r^n are zero. Hence
   $$S_n = \frac{r - (n+1)r^{n+1} + nr^{n+2}}{(1-r)^2}.$$
   When $n \to \infty$, we need $-1 < r < 1$ in order that the second and third term in the numerator vanish, and then we have
   $$\sum_{i=1}^{\infty} ir^i = \frac{r}{(1-r)^2}.$$

5. Multiplying by $(1-r)^3$, we obtain
   $$\sum_{i=1}^{n} i^2 r^i = \frac{r + r^2 - (n+1)^2 r^{n+1} + (2n^2+2n-1)r^{n+2} - n^2 r^{n+3}}{(1-r)^3}$$
   and, so long as $-1 < r < 1$,
   $$\sum_{i=1}^{\infty} i^2 r^i = \frac{r(1+r)}{(1-r)^3}.$$

Exercise F

1. (a) $169 + 489 \equiv 2 \pmod{16}$.
   (b) $57 \times 73 \equiv 1 \pmod{8}$.
   (c) $1542^2 \equiv 4 \pmod{10}$.
   (d) $599 \times 1512 \equiv 3 \pmod{15}$.
   (e) $13^8 \equiv 1 \pmod{17}$

2. (a) True.
   (b) False; any multiple of 7 is a counterexample.
   (c) True.
   (d) True.
   (e) False; 5 is a counterexample.
   (f) False; 3 is a counterexample.
   (g) True.
       If $x^2 \equiv 5 \pmod{11}$, then $x^2 - 16 \equiv 0 \pmod{11}$. This means that 11 divides $(x-4)(x+4)$. Now the fact that 11 is prime implies that 11 divides one of the terms in brackets.
   (h) True. This can be seen by considering the equation modulo 4.

Bibliography

[1] C. J. Bradley. *Introduction to Inequalities*. UKMT, 2010.
ISBN: 9781906001117.

[2] C. J. Bradley. *Introduction to Number Theory*. UKMT, 2010.
ISBN: 9781906001124.

[3] Gerry Leversha. "A direct derivation of the Catalan formula".
In: *The Mathematical Gazette* 97 (Mar. 2013), pp. 53–60.

[4] Josef Rukavicka. "On Generalized Dyck Paths".
In: *The Electronic Journal of Combinatorics* 18.1 (2011).
URL: http://www.combinatorics.org/ojs/index.php/eljc/article/view/v18i1p40.

[5] Stan Wagon. "Fourteen proofs of a result about tiling a rectangle".
In: *American Mathematical Monthly* 94 (1987), pp. 601–17.

We recommend the following books for further reading.

R. B. J. T. Allenby and Alan Slomson.
How to Count: an Introduction to Combinatorics. 2nd edition.
Chapman and Hall, 2010. ISBN: 9781420082609.

Victor Bryant. *Aspects of Combinatorics*. Cambridge University Press, 1992.
ISBN: 9780521429979.

Arthur Engel. *Problem-Solving Strategies*. Problem Books in Mathematics.
Springer, 2008. ISBN: 9780387982199.

Solomon W. Golomb. *Polyominoes: Puzzles, Patterns, Problems and Packings*.
2nd edition. Princeton University Press, 1996. ISBN: 9780691024448.

George E. Martin. *Counting: the Art of Enumerative Combinatorics*.
2nd edition. Springer, 2010. ISBN: 9781441929150.

Paul Zeitz. *The Art and Craft of Problem Solving*. 2nd edition. John Wiley & Sons, 2006. ISBN: 9780471789017.

Index

AM-GM inequality, 206, 334
annulus, 326
argument
    colouring ∼, 155
    double-counting ∼, 47
    parity ∼, 161
    recursive ∼, 4
arithmetic
    ∼ mean, 202
    fundamental theorem of ∼, 237
auxiliary equation, 101
averaging principle, 141

base, 255
Bezout's lemma, 237
bijection, 53
binary family tree, 84
Binet formula, 102
binomial
    ∼ coefficient, 33
    ∼ theorem, 33

cardinality, 53
Catalan number, 86
Chinese remainder theorem, 151
closed-form formula, 71
coding, 36, 37
coefficient, 253
    binomial ∼, 33
    multinomial ∼, 34

colex, 9
colexicographic ordering, 9
colouring argument, 155
combination, 30
    ∼ with replacement, 42
complement, 58, 244
composition, 38
concatenation, 83
conditions, initial ∼, 72
convergent, 260
convex, 144
Conway's soldiers, 358
counting criteria, 2
cubic, 253

degree, 253
derangement, 66
diagram
    Ferrers ∼, 55
    Venn ∼, 58, 244
Dijkstra, Edsger W., 141
Diophantine equation, 38
Dirichlet's
    ∼ approximation theorem, 141
    ∼ principle, 124
distance, taxicab ∼, 207
divergent, 260
domino, 148
double-counting argument, 47
dummy variable, 248

element, 243
ellipsis, 247
equation
    auxiliary ∼, 101
    Diophantine ∼, 38
Eratosthenes, sieve of ∼, 62

factorial, 5
family, binary ∼ tree, 84
Ferrers diagram, 55
Fibonacci, 76
    ∼ recurrence, 74
floor function, 62
formula
    Binet ∼, 102
    closed-form ∼, 71
fractional part, 138
fractions, partial ∼, 119
function
    floor ∼, 62
    generating ∼, 110
    phi ∼, 65
fundamental theorem of arithmetic, 237

Galton, Francis, 13
generating function, 110
geometric progression, 259
golden ratio, 103

Hanoi, Tower of ∼, 72
hockey stick theorem, 36
hypothesis, inductive ∼, 255

inclusion-exclusion principle, 60
index, 248
induction, 255
    mathematical ∼, 255
inductive hypothesis, 255
inequality
    ∼ principle, 147
    AM-GM ∼, 206, 334
    rearrangement ∼, 207

infinity, sum to ∼, 260
initial conditions, 72
injection, 65
intersection, 243
invariant, 183
irrational, 141

leading term, 253
lemma, Bezout's ∼, 237
Leonardo of Pisa, 76
Lucas, Edouard, 78

mathematical induction, 255
mean
    arithmetic ∼, 202
    quadratic ∼, 202
monovariant, 193
multinomial coefficient, 34
multiplication principle, 6

Narayana Pandit, 273
necklace, 23
number, Catalan ∼, 86

one-sided, 159
ordering, colexicographic ∼, 9
overcounting, 47

paradox, poker ∼, 287
parity argument, 161
part, fractional ∼, 138
partial
    ∼ fractions, 119
    ∼ sum, 259
partition, 10
Pascal's
    ∼ identity, 32
    ∼ triangle, 14
pattern-spotting, 288
permutation, 6, 19
    ∼ with replacement, 21
phi function, 65
PIE, 60

pigeonhole principle, 124
poker paradox, 287
polyhedron, 144
polynomial, 253
power series, 112
principle
    averaging ∼, 141
    Dirichlet's ∼, 124
    inclusion-exclusion ∼, 60
    inequality ∼, 147
    multiplication ∼, 6
    pigeonhole ∼, 124
    reflection ∼, 93
product, 249
progression, geometric ∼, 259

quadratic, 253
    ∼ mean, 202
quartic, 253
quincunx, 13
quintic, 253

range, 247
ranking, 8
ratio, golden ∼, 103
rearrangement inequality, 207
recurrence
    ∼ relation, 72
    Fibonacci ∼, 74
recursive argument, 4
reflection principle, 93
relation, recurrence ∼, 72
remainder, Chinese ∼ theorem, 151
replacement
    combination with ∼, 42
    permutation with ∼, 21
repunits, 137
round table, 23
row-neighbour, 145

self-conjugate, 56

series, 259
    power ∼, 112
set, 243
sieve of Eratosthenes, 62
skeleton, 162
smoothing, 203
soldiers, Conway's ∼, 358
step, 255
subset, 243
sum
    ∼ to infinity, 260
    partial ∼, 259
summand, 247
surjection, 65

table, round ∼, 23
taxicab distance, 207
term, 253
    leading ∼, 253
tetromino, 159
theorem
    binomial ∼, 33
    Chinese remainder ∼, 151
    Dirichlet's approximation ∼, 141
    fundamental ∼ of arithmetic, 237
    hockey stick ∼, 36
Tower of Hanoi, 72
tree, binary family ∼, 84
triangle, Pascal's ∼, 14
tromino, 159
two-sided, 159

union, 243
unranking, 8

Vandermonde's identity, 51
variable, dummy ∼, 248
Venn diagram, 58, 244